THE TECHNIQUE
of
FILM EDITING
Second edition

THE TECHNIQUE OF

FILM EDITING

Second edition

Written and compiled by

KAREL REISZ AND GAVIN MILLAR

*with the guidance of the following Committee
appointed by
The British Film Academy*

**Thorold Dickinson (Chairman)
Reginald Beck, Roy Boulting, Sidney Cole, Robert Hamer
Jack Harris, David Lean, Ernest Lindgren, Harry Miller
Basil Wright**

Introduced by

THOROLD DICKINSON

Focal Press
An imprint of Butterworth-Heinemann
Linacre House, Jordan Hill, Oxford OX2 8DP
A division of Reed Educational and Professional Publishing Ltd

Ɛ A member of the Reed Elsevier plc group

OXFORD   LONDON   GUILDFORD   BOSTON
NEW DELHI   SINGAPORE   SYDNEY
TOKYO   TORONTO   WELLINGTON

First published 1953
Thirteenth reprint 1967
Second edition 1968
Sixth reprint 1978
Reprinted 1982, 1983, 1984, 1987, 1988, 1989, 1991, 1995, 1996

ISBN 0 240 51437 8

Printed and bound in Great Britain
by Hartnolls Ltd, Bodmin, Cornwall

PUBLISHER'S NOTE TO THE ENLARGED EDITION

THE TECHNIQUE OF FILM EDITING by Karel Reisz was first published in 1953.

It not only had a strong immediate impact, but has remained the standard introduction to its subject ever since and wherever young film-makers are trained.

The original English version of the book has been reprinted 13 times without a word being changed. So it still reflects the outlook of a time when the craft of film-making seemed to have arrived at conventions and methods of lasting validity.

Close on 15 years later, many of them have changed considerably. Confronted with the need to take note of these changes, the author decided to update his work by adding a fourth Section to it.

This new Section was contributed by *Gavin Millar*, in consultation with *Karel Reisz*. It surveys and records the contemporary approach to film editing by new " schools " of film-makers all over the world.

Karel Reisz's original text is reprinted as it was. Any attempt to revise or re-interpret it could only blur its spirit. It would also handicap the reader in forming his own views about the ever-growing momentum of sophistication that went into cinematic expression and perception during the last decade and a half.

Professor Thorold Dickinson, then of London University, who twenty-five years ago chaired the guiding committee of the *British Film Academy* assisting the author in writing this book and who himself wrote the Introduction to its first edition, has now contributed a new Introduction (page 275) followed by a series of notes on passages in the original text which, in his opinion, are no longer valid.

A. Kraszna-Krausz

CONTENTS

INTRODUCTION

GREAT BRITAIN has no educational centre where would-be craftsmen can study the technique of the film. Neither is it within the scope or the resources of the *British Film Academy* to fulfil this need. The excellent book and film libraries attached to the *British Film Institute* provide the only reasonable stop-gap for those who are capable of guiding their own education.

We, members of the B.F.A. Council, have examined the literature of the cinema, haphazard as it is, with the idea of helping to fill the gaps among those subjects which the existing text-books fail to cover. We have found that some crafts like sound recording, set design (or art direction), script writing, even film direction, have in fact been discussed in an articulate manner, but that the pivotal contribution of the film editor has never been analysed objectively. Film editing has only been dealt with in the personal theories of Eisenstein, Pudovkin and others, and only in relation to the styles of cinema of which they have had experience.

To fill the gap, we approached those among our members who are practised in film editing and found nine volunteers willing to pool their joint experience of a wide range of film styles in shaping an objective introduction to their craft.

To compile the book we chose, not a film editor who might be biased towards the style of film in which he is expert, but a layman with a scientific background and an analytical skill in sifting a maze of material, most of which has never been stated articulately before. Karel Reisz, over months of gruelling experiment, has patiently sifted the relevant technique from the personal reminiscence and has projected miles of film in search of the apt sequence, analysing on a hand projector the chosen sequences, noting every detail and measuring every foot.

This collaboration of enthusiasts has resulted in a work which falls into three sections.

The first and third are general ; the second is drawn from a series of particular statements, each under the control of the appropriate expert or experts. The whole may therefore be regarded as a symposium, bound together by a prologue and an epilogue.

*   *   *   *   *

Now a word about our use of the words *film editing* and *editor*. The responsibility for the editing of a film rests with a number of people—the writer, the director, the editor, the sound-editor and so on. No attempt has been made to differentiate between these functions. When the word *editor* is used, it is not necessarily to be taken as reference to the technician working in the cutting room. It simply refers to the person—whoever he may have been—who was responsible for the particular editing decision being discussed. The whole of this book is, in fact, not so much about the specific work of the editor as about the process of *editing* which is usually a far wider responsibility.

*   *   *   *   *

I must emphasise that we have not tried to write a book of editing *theory*. With nine film-makers working by choice in different styles—some of whom did not in the first place recognise the value of a theoretical approach—this would surely have proved an impossible task. As I have indicated, we decided to make the best use of our panel by letting each expert supervise the chapter dealing with his own *genre*. The bulk of the book—contained in Section II—is therefore devoted to practical examples which are analysed by their directors or editors. The generalisations which can be drawn from these practical issues are gathered together and summarised in Section III.

In dividing Section II into the chapters we chose, we were aware that the divisions must inevitably remain somewhat arbitrary. It is not possible to divide all the problems of film presentation into a series of self-contained compartments for specialists, and this has not been our aim. Our choice of chapter headings does not so much represent a division into self-contained *genres* as a grouping of related editing problems.

For instance : a lucid exposition of the action being depicted on the screen is, of course, always desirable, but we have found it most convenient to consider this specific problem under the heading of Educational Films where lucid exposition is the first need. Similarly, the chapter on Newsreels deals primarily with *ad hoc* problems of editing technique, the chapter on Dialogue Sequences primarily with questions of timing. In this way we hope that the cumulative effect of the book will be reasonably comprehensive.

We have allowed ourselves some latitude in our approach to the practical examples. The chapters are uneven in length simply because some editing problems are more complex than others and since the editor's contribution to the total effect is—to take a simple example—more considerable in a compilation film than in a newsreel.

Again, in some instances the nature of the editing problems is so much subject to personal interpretation that we have found it suitable to quote the editor's own comments on his work ; in other cases, where a more general approach is permissible, the editor's comments have been incorporated in the text. These slight unevennesses in approach spring from the diverse nature of the material and to standardise it would have meant breaking faith with our subject.

One word of explanation about the examples. Except where otherwise stated, they are presented in the form of break-downs of finished sequences and are not taken from scripts. They are chosen to represent typical problems, where possible, from films which have had a wide showing. No claims are made for the films on which we have drawn : we have simply taken examples, good or bad, which were most useful to our exposition. (No foreign language films have been used because of the difficulty of reproducing foreign dialogue in the break-downs.)

*　　*　　*　　*　　*

I hope most of the readers of this book will be those who normally cannot afford a book published at this price. Faced with the problem of producing a comprehensive book on so large a subject, we decided, with the loyal help of the publisher, not to restrict the scope of text and illustrations. We hope that friends will club together to share a copy, that film societies here and abroad will find it worth while to invest in more than one copy.

This is not a book to be absorbed at one reading. For full appreciation the keen student may want to avail himself of the hand projector and viewing machines which the *National Film Library* (of the *British Film Institute*) provides for the close examination of films in its collection.

I mentioned earlier the pivotal nature of the editing process in films. Only those who know the craft can estimate the essential contribution of the editing process not only to the art but also to the physical (and that means also financial) economy of the film.

Thorold Dickinson,

October, 1952. *British Film Academy.*

PART I
SECTION 1

THE HISTORY OF EDITING

1

EDITING AND THE SILENT FILM

" ONCE more I repeat, that editing is the creative force of filmic reality, and that nature provides only the raw material with which it works. That, precisely, is the relationship between editing and the film."[1] This confident statement, from the pen of one of the silent cinema's most noted directors, was written in 1928. By examining the films produced in the first thirty years of the cinema's history and by drawing on his own extensive experience as a practising director, Pudovkin came to the conclusion that the process of editing—the selection, timing and arrangement of given shots into a film continuity—was the crucial creative act in the production of a film. It would be difficult to-day to be so emphatic. Contemporary film-makers have raised other elements of film production—most notably acting and dialogue writing—to a level of importance which is incompatible with Pudovkin's statement. The tradition of expressive visual juxtaposition, which is characteristic of the best silent films, has been largely neglected since the advent of sound. It will be one of the main arguments of this book that this neglect has brought with it a great loss to the cinema.

Meanwhile, the history of the silent cinema provides ample corroboration for Pudovkin's belief. The growth in the expressiveness of the film medium from the simple film records of the Lumière brothers to the sophisticated continuities of the late twenties was the result of a corresponding development in editing technique. Pudovkin, in 1928, was able to convey infinitely more complex ideas and emotions in his films than were the Lumière brothers thirty years earlier, precisely because he had learnt to use editing methods through which to do so.

The history of the silent cinema is by now so well documented that there is no need to restate the precise historical events in this evolution : when a particular editing device was first used, or who

[1] Film Technique *by V. I. Pudovkin. Newnes, 1929, p. xvi.*

15

should be given credit for its first application, are questions for the film historian. What concerns us is the significance of new editing constructions, the cause of their development and their relevance to contemporary usage. The brief historical notes that follow are designed not so much to summarise the research of historians as to provide a logical starting point for a study of the art of film editing.

The beginnings of film continuity

In making their earliest films, the Lumière brothers adopted a simple procedure : they chose a subject which they thought might be interesting to record, set up their camera in front of it, and went on shooting until the stock ran out. Any common event— *Baby at the Lunch Table, A Boat Leaving Harbour*—served their purpose, which was simply to record events in motion. They used the film camera as a recording instrument whose sole advantage over the still camera was that it could capture the element of movement : indeed, the essence of a film like *A Boat Leaving Harbour* could have been equally conveyed in a still photograph.

Although most of the Lumière films were records of simple unrehearsed events, one of the earliest already shows a conscious control of the material being shot. In *Watering the Gardener* the Lumières recorded for the first time a prearranged comic scene in which they exercised conscious control over their material : a small boy steps on the hose with which a gardener is watering his flowers ; the gardener is puzzled when the flow stops, looks at the nozzle ; the boy takes his foot off the hose and the gardener is drenched with water. The action itself, as well as the fact that it moved, was designed to capture the spectator's interest.

The films of George Méliès are to-day mainly remembered for the ingenuity of their trick-work and for their primitive charm. At the time of production, however, they marked an important advance on previous work in that they enlarged the scope of film story-telling beyond the single shot. *Cinderella* (1899), Méliès' second long film, ran 410 feet (where the Lumière films had been around 50 feet) and told its story in twenty motion *tableaux* : (1) Cinderella in her Kitchen ; (2) The Fairy, Mice and Lackeys ; (3) The Transformation of the Rat ; . . . (20) The Triumph of Cinderella.[1] Each *tableau* was similar in kind to the Lumières'

[1] An Index to the Creative Work of Georges Méliès, *by Georges Sadoul. The British Film Institute, 1947.*

16

Watering the Gardener in that a relatively simple incident was prearranged and then recorded on to a single continuous strip of film. But whereas the Lumières had confined themselves to recording short single-incident events, Méliès here attempted to tell a story of several episodes. The continuity of *Cinderella* established a connection between separate shots. The twenty *tableaux*—presented rather like a series of lecture-slides—acquired an elementary kind of unity by virtue of revolving around a central character : seen together, they told a story of greater complexity than was possible in the single shot film.

The limitations of *Cinderella*, as of most of Méliès' subsequent films, are the limitations of theatrical presentation : each incident —like each act in a play—is set against a single background and is self-contained in time and place ; scenes are never started in one place and continued in another ; the camera, always stationed at a distance from the actors and facing the backcloth head-on, remains stationary and outside the scene of the action—precisely as does the spectator in the theatre auditorium. Further, the continuity of *Cinderella* is purely one of subject : there is no continuity of action from shot to shot and the time relationship between consecutive shots is left undefined.

While Méliès continued for many years to produce increasingly sophisticated films on the theatrical pattern of *Cinderella*, some of his contemporaries were beginning to work on entirely different lines. In 1902, the American Edwin S. Porter, one of Edison's first cameramen, made *The Life of an American Fireman*. His very approach to the task of making a film contrasts sharply with hitherto accepted practice :

Porter rummaged through the stock of Edison's old films, searching for suitable scenes around which to build a story. He found quantities of pictures of fire department activities. Since fire departments had such a strong popular appeal, with their colour and action, Porter chose them as his subject. But he still needed some central idea or incident by which to organise the scenes of the fire department in action . . . Porter therefore concocted a scheme that was as startling as it was different : a mother and child were to be caught in a burning building and rescued at the last moment by the fire department.[1]

Porter's decision to construct a story film from previously shot material was unprecedented. It implied that the meaning of a shot was not necessarily self-contained but could be modified by joining the shot to others. A description of the last episode of *The Life of an American Fireman* will suffice to give an idea of the film's revolutionary method of construction.

[1] The Rise of the American Film *by Lewis Jacobs. Harcourt, Brace and Co., New York, 1939, p. 37.*

17

Scene 7. *Arrival at the fire.*

In this wonderful scene we show the entire fire department . . . arriving at the scene of action. An actual burning building is in the centre foreground. On the right background the fire department is seen coming at great speed. Upon the arrival of the different apparatus, the engines are ordered to their places, hose is quickly run out from the carriages, ladders are adjusted to the windows and streams of water are poured into the burning structure. At this crucial moment comes the great climax of the series.

We dissolve to the interior of the building and show a bedchamber with a woman and child enveloped in flame and suffocating smoke. The woman rushes back and forth in the room endeavouring to escape, and in her desperation throws open the window and appeals to the crowd below. She is finally overcome by the smoke and falls upon the bed. At this moment the door is smashed in by an axe in the hands of a powerful fire hero. Rushing into the room, he tears the burning draperies from the window and smashes out the entire window frame, ordering his comrades to run up a ladder. Immediately the ladder appears, he seizes the prostrate form of the woman and throws it over his shoulders as if it were an infant, and quickly descends to the ground.

We now dissolve to the exterior of the burning building. The frantic mother having returned to consciousness, and clad only in her night clothes, is kneeling on the ground imploring the fireman to return for her child. Volunteers are called for and the same fireman who rescued the mother quickly steps out and offers to return for the babe. He is given permission to once more enter the doomed building and without hesitation rushes up the ladder, enters the window and after a breathless wait, in which it appears he must have been overcome with smoke, he appears with the child in his arms and returns safely to the ground. The child, being released and upon seeing its mother, rushes to her and is clasped in her arms, thus making a most realistic and touching ending of the series.[1]

The events which form the climax of *The Life of an American Fireman* are rendered in three stages. A dramatic problem is set in the first shot which is not resolved till the end of the third. The action is carried over from shot to shot and an illusion of continuous development is created. Instead of splitting the action into three self-contained sections joined by titles—which is how Méliès might have tackled the situation—Porter simply joined the shots together. As a result, the spectator felt that he was witnessing a single continuous event.

By constructing his film in this way, Porter was able to present a long, physically complicated incident without resorting to the jerky, one-point-at-a-time continuity of a Méliès film. But the gain derived from the new method is more than a gain in fluency. For one thing it gives the director an almost limitless freedom of movement since he can split up the action into small, manageable units. In the climax of *The Life of an American Fireman*, Porter combined the two hitherto separate styles of film-making : he

[1] The Rise of the American Film *by Lewis Jacobs. Harcourt, Brace and Co., New York, 1939, p. 40. Quoted from the Edison catalogue of 1903.*

18

joined an actuality shot to a staged studio shot without apparently breaking the thread of the action.

Another equally fundamental advantage of Porter's method of assembly is that the director is able to convey a sense of time to the spectator. *The Life of an American Fireman* opens with a shot of a fireman asleep in his chair, dreaming of a woman and child trapped in a burning house (the dream is shown in a 'dream balloon'). The next shot shows the fire alarm being raised and is followed by four shots of the firemen hurrying towards the scene of the disaster. These, in turn, are followed by the climax which we have already quoted. An operation taking a considerable length of time is compressed into the space of a one-reeler without, apparently, any discontinuity in the narrative : only the significant parts of the story are selected and joined to form an acceptable, logically developing continuity. Porter had demonstrated that the single shot, recording an incomplete piece of action, is the unit of which films must be constructed and thereby established the basic principle of editing.

Porter's next important film, *The Great Train Robbery* (1903), shows a more confident use of the newly discovered editing principle. It contains, moreover, one shot transition which is more sophisticated than anything in his earlier film.

Scene 9. *A beautiful scene in the valley.*

The bandits come down the side of the hill, across a narrow stream, mounting their horses, and make for the wilderness.

Scene 10. *Interior of telegraph office.*

The operator lies bound and gagged on the floor. After struggling to his feet, he leans on the table and telegraphs for assistance by manipulating the key with his chin, and then faints from exhaustion. His little daughter enters with his dinner pail. She cuts the rope, throws a glass of water in his face and restores him to consciousness, and, recalling his thrilling experience, he rushes out to give the alarm.

Scene 11. *Interior of a typical Western dance hall.*

Shows a number of men and women in a lively quadrille. A " tenderfoot " is quickly spotted and pushed to the centre of the hall, and compelled to do a jig, while bystanders amuse themselves by shooting dangerously close to his feet. Suddenly the door opens and the half-dead telegraph operator staggers in. The dance breaks up in confusion. The men secure their rifles and hastily leave the room.[1]

The most significant feature of this short excerpt is its freedom

[1] The Rise of the American Film *by Lewis Jacobs. Harcourt, Brace and Co., New York, 1939, p. 45. Quoted from the Edison catalogue of 1904.*

of movement. The cut from *9* to *10* takes us from one set of characters to another—from the shot of the escaping bandits, to the office where the operator (whom the bandits gagged in the first scene) lies helpless. There is no direct physical connection between the shots : *10* does not take up the action started in *9*. The two events shown in *9* and *10* are happening in parallel and are linked by a continuity of idea.

This passage marks a distinct advance on the simple continuity of action of *The Life of an American Fireman*. Porter himself developed this kind of parallel action editing further in his subsequent films, but it was not till Griffith's time that the device found its full application.

Griffith : dramatic emphasis

By evolving the simple method of action continuity, Edwin S. Porter showed how a developing story could be presented in terms of the film medium. His control of the presentation was, however, limited. The events of his films were rendered unselectively since each incident was staged at a fixed distance from the camera : there was, as yet, no means by which the director could vary the emphasis of his narrative. Such variations in dramatic intensity as could be achieved had to be conveyed solely through the actors' gestures.

Let us now look at an excerpt from a film made some twelve years after *The Great Train Robbery*—D. W. Griffith's *The Birth of a Nation*. A comparison of the methods of the two films shows the manner in which Porter's simple action continuities were developed by Griffith into a subtle instrument for creating and controlling dramatic tension.

THE BIRTH OF A NATION

Excerpt from Reel 6 : The assassination of Lincoln

TITLE : " *And then, when the terrible days were over and a healing time of peace was at hand* " . . . *came the fated night of 14th April, 1865.*

There follows a short scene in which Benjamin Cameron (Henry B. Walthall) fetches Elsie Stoneman (Lillian Gish) from the Stonemans' house and they leave together for the theatre. They are attending a special gala performance at which President Lincoln is to be present. The performance has already begun.

TITLE :   *Time : 8.30*
                     The arrival of the President

20

1	F.S.² of Lincoln's party as, one by one, they reach the top of the stairs inside the theatre and turn off towards the President's box. Lincoln's bodyguard comes up first, Lincoln himself last.	7
2	The President's box, viewed from inside the theatre. Members of Lincoln's party appear inside.	4
3	F.S. President Lincoln, outside his box, giving up his hat to an attendant.	3
4	The President's box. As in 2. Lincoln appears in the box.	5
5	M.S. Elsie Stoneman and Ben Cameron sitting in the auditorium. They look up towards Lincoln's box, then start clapping and rise from their seats.	7
6	Shooting from the back of the auditorium towards the stage. The President's box is to the right. The audience, backs to camera, are standing in foreground, clapping and cheering the President.	3
7	The President's box. As in 4. Lincoln and Mrs. Lincoln bow to the audience.	3
8	As in 6.	3
9	The President's box. As in 7. The President bows, then sits down.	5

TITLE : Mr. Lincoln's personal bodyguard takes his post outside the box.

10	F.S. The bodyguard coming into the passage outside the box and sitting down. He starts rubbing his knees impatiently.	10
11	Shooting from the back of the auditorium towards the stage. The play is in progress.	5
12	The President's box. As in 9. Lincoln takes his wife's hand. He is watching the play approvingly.	9
13	As in 11. The spectators stop clapping.	4
14	Closer view of the stage. The actors are continuing with the play.	10

TITLE : To get a view of the play, the bodyguard leaves his post.

15	F.S. Bodyguard. As in 10. He is clearly impatient.	5
16	Close view of the stage. As in 14.	2
17	F.S. The bodyguard. As in 15. He gets up and puts his chair away behind a side door.	6
18	As in 6. Shooting towards a box near Lincoln's, as the bodyguard enters and takes his place.	3
19	Within a circular mask, we see a closer view of the action of 18. The bodyguard takes his place in the box.	5

TITLE :   Time : 10.30
                         Act III, Scene 2

20	A general view of the theatre from the back of the auditorium ; a diagonal mask leaves only Lincoln's box visible.	5
21	M.S. Elsie and Ben. Elsie points to something in Lincoln's direction.	6

TITLE :   John Wilkes Booth

22	The head and shoulders of John Wilkes Booth seen within a circular mask.	3
23	As in 21. Elsie is now happily watching the play again.	6
24	Booth. As in 22.	2½
25	Close view of Lincoln's box.	5
26	Booth. As in 22.	4
27	Close view of the stage. As in 14.	4
28	Close view of the box. As in 25. Lincoln smiles approvingly at the play. He makes a gesture with his shoulders as if he were cold and starts to pull his coat on.	8
29	Booth. As in 22. He moves his head up in the act of rising from his seat.	4
30	28 continued. Lincoln finishes putting on his coat.	6

¹ The length of each shot is indicated in feet of film.
At silent speed 1 foot is equivalent to a running time of 1 second.
At sound speed 1 foot is equivalent to a running time of ⅔ second.
² These abbreviations are explained and defined in the Glossary of Terms.

		Ft.
31	The theatre viewed from the back of the auditorium. *As in* 20. *The mask spreads* to reveal the whole theatre.	4
32	*C.S.* The bodyguard, enjoying the play. *As in* 19, *within circular mask*.	1½
33	*F.S.* Booth. He comes through the door at the end of the passage outside Lincoln's box. He stoops to look through the key-hole into Lincoln's box. He pulls out a revolver and braces himself for the deed.	14
34	*C.S.* The revolver.	3
35	33 *continued.* Booth comes up to the door, has momentary difficulty in opening it, then steps into Lincoln's box.	8
36	*Close view* of Lincoln's box. *As in* 25. Booth appears behind Lincoln.	5
37	The stage. *As in* 14. The actors are performing.	4
38	*As in* 36. Booth shoots Lincoln in the back. Lincoln collapses. Booth climbs on to the side of the box and jumps over on to the stage.	5
39	*L.S.* Booth on the stage. He throws his arms up and shouts.	
	TITLE : *Sic Semper Tyrannis*	

The plot of this passage is relatively simple : President Lincoln is assassinated at a theatre while his bodyguard has carelessly left his post. In Porter's time, the events might have been rendered in half a dozen shots and been clear to an audience. Griffith, however, is concerned with more than simply reproducing the plot. He has constructed his scene around four groups of characters : Lincoln's party, including the bodyguard ; Elsie Stoneman and Ben Cameron ; Booth, the assassin ; and the actors on the stage. Each time he cuts from one to another, the transition is acceptable because it has been established that all the characters are present at the scene. Thus although the main action (which concerns Lincoln, the bodyguard and Booth only) is repeatedly interrupted to reveal the surrounding events, there is no apparent discontinuity : Porter's continuity principle is in no way violated.

There is, however, a marked difference between Porter's and Griffith's reasons for splitting the action into short fragments. When Porter cut from one image to another, it was usually because, for physical reasons, it had become impossible to accommodate the events he wanted to show in a single shot. In Griffith's continuity, the action is only rarely carried over from one shot to the next. The viewpoint is changed not for physical but for *dramatic* reasons—to show the spectator a fresh detail of the larger scene which has become most relevant to the drama at the particular moment.

Griffith's approach to editing is thus radically different from Porter's. The excerpt from *The Birth of a Nation* creates its effects through the cumulative impression of a series of details. Griffith has divided the whole action into a number of components and has then re-created the scene from them. The advantage over the earlier editing method is twofold. Firstly, it enables the director to

22

create a sense of depth in his narrative : the various details add up to a fuller, more persuasively life-like picture of a situation than can a single shot, played against a constant background. Secondly, the director is in a far stronger position to guide the spectator's reactions, because he is able to *choose* what particular detail the spectator is to see at any particular moment. A short analysis of the excerpt quoted should amplify the point.

The first fourteen shots establish Lincoln's arrival and reception at the theatre.

Then, a title gives the first hint of the impending danger.

The following five shots present an interesting comparison with Porter's simple action continuity because they depict a single character's continuous movements.

15 shows the bodyguard waiting impatiently.

Then, instead of showing what he does next, shot *16* establishes the cause of the bodyguard's impatience—the stage which he wishes to see.

17, *18* and *19* show him getting up, moving through the door and settling down in the box. There is a perfectly logical continuity of theme running through the sequence. The cut from *17* to *18* is straightforward : it merely changes the location of the action as the bodyguard moves into the box.

18 and *19*, by contrast, are both views of the same action—*19* merely draws attention to a detail of the previous larger image. Clearly, this cut is not physically necessary : it is made because it is dramatically effective.

There follows another ominous hint in the title and *20* and *21* reveal the theatre audience, unaware of the danger.

In the shots that follow (*22–30*), the haunting static image of John Wilkes Booth is cut in after each detail of the general scene, partly to create suspense, partly to establish that Booth is, in fact, unidentified and unsuspected.

Then, after a reminder that the bodyguard is not at his post (*32*), Booth is seen going into action (*33–36*).

At this point, instead of showing the assassination, Griffith interrupts the action of *36*, which was probably shot as a continuous take with *38*, to give a glimpse of the stage (*37*). The last two cuts form a concise illustration of Griffith's newly developed editing method. The view of the stage in *37* adds nothing to our knowledge of the scene. It is inserted for purely dramatic reasons : the suspense is artificially kept up a while longer and Lincoln's complete unawareness of Booth's presence is indirectly stressed.

23

We have said that Griffith's editing allows for a more detailed and persuasive rendering of the drama. Two instances in this brief excerpt illustrate the point. In shot *21* Elsie points in the direction of Lincoln's box : for a moment it looks as if she has spotted the assassin, then the suspicion is allowed to die. The tantalising moment of uncertainty adds greatly to the suspense of the scene.

Again, before Lincoln is shot, we see him making the curious gesture—as if he were sitting in a draught—which suggests a momentary premonition of what is about to happen. It is a detail which poignantly foreshadows his sudden death.

Griffith's fundamental discovery, then, lies in his realisation that a film sequence must be made up of incomplete shots whose order and selection are governed by dramatic necessity. Where Porter's camera had impartially recorded the action from a distance (i.e., in long shot), Griffith demonstrated that the camera could play a positive part in telling the story. By splitting an event into short fragments and recording each from the most suitable camera position, he could vary the emphasis from shot to shot and thereby control the dramatic intensity of the events as the story progressed.

We have already noticed one application of this principle in the cross-cutting of four streams of action in the excerpt from *The Birth of a Nation*. Another application of the same principle is to be found in Griffith's use of close shots.

Early in his career, Griffith became aware of the limitations of staging an entire scene at a fixed distance from the camera. Where he wanted to convey a character's thoughts or emotions, Griffith saw that he could best do so by taking his camera closer to the actor and recording his facial expressions in greater detail. Thus, at the moment when an actor's emotional reaction became the focal point of the scene, Griffith simply cut from the establishing long shot to a closer view ; later, when the scene again reverted to broader movement, he cut back to the more comprehensive long shot.

There would be no point in quoting extensive examples of Griffith's use of close shots, for the device is completely familiar to-day. We may recall, in passing, the striking use made of it in the trial scene from *Intolerance* : close shots of The Dear One's hands, working in an agony of suspense, together with close shots of her anxious face, convey all we need to know of her state of mind as she awaits the court's judgment.

The introduction of extreme long shots is another example of Griffith's use of images which have no direct part in the plot and

24

are employed for purely dramatic effect. The memorable panoramic views of the battlefields in *The Birth of a Nation* give an impression of the nation-wide disaster against which the story of the Camerons and the Stonemans is told. They establish the wider context which the story's gravity demands.

An innovation similar in purpose is Griffith's use of the flashback. Here, again, Griffith saw that a character's actions could often be more clearly motivated by letting the spectator see certain thoughts or memories passing through the character's mind. In *Intolerance*, for example, when The Friendless One is just about to implicate The Boy in the murder of The Musketeer of the Slums, she has a momentary pang of conscience as she recalls the time when The Boy did her a kindness. From the scene in the present, Griffith simply mixed to the earlier scene and then mixed back again. The continuity of dramatic ideas was sufficiently forceful for the scene to be completely lucid.

The revolution in film craftsmanship which followed Griffith's many innovations was felt in various ways in the routine of production. Armed with his new editing methods, Griffith was no longer obliged to stage scenes in their entirety. Where Porter might have staged an elaborate chase sequence and photographed it as it might be seen by a spectator present on the spot, Griffith took separate shots of the pursuer and the pursued. It was only when the scenes came to be edited that they conveyed the desired picture of a chase. Scenes which could previously only be recorded with great difficulty, could now be assembled from easily staged shots : huge battle scenes, fatal accidents, hair-raising chases—all these could now be conveyed to the spectator by appropriate editing. The massacres of the Babylonians in *Intolerance* are presented with conviction by being reconstructed from shots of manageable length. A continuity consisting of one shot of a Persian releasing an arrow, followed by a second shot of a Babylonian, struck and falling to the ground, gives an entirely convincing picture of a scene which would have been difficult to handle in a single shot.

If Griffith's methods made the staging of spectacle scenes easier, they made the actor's task in films considerably more difficult. Acting in close shot demanded greater control and subtlety of expression than had hitherto been necessary. Whereas in Porter's time it had been necessary to over-act to convey an effect at all, the camera's proximity imposed on the actor the new discipline of restraint.

25

Yet, while the actor's task became more exacting, the prime responsibility for conveying an effect passed from his hands into those of the director. The suspense leading up to the murder of Lincoln (achieved by devices like the quick cut-away to shot 37) is conveyed not primarily by the actors but by the manner in which the events are arranged. The director controls the order and manner in which the spectator sees consecutive shots and can therefore highlight or flatten a scene as he chooses. If he cuts to a close shot, the very appearance of the larger image implies to the spectator that a moment of greater dramatic intensity has arrived. The effect of an actor's performance in a shot is thus conditioned by the way the director decides to place the camera and by the context in which he chooses to show it.

The control of the element of timing is equally transferred from the actor to the director in Griffith's films. Griffith's splitting up of scenes into small components raises a new question for the editor. How long should each shot be left on the screen? An examination of the excerpt from *The Birth of a Nation* reveals how the timing of shots can be made to play a significant part in controlling the impact of a scene. The pace of cutting is increased towards the climax to give an impression of mounting tension. Griffith's famous chase sequences—the technique of cross-cutting in the final chase of an action picture was, for a long time, known in the industry as the " Griffith last minute rescue "—all gained a great deal of their effectiveness from the tempo at which they were edited. The cutting rate was invariably increased towards the climax, giving the impression that the excitement was steadily mounting.

Rhythmic effects of this kind are, unfortunately, extremely difficult to analyse without direct reference to the film itself and we shall have to content ourselves, at this stage, with drawing attention to Griffith's awareness of their importance. Since a consideration of the control of tempo and rhythm in Griffith's films would cover points we shall consider later, more detailed discussion is held over to Chapter 14.

Pudovkin : constructive editing

D. W. Griffith's genius was essentially the genius of a story-teller ; his great achievement lay in his discovery and application of editing methods which enabled him to enrich and strengthen the narrative power of the film medium. The Russian director

Sergei Eisenstein, in his essay, *Dickens, Griffith, and the Film To-day*,[1] describes the manner in which Griffith translated the literary devices and conventions of the novelist (particularly of Dickens) into their film equivalents. Eisenstein points out that devices such as cross-cutting, close shots, flash-backs, even dissolves, have literary parallels and that all Griffith did was to find them. Having analysed the origin of Griffith's methods, Eisenstein goes on to explain their influence on the young Russian directors. Deeply impressed by Griffith's pioneer work, they nevertheless felt it was lacking in one important respect.

To the parallelism of alternating close-ups of America [i.e., of Griffith] we [i.e., the young Russian directors] offer the contrast of uniting these in fusion ; the montage trope.

In the theory of literature a *trope* is defined thus : a figure of speech which consists in the use of a word or phrase in a sense other than that which is proper to it, for example, a *sharp* wit (normally, a *sharp* sword).

Griffith's cinema does not know this type of montage construction. His close-ups create atmosphere, outline traits of characters, alternate in dialogues of leading characters, and close-ups of the chaser and the chased speed up the tempo of the chase. But Griffith at all times remains on a level of *representation and objectivity* and nowhere does he try through the *juxtaposition* of shots to shape *import and image*.[2]

In other words, where Griffith was content to tell his stories by means of the kind of editing construction we have already seen in the excerpt from *The Birth of a Nation*, the young Russian directors felt that they could take the film director's control over his material a stage further. They planned, by means of new editing methods, not only to tell stories but to interpret and draw intellectual conclusions from them.

Griffith had attempted just this in *Intolerance*. By telling four stories, each illustrating his title theme, and presenting them in parallel, he meant to express his central idea. Eisenstein conceded that the four stories of *Intolerance* were well told but maintained that the central idea failed to get across : the generalisation Griffith wanted to make failed to reach the audience because it was nowhere directly expressed. This failure, Eisenstein argued, arose from Griffith's misunderstanding of the nature of editing.

Out of this [*misunderstanding*] came his unsuccessful use of the repeated refrain shot : Lillian Gish rocking a cradle. Griffith had been inspired to translate these lines of Walt Whitman :

" . . . endlessly rocks the cradle, Uniter of Here and Hereafter."

not in structure, nor in *the harmonic recurrence of montage expressiveness*, but in *an isolated picture*, with the result that the cradle could not possibly

[1] Film Form *by Sergei Eisenstein. Dobson, 1951.*
[2] Ibid., *p. 240.*

be *abstracted into an image of eternally reborn epochs* and remained inevitably simply a *life-like cradle*, calling forth derision, surprise or vexation in the spectator.[1]

Eisenstein concluded that if generalised ideas of the kind Griffith attempted to express in *Intolerance* were to be conveyed in the film medium, then entirely new methods of editing—of montage—would have to be evolved. And this he understood to be the task of the young Russian directors.

To understand the unique contribution to the cinema made by the early Russian film-makers, it is necessary to know a little of the state of the Soviet film industry in the silent period. Eisenstein has described how he and his colleagues, starting their work in the cinema, found themselves in an industry almost completely devoid of native traditions. Such films as had been made in Russia before the revolution were mainly undistinguished commercial quickies whose artificiality was alien to the young revolutionary directors who saw themselves as propagandists and teachers rather than as conventional entertainers. As such, their task was twofold : to use the film medium as a means of instructing the masses in the history and theory of their political movement ; and to train a young generation of film-makers to fulfil this task.

These circumstances produced two noteworthy results. First, the young directors set about finding new ways by which to express ideas in the film medium so that they could communicate these in their political cause. Second, they went about developing a theory of film-making which Griffith, busy and essentially instinctive worker that he was, had never attempted to do.

The theoretical writing of the Russian directors falls into two separate schools. On the one hand, are the views of Pudovkin and Kuleshov, most succinctly laid down in Pudovkin's book, *Film Technique* ; on the other, the more erratic, less systematically presented writing of Eisenstein. Pudovkin's contribution to film theory is to a large extent a rationalisation of Griffith's work. Where Griffith was content to solve his problems as they arose, Pudovkin formulated a theory of editing which could be used as a general guiding system. He started from first principles.

If we consider the work of the film director, then it appears that the active raw material is no other than those *pieces of celluloid* on which, from various viewpoints, the separate movements of the action have been shot. From nothing but these pieces is created those appearances upon the screen that form the filmic representation of the action shot. And thus the material

[1] Film Form *by Sergei Eisenstein. Dobson, 1951, p. 241.*

28

of the film director consists not of real processes happening in real space and real time, but of those pieces of celluloid on which these processes have been recorded. This celluloid is entirely subject to the will of the director who edits it. He can, in the composition of the filmic form of any given appearance, eliminate all points of interval, and thus concentrate the action in time to the highest degree he may require.[1]

Having thus stated the principle of what he called *constructive editing*, Pudovkin went on to demonstrate how it could be applied —and, indeed, had been applied by Griffith—in the course of film narrative.

In order to show on the screen the fall of a man from a window five storeys high, the shots can be taken in the following way :
First, the man is shot falling from the window into a net, in such a way that the net is not visible on the screen ; then the same man is shot falling from a slight height to the ground. Joined together, the two shots give in projection the desired impression. The catastrophic fall never occurs in reality, it occurs only on the screen, and is the resultant of two pieces of celluloid joined together. From the event of a real, actual fall of a person from an appalling height, two points only are selected : the beginning of the fall and its end. The intervening passage through the air is eliminated. It is not proper to call the process a trick ; it is a method of filmic representation exactly corresponding to the elimination of the five years that divide a first act from a second upon a stage.[2]

Up to this point, Pudovkin's writing merely provides a theoretical explanation of what Griffith had already done in practice. From here onward, however, Pudovkin's theory begins to diverge from Griffith's work. Where Griffith staged scenes in long shot and used inserted close shots of details to heighten the drama, Pudovkin held that a more impressive continuity could be obtained by constructing a sequence purely from these significant details. This change of attitude, as will be seen from one of Pudovkin's examples, is more than a matter of differently explaining a given method, for it affects the director's approach to his subject from the moment the script is conceived.

Scene 1. A peasant waggon, sinking in the mud, slowly trails along a country road. Sadly and reluctantly the hooded driver urges on his tired horse. A figure cowers into the corner of the waggon, trying to wrap itself in an old soldier's cloak for protection against the penetrating wind. A passer-by, coming towards the waggon, pauses, standing inquisitively. The driver turns to him.
Title : *Is it far to Nakhabin ?*
The pedestrian answers, pointing with his hand. The waggon sets onward, while the passer-by stares after it and then continues on his way . . .

A scenario written in this way, already divided into separate scenes and with titles, forms the first phase of filmic overhaul . . . Note that there is

[1] Film Technique *by V. I. Pudovkin. Newnes, 1929, p. 56.*
[2] Ibid., *p. 57.*

a whole series of details characteristic for the given scene and emphasised by their literary form, such as, for example, " sinking in the mud," " sadly the driver," " a passenger, wrapped in a soldier's cloak," " the piercing wind "— none of these details will reach the spectator if they are introduced merely as incidentals in shooting the scene as a whole, just as it is written. The film possesses essentially specific and highly effective methods by means of which the spectator can be made to notice each separate detail (mud, wind, behaviour of driver, behaviour of fare), showing them one by one, just as we should describe them in separate sequence in literary work, and not just simply to note " bad weather," " two men in a waggon." This method is called constructive editing.[1]

Pudovkin held that if a film narrative was to be kept continually effective, each shot must make a new and specific point. He is scornful of directors who tell their stories in long-lasting shots of an actor playing a scene, and merely punctuate them by occasional close shots of details.

Such interpolated close-ups had better be omitted—they have nothing to do with creative editing. Terms such as interpolation and cut-in are absurd expressions, the remnants of an old misunderstanding of the technical methods of the film. The details organically belonging to scenes . . . must not be interpolated into the scene, but the latter must be built out of them.[2]

Pudovkin arrived at these conclusions, partly from the experiments of his senior colleague Kuleshov, partly from his own experiences as a director. Kuleshov's experiments had revealed to him that the process of editing is more than a method for telling a continuous story. He found that by suitable juxtaposition, shots could be given meanings which they had hitherto not possessed. If, Pudovkin argued, one were to join a shot of a smiling actor to a close shot of a revolver, and follow this by another shot of the actor, now terrified, the total impression of the sequence would be to suggest that the actor was behaving in a cowardly manner. If, on the other hand, the two shots of the actor were reversed, the audience would see the actor's behaviour as heroic. Thus, although the same shots would have been used in the two cases, a different emotional effect would be achieved by simply reversing their order.

In another experiment, Pudovkin and Kuleshov took close-ups of the actor Mosjukhin and used them to edit three experimental sequences. In the first, they joined the shots of the actor—whose expression in them was neutral—to shots of a plate of soup standing on a table ; in the second, to a shot of a coffin in which lay a dead woman ; in the third, to a shot of a little girl playing with a toy.

[1] Film Technique by V. I. Pudovkin. Newnes, 1929, pp. 22, 23.
[2] Ibid., p. 23.

When we showed the three combinations to an audience which had not been let into the secret the result was terrific. The public raved about the acting of the artist. They pointed out the heavy pensiveness of his mood over the forgotten soup, were touched and moved by the deep sorrow with which he looked on the dead woman, and admired the light, happy smile with which he surveyed the girl at play. But we knew that in all three cases the face was exactly the same.[1]

So impressed were Pudovkin and Kuleshov with this ability to create effects by shot juxtaposition that they formulated the method into an aesthetic credo :

From our contemporary point of view, Kuleshov's ideas were extremely simple. All he said was this : " In every art there must be firstly a material, and secondly a method of composing this material specially adapted to this art." The musician has sounds as material and composes them in time. The painter's materials are colour, and he combines them in space on the surface of the canvas . . .

Kuleshov maintained that the material in filmwork consists of pieces of film, and that the composition method is their joining together in a particular, creatively discovered order. He maintained that film art does not begin when the artists act and the various scenes are shot—this is only the preparation of the material. Film art begins from the moment when the director begins to combine and join together the various pieces of film. By joining them in various combinations in different orders, he obtains differing results.[2]

Although this appears to-day an almost absurdly exaggerated statement of the importance of the editing process, Pudovkin achieved remarkable results when he put it into practice. Comparing his silent films with those of Griffith, one finds the very differences which Pudovkin's theoretical writings might have led one to expect. Where the narrative of Griffith's films reaches the spectator through the behaviour and movement of the actors, Pudovkin builds his scenes from carefully planned series of details and achieves his effects by their juxtapositions. As a result his narrative passages are more concentrated in their effect but less personal in their appeal.

This difference in editing style and therefore of emotional effect is, of course, primarily a reflection of the two directors' differing dramatic intentions. While Griffith is usually most concerned with human conflicts, Pudovkin is often more interested in the sidelights and overtones of the story than in the conflicts themselves. Pudovkin's plots are always, in sheer quantity of incident, simpler than Griffith's and he allots a greater proportion of screen time to exploring their implications and significance.

In *The End of St. Petersburg* Pudovkin has a sequence of the

[1] Film Technique *by V. I. Pudovkin. Newnes, 1929, p. 140.*
[2] Ibid., *pp. 138, 139.*

1914–1918 war in which soldiers are fighting and dying in the muddy trenches. To strengthen the impact of this, he cross-cuts the shots of the trenches with a sequence showing the city-dwelling financiers crazily rushing to the stock exchange to cash in on the rising market prices. One feels that Pudovkin's aim in editing his scene in this way was not so much to score a political point as to strengthen the emotional effect of the trench scenes. These, indeed, depend for their effect almost entirely upon the juxtaposition of the two actions, for the soldiers at the front are shown almost exclusively in long shot and none of them is individually identified.

Another equally characteristic Pudovkin continuity occurs in *Mother* when the son is just about to be released from prison. Pudovkin has described its making as follows :

> In . . . *Mother*, I tried to affect the spectators not by the psychological performance of an actor, but by plastic synthesis through editing. The son sits in prison. Suddenly, passed in to him surreptitiously, he receives a note that next day he is to be set free. The problem was the expression, filmically, of his joy. The photographing of a face lighting up with joy would have been flat and void of effect. I show, therefore, the nervous play of his hands and a big close-up of the lower half of his face, the corners of the smile. These shots I cut in with other and varied material—shots of a brook, swollen with the rapid flow of spring, of the play of sunlight broken on the water, birds splashing in the village pond, and finally, a laughing child. By the junction of these components our expression of prisoner's joy takes shape.[1]

In *The Art of the Film* Ernest Lindgren puts forward a detailed and highly illuminating analysis of this passage. He points out, among other things, that Pudovkin's description of the sequence is incomplete and hardly does justice to it. From our point of view, however, the director's account is sufficiently full to make its main point : that instead of attempting to play the scene on the actor's face, a complex montage sequence is employed to convey an emotional effect.

Pudovkin's films abound in passages of this kind, where the relationship between shots is purely one of idea or emotion (although, as Lindgren has pointed out in this case, Pudovkin makes the images of the stream, birds, etc., appear to be a natural part of the continuity by prefacing them with the title, " And outside it is spring "). In this sense, his films already contain hints of the sort of continuities employed by Eisenstein which, as we shall see, are even further removed from Griffith's straightforward narratives.

[1] Film Technique *by V. I. Pudovkin. Newnes, 1929, p. xviii.*

Eisenstein : intellectual montage

In Pudovkin's silent films it is always the dramatic situation which remains foremost in the spectator's mind : the indirect comments on the story never become an end in themselves, they merely serve to heighten the drama. In Eisenstein's silent films, particularly in *October* and *Old and New*, the balance between plot and comment is, as it were, tipped the other way. To Eisenstein—and we are here speaking of his silent films only—the story merely provides a convenient structure upon which to build an exposition of ideas ; to him, it is the conclusions and abstractions which can be drawn from the actual events which are of first interest.

Eisenstein's methods of what he himself has called *intellectual montage* are fully described in his own theoretical writings. These, in translation, are often extremely obscure and, since they depend on a series of definitions peculiar to the writer's method, difficult to summarise. Let us therefore, before passing on to the theory, look at a passage of intellectual cinema from one of Eisenstein's silent films and attempt to analyse the difference between his and his predecessors' editing techniques. In doing so, we shall keep faith with Eisenstein's theoretical approach, which was always a direct rationalisation of his practical work.

OCTOBER

Reel 3

1–17	The interior of the Winter Palace in St. Petersburg. Kerensky, head of the provisional government, attended by two lieutenants, is slowly walking down the vast palatial corridor. He moves up the stairs : *inter-cut* with a number of slow-moving shots of Kerensky proudly ascending the stairway, are separate *titles* describing Kerensky's rank : *Commander-in-Chief, Minister of War and Marine, etcetera, etcetera, etcetera.*
18	*C.S.* A garland in the hands of one of the palace statues.
19	*F.S.* The whole statue, holding the garland.
20	*C.S.* Garland, *as in* 18.
21	*Title : Hope of his Country and the Revolution.*
22	*Shooting up* towards another statue holding a garland. (*The angle of the camera makes it appear as if the statue were just about to deposit the garland on Kerensky's head.*)
23	*Title : Alexander Fedorovitch Kerensky.*
24	*C.U.* Kerensky's face, still and intense.
25	*C.S.* Garland in the statue's hands.
26	*C.U.* Kerensky, *as in* 24. His expression relaxes into a smile.
27	*C.S.* Garland, *as in* 25.
28–39	Kerensky ascends the stairway farther and is greeted by the Czar's large, richly decorated footman. Kerensky, despite attempts at dignity, looks small beside this imposing figure. He is introduced to a whole line of footmen and shakes hands with each one. *What a democrat* !
40–74	Kerensky waits before the huge ornate palace doors leading to the Czar's private quarters. We see the Czar's coat-of-arms on the doors. Kerensky waits helplessly for the doors to open. Two footmen smile. Kerensky's boots, then his gloved hands, seen in *close-up*, moving in impatient gestures.

The two Lieutenants are ill at ease. *We cut* to the head of an ornamental toy peacock ; it wags its head, then proudly spreads its tail into a fan ; it starts revolving, performing a sort of dance, its wings shining. The huge doors open. A footman smiles. Kerensky walks through the doors and farther doors ahead of him are opened one by one. (*The action of opening the doors is repeated several times without matching the movements on the cuts.*) The peacock's head comes to rest and stares, as if in admiration, after Kerensky's receding figure.

75–79 *Cut to* soldiers, sailors and Bolshevik workers, listlessly waiting in prison; then to Lenin, hiding in the misty marshes.

80–99 Kerensky in the private apartment of the Czar. Close shots of rows of crockery, the Czarist initial *A* on everything including the imperial chamber pots. *In the apartments of the Czarina—Alexandra Fedorovna :* more shots of rows of crockery, ornamental furniture, tassels, the Czarina's bed. Kerensky lying on the bed (*shown in three consecutive shots from different angles*). Alexander Fedorovitch. More ornamental tassels, etc.

100–105 *In the library of Nicholas II.* Kerensky, standing by the desk in the Czar's library, a very small figure in these grand surroundings. Three more shots of Kerensky *from progressively farther away* and emphasising Kerensky's smallness in this huge palatial room. Kerensky picks up a piece of paper from the desk.

106 *Title : The Decree Restoring the Death Penalty.*
107 *M.S.* Kerensky sitting at the desk, thinking.
108 *L.S.* Kerensky. He leans over the desk and signs.
109 *Shooting down* from the top of a palace staircase towards Kerensky, as, slowly, he approaches the foot of the stairs.
110 *C.S.* A servant watching.
111–124 Kerensky, head bowed, hand in his jacket Napoleon-fashion, slowly ascends the stairs. A servant and one of the Lieutenants are watching. *M.S.* Kerensky, looking down, arms folded. Statuette of Napoleon in the same attitude. The servant and Lieutenant salute. A row of tall, palace wine glasses. Another row of glasses. A row of tin soldiers, *similarly disposed about the screen.*
125 *C.S.* Kerensky, sitting at a table. In front of him stand four separate quarters of a four-way decanter. They are standing side by side on the table ; Kerensky stares down at them.
126 *C.S.* Kerensky's hands manipulating the four decanter bottles into position.
127 *M.S.* Kerensky.
128 *C.S.* Kerensky's hands.
129 *M.S.* Kerensky. He stares at the bottles.
130 *C.U.* Kerensky's hand as it opens a drawer in the table and withdraws the fitting cap of the decanter—shaped like a crown—from the drawer.
131 *M.S.* Kerensky ; he raises the crown before his eyes.
132 *B.C.U.* The crown.
133 *M.S.* Kerensky ; he places the crown on top of the bottles.
134 *B.C.U.* The crown, now fitting over the decanter.
135 A factory steam whistle blowing steam.
136 *B.C.U.* The crown.
137 The steam whistle.
138 *Title : The Revolution in Danger.*
139 *B.C.U.* The crown.
140 *M.S.* Kerensky, settling down to admire the crown on the top of the decanter.
141 *B.C.U.* The crown.
142 The steam whistle.
143–150 Inter-cut with the single words of the title *General Kornilov is advancing,* we see shots of the steam whistle.
151 *Title : All Hands to the Defence of Petrograd.*
152 *L.S.* of a factory. Men (Bolsheviks) holding rifles and banners, rush past the camera.
153 The steam whistle.
154 *Title : For God and Country.*
155 *Title : For*
156 *Title : God*

34

Sc.	
157	The cupola of a church.
158	C.S. a highly ornate ikon.
159	A tall church spire, *the image being tilted through 45 deg. to the left.*
160	A tall church spire (the same as above), *the image being tilted through 45 deg. to the right.*
161–186	Shots of grotesque religious effigies, temples, Buddhas, primitive African masks, etc.
187	*Title : For*
188	*Title : Country*
189–199	*Close shots of medals, ornate uniforms, officers' lapels, etc.*
200	*Title : Hurrah !*
201	The pedestal of a statue of the Czar. (The statue itself was torn down by workers in the first reel.) Fragments of the torso of the statue, lying on the ground, swing back into position on top of the pedestal.
202	*Title : Hurrah !*
203	*The same action seen in 201 from a different angle.*
204	*Title : Hurrah !*
205–209	Six short images of the religious effigies seen earlier. They appear to be smiling.
210–219	Other fragments of the torn-down statue of the Czar reassembling. Finally, the sceptre and then the head of the statue wobbles and settles back into position.
220–233	Several shots of church spires, *tilted, as before.* Church spire, *upside down.* Censers swinging. Head of Czar's statue, proudly back in position. A priest, holding a cross.
234–259	General Kornilov, leader of the anti-revolutionary army, sits on his horse and surveys his troops. A statue of Napoleon, astride a horse, his arm stretched forward. A similar shot of Kornilov as he raises his arm. Kerensky, still in the palace, staring at the crown at the top of the decanter, arms folded. *Title : Two Bonapartes.* Several more images of the statue of Napoleon. A head of Napoleon *facing left.* A head of Napoleon *facing right.* The two heads on screen together, facing each other. Two grotesque figures—seen earlier—facing each other. More shots of Napoleon and another sequence of religious effigies.
260	Kornilov, on his horse, giving the command to march.
261	A tank moves forward, hurls itself over a ditch.
262	Kerensky, in the Czarina's bedroom, hopelessly hurls himself on to the bed.
263	Fragments of the bust of Napoleon, lying scattered on the ground.

Eisenstein's aim in making *October* was not so much to recount an historical episode as to explain the significance and ideological background of the political conflict. The film's appeal, therefore, comes from the manner in which Eisenstein has exposed certain ideas rather than from its excitement as a dramatic story. Indeed, as a piece of *narrative*, the passage we have quoted is extremely unsatisfactory. The incidents are loosely constructed and do not follow each other with the dramatic inevitability which a well-told story demands : we are not, for instance, shown Kerensky's character through a series of dramatically motivated episodes but through a number of random incidents, each suggesting a further aspect of Kerensky's vanity or incompetence. The time relationship between consecutive shots and scenes is left undefined and no sense of continuous development emerges : the cut from *108* to *109*, for example, takes us—without reason or explanation—from the

Czar's study to a staircase somewhere in the palace. No attempt is made to explain or to conceal the time lapse between the shots, as could easily have been done with a dissolve. The reel abounds in similar examples, showing Eisenstein's lack of interest in the simple mechanics of story-telling and his ruthless suppression of any footage not directly relevant to his thesis.

This contempt for the simplest requirement of a story-film—the ability to create the illusion of events unfolding in logical sequence—is manifested in Eisenstein's films in another way. Just as in the cut from *108* to *109* he jumps forward through time, so on other occasions he may play a scene for longer than its natural duration. In the well-known sequence of the raising of the bridges in *October*, Eisenstein photographed the action from two viewpoints : from beneath the bridge and from above. Then, in editing the material, he used both these series of shots and thereby considerably extended the screen time of the actual event. Clearly, this creates a laboured effect : the extreme emphasis Eisenstein meant to place upon the event is achieved at the expense of drawing the spectator's attention to an artificial device.

A similar instance occurs in the reel we have quoted. When Kerensky is about to enter the Czar's private quarters, the incident is stressed by repeating the shot of the opening doors without matching the cuts, i.e., by cutting back to an earlier stage in the movement of opening the doors than that with which the previous shot ended. (The whole question of matching cuts is discussed in greater detail in Chapter 14.)

Eisenstein's aim in thus breaking away from the narrative editing methods of his predecessors was to extend the power of the film medium beyond simple story-telling. " While the conventional film directs *emotions*," he wrote, " [intellectual montage] suggests an opportunity to direct the whole *thought process* as well."[1] How he, in practice, availed himself of this opportunity, we shall perhaps most easily assess from his own analyses of the sequence we have quoted in detail.

Eisenstein describes his intentions at the opening of reel 3 (shots 1–27) as follows :

Kerensky's rise to power and dictatorship after the July uprising of 1917. A comic effect was gained by sub-titles indicating regular ascending ranks ("Dictator," "Generalissimo," "Minister of Navy and of Army," etc.) climbing higher and higher—cut into five or six shots of Kerensky, climbing the stairs of the Winter Palace, all with exactly the *same* pace. Here a conflict between the flummery of the ascending ranks and the hero's trotting up the same

[1] Film Form *by Sergei Eisenstein. Dobson, 1951, p. 62.*

36

unchanging flight of stairs yields an intellectual result : Kerensky's essential nonentity is shown satirically. We have the counterpoint of a literally expressed conventional idea with the *pictured* action of a particular person who is unequal to his swiftly increasing duties. The incongruence of these two factors results in the spectator's purely *intellectual* decision at the expense of this particular person.[1]

In addition to this consciously satirical staging of the scene, Eisenstein achieved a further ironic effect by continually cutting back to the statues holding the ornamental garlands as if just about to place them upon Kerensky's head. The whole passage is typical of Eisenstein's method : its " plot " is almost non-existent—Kerensky is simply walking up a staircase ; it is in the comments and symbolic allusions that the meaning is conveyed.

The next incident is relatively simple : more ridicule is heaped upon Kerensky in a straightforward narrative passage. After this, in *40–74*, Eisenstein resumes his oblique approach : throughout this section Kerensky stands still and all the significant meaning is conveyed by the sequence of close shots—gloves, boots, door-locks, the peacock—which produce ironic overtones quite outside the range of a more conventionally staged scene. Then, after a brief glimpse of the revolutionary fighters, Eisenstein returns to the attack, this time exposing Kerensky's petty enjoyment of the Czarist palace, seen side by side with his inability to assume the responsibilities of a ruler.

There now follows a satirical rendering of Kerensky's dreams of power. The image of Kerensky is compared with a shot of a bust of Napoleon, but the row of wine glasses, followed by the similar row of tin soldiers, promptly throws scorn on the empty pretence : the continuity suggests how temporary and meaningless are Kerensky's present surroundings and implies that his position is that of a figurehead, not in command of any real forces or authority. The image of the crown-shaped decanter stopper becomes a symbol of Kerensky's ambition (*136–153*) and this is inter-cut with the shot of the factory whistle—the symbol of the power of the revolutionaries. The conflict, it will be noted, is not established in terms of armies or political statements but by symbols of the two opposing ideologies. The potential drama of the situation is rendered as a clash of ideas.

Up to this point, though the continuity has abounded in side-allusions, all the images which have been used for symbolic effect were taken from Kerensky's actual surroundings. From here onward Eisenstein chooses his images at random, without reference

[1] Ibid., *pp. 61, 62.*

to the story's locale. Having established that Kornilov represents the military danger, he proceeds to discredit the regime which, under the banner " For God and Country," is about to attack the Bolsheviks (see *157–186*).

> Kornilov's march on Petrograd was under the banner of " In the Name of God and Country." Here we attempted to reveal the religious significance of this episode in a rationalistic way. A number of religious images, from a magnificent Baroque Christ to an Eskimo idol, were cut together. The conflict in this case was between the concept and the symbolisation of God. While idea and image appear to accord completely in the first statue shown, the two elements move further from each other with each successive image. Maintaining the denotation of " God," the images increasingly disagree with our conception of God, inevitably leading to individual conclusions about the true nature of all deities. In this case, too, a chain of images attempted to achieve a purely intellectual resolution, resulting from a conflict between a preconception and a gradual discrediting of it in purposeful steps.[1]

Here, the whole narrative structure of the story-film is thrown aside and a continuity of purely intellectual significance is constructed. Each cut carries forward an idea instead of continuing the action of the previous shot : in continuity, the images convey an argument, not an incident. The same method is maintained in the next few shots (*189–219*) when the idea of " Country " is rendered in terms of the outdated military paraphernalia and, later, as the battered statue of the Czar reassembling itself. The separate threads of the argument are then tied together in *220–259* and the two figures of Kornilov and Kerensky are reduced to insignificance by satirically identifying them with " two Bonapartes."

The final touch (*261–263*) is achieved by a (not altogether lucid) device which Eisenstein describes as follows :

> . . . the scene of Kornilov's *putsch*, which puts an end to Kerensky's Bonapartist dreams. Here one of Kornilov's tanks climbs up and crushes a plaster-of-Paris Napoleon standing on Kerensky's desk in the Winter Palace, a juxtaposition of purely symbolic significance.[2]

In examples of this sort Eisenstein saw pointers to what could be achieved by " [liberating] the whole action from the definitions of time and space."[3] He envisaged that experiments along these lines would lead " towards a purely intellectual film, freed from traditional limitations, achieving direct forms for ideas, systems and concepts, without any need for transitions or paraphrases."[4]

Pudovkin, in his theory of constructive editing, claimed that a scene is most effectively presented by linking together a series of

[1] Film Form *by Sergei Eisenstein. Dobson, 1951, p. 62.*
[2] Ibid., *p. 58.*
[3] Ibid., *p. 58.*
[4] Ibid., *p. 63.*

specially chosen details of the scene's action. Eisenstein emphatically opposed this view. He believed that to build up an impression by simply adding together a series of details was only the most elementary application of film editing. Instead of linking shots in smooth sequence, Eisenstein held that a proper film continuity should proceed by a series of shocks ; that each cut should give rise to a conflict between the two shots being spliced and thereby create a fresh impression in the spectator's mind. " If montage is to be compared with something," he wrote, " then a phalanx of montage pieces, of shots, should be compared to the series of explosions of an internal combustion engine, driving forward its automobile or tractor : for, similarly, the dynamics of montage serve as impulses driving forward the total film."[1] And again : " the juxtaposition of two shots by splicing them together resembles not so much the simple sum of one shot plus another—as it does a creation."[2]

How the film-maker should set about producing and controlling these " creations " Eisenstein explained by pointing to analogies between the cinema and the other arts. He stated the principle of intellectual montage most succinctly by comparing it with the workings of hieroglyphs.

. . the picture of water and the picture of an eye signifies to weep ; the picture of an ear near the drawing of a door = to listen ; a dog + a mouth = to bark ; a mouth + a child = to scream ; a mouth + a bird = to sing ; a knife + a heart = sorrow, and so on. But this is — montage ! Yes. It is exactly what we do in the cinema, combining shots that are *depictive*, single in meaning, neutral in content—into *intellectual* contexts and series.[3]

A number of obvious instances of this method occur in the excerpt we have quoted from *October* : " Kerensky's essential nonentity " is shown by juxtaposing shots of his ceremonial ascent of the palace staircase with the titles (" Dictator, Generalissimo," etc.) and with the shots of the statues holding garlands ; his ambition is rendered in the contrast with the shots of the bust of Napoleon ; the shot of the tank hurling itself over a ditch followed by Kerensky, flinging himself on a bed, conveys the impression of Kerensky's incapacity as a ruler.

Eisenstein believed that the director's function was to evolve series of shot conflicts of this sort and to express his ideas through the new meanings which arose from them. He held that the ideal film continuity was one in which every cut produced this momentary shock. There is nowhere in his films any attempt at smooth

[1] Film Form *by Sergei Eisenstein. Dobson, 1951, p. 38.*
[2] Film Sense *by Sergei Eisenstein. Faber & Faber, 1943, p. 18.*
[3] Film Form, *p. 30.*

39

cutting : his continuities proceed by a series of collisions, giving an impression of a constantly shifting and developing argument.

Eisenstein classified the various kinds of conflict possible between adjacent images in terms of contrasting composition, scale, depth of field, photographic key and so on. Any feature of the picture could be abruptly varied in adjacent shots in order to give rise to the desired conflict. Here, for instance, is his description of one of the juxtapositions from the anti-religious passage we have quoted in which the contrasting shapes of the objects photographed produce the momentary shock.

> In illustrating the monarchist *putsch* attempted by General Kornilov, it occurred to me that his militarist *tendency* could be shown in a montage that would employ religious details for its material. For Kornilov had revealed his intention in the guise of a peculiar Crusade of Moslems (!), . . . against the Bolsheviki. So we intercut shots of a Baroque Christ (apparently exploding in the radiant beams of his halo) with shots of an egg-shaped mask of Uzume, Goddess of Mirth, completely self-contained. The temporal conflict between the closed egg-form and the graphic star-form produced the effect of an instantaneous *burst*—of a bomb, or shrapnel.[1]

This example, while it illustrates Eisenstein's intellectual montage at its most complex, also gives a hint of the method's main weakness —its frequent obscurity. The conflicting compositions of the two images create, according to Eisenstein's analysis, " the effect of instantaneous *burst*—of a bomb, or shrapnel," and therefore indirectly throw light on Kornilov's militarism. It is pertinent to ask whether the intended effect does, in practice, reach the audience. The " burst," as seen by the spectator, is a purely pictorial one and it is difficult to see why he should associate it with Kornilov's " military tendency." The effect, which on paper looks ingeniously double-edged, fails when put on the screen because it remains obscure.

This is perhaps an extreme example of the obscurities which occur fairly frequently in Eisenstein's films. In most instances, the difficulty is not so much that the passages of intellectual cinema are incomprehensible, as that many of the references escape the spectator on first viewing, and demand from him an amount of study and analysis that few are in the position to devote to a film. Whether this obscurity is inherent in Eisenstein's method, it is difficult to say. He only worked with the *genre* consistently in two films and the whole system of intellectual cinema may perhaps be said never to have got beyond the experimental stage.

[1] Film Form *by Sergei Eisenstein. Dobson, 1951, p. 56.*

2

EDITING AND THE SOUND FILM

General

" THE development of film technique . . . has been primarily
the development of editing." If one is thinking of the silent cinema
alone, Ernest Lindgren's statement remains an indisputable truism.
Men like Porter, Griffith and Eisenstein, together with many lesser
innovators, evolved editing techniques which gradually transformed
cinematography from a simple means of recording actuality to a
highly sensitive aesthetic medium. The history of silent film-making
is the history of the struggle to widen the cinema's visual appeal
through more and more elaborate editing. The desire to tackle
increasingly complex intellectual and emotional themes forced
directors to experiment with fresh, more evocative patterns of
visual continuity, and produced by the end of the silent period a
fairly comprehensive " grammar " of film construction.

The introduction of sound brought with it a temporary reversal
of this process. *All* the dramatic effects were, for a time, derived
from the sound-track. While film theorists claimed on the one hand
that dialogue could only lessen a film's total appeal,[1] and on the
other, that sound must be used in counterpoint, not in synchronisation with the picture,[2] commercial film-makers eagerly went about
making the (highly successful) *hundred per cent talkies.*

Looking back, it is easy to say that these films showed a retro-
gressive development, but that is to ignore the background against
which they were made. The majority of silent films made in the
twenties in this country and in U.S.A. relied on the use of numerous
long subtitles : it was natural that their makers should welcome
the advent of actual sound. (The adjective actual, as applied to

[1] *See, for instance, Paul Rotha's theoretical section in* The Film Till Now. *Cape,
1929.*
[2] *See* A Statement, *signed by S. M. Eisenstein, V. I. Pudovkin and G. V. Alexandrov,
first published in Moscow in 1928.* Film Form. *Denis Dobson, 1951.*

sound effects, is used in this book in a specially defined sense. For the definition, see p. 278.) In retrospect, it seems unreasonable to condemn the directors of the numerous hundred per cent talkies for misusing their new toy : their films were the sort of products which, had they been made a few years earlier, would certainly not have utilised the full resources of Griffith's (much less Eisenstein's) silent editing methods and would have received no serious critical attention.

Yet the hundred per cent talkies—that is to say musicals and stage adaptations which relied solely on the appeal of spoken dialogue and songs, and made the picture into a static, unimportant background for the sounds—proved, after the novelty had worn off, dull and unimaginative. Part of the trouble was undoubtedly that in the early days of sound recording the microphone had to be kept static on the set : a scene which would previously have been shot from a large number of set-ups, some of them with a panning or tracking camera, now had to be shot from one fixed position. More important, the makers of the hundred per cent talkies failed to realise that conveying events through an unceasing and unselective flow of actual sound does not correspond to the mode in which real life is normally experienced.

Just as we did not dwell at any length on the earliest years of the silent cinema, so there is no need here to give detailed consideration to the first days of the talkies : both were periods of instability and technical fumbling which are now of little more than academic interest. Instead, we must attempt to use the experience of the last twenty years of sound film-making to establish a consistent theory about how actual sound can or cannot be used to strengthen a film's total appeal.

In discussing the use of sound in the early talkies, Lindgren has said :

. . . the compensating gain from synchronism was negligible. A silent film can show a dog barking ; to add the sound of his bark is certainly a gain in realism, but it tells us nothing more than we knew before, it adds nothing to the expressive qualities of the image ; it is still merely a dog barking. Even dialogue was often used to say in words what the films were able to express as well by images alone. The picture of the angry father pointing his erring son to the door is made no more significant if we add the words : " Get out of here and never darken these doors again." The silent image, in such a case, may well be more, rather than less, impressive.[1]

These remarks were written as a criticism of the thoughtless use of actual sound with *all* images, and as such one must agree

[1] The Art of the Film *by Ernest Lindgren. Allen & Unwin, 1948, p. 99.*

with them. As a general indictment against the use of actual sound itself, they seem unnecessarily emphatic.

Although it is true that both the silent and sound versions of the father evicting his son convey the same facts, to argue from this that one is more or less impressive than the other is to make a meaningless comparison. Assuming the father is given a less outrageous line than Lindgren gives him, the fact that we hear him say *something* means that the scene becomes more realistic. The silent version, expressed through the father's mime, may be equally " impressive," but it will be so on a different plane of realism. If a comparison must be made, it will depend on the standard of direction and acting, and the context of the scene within the film. The fact that one uses sound and the other does not merely places the two scenes in two different artistic conventions, and there can be no question of relative merits.

The case of the barking dog could be equally misleading. Clearly, the sound of the bark gives us no fresh information, but that is by no means to say that " it adds nothing to the expressive qualities of the image." Depending on the quality of the sound used and the general context of the bark within the rest of the sound-track, it could give the picture a variety of emotional meanings which were not necessarily inherent in the picture alone. (The example quoted from *Odd Man Out* on p. 261 is a case in point.) In both cases, the sound could not only strengthen the realism of the rendering but also sharpen the dramatic impressiveness.

Besides this, the use of actual sound has brought with it a more fundamental change in film story-telling. Using sound and dialogue in synchronisation with the picture has enabled directors to practise a much greater economy than was possible in the silent film. The character of a place or a person can be conveyed more directly, because it comes to the spectator in terms more nearly akin to those of everyday life. A line of dialogue may convey an amount of information which the silent film-maker could only express in a subtitle or through an awkward, visually self-explanatory scene. Inessentials can be conveyed economically through hints on the dialogue or sound track. The director of a sound film has greater freedom to distribute the dramatic emphasis as he wishes, because he is not bound to spend time on dramatically ineffectual scenes which are nevertheless necessary to the sense of the story. Whereas Griffith—in *Birth of a Nation*, for instance—often needed to open his films with long, dramatically rather flat scenes to set the situation, the director of a sound film can establish the character of the players and the scene in a few well-chosen shots and lines of dialogue. (This becomes especially apparent in scenes of transition : where the silent film-maker normally used a subtitle and a long establishing scene when he took the story from one place to another, a simple hint in the dialogue can quite effortlessly accomplish a similar transition to-day.)

These, then, are the two main changes that sound has brought with it : a greater economy is story-telling means, which has enabled the narrative of sound films to become more and more complex ; and a high standard of realistic presentation which has become the aim of the majority of film makers of the sound period. Whereas the tendency in the best silent films was towards perfecting a style which would affect audiences by various indirect suggestions peculiar to the medium—by over-expressive visual compositions, evocative cutting effects, symbolic devices and so on—the sound film makes a more direct appeal, expressed more nearly in the terms of ordinary experience.

This fundamental change of approach becomes immediately obvious nowadays when one goes to see a silent film. One is conscious with films like *Intolerance, Battleship Potemkin, Cabinet of Dr. Caligari*—to take three widely different instances—that the directors have contrived visual effects which are somehow larger than life ; they attempt to make an exaggerated appeal to the eyes in order to express themselves comprehensively on a single plane. One is conscious of an artistic convention which, being unable to use the element of sound, needs to enlarge and distort the visual plane of appeal. To react by saying that this very need for highly expressive images made silent films superior to sound, or, conversely, to claim that inability to use sound reduced the silent cinema to a series of inadequate approximations, is to misunderstand the strength of either medium. Silent and sound films operate on two different levels of realistic presentation : there can be no question of relative merits, only a recognition of differences.

The interrelation of sound and picture, the relative amount of attention each factor requires or should require from an audience —these are problems which can be discussed only in general terms. Films like Ford's *The Informer*, de Sica's *Bicycle Thieves* or some of Carné's pre-war films, all display an admirable economy in the use of dialogue which has led to works of great distinction. But this does not in itself justify the conclusion that a sparing use of dialogue is necessarily an essential prerequisite of every good film. Any theory which rules out films like *The Little Foxes, Citizen Kane* or the early Marx Brothers comedies, must be suspect from the beginning. It is more relevant to stress that although these films use dialogue to a considerable extent, they make their essential impression by the images : *The Little Foxes* and *Citizen Kane* are among the most visually interesting films to have come from Hollywood ; the visual contribution to his gags of Groucho Marx' eyebrows is incalculable, and Harpo never says a word. Making a quantitative estimate between the amount of visual and aural appeal can serve no useful purpose. It is not so much the quantitative balance between sound and picture, as the insistence on a primarily visual emphasis which needs to be kept in mind.

Who edits a film ?

The fundamental editing principles which were evolved in the silent cinema have now become common knowledge. The use of close shots, flash-backs, dissolves, panning and tracking shots is now common practice in every studio. These devices form an accepted part of every film-maker's resources : the way in which any of them are used to-day may vary in detail from the silent days, but their dramatic usefulness has remained substantially unaltered.

Sound and other technical innovations have brought about some minor changes : the determination of pace, which in the silent days was entirely a matter of the rate of cutting, can now to some extent be aided by the control of the volume and urgency of the sound-track ; passages of time, previously conveyed by subtitles, can now be suggested in the dialogue ; on a more routine level, devices like inter-cutting shots of the passing landscape with interior shots of a train compartment to convey that the train is moving, are no longer necessary because back-projection can be used to convey the idea in a single shot. These and many other small technical differences have arisen but they are all of an essentially practical nature.

More important changes of editing technique have arisen out of the very marked change of style which followed the advent of sound. A much greater insistence on realism has been a notable feature of the last two decades of film-making. This is strongly reflected in contemporary editing practice. Effects which were commonly used in the silent cinema but which now seem to detract from the realism of the presentation have fallen into disfavour : iris shots which were so often used to focus the attention to a detail are now out of fashion because they constitute an artificial pictorial

45

effect ; masking, which was used by Griffith, is now rarely employed, again because it is unnaturalistic ; quick, momentary flash-backs, such as Griffith has in *The Birth of a Nation*, are rarely used since they tend to look arbitrarily planted. It would be rash to say that these devices will never be used again, but they have at present fallen into disfavour because they draw attention to technique and disturb the illusion of reality.

Larger problems of planning and editing the story continuity have considerably changed since the advent of sound because it is now no longer necessary to show everything visually. In *The Birth of a Nation*, for instance, there is a scene where a mother promises her son who is lying wounded in hospital and is later to be court-martialled, that she will go to see President Lincoln and plead on his behalf. From the shot of the mother in hospital, Griffith cuts to a shot of Lincoln in his study, and then, after an explanatory title, cuts back again. The insert is necessary if the audience is to become aware of what the two characters are discussing and is a much more elegant way of conveying it than would be a title alone. In a sound film, obviously, this sort of explanatory editing is no longer necessary since we would hear the mother's words.

A detailed comparison between the editing of silent and sound films will perhaps emerge, if we consider the whole complex of problems which constitute editing under four separate headings :

The Order of Shots

In the silent days, the director and editor (they were usually the same person) worked with a great deal of freedom. The only factor which decided the order of shots was the desire to achieve the most satisfactory visual continuity.

Often a great deal of material was shot which only found its appropriate place in the final scheme of continuity on the cutting bench. Griffith is said to have shot most of his films " off the cuff," shooting a certain amount of cover which allowed him enough footage to experiment with the material when he came to edit it. Eisenstein worked on his scripts in much greater detail, but he too relied to a great extent on the cutting stage of production to shape and reorganise the shot material. German film-makers, on the other hand (Carl Mayer, for instance), tended to work with much tighter scripts ; but the point is that in the silent cinema it was possible, creatively and economically, to let even the broader outlines of continuity take shape after the shooting was finished. The medium was extremely flexible in that there was no *physical*

46

reason why one should not cut from practically anything to anything else : indeed, one suspects that Eisenstein, for example, arrived at some of his most telling juxtapositions in the cutting room.

In sound films this freedom to rearrange and experiment with the material in the cutting room has been considerably reduced : partly because synchronised sound " anchors " the visuals ; partly because production costs of sound shooting are so high that it is normally impracticable to shoot a large footage which may not in the end be used. Dialogue often carries essential plot-information which cannot be given anywhere except in one specific context, and the image going with it is therefore " anchored " from the moment it is shot. This does not mean—as some writers have suggested—that editing patterns in the sound film need be any less complex or expressive than they were in the silent days. What it does mean is that the final order of shots in sequences employing actual sound needs to be planned at an earlier stage in production. In this sense the responsibility for the editing has shifted from the editor to the writer.

Selection of Camera Set-ups : Emphasis

The principle of using long, medium and close shots for various degrees of emphasis has remained substantially the same since Griffith first applied it. In contemporary films the writer will usually indicate the kind of camera set-up he thinks most suitable, and even if he does not, the director should have a fairly clear idea as to which set-ups will be used in the assembled continuity. When a scene requires a number of different camera set-ups, the whole scene is frequently shot from each separate position and subsequently assembled by the editor as he sees most fit. This, however, is not ideal policy : however much cover has been taken, a scene shot by a director who is uncertain as to how it will be edited is not likely to have the precision of effect which can be achieved by planned shooting.

Timing

In a silent film the state of tension of a passage was largely conveyed through the rate of cutting. Griffith constantly varied the pace of his films to convey (and control) the changing of dramatic tension ; and the climax was almost always a rapidly cross-cut sequence, usually a chase. Eisenstein evolved an extremely elaborate theory of timing which can perhaps be best appreciated in the sharp

47

changes of tempo in the Odessa Steps sequence. Whatever the theory, however, the timing of shots was solely determined by their visual content.

In the sound film this is no longer the case. By timing the picture in relation to the sound-track the editor can achieve a whole range of effects which are not necessarily inherent in either the picture or the sound alone. With dialogue he can frequently carry the words from a shot of the speaker over to the reaction shot ; he can delay reactions or give pre-warning of what is about to happen ; he can play sound and picture in parallel or he can use them in counterpoint.

These detailed points of timing are normally left to the editor and sound editor. Often the effects depend on minute adjustments which are difficult to envisage before the material is shot, and they present the contemporary editor with one of his chief problems.

Presentation : Smoothness

Although the process of cutting from one shot to another is comparable to the sharp changes of attention one registers in everyday life, this does not mean that *any* cut will automatically pass unnoticed. In most silent films one remains conscious of the many abrupt transitions ; in many of Griffith's films one is aware of the constant changing of camera angles and it requires a certain amount of practice and adjustment to accept the jerkiness of the continuity without irritation. Eisenstein, far from wanting a smoothly flowing series of images, deliberately set out to exploit the conflict implied at the junction of any two shots. Against this it must be said that the German film-makers of the late twenties, using a much more fluid camera technique, often made deliberate attempts to achieve a smooth-flowing continuity. (Pabst may have been one of the first film-makers to time most of his cuts on specific movements within the picture in an attempt to make the transitions as unnoticeable as possible.)

Owing to the sound cinema's insistence on realistic presentation the problem of achieving a smooth flow of images is much more acute to-day. Harsh, noticeable cuts tend to draw attention to technique and therefore tend to destroy the spectator's illusion of seeing a continuous stream of action. Constructing a smoothly flowing continuity has, indeed, become one of the modern editor's main preoccupations.

It must be stressed again that this grouping of the various

functions which together make up the process of editing does not correspond to anything like four stages in production or even to four separate creative processes. Nevertheless, it shows how the responsibility for the larger editing issues has shifted from the editor to the writer and director, and how the new problems which have arisen since the advent of sound have remained the responsibility of the editor. A quotation from a modern shooting script, set side by side with a post-production break-down of the finished sequence, is given below. A comparision between the two columns should indicate how the responsibility for the editing has been divided between writer, director and editor in a contemporary film.

BRIGHTON ROCK[1]

Extract from Shooting Script and Reel 7 of the film

> Pinkie Brown (Richard Attenborough), the leader of a gang of toughs, has been trying to kill Spicer (Wylie Watson) who possesses some incriminating evidence. Pinkie arranges to have Spicer killed by a rival gang but the arrangements go wrong and both Pinkie and Spicer are beaten up. Pinkie, however, believes that Spicer has been killed.
>
> In the following scene Pinkie is seen talking to his lawyer Prewitt (Harcourt Williams), when Dallow (William Hartnell), a member of Pinkie's gang, enters the room.

SHOOTING SCRIPT	POST-PRODUCTION SCRIPT	Ft. fr.

34   M.S. The Door
It opens and Dallow comes in.
Dallow :
  What's up with Spicer ?
We pan him across to the end of the bed bringing Pinkie *into* shot.
Pinkie :
  Colleoni's men got him. They nearly did for me, too.
Dallow :
  Did for . . . but Spicer's in his room now. I heard him.
	
	Dallow :
	  Killed him ? I've just seen him—	

35   M.C.S. Pinkie
He turns a horrified gaze on Dallow and rises slowly from the bed.
Pinkie :
  You're imagining things.
	1. M.C.S. Pinkie, *back to camera.*
	He turns his head *towards camera.*
	Dallow : (contd.)
	  —he's in his room.
	Pinkie :
	  You're imagining things, Dallow.
		23

36   M.C.S. Dallow
Dallow :
  I tell you he's in his room.
	Dallow :
	  I tell you I've just seen him—
	NOW !
	Pinkie hesitates for a moment, then walks across right.
	Loud, dramatic music begins.	

[1] *Director : John Boulting. Editor : Peter Graham-Scott. Shooting script and production : Roy Boulting. Associated British Picture Corporation, 1947.*

1

2

3

4

5a

5b

5c

6

7

8

9

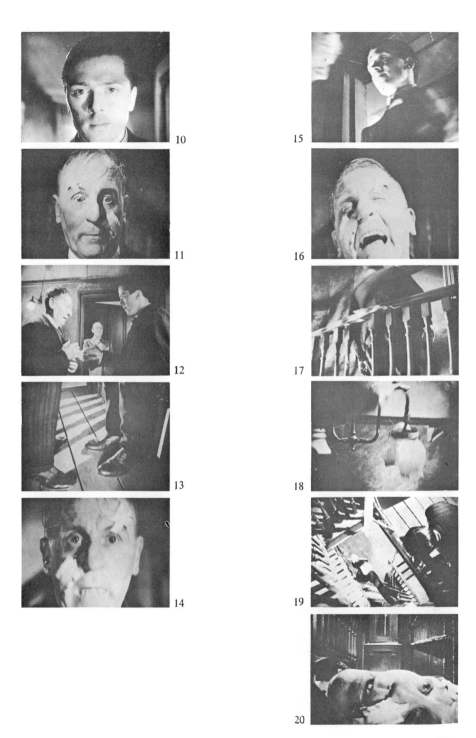

10
11
12
13
14
15
16
17
18
19
20

37   M.C.S. Pinkie
Pinkie rises slowly from the bed and moves through the door into the passage outside. The *camera pans* and *tracks* out on to the landing. The door of Spicer's bedroom is open and swings to and fro in the draught, making little creaking sounds. The *camera* is stationary. Pinkie moves towards it.

2. *M.L.S.* Pinkie, Dallow in right 2 5 foreground. Pinkie walks across room to right, *camera pans with him* up to the door.

38   M.S. Outside Spicer's bedroom
Pinkie *enters frame* from behind *camera* and stands listening with one hand on the banisters. He shivers suddenly as a tinny noise comes from inside. His hand tightens on the banister rail and it moves visibly. He looks at it and then back to the half open door. He enters. The *camera* stays outside on the shadows and the swinging door. Once inside the doorway there is sudden and complete silence from the bedroom.

3. Landing outside Pinkie's room 18 *Camera facing door* of Pinkie's room, banisters left, door to Spicer's bedroom right. Pinkie comes out through door, pauses, and then walks cautiously towards Spicer's door.
4. *M.S.* Interior Pinkie's room.   3 Prewitt examining the money Pinkie gave him.
5. *As in* 3. Pinkie looks back 83 at the banisters behind him. He puts his hand on the banister rail ; he pushes it sideways to make sure it is broken.
Music stops.
He slowly walks forward into Spicer's bedroom. Dallow appears in Pinkie's bedroom door, stops there, hand in coat pocket.
Camera pans slowly left below level of banister rail, until the half-open door to Spicer's bedroom is seen through banister uprights in *centre of frame.*

Pinkie : (off)
  So you're alive !

Pinkie : (off, from Spicer's bedroom)
  So you're alive, Spicer !

Spicer : (off)
  I got away, Pinkie.
The sound of footsteps moving into the room. The door gives a loud creak in the draught, then more footsteps as Spicer starts backing away talking rapidly.

Spicer : (off)
  I got away, Pinkie !—
While Spicer is heard talking, the door opens and Spicer appears, retreating *back towards camera* and being followed by Pinkie. Spicer is terrified.

Spicer : (off)
  I'm clearing right out, Pinkie. I'm too old.
Spicer comes backing out on to the landing.   Pinkie follows closely.

Spicer :
  —I got away. I'm clearing out, Pinkie—right out. I'm too old for this game, I—I'm far too old. Nobody wants an old man. I'll go to my cousin in Nottingham—the Blue Anchor. Yeah, —I can stay there as long as I like. You can find me there if you want to, Pinkie.—

Spicer :
  Don't do anything, Pinkie. I'm clearing out I tell you— I'm too old—that pub in Nottingham.
He is right up against the broken banisters now.

SHOOTING SCRIPT	T-PRODUCTION SCRIPT	Ft. fr

39 Low Angle landing from hall
Pinkie has Spicer backed up
against the banister rail.

Spicer :
   . . . You're always welcome.

—You're always welcome,
Pinkie.

6. C.U. Pinkie, staring menacingly. 3

40 C.U. Spicer
Terrified he watches Pinkie's
eyes and hands in turn.

7. C.U. Spicer, terrified. He 3
glances down towards the banister
rail.

41 C.U. Pinkie
He raises his bandaged hand
slowly.

8. C.U. Pinkie (as in 6). He has 2 4
raised his right hand ; he glances
towards the banister rail without
moving his head.

42 C.U. Spicer
His hands rise defensively.

43 C.U. Pinkie
His eyes go to the banisters.

44 C.U. Banister rail

9. C.S. Crack in the banister I 4
rail.

45 C.U. Pinkie
His expression changes with his
resolution.

10. C.U. Pinkie (as in 8). He I II
glances up to look straight at
Spicer.

11. C.U. Spicer (as in 7), terrified. I 9
Spicer :
  Don't do anything, Pinkie !

46 M.C.S. Pinkie and Spicer
Pinkie's fingers flatten. He holds
his hand towards Spicer.

Pinkie :
  Good-bye, Spicer.
Spicer, fearful, relieved, dis-
believing and joyful all at once,
offers a trembling hand.

12. M.C.S. Pinkie and Spicer. I2
Dallow is seen in background
between them, picking his teeth.
Pinkie slowly lowers his right hand
to shake hands with Spicer.
Pinkie :
  Why, Spicer ?
He suddenly grips Spicer's hand
really hard.
Pinkie :
  Good-bye.

47 C.U. Pinkie's feet
His left foot goes back and then
he shoots it forward with terrible
force against Spicer's shin (dummy
legs).

13. C.S. Spicer's and Pinkie's legs. I0
from the knees down. Pinkie's left
foot suddenly kicks Spicer's shin.

48 C.U. Spicer
His face contorts with agony as
he comes forward in an involun-
tary movement.

14. C.U. Spicer ; his mouth opens I2
in a loud scream.

49 C.U. Pinkie
Spicer's head and shoulders come
forward into frame towards Pinkie.
Pinkie's left hand comes up and
thrusts him sharply against the
banister rail.

15. Shooting up to M.C.S. Pinkie I4
from low angle. Spicer's body
lurches forward into frame.
Pinkie pushes him violently towards the banister.

53

SHOOTING SCRIPT	POST-PRODUCTION SCRIPT Ft. fr.
50 C.U. Spicer's face *It fills the screen.* His mouth opens in a scream, his eyes wide. The face goes back with the thrust.	16. C.U. Spicer as he falls back- 8 wards. *Long whine of pain (continuing to shot 20).*
51 M.C.S. Banisters, *low angle* Spicer breaks through the broken rail and hurtles down past *camera.*	17. *Shooting up* towards banister. 1 3 Spicer's back breaks through the crack in the banister and he falls backwards. 18. C.S. Gas-lamp. As the body 11 falls it breaks the lamp and a jet of flame comes out.
52 L.S. *from above landing shooting down* through broken rail to hall below. Spicer's body (dummy) falls. We see it spread-eagled below in the hall. Pinkie steps forward to the gap and looks down. *We shoot over* his head.	19. *Shooting down* from above 11 Pinkie's head. Spicer's body falling down. 20. Ground floor ; *shooting* along 1 14 ground level. Base of tall grand-father clock in background. Spicer's body falls *into frame* and his head rests in C.U. *across the screen.*

The passage from *Brighton Rock* is noteworthy for two reasons. Firstly, it is a sequence which depends for its effects largely on the editing. Secondly, the script is very near to the finished film and dem-onstrates that it is possible to plan a large proportion of the editing effects before the film goes on the floor. The selection of set-ups and the order of shots have been preserved practically unaltered. The changes which *were* made are interesting because they throw light on the relative functions of the writer, the director, and the editor. (In practice, of course, writer, director and editor may be the same person : the functions performed by each are here considered separately merely to indicate the work done before, during and after shooting, i.e., in the script, on the floor and in the cutting room.)

There are a number of minor alterations in the order of shots where the director and editor have felt that they could improve on the scripted continuity. Scene *36* has been left out completely, presumably on the grounds that it is more important to show Pinkie reacting to Dallow's baffling news than to show Dallow—who simply happens to be the person bringing it—delivering his lines. Similarly, shot *20* has been introduced to strengthen the scripted effect. These and one or two other changes have been made on the floor and in the cutting room, but they are all essentially matters of detail.

The more important alterations of continuity are all concerned with smoothness of presentation. They are introduced at points where the scripted continuity has, for one reason or another, given rise to physical difficulties. The insert of the shot of Prewitt (*4*) was almost certainly a necessity arising out of the shooting. One imagines that shots *3* and *5* might have been used as one continuous take : possibly this was intended, but the end of the take used in shot *3* was for some reason unsatisfactory (or the take used in shot *5* unsatisfactory towards the beginning, or both) and the two takes had to be bridged by cutting away to shot *4*.

Similarly, it will be noticed that the camera set-up used in shot *3* is from the opposite side to that envisaged in script-scene *38*. The reasons for this are a little more complex. Immediately following *5*, a series of rapid close-ups is used : coming after an extremely long, slow-moving shot (shot *5* is 83 feet long) they make a striking effect. Now if the script order of scenes had been followed, it would have been necessary to *cut* to a shot of Spicer's back against the broken railing, and this would have considerably softened the impact of the rapidly following close-ups. Further, the slow panning movement of the camera transfers the attention to the door of Spicer's room : we can hear voices coming from within and the slow panning of the camera visually strengthens the atmosphere of anticipation. Lastly, the camera set-up which was used allowed the director to show Dallow nonchalantly watching the whole incident : the dramatic advantage of this is obvious.

Since it is often necessary to write the shooting script before the final details of the construction of sets is known, physical difficulties may arise in the shooting which the writer cannot envisage. Script scene *38* is a case in point. The panning movement of the camera in shot *3* would have been physically impossible had the camera been facing in the direction suggested in the script.

The most striking difference between the shooting script and the finished sequence becomes apparent when one looks at the third column indicating the length of each shot. It becomes clear to what a great extent the element of timing brings life to the inert shot material. The speed with which the shots follow each other and the changes in the rate of cutting, both of which are finally determined in the cutting room, are the very basis of the scene's effectiveness.

This is particularly so in this sequence where two slow, expectant periods are contrasted with two extremely fast volleys of shots. Shot *5*, for example, has been quite deliberately left on the screen for a great length of time : by preceding the series of short, incisive close-ups (*6–11*) which convey the conflict between the two men, it considerably adds to their effect.

Again, the relatively long-lasting shot *12* provides a brief period of respite—a moment of false security for Spicer—which suddenly gives way to the feverishly fast cutting of the actual fall. This contrast was evidently partially planned in the shooting, for shot *12* was made intentionally slow-moving : Pinkie's movement is slow and deliberate, and Dallow is seen in the background watching the proceedings with feigned boredom. After this, the quick group of shots, each in the region of one foot long, comes as a sudden dramatic switch into action.

Looking again at the way this sequence has been conceived and edited, we see that the credit for the editing must go not only to the editor but also to the writer and director. The larger editing decisions, such as the rough order of shots and the first planning of the set-ups, have been tentatively decided in the script. Decisions of timing and smoothness have been left over to the cutting room and when necessary have been made to override previously made plans. This is of course an over-simplification—it is certainly not possible to say categorically that the writer has been responsible for one particular point, the director or editor for another—but it gives an overall picture of the procedure. Certainly, it shows that the editing of a sound film begins long before it reaches the cutting room.

The contribution of editing

The division of responsibility for the editing of a film must necessarily vary from one unit to another. An experienced writer, able to visualise effects which can be achieved through editing, may take most of the responsibility upon himself ; an experienced director will insist on making his own decisions. If writer and director have been uncertain about the precise continuity, the main responsibility will remain with the editor. Depending on the traditions of the industry as a whole or the studio in particular, the personality and ability of the various technicians, the exact set-up will vary from production to production.

In British studios the director is usually the key figure in production. He collaborates on the shooting script and supervises the editing. The responsibility for the final continuity of a film rests with him and the editor. In Hollywood, the reverse normally happens. Writers normally prepare their scripts in much greater

56

detail and leave the director with the comparatively minor role of following the written instructions. In America, moreover, the producer is generally much more closely concerned with the creative part of production than is his British counterpart. The American producer almost invariably supervises the editing of the film—a stage of production which in most Hollywood studios is no longer held to be the director's responsibility.

> There are only half a dozen directors in Hollywood who are allowed to shoot as they please and who have any supervision over their editing . . . We have tried for three years to establish a Directors Guild, and the only demands we have made on the producers as a Guild were to have two weeks' preparation for " A " pictures, one week preparation time for " B " pictures, and to have supervision of just the first rough cut of the picture . . . We have only asked that the director be allowed to read the script he is going to do and to assemble the film in its first rough form for presentation to the head of the studio. It has taken three years of constant battling to achieve any part of this . . . I would say that 80 per cent of the directors to-day shoot scenes exactly as they are told to shoot them without any change whatsoever, and that 90 per cent of them have no voice in the story or in the editing. Truly a sad situation for a medium that is supposed to be the director's medium.[1]

While Capra's letter gives a picture which is no longer quite accurate, the improvement does not seem to be very marked. Against it, it must be said that some of Hollywood's leading directors have managed to get round this seemingly hopeless situation : Preston Sturges and John Huston write and direct their own films ; Chaplin writes, produces and directs ; Ford is generally his own producer ; Orson Welles was in sole charge of *Citizen Kane*. The success of the films made by these directors would seem to prove beyond doubt, what common sense alone indicates : that the editing (whether planned before shooting in the script, or supervised after shooting in the cutting room) and the direction should be done, or at least controlled, by one person.

But who should ideally be responsible for the writing ? Some directors, as we have seen, appear to be at their best with their own scripts. (This does not necessarily mean—as in the case of Sturges—that the director needs to invent his own story : he may only collaborate on or supervise the writing of the shooting script.) Thorold Dickinson has put forward a strong case for this arrangement as being the only possible one.[2] But it does not necessarily apply to all directors. John Ford is said to direct his films (*The Grapes of Wrath*, for instance) very faithfully from other people's

---

[1] *From a letter to* The New York Times, *published 2nd April, 1939. Quoted in* America at the Movies *by Margaret Thorp. Yale University Press, 1939, pp. 146-7.*
[2] Sight and Sound. *March, 1950.* The Filmwright and the Audience.

scripts. Others have found it most congenial to form a director-writer partnership in which through a long period of collaboration their two contributions have led to a complementary and harmonious fusion of talents. Whatever the precise nature of the producer-director-writer-editor relationship which obtains on any film, the essential condition would seem to be that the ultimately controlling mind should conceive and execute the continuity in primarily visual terms, in terms of the choreography and editing of visually telling strips of film.

In practice this means that the director should normally be in charge. It is he who is responsible for planning the visual continuity during shooting, and he is therefore in the best position to exercise a unifying control over the whole production. This implies that he must also be in charge of the editing and be allowed to interpret the material in the cutting room as he visualised it on the floor.

Although most directors, if given the choice, would certainly wish to retain the ultimate responsibility for their films, most of them do not insist on writing the first treatment of their stories. The invention of incidents and the writing of dialogue requires a talent which does not necessarily coincide in one person with a talent for imaginative visual treatment. Writer-director collaboration such as is practised by many British directors has been found to lead to a satisfactory balance.

A clue to the ideal working relationship between writer and director is perhaps best provided by a concrete instance. Discussing Marcel Carné's long period of collaboration with the writer Jacques Prévert, and in particular, their work on *Les Enfants du Paradis*, the French critic Jean Mitry has written :

In the past—when it was a question of works into which [Prévert and Carné] put all their resources, *Quai des Brumes*, *Drôle de Drame* or *Le Jour Se Lève* —which I take not only to be his masterpiece but one of the rare masterpieces of the French cinema—in the past although the scenarios had always been the result of a close collaboration, Carné had the upper hand in the breakdown into the shooting script and in the cinematographic construction of the film. After Carné had made a suitable adaptation of the subject chosen, and had sketched the main lines of the continuity, Prévert was content to write the dialogue and to fit this into the limited and prearranged framework which had already been determined by Carné. The latter, working in terms of cinema, tried to express himself visually and only allowed the dialogue to act as a reinforcing support on which to rest the images and to allow them to take their full value.

Since *Les Visiteurs du Soir*, the jobs have been reversed. It is Prévert who conceives the subject of the film, who develops it, writes the continuity and often breaks it down into an extremely detailed form. Carné's job is then confined to writing into the script the necessary technical notes and to planning the changes of camera angles. They are no longer Carné's films with dialogue by Prévert, but Prévert's films, directed by Carné. It is another world.

Where Carné makes a point visually, Prévert makes his point with words. He allows the visuals the sole purpose of showing, presenting and placing the characters in situations cleverly contrived, but controlled by his text. Hence the visuals emptily serve only to identify outwardly characters of whom we know nothing except from what they say ; the visuals serve only to illustrate a story whose development is never indicated except in words. The text becomes the pivot, the life, the structure of the film, and the visuals serve as the reinforcing support by showing the shapes which the words represent.[1]

Mitry's account suggests a reason for the extraordinary visual emptiness of Carné's post-war films. It is not that the images are dull—they are, if anything (in *Les Visiteurs du Soir*, particularly), too striking : but they serve to illustrate rather than to tell the story.

It may be objected that dialogue-bound scripts are not necessarily written by all writers, but only by bad ones. Experience shows, however, that where the writer is given ultimate control, where the director is made to shoot to a tight script which he is not allowed to modify, films tend to become static and wordy. Often, this is a matter of deliberate choice. The normal Hollywood practice of making the writer and producer the controlling members of the unit is, no doubt, made possible by the comparatively great skill of the writers. But it is also a symptom of the Hollywood system of film-making in a much wider sense.

Behind a great proportion of films made in Hollywood is the simple intention to exploit the box-office appeal of the studio's contracted stars. Films are written, directed (and edited) around the particular talents of the leading players. Scripts are written primarily in terms of dialogue which can most economically bring out the special box-office attractions of the actors involved, and the visuals are designed to flatter the stars' appearance. The effect on editing is equally strong : it becomes not so much a matter of working to the specific dramatic needs of the story, as of presenting the leading players in the most favourable light. The most obvious effect of this is the superabundance of dramatically meaningless close-ups which so often ruins a film's pace and movement.

As anyone who goes to the cinema at all regularly can testify, the outcome of this star-centred system of film-making is a consistent level of dramatic mediocrity.

[1] Sight and Sound, *March, 1950. Translated by Thorold Dickinson.* The Filmwright and his Audience.

But there are exceptions. Many of the films built round the personality of Greta Garbo, some of the Paul Muni biographies or Marcel Pagnol's films featuring Raimu, are little more than ingeniously contrived star-vehicles, yet they cannot be dismissed as worthless. Here, all the various creative elements of sound film-making are sacrificed to the one element of acting, and the appeal comes to depend on the virtuosity of the central player. With performers of the stature of Garbo good films occasionally emerge, but the same technique applied to a star who may happen to be a current box-office favourite can only lead to a formula success, or boredom. One need only imagine *Queen Christina* without Garbo or *La Femme du Boulanger* without Raimu to perceive the weakness of this star-centred production technique as a general method.

There are other kinds of film which do not owe their primary appeal to the director : the films of Preston Sturges are essentially the work of a brilliant dialogue writer ; the main credit for many good musicals may often be justly assigned to the dance director ; a good case could be made out for the set designer as being the key figure in a de Mille epic. These films are first and foremost the work of a technician other than the director.

But it should be noticed that they are all unrealistic in their approach to their material. In various ways, they create their own level, their own distorted atmosphere : the caricature figures of a Sturges comedy, the majestic, larger-than-life figures created by Garbo, the light-hearted abandon of a good musical or the spectacular excesses of a de Mille epic, all these make an appeal on their own artificial level. They do not attempt to show events realistically but gain their strength through their own particular stylistic distortion.

When one comes to consider films which attempt a more rigidly authentic approach to reality, it becomes obvious that here the director must be mainly in charge. The great films of the sound period—*The Grapes of Wrath, Le Jour Se Lève, Bicycle Thieves*—are all essentially " directors' films." The story and characterisation is conveyed in the first instance in the pictures—through the " choreography " and editing of significant images. The major creative impulse (whether it comes from the man who is given on the credit titles as the writer, the director or the producer) finds expression in the making of significant images. Dialogue-writing, set-design and acting all become subjugated to this central purpose.

60

Special styles of editing

The ability to use actual sound has allowed film makers to tell more complex stories than was possible in the silent cinema. As a result the tendency in the sound cinema has been to concentrate on incident and narrative rather than on indirect forms of comment and description.

Whereas the best silent film directors tended to work with simple plots and to elaborate them through various personal symbols and comments, directors of sound films have so far, on the whole, employed more straightforward narrative techniques. Methods of film-making are to-day much more direct in their appeal, much more closely geared to the taste of the average audience. Fast, dramatic story-telling seems to be the key to box-office success and is therefore the aim of the majority of directors. It seems inconceivable that a project which was designed to appeal on the emotional level of, say, Dovzhenko's *Earth* or on the intellectual level of *October* or even *Intolerance* would find commercial backing to-day. (None of these films was, in fact, commercially backed. Griffith financed *Intolerance* largely himself and the Soviet film industry was not organised on a profit-making basis. To-day, the cost of film-making is incomparably higher than it was in the silent days and any similar project would have to receive commercial backing to reach the screen at all.)

Apart from this obvious commercial reason which has led to the neglect of any but the most direct story-telling devices, there is also a new technical problem associated with the use of sound. We have seen that the use of actual sound does not necessarily mean that the editing of sound films needs to become any less complex or expressive. That is true if one is thinking of sequences of a straight narrative character, where each shot continues the action of the previous one. In sequences which employ a less direct visual continuity, where the juxtaposition of shots is determined by an intellectual or emotional as opposed to a physical relationship, actual sound may become an insuperable obstacle. Two examples should clarify the distinction.

Imagine a simple scene. A man is shown walking along a hotel corridor and we can hear his footsteps. He walks up to the door of a room and opens it : we hear the sound of the lock opening. Half way through his movement of opening the door we cut to another shot from the inside of the room which takes up his movement from the previous shot. He shuts the door behind him and we hear the sound. He walks over to another character who is already in the room and we see and hear a scene of dialogue. While the lines are heard we first cut to a closer two-shot, and then to alternating close shots of the two men, one at a time : in each case the dialogue comes from the character on screen. Later, a reaction shot is shown and held while the character off screen is speaking his lines . . . etc. This is a straight narrative sequence in which each cut continues the physical action of the previous shot. Clearly, using actual sound presents no difficulty, even if the cutting rate becomes very fast.

Now take an instance where the editing does not join physically continuous actions, where several physically unrelated events are woven into a single sequence.

The great pianist is approaching the climax of the Tchaikovski Concerto in the Albert Hall. In a box sits the Crown Prince of Ruritania. Under the box a revolutionary is fixing the fuse of a bomb. In a taxi rushing to warn the Prince is Rose Rowntree, a simple English girl who loves him for himself alone. In a silent film as the sequence reached its climax the shots of the pianist's hands, the Prince, the fire creeping up the fuse, the taxi swaying around the corner on two wheels, would alternate at ever increasing speeds. The eye already accustomed to the images could identify them in a fraction of a second, and the fact that the images might have elements of movement in common—the hands running up the piano, the flame moving along the fuse, the taxi seeming to hurtle over the camera—this common movement would in spite of the contrasts preserve the visual unity ; but if we try to imagine the same contrasts in terms of sound—the piano music, the hiss of the fuse, the roar of the taxi engine—we realise at once that these contrasts even to be intelligible, let alone effective, need ten times the space.

. . . In the kind of quick cutting I have been describing a foot, half a foot or even less, is visually intelligible, but aurally unintelligible. Further, there is no underlying unity in the sounds as there was in the movement of images. There can only be accelerando in sound where the sound itself remains constant in kind. The tempo of the music may quicken, the noise of the motor may rise to a scream, but no climax will be achieved by jumping from one to another with increasing speed, as can be done visually. The result would be merely a meaningless jumble of unrecognisable sounds. The obvious way to make this sequence in terms of sound would be to keep the music of the Concerto continuous throughout and cut the picture to its rhythm regardless of naturalism, making the visual climax coincide with the musical climax.[1]

In the above continuity, each cut takes us to a piece of action which is physically unrelated with the action of the previous shot : there is, in each case, only an emotional link between adjacent images. In sequences of this sort, as Asquith points out, using the actual sound of each image would produce a meaningless effect. A continuous sound track, employing a sound of *one kind*, has to be used over all the images and this is, of course, standard practice.

[1] The Cinema, *1950. Edited by Roger Manvell. Penguin Books, 1950. The quotation is from the essay* The Tenth Muse Takes Stock *by Anthony Asquith.*

Car chases which require a similar kind of rapid cross-cutting are commonly accompanied by a continuous and mounting sound of police sirens. Other scenes of this type do not employ natural sound at all, but are supported by a " background " music track which rises to a climax at the same point as the picture. (If the sequence described by Asquith were to take place in a theatre instead of in a concert hall, then a superimposed music score—or some other continuous sound—would have to be used.)

There is another entirely different editing effect which cannot be used with actual sound. We have described how Griffith, and to a greater extent the Russians, made use of what Pudovkin called " relational editing." Instances of this have already been given (e.g., the Stock Exchange sequence from *The End of St. Petersburg*). The method depends on using numbers of physically disconnected images and arranging them into a pattern which will convey certain emotional or intellectual impressions. Often isolated images, quite unconnected with the " story " are cut in. (For instance, the shots of Chinese religious effigies which form part of a sequence centred on St. Petersburg in *October*.) Clearly, the problem of fitting a synchronous track composed of actual sounds to series of images of this kind is exactly the same as it is in the example quoted by Asquith. It is, in fact, insuperable because the many short sound impressions would not add up to a significant total.

Some early film-makers of the sound period have tried to introduce certain symbolic effects into the action of their stories and thereby obviated the necessity of cutting to extraneous objects for their effects. Hitchcock, in *Blackmail* (1929), makes use of a painting of a laughing clown which is introduced into the action at several points and carries rather laboured symbolic overtones. Mamoulian, in *City Streets* (1931), introduces shots of ornamental figures of cats in a woman's bedroom to make a simile of her jealousy ; he shows a shot of birds in flight outside a prison window to symbolise the freedom beyond the bars ; he makes the snuffing out of a match symbolise a murder. Earlier, Mamoulian had experimented with similar effects in *Applause* which were severely criticised.

One of the most effective moments in *Applause* comes when the lover of the fading burlesque queen tells her she is old, ugly, finished. The camera hovers for an instant over Miss Morgan's face, moves slowly to the framed picture of her in her lovely youth, and then comes back to her. The movement of the camera and the continuing bitter voice over it combine to intensify the effect enormously. In another scene, as the dancer's daughter in a restaurant lifts a glass of water, the music fades slowly and the picture dissolves to the identical movement of her mother's arm, lifting a glass of poison to her lips. Obvious though such touches appear now, they were uncommonly good in the early days of sound.[1]

Jacobs' last comment seems unduly harsh. It seems ungenerous to dismiss Mamoulian's effects as obvious, simply because it is no longer fashionable to use them. The fashion to-day is for slick, dramatic story-telling and symbolic devices of the kind Mamoulian used have fallen into disfavour. None of them " help to get on with the story " and are therefore regarded by most film-makers as unnecessary complications of the continuity. Jacobs' judgment (" Obvious though such touches appear now . . . ") is written from the point of view of the contemporary audience which, through years of experience in seeing simple narrative movies, is no longer properly receptive to side-allusions, symbols and other subjective refinements.

The introduction of sound has, then, largely caused film-makers to concentrate on realistic narrative and to discard the silent cinema's methods of indirect visual allusion. In saying this, it is important to realise that this change of approach has been a matter of choice, not of necessity arising out of some new limitation of the sound medium.

There is no reason at all why a sound film should not make use of pictorially expressive devices of the kind Mamoulian used. The path of realism is not necessarily the only one along which the sound cinema can develop. There have been hints in many sound films indicating that personal, essentially undramatic devices can be used with great effect, provided that the whole film is conceived in a style which allows the symbols and images to take their place naturally in the continuity. If using the sleek ornamental cats as a simile to a girl's jealousy in *City Streets* is not entirely successful, it is not because the device itself is at fault. Rather, it is because the effect is introduced in the course of otherwise straightforward realistic narrative. The sudden transition from realism to highly sophisticated, contrived imagery becomes unacceptable because the spectator is abruptly asked to view the action, as it were, through different eyes. Mamoulian's effects, as Jacobs says, remain " touches," they never become an integral part of the narrative. The essential stylistic unity is missing.

One of the few sound films of recent years in which extensive use has been made of a personal imagery was the adaptation of

[1] The Rise of the American Film *by Lewis Jacobs. Harcourt, Brace & Co., 1939, pp. 170-1.*

Pushkin's *The Queen of Spades*. An image of a spider's web is used as a recurring symbol ; the sound of the old Countess's dress is made to assume a symbolic significance of its own ; when, in the scene where the young Countess has " sold her soul " and returns to her room to kneel before the Madonna, a gust of wind blows out the candle and leaves the room in darkness, it is as if the Virgin were rejecting the young girl's prayer. These effects are acceptable in *The Queen of Spades* because the film as a whole was conceived and executed in a style which can accommodate a use of symbols of this kind. The nature of the film's story, the ornate richness of the sets, the elegant low-key lighting (which is utterly unrealistic) and the powerful, larger-than-life portrayals of character give the film a style in which visual symbolism can form an acceptable part : the symbols are not " added " to the story, they form an integral part of its style. *The Queen of Spades* demonstrates that the sound cinema lends itself to this obliquely evocative style provided that a stylistic unity is preserved throughout the whole film.

All the effects described so far arise out of the setting of the story. The subjective comments spring naturally from a selective observation of the background. Ernest Lindgren has argued that this is as it always should be : that the visual simile or symbol is always more effective if it forms a natural part of the story's setting. Yet it must be remembered that the Russians produced some of their most telling visual contrasts by completely ignoring the story's natural locale and cutting to images which have no physical connection with the rest of the film. In the sequence in *October*, where Eisenstein wishes to satirise the mumbo-jumbo of religious ceremonies, he cuts from his title to shots of ikons, churches, and leaning spires, to Egyptian, Chinese and primitive African effigies. The sequence of shots is not linked by any sort of physical connection but by an abstract concept.

Obviously, there can be no question of making a continuity of this kind with actual sound. The sequence is composed of shots which are heterogeneous in time and space and any kind of naturalistic sound would merely draw attention to their diversity.

One may conclude that the sound medium is not capable of this kind of editing to an idea. But this is not necessarily so. Nor does the fact that Eisenstein himself never quite assimilated the element of sound prove anything except that he personally did not do so. British documentary directors of the thirties, particularly Basil Wright and Humphrey Jennings, showed that

Eisenstein's methods could be further developed in the sound cinema. Passages in *Song of Ceylon* (a sequence is analysed on p. 157) show that the film of ideas can be greatly enriched by the imaginative use of sound. By his experiments with sound, by evolving an extremely intricate sound continuity which alternately contrasts and blends with the picture, Wright showed that Eisenstein's conception of relational editing—editing to an idea, without respect for the unity of time and space between adjacent shots—could be further developed in the sound film.

The fact that the experiments of the thirties—Wright's, Jennings', and to a lesser degree Lorentz's in *The City*—have not been sufficiently followed up, does not prove that this could not be done. It is rather that documentary film sponsorship seems to have considerably tightened in recent years, with fewer and fewer sponsors being prepared (as the Soviets were in the twenties) to allow directors freedom to experiment with more abstract techniques. Yet in this direction lies a vast field for experiment.

In the section on documentary film making we will try to analyse some of the films which achieve their effects through relational editing. Meanwhile, it is worth noting that in these films, as also in compilations, the editor again assumes something of the importance he had in the silent cinema. Wright's method of shooting (and, in a rather different way, Flaherty's) again leaves much of the creative work over to the cutting room stage of production. The quality of films like *Louisiana Story* and *Song of Ceylon* must make one regret that their directors' methods of production are not practicable in more films. There are, as we have already suggested, good economic reasons for this, reasons why a more closely planned, plot-centred continuity is at present favoured. When these are in one way or another overcome, a whole new range of themes will again come within the scope of the sound cinema. At present, one can only hopefully anticipate the films of some future director, working in the sound medium, but with the freedom of a Griffith, an Eisenstein or a Dovzhenko.

SECTION 2

THE PRACTICE OF EDITING

3

ACTION SEQUENCES

THE ability of the cinema to record movement, to take the action of a story instantaneously from one place to another, remains one of its main sources of appeal. Many different styles of film-making have been developed around this central asset. The Western, almost as old as the cinema itself, the tough " sociological " gangster cycle of the thirties, the post-war semi-documentary police films, all with their compulsory chase endings, as well as the more sophisticated thrillers of Lang and Hitchcock, have based their appeal largely on the use of fast, exciting action scenes. Passages of movement, fighting and action are uniquely presented by the movies and remain perennially popular.

In the silent cinema the development of the action picture was inextricably bound up with the development of film editing. Characteristically, the first films to employ a rudimentary editing technique were Porter's chase films. Griffith developed the device of cross-cutting and thereby gave his action scenes a further dimension—by *timing* the conflicting shots he was able to give now the pursuer, now the pursued, the advantage of the chase. Later, the reaction shot—usually a static image of an observer— was used to punctuate the moving shots and to produce the visual contrast which accentuates the effect of movement. All these devices of presentation have remained essentially unaltered to the present day.

The use of cross-cutting gives the director a unique instrument with which to suggest physical conflict on the screen. By alternately cutting from the man chasing to the man being chased, the conflict is constantly kept in front of the audience, and the illusion of a continuous scene is preserved. Yet this very asset presents problems to the editor which are in some ways more difficult than those faced in passages of straight story-telling where each cut merely continues the action of the previous shot. There is first the elementary difficulty of keeping the spectator clearly informed of what is going on. Since in many cases the pursuer may be a long way behind his victim, it may become necessary to cross-cut between two locales which have no obvious visual connection. In such cases it is all the more important not to confuse the audience about the geographical relationship between the two `parallel streams of action. There may sometimes be a temptation to cut an action sequence too fast in the attempt to generate greater excitement : if this involves confusing the spectator about the physical details of the scene, then the editor will have defeated his object.

A further problem is to convey the varying fortunes of the contestants. This is largely a matter of timing : altering the rate of cutting to reflect the changing tension, lengthening a cut here or there to switch the emphasis from pursuer to pursued or vice versa. All these problems are so closely bound up with the particular dramatic requirements of any given sequence that a theoretical discussion must remain too vague to be useful. Here is a practical example of a straightforward chase sequence.

NAKED CITY[1]

Extract from Reel 10

> After a long search, Willie Garza (the murderer) is tracked down by Detective Halloran in Garza's apartment. While being interrogated, Garza tricks the detective, knocks him to the floor and runs away, unaware that the detective is still conscious. In the chase which follows Garza gets away and Detective Halloran reports the situation to headquarters. Lieut. Dan Muldoon is in charge of the case.
>
> Garza is seen running up the steps of a subway. As he reaches the top, he looks round to see if he is being pursued and accidentally runs into a blind man coming round the corner. The blind man's Alsatian dog pounces on Garza :
>
> The commentator throughout the film is the producer, Mark Hellinger.

Ft. fr.

	Commentator : (as if giving Garza kindly advice) It's only an accident, Garza. Pass it off !		
1	M.L.S. Garza. The dog has got hold of Garza's left arm and he is running along, struggling to get free.	Fast dramatic music.	2 2

[1] *Director : Jules Dassin. Editor : Paul Weatherwax. Universal International, 1948.*

2	M.S. Garza's back. His right hand is reaching for his revolver as he struggles with the dog.	*Commentator :* Don't lose your head ! Don't lose your head ! *Music continues.*	5 2
3	M.L.S. Lieut. Muldoon sitting in his car. The car door is open, Det. Halloran and others standing by. Lieut. Muldoon hands over a revolver to Halloran. They all look in the direction of the shot. Halloran and an assistant run away to see what is happening. Car door is slammed.	*Lieut. Muldoon :* —in a crowded neighbourhood. Now here's what you do— *A loud report is heard.*	10
4	*Shooting down* a wide street with a railway station in the background. Halloran and an assistant come running *into frame* going *away from camera* and the car follows.	*Music continues.* *Police whistles.* *Sound of accelerating car.*	16 8
5	Garza running down a long bridge *towards camera*. A small child is in his way. Its mother rushes towards the child just in time to pick it up and let Garza run past the *camera right*.	*Music continues.*	6 13
6	*Shooting up* subway steps. The blind man stands helpless at the top. Halloran and assistant running up towards him.	*Music continues*	
7	L.S. Blind man. A small boy is helping him. Dog lies dead to the right, bridge in background. The two detectives come *into frame* from below. Halloran stoops to look at the dead dog.	*Music continues.*	5 10
8	M.C.S. Halloran. He looks up in the direction of the bridge (trying to spot Garza).	*Music continues.*	2 8
9	*Shooting along* bridge as from Halloran's viewpoint. Garza running *away from camera* in V.L.S.	*Music continues.*	3 4
10	As *in* 8. Halloran turns back towards his assistant, speaks and runs *past camera*, to follow Garza.	*Halloran :* (to assistant) It's Garza !	3 14
11	*Shooting down* from top of subway steps. Lieut. Muldoon and two assistants run *into frame* at the bottom of steps.	*Halloran's assistant :* (off) Dan ! It's Garza ! *Music continues.*	4 9
12	Halloran's assistant at top of steps. *Shooting* from about halfway up the steps.	*Halloran's assistant :* (shouting) Halloran's after him, they're running towards the Brooklyn end.	3 8

13   M.L.S. Muldoon and assistants at bottom steps.

Muldoon (shouting up)   8 2
You stay with Halloran.
Don't shoot unless you have to.

Muldoon turns to assistants and speaks. They run up steps *past camera.*

You two stay with him.

Muldoon and other assistants run back towards car.

14   *Shooting along* bridge. *As in 5, but much farther along.* Garza *running towards camera and past it.*

Music continues.   8 12

15   *As above* (14), but nearer end of bridge.   Halloran *running towards camera and past it.*
Mother holding her child stands right.

Music continues.   5 1

16   M.S. Muldoon and a cop. 'Phone box in background.

Muldoon :   5 13
Get the radio !

Cop runs to 'phone box. Muldoon runs *off left.*

Have 'em send a car to the Brooklyn end.

17   M.S. Muldoon's car.
Muldoon's assistant gets into the car.
Two cops standing behind car.

15 6

Two other cops standing in front of car.
Muldoon gets into the car and it moves away right. *Camera pans as car moves off round the corner.*

Muldoon :
You both, get in !
You two ! Up at this **end.**

Police sirens.

18   M.S. Garza running towards camera. *Camera tracks back in front of him, keeping him in M.S.*

2 7

19   M.S. Halloran running *towards camera. Camera tracks back in front of him, keeping him in M.S.*

3 8

20   *As in* 18.   M.S. Garza running *towards camera.*

4 5

21   Interior moving car.   Muldoon sitting beside driver.
Camera shooting from back of car in direction of the car's movement along the bridge.

3 2

22   Overhead crossing. Garza comes *into frame* bottom left and runs up the steps.

9 7

23   *As in* 19. Halloran running *towards camera which is tracking before him.*

2 11

1

15

5

18

8

19

9

20

14

23

24	*As in* 21. Interior moving car.	Muldoon : (turning to cops sitting in back of car) That tower up ahead on the left—you boys can get out there. Watch for Garza from that end. Cop : Right.	8
25	Garza running down steps at the other side of the overhead crossing.		5 14
26	M.C.S. Garza as he climbs on to a fence. He looks down.		1 13
27	*From Garza's viewpoint.* Muldoon's car draws up below.		5 3
28	*As in* 26. Garza has spotted the car and momentarily attempts to hide behind the fence.		2 3
29	M.S. Car. Two cops get out.		1 12
30	*As in* 28. Garza panics and shoots.	*Report of shot.*	2 3
31	*As in* 29. Cops both crouch on one knee and shoot up at Garza. They run towards overhead crossing.		6 1
32	Garza running down some steps. He suddenly stops as he sees somebody in the opposite direction.		4 2
33	*Shooting* across the railway line. Halloran is seen approaching. Just as he is about to jump the railing, a train speeds *across screen left to right,* thereby cutting Halloran off from Garza.		3 10

Let us try to follow the relative positions of Garza and his pursuers throughout the sequence in order to see how the editor has contrived this perfectly lucid continuity.

Up to half way through shot *3* the two parties are unaware of each other's whereabouts.

This is confirmed in *4*, when we see Halloran running towards the railway station, and in *5*, when Garza is seen to be already some way along the bridge. Specific attention is unobtrusively drawn to Garza's position by the presence of the mother with her small child.

The next three shots (*6–8*) show Halloran running in the direction from which the gun was fired, and take him to the top of the flight of steps—to the exact spot where Garza was at the opening of the incident.

In *9*, he catches sight of Garza and contact is established. Halloran quickly gives the news to Muldoon and the chase begins.

Garza is still running (*14*) but we see that he has meanwhile got some way ahead.

The next shot (*15*) places Halloran quite clearly in relation to Garza : he is just passing the woman and child whom we saw in *5* (note that the camera set-up in *5* and *15* is the same). This implies that while Muldoon has been giving instructions, Halloran has just had time to reach the place from which Garza started running during shot *3*.

We cut back to Muldoon (*16–17*) and hear that he is going to try to cut off Garza's escape from the other side.

Meanwhile, *18* shows Garza slowing down through exhaustion.

He is followed by Halloran (*19*) and we see that the detective is drawing closer. (The two stills may be a little confusing at this point. *18* is taken from the very beginning of the shot and *19* from near the end. Thus the two men do not appear in the film to be in quite such close pursuit as the stills suggest.)

In *20* we see that Garza has become aware of Halloran's presence and is putting on a fresh spurt.

Again, we cut away from the main action. *21* keeps us aware of Muldoon's movements, and implies, when we cut to shot *22*, that Garza has had time to reach the overhead crossing.

At this point the editor has slightly distorted the true continuity of events. Shot *23* shows Halloran barely farther along the bridge than he was in *19*—not nearly as far along, in fact, as the duration of shots *20–22* would suggest. The purpose of taking this liberty— it is not noticeable at a first viewing—is to show that Garza has once more succeeded in leaving Halloran far behind.

Again we cut back to Muldoon, and the conflict changes : it is now between Garza and Muldoon's men, Halloran having been left behind. The gun-fight is simply presented in to-and-fro reaction shots *26–31*.

Then, in *32*, Garza realises that he cannot get past the cops and decides to turn back. He sees Halloran behind him (*33*) and is cornered.

Thus : Garza is sighted in *9* ; in *14–15* he is seen to be a long way ahead ; in *18–19* Halloran has nearly caught up ; in *20* Garza puts on an extra spurt ; and we see in *22–23* that he has again succeeded in getting away. Then follows the quick interchange of gunfire (*24–31*) and finally the presence of Halloran in

33 indicates that Garza is caught. During the entire passage, the geography of the locale and each stage of the chase have been clearly conveyed.

The rate of cutting is continuously made to underline the changing tension of the situation. Shot *3* is 10 feet long : the chase has not yet begun and the revolver shot takes the cops unawares in the midst of a lull in the action. The beginning of the chase is rendered as being long and exhausting rather than particularly eventful. Shots *5, 14* and *15* are relatively long : Garza's desperate struggle to get away rather than any new dramatic development is stressed. After this, the cutting becomes a little quicker as Halloran begins to draw nearer and then farther away again. Finally, the rate of cutting is further speeded up into a climax as the gunfire begins.

It is worth commenting on the particular methods the editor has adopted to convey the effect of speed and excitement. Earlier in the film Garza has been characterised as cunning as well as ruthless, and the final chase therefore was best presented as a " battle of wits," instead of a wild action-packed shooting-match. The editor has adapted his technique to this demand of the story. He has not cut the passage particularly fast, but has concentrated in switching the action around quickly among the three participants, in order to give the impression of the smoothly co-ordinated action of the two police contingents working together against the criminal. It is, for instance, particularly noticeable that from shot *13* onwards each cut takes us to another part of the action : there are no cuts which continue the action of a previous shot. This constant switching of the focus of attention creates an impression of fast action even though the cutting—except at the very end—is not particularly quick.

A conspicuous feature of the editing of this passage as compared to most other action scenes is the complete absence of any establishing long shots in which the opposing parties can be seen at once, and of any static reaction shots of observers. Close attention to the details of the locale which is cleverly used to placeeach character in a recognisable position obviates the use of establishing long shots. Similarly, the editor has not resorted to using any reaction shots of observers because the three groups of people concerned in the chase always provide him with something to cut away to.

Nevertheless, both these devices form a useful and often indispensable feature of the editing of action scenes. Their use is shown in the next example.

ONCE A JOLLY SWAGMAN[1]
Extract from Reel 11

Bill Fox (Dirk Bogarde) had been an ace speedway rider before the war. When he returns from the army, his wife urges him to get a steady job instead of returning to the track. They quarrel, and Bill decides to attempt to make a come-back. As a test to find out whether Bill has not lost his touch during his absence, Tommy Possey (Bonar Colleano) makes Bill run a trial race with Chick, the current champion rider. Preceding this sequence we have seen shots which show Chick to be perfectly calm, Bill very nervous.

			Ft.	fr.
1	L.S. of Bill, Chick, Tommy and a mechanic (Taffy) walking towards the bikes in foreground.	Music : the speedway-riders' march as used previously in the film. Tommy : We might as well do this proper-ly. We'll toss for it. Call.	39	6

	They stop in M.S. in front of camera.
	Tommy tosses a coin.
	
	Tommy looks at the coin.
		Bill :
		  Tails.
		Tommy :
		  Heads.
		Chick :
		  I'll take the outside.
		Tommy : (to Taffy, off)
		  Give them " Go," will you, Taffy.		

	Camera pans with Chick as he mounts his bike.			

2	M.L.S. Bill, Tommy and Chick.
	
	Mechanics push Chick's bike.
		Tommy: (to Bill)
		  Watch him, boy—he's good
		Bill :
		  O.K. Tommy, don't worry. I'll be all right.
		Chick :
		  Up !
		Music stops.
		Roar of bikes begins.
		Bill :
		  Come on, let's get going.
		Tommy :
		  All right.
			28	7

	Tommy pushes Bill's bike until it starts. Camera pans with them until Bill rides out of frame.			
3	L.S. Taffy running towards camera. He stands right ; Bill and Chick take up their positions near him.		17	1
4	M.C.S. Taffy holding up his handkerchief as a starting flag.		2	12
5	M.S. Bill and Chick looking to-wards Taffy (off). Bill looks at Chick to see if he is ready.		4	3

[1] *Director : Jack Lee. Editor : Jack Harris. A Wessex production, 1948.*

			Ft. fr.
6	C.S. handkerchief in Taffy's hand.		2 2
7	C.U. Bill.		1 12
8	C.S. handkerchief as it is jerked down.		15
9	L.S. Chick and Bill starting the race. Chick's front wheel goes off the ground as he accelerates.	*Roar of bikes suddenly increases.*	2 2
10	L.S. Bill and Chick riding *towards camera which pans with them* as they go all the way round the first bend. They ride *out of frame left.*		10 12
11	M.S. Tommy watching.		3 4
12	L.S. Chick and Bill. *Camera pans left to right with them* as they go round the bend. Bill is slightly ahead.		8 10
13	M.S. Bill and Chick riding *towards camera which is tracking back in front of them.* Bill still slightly ahead.		7 11
14	M.L.S. Chick and Bill going round the bend : *camera pans left to right with them.* Chick moves slightly ahead.		11 11
15	L.S. Chick and Bill : as Bill passes Chick, *camera pans left to right into a M.S. of Tommy.*		9
16	C.S. Bill. *Camera tracks back in front of him, keeping Bill in C.S.*	*Music starts.*	3 6
17	C.S. of Chick. *Camera tracks back in front of him, keeping Chick in C.S.*		3 3
18	L.S. Bill and Chick. *Camera pans left to right with them* as they go round a bend. Chick is slightly ahead.		8
19	M.S. Chick. He is riding *towards camera.*		4 3
20	M.S. Bill, riding *towards camera.*		3 1
21	M.S. Chick, *as in* 19. His bike tilts as he goes round a bend.		4
22	V.L.S. Chick and Bill riding *towards camera,* past the Start. They ride *out of frame* right, with Chick ahead.		6 12
23	C.S. Tommy, anxiously watching.		1 10
24	L.S. Bill and Chick : *camera pans round the bend with them.* Chick slightly ahead.		5 5

78

" Once a Jolly Swagman "

9

15

10

18

11

22

12

24

13

28

14

31

		Ft. fr.
25	C.S. Bill : *camera tracks back in front of him.*	2 7
26	C.S. Chick : *camera tracks back in front of him.*	2 12
27	C.S. Bill. As in 25.	2 11
28	L.S. Bill and Chick riding *towards camera* as they come round the bend. They are almost level.	4 13
29	C.S. Tommy. He takes his pipe from his mouth, watches anxiously.	1 9
30	L.S. Chick and Bill : they are going *across screen left to right,* almost level.	4 7
31	V.L.S. Chick and Bill riding *towards camera* from the distance. At the winning post, Bill just passes Chick. *Music stops.*	4 6
32	M.L.S. Tommy. He puts his pipe in his mouth and walks on to the track. He looks pleased.	7 7
33	L.S. Chick and Bill coming *towards camera.* Chick goes *out of frame right* and Bill stops in M.S. He rests in front of camera, takes off his goggles and looks up, relieved. *Crowd cheers (as in Bill's mind). Roar of bikes dies down. Music starts.*	23 5

From an editor's point of view,[1] I was faced with one great advantage and a number of difficulties. In most race or fight sequences of this kind, the audience gets a prior knowledge as to what the final result will have to be if the story is to continue. In this case, however, the situation before the race is that Bill himself is uncertain whether he can make a come-back. If he wins, he knows that he will get his old job again, but that he will never get his wife back. On balance, therefore, the audience should anticipate that Bill will lose. This uncertainty made it easier for us to hold the audience's interest.

The difficulties were more numerous. Previous to this, there had already been four racing sequences in the film, so that we had to introduce certain variations here. There could only be very few reaction shots—only two onlookers were present—and there were only two competitors in the race. This narrowed the choice of shots. Finally, for various reasons, we were unable to cover the sequence with as many shots as we would have liked.

The sequence starts with a sort of musical echo effect of the speedway riders' march. We used this in order to contrast the emptiness of the arena with the crowd and bustle of the earlier race sequences. The mechanics standing idly by instead of being on their toes, and Bill's old mechanic acting as starter with a handkerchief instead of using the elaborate mechanical starting gate were both points of difference from the earlier visits to the track. So far so good. But it was the race itself which was the difficulty.

With the shortage of material it became obvious that we would have to concentrate on shots of the race itself and use only occasional reaction shots of Tommy. We could not let either of the riders get too far ahead of the other : Bill had to be the eventual winner, but Chick was, after all, the ace rider and

[1] *Notes by Jack Harris.*

80

it would have been ridiculous for Bill to come from behind to win. The medium and long shots were therefore used to indicate the ding-dong battle and the close-ups to show the riders' reactions—with Chick to show that he at least had no doubts as to the result, and with Bill to show his confidence gradually returning until he just wins on the post.

As in the sequence from *Naked City*, great care has been taken here to keep the spectator clearly informed about the precise state of the race at each stage. Here, however, this does not present much of a problem : the aim is not so much to elucidate a complicated chase as to convey something of the suspense of the contest. This is done partly through the use of the self-explanatory long shots, partly through the suggestive use of reaction shots.

The first three shots leading up to the beginning of the race are all deliberately slow. In the opening shot the three men are silently walking towards the camera: the music is a reminder of Bill's previous triumphs on this track and of his nervousness about making a come-back.

Again, *2* and *3* are both long-lasting shots in which the preparations for the race are made at leisurely tempo.

Following on this slow introduction, the quick group of shots *4-9* conveys the sudden release of the stored-up tension. This is the moment when Bill's nerve is being most severely tested and constitutes, in effect, the first climax of the sequence.

As the race progresses, the action shots (*10, 12-15, 18, 22, 24*) are all kept on the screen for a relatively long time. The end of the race, as Jack Harris points out, could not be made in any way spectacular because that would have been out of keeping with the story. Accordingly, the rate of cutting is not appreciably increased towards the finish. In this sense, the editing is quite different from the *Naked City* chase where the story required a mounting tension. The end of the race is here shown in long shot and gives a straight objective view of the riders crossing the finishing line. There is no attempt to force another climax.

The final shot of the sequence conveys the slow dying down of the physical excitement : in a long-lasting shot (*33*) Bill slows down as he approaches the camera and finally comes to rest in medium shot. The race itself is over by the time *31* has been seen and Tommy's reaction (*32*)—he is known to be sympathetic to Bill—leaves no doubt as to the result. Shot *33* is therefore merely used to suggest the lull after the excitement. This is an important dramatic point in the story because the lull contrasts with what would happen in a real race meeting and leads naturally to the

81

phantom sounds which are heard as though through Bill's ears. The imaginary sounds *could* have been introduced during the race but this would have been less effective because they would have competed for attention with the roar of the bikes. ("The music[1] starting on shot *16* was deliberately introduced there not to add to the excitement of the race but to take the realism out of the track and to prepare for the phantom cheers which grew out of it as Bill finally brings his bike to a stop.")

In the course of the sequence, the editor has cut away five times to shots of Tommy. Static shots of this kind used in a sequence intended primarily to convey swift, exciting movement, may at first sight appear unsuitable. In fact, they perform several important functions.

In the first place, it is necessary here to suggest that in the course of the contest the riders have gone round the track four times. If this were to be shown in full, it might become unnecessarily tedious. The use of the reaction shots (or, for that matter, the individual close shots of Chick and Bill) bridges the time gaps between the long shots of the race itself. By cutting away from the race and then cutting back again, a lapse of time is implied which makes it acceptable to the spectator to see that the race has meanwhile progressed. In this way the editor can unobtrusively cut down the screen duration of the race and yet make the spectator believe that he has seen it in its entirety. (See, for instance, *22* and *24*. Both shots show the riders covering the same stretch of track. The short insert (*23*) makes the audience accept the implication that while they have been seeing Tommy, the riders have had time to cover a whole lap.)

In addition, the static reaction shots break up the movement of the fast action shots and make them all the more impressive by contrast. If a sequence of this length were to be composed entirely of long shots of the race the effect of movement would be slowly frittered away by the lack of variety in the images. It is precisely through the *variation* of the images that an effect of speed is conveyed.

The further purpose of the reaction shots is to guide the spectator's response. The variations in Tommy's facial expression set the key to the spectator's appreciation of what is happening in the race and form an important factor in producing the desired emotional effect.

As in the previous extract, all the cuts in this sequence are

[1] *Notes by Jack Harris.*

either to a piece of parallel action or to a sharply contrasting image of the action in the previous shot. In the sequence *12–15* each cut continues the action of the previous shot, but it always takes us to an entirely different angle of view : *12* is a long shot with the movement from left to right ; *13* is a medium shot with a tracking camera ; in *14* the movement is from left to right and the camera pans with the riders as they move into the distance ; *15* is a left to right shot finishing on a quick pan on to Tommy. Four shots of a continuous action are shown but they are all from different angles and distances. In this way a sense of speed and excitement is conveyed which could not be achieved by a series of smooth cuts.

An examination of the footages does not in itself give an accurate idea of the effective pace at which the sequence is edited. It is particularly noticeable that the close shots are always left on the screen for a much briefer interval than the long shots. This is because a close shot in which the image of the figure remains still within the frame conveys all it has to say in a short time. A long shot, on the other hand, in which the movement takes place across the frame, is a source of more sustained interest because it is continually changing.

This is a most important distinction to understand when editing an action scene. Five feet of a static reaction shot (e.g., the shot of Tommy in *11*) or of a tracking shot which keeps a figure in the frame at constant size (e.g., *25*, *26*, *27*) appears to a spectator to last much longer than five feet of a long shot in which the bikes travel across the screen. The absolute lengths of the shots only make a significant measure for comparison if the nature of each shot is taken into account.

The two sequences we have quoted provide fairly representative examples of problems the editor faces in conveying movement and action. The points which are of first importance can be summarised as follows :

(1) to keep the " plot " of the passage clearly in front of the spectator ; i.e., to see that the cross-cutting does not confuse the continuity ;

(2) to vary the pace of the cutting in order to obtain the desired variations of dramatic tension ;

(3) to cut away to reaction shots of static observers in order to bridge time lapses between adjacent action shots and in order to guide the audience's emotional response ;

(4) to give visual variety and the illusion of continuous movement by frequent cross-cutting and by varying the angles of view on a single piece of action.

It will be seen that all these points cannot be finally settled until the film reaches the cutting room. This does not mean that the broad outlines of the continuity should not be planned earlier. It is obviously desirable that the director, while shooting the material, should attempt to visualise the steps by which the sequence will develop. Even then, however clear the director may be about the continuity while he is shooting, he will usually provide a certain amount of cover. It is in the finer variations of the timing and the precise correlation of the shots that the scene will finally attain its effects, and it is important that the editor should be given enough material with which to elaborate minor points. More than this, the editor often finds that rearranging the order of shots throws fresh light on the material ; in such instances, to hinder his work through lack of footage might waste good opportunities.

On some occasions it is practically impossible to shoot material with any definite preconceived sequence of shots in mind. In war-time scenes of fighting it is often impossible for the director—or the newsreel cameraman whose material will later be used—to shoot to anything like a preconceived plan ; he can only shoot the scenes which happen to be to hand. Provided enough material has been shot, however, this should not prevent the editor from assembling a dramatically effective sequence which makes film sense. For even if the shooting has been carefully planned, the prime responsibility for giving an action sequence its essential precision and tempo rests with the editor. The elucidation of the continuity and the timing of shots are the two crucial processes and they must, in any event, be left over to the cutting room.

In assembling an action sequence the editor works with a much greater degree of freedom than in more static scenes where dialogue plays the predominant role. In a dialogue scene most of the visuals form an essential and unavoidable counterpart to the words and the editor is constantly tied down by the continuity of the words when cutting the picture. The visuals are anchored from the moment they are shot : the editor is merely able to choose between alternative shots and to time the cuts to the greatest dramatic effect. He remains the interpreter of the small details rather than the prime creator of the continuity. In action sequences, on the other hand, it is the pictures which tell the story, and the editor is free

84

to arrange them in any order he thinks most telling. Here he has the major creative responsibility, for it is only in the process of editing that the shots acquire their significance. Unhampered by the restrictions imposed by synchronised dialogue, the editor is able to work with much the same freedom as he enjoyed in the silent cinema. Even to-day, however good the director's raw material, it is the editor who makes or mars a sequence of action.

4

DIALOGUE SEQUENCES

THE effective editing of dialogue passages presents the director and editor with both the simplest and the most difficult problems. If the dialogue is well written, then the scene is easy to assemble—indifferently well. The words carry the scene and the director only has to see to it that the emphasis is clear and correctly placed. On the other hand, if the director is not prepared to let the words do all the work, but insists on bringing a positive visual contribution to the scene, then his problem is much more difficult.

Let us take the first case first. Frequently dialogue scenes are shot something like this : (1) two characters are shown talking to each other in medium or long shot to establish the situation ; (2) the camera tracks in towards the characters or we cut to a closer two-shot in the same line of vision as shot (1) ; (3) finally, we are shown a series of alternating close shots of the two players—usually over the opposite character's shoulder—either speaking lines or reacting. At the main point of interest, close-ups may be used and the camera generally eases away from the actors at the end of the scene.

Up to a point, this method is satisfactory. The words are presented clearly, with no " distraction " from the visuals. Shooting over the shoulder of one player keeps the audience aware of the essential conflict between the two players. Isolating the characters in close shots makes it possible to show their faces in head-on view rather than in profile—as necessarily happens when they are both shown talking to each other. Finally, there is a good opportunity to show close-ups of stars which the public like to see.

But there are two more positive reasons why the method outlined is on the whole satisfactory. Firstly, a dialogue scene is normally rather static : it is what the characters *say*, not what they *do*, that matters. Using two-shots and individual close shots gives a certain visual variety and movement to the presentation, while leaving the characters—as they normally would be—sitting or standing more or less stationary. Secondly, the editor is given a great deal of freedom in cutting the scene in a variety of dramatically effective ways. He must judge the right point at which to cut from the establishing shot to one of the close shots and has an infinite variety of possibilities of timing the cuts between the individual close shots. Often he does not cut the dialogue track at the same point as the visuals, that is to say, he does not show the speaking characters all the time. (It is, of course, frequently more important for the story to show a character reacting rather than speaking a line.) By a variety of small tricks of presentation— by the choice of the exact moment in a scene to cut to a close-up, the timing of delayed reactions, the overlapping of dialogue, and so on—the editor can accentuate and control the drama of a given scene. Often, by a suitable timing of words and images, he can produce dramatic overtones, which the visuals alone did not have.

Here is a simple example, chosen at random.

TOPPER RETURNS[1]

Extract from Reel 2

> *This is one of the Topper series of comedy films. A rather slight but gruesome murder plot forms the background for the comedy action.*
> *The grown-up daughter has just arrived in America and has been greeted by her father, whom she has never seen before. She questions him about the death of her mother. So far everything has been perfectly straightforward and amiable between them. A doctor, who is present, has previously warned the girl not to excite her father too much since he is very ill.*

			Ft.
1	M.C.S. Father. He gets very excited towards the end of his speech.	Father : My partner was a man called Walter Harburg. One day he was showing your mother through the mine, when suddenly there was an earthquake, the tunnel collapsed . . . Doctor : (off : a deep. authoritative voice) You've talked enough,—	1
2	M.C.S. Doctor.	—Mr. Carrington.	3
3	M.S. Father, daughter and doctor.	Doctor : (continues amiably) I'm sorry to interrupt, but we must not tire your father.	

[1] *Director : Roy del Ruth. Editor : James Newcom. United Artists, 1941.*

87

A reading of the dialogue alone conveys simply that a sick old man is telling a rather distressing story when his doctor stops him, advising that he should not get too excited. The sequence, as shot and edited, however, presents a rather more complex situation.

The line, " You've talked enough . . . " is spoken " off " ; the daughter has been talking to her father for some time and although we saw the doctor enter, we have not seen him in the room since. When his voice is suddenly heard (over shot *1*) it comes as rather a surprise and produces an air of mystery around the man. The spectator becomes subconsciously aware that the doctor has been in the room all this time without saying a word ; suddenly, when the father is getting to the point of his story, the doctor mysteriously stops him. So while there is nothing strange about the doctor's words—the daughter suspects nothing—the spectator is given a foreboding hint by the way the cuts are timed.

If shot *2* had not been used at all, and the cut from *1* to *3* had been made on the doctor's first words, the whole action would have been perfectly straightforward—just a doctor looking after his patient. If the whole line (" You've talked enough, Mr. Carrington ! ") had been given with *3*, the surprise effect would have been lost because the spectator would have been aware of the doctor's presence before hearing his words. Indeed, throughout the whole scene, the lines of dialogue are in themselves quite ordinary—the daughter hears them all without astonishment ; it is the way the scene is edited that gives it its air of mystery. (This is precisely what is wanted : the doctor and father later turn out to be impostors.)

It would be absurd to suggest that the whole of this effect is conveyed by the timing of the cuts alone ; clearly, the lighting adds an air of mystery and the actors play a most important role— the doctor's tone of voice, for instance, suddenly becomes more kindly over shot *3*. The point is that the shots *could* have been made into a colourless narrative sequence with none of the mysterious overtones. By introducing the shot of the doctor *after* he has started his line, the spectator is, so to speak, one jump ahead of the story as seen by the daughter, and the upward tilt of the camera momentarily strengthens the sinister suspicion. After that, the scene continues in an ordinary matter-of-fact way. The suspicion has been planted and that is enough, for of course the doctor's behaviour must remain plausible.

This is a simple example, quoted to illustrate the importance of precise timing of action and reaction shots, and to show how the elementary device of overlaying a piece of dialogue can make a

1

2

3

definite dramatic point. Any number of other examples could be cited to show how this process works in dramatic or humorous scenes, but they would not lead us to any universally applicable principle : the editor's point of departure must always be the particular dramatic requirement of his scene.

The simple editing pattern of two-shot and alternating close shots, used simply or with minor variations, is by no means the ideal way of directing a scene of dialogue. Most passages shot in this way are visually dull and gain little in translation from script to screen. The formula is used so extensively because writers so frequently give little indication of what visual action is to accompany the spoken words, and because it is easiest to handle : the director merely needs to cover the scene from, say, half a dozen different set-ups, and let the editor do the best he can with the result.

Mention of the writer brings us to the crux of the problem of successful direction of dialogue. If the scene is to be wholly successful then it must be *visually* interesting as well as worth listening to, and that requires planning in the script stage. If a writer has been satisfied to write a scene in terms of dialogue alone, leaving the images to be taken care of later, a director, able to improvise, may still succeed in producing an exciting sequence (or he may not). The point at issue is that the visual action needs at least as much creative attention as the dialogue itself and should certainly be given the benefit of a carefully planned script. As sometimes happens, the director, faced with a script which gives him no lead as to the appearance of the scene, chooses the simplest way out and merely covers the scene from a number of camera set-ups. The result, if well edited, is usually quite presentable and may, depending on the director, sometimes be dramatically effective. But the chances of scenes shot in this way being really successful are small ; mostly, they turn out rather flat.

In a more adventurous approach to dialogue scenes the visuals can be used to contribute more positively to the total effect. Even if the words convey most of the facts and information, the images must still remain the primary vehicle for the dramatic interpretation. Before discussing this question more fully, let us take an example.

THE PASSIONATE FRIENDS[1]
Excerpt from Reel 5
Howard Justin (Claude Rains), a wealthy and influential banker, has gone off on a business trip to Germany. During his

[1] *Director : David Lean. Editor · Geoffrey Foot. Cineguild, 1948.*

90

absence, his wife Mary (Ann Todd) meets Steven Stratton (Trevor Howard) with whom she was once in love. During Howard's absence they see a great deal of each other and fall in love again. Howard returns from Germany earlier than expected and Mary informs him that she has arranged to go to the theatre that night with Steven. Later in the evening, Howard finds that Mary has left the theatre tickets behind ; he goes to the theatre with the tickets, buys a programme at the door and finds that Mary and Steven are not there. He goes home and carefully places the programme on a table in the centre of the room. When Steven and Mary arrive home Howard insists that Steven should come in for a drink. Steven consents and, while Mary is upstairs changing, Howard tells Steven all about his visit to Germany in terms referring to treachery, sentimentality, etc., which are obviously an indirect and ironic allusion to Steven's affair with Mary. Then Mary enters.

		Ft.	fr.

1   M.L.S. Mary coming through half-open door right. *Camera pans left with her* to bring Howard (pouring a drink in background) and Steven (standing left) *into frame.*

Mary takes off her jacket and then turns to walk away to radio-gram in right background. Howard walks forward, glass in hand. *Camera pans left to keep Howard and Steven in frame ; Mary is off right.*

Howard picks up a lighter and lights Steven's cigarette.

42   7

Howard :
Had a good evening ?
Mary :
Yes, fine.

Shall we have some music ?
Howard :
Help yourself to a cigarette, Stratton.
Steven :
Oh, thank you.
Howard :
Where did you dine ?

2   M.L.S. Mary standing at radio-gram, *back to camera.* On hearing Howard's question she turns abruptly and bangs down the lid of the gramophone.
She walks forward towards a table with a bowl of flowers and starts rearranging them.

14   5

Mary : (to Howard, off)
Oh, that French place with the mad waiter.

I do wish they wouldn't keep sending irises. I told them about it before. They're so spiky and unfriendly.

3   M.S. Steven and Howard. Howard turns *away from camera* and walks towards fireplace, *camera tracking after him.*

11   7

Howard : (to Mary, off)
How was the show ?

4   M.C.S. Mary.

Mary : (to Howard, off)
Oh, fine.

3   1

5   M.C.S. Howard. He turns his head towards Mary (off) and smiles ironically.

3   14

Howard : (to Mary, off)
Good seats ?

6   C.S. Mary. She glances up embarrassed and moves *out of frame* right.

Mary : (to Howard, off)
Very.

5   1

91

1a

1b

1c

1d

2

3

4

5

6

7a

7b

8

9

10

11

12

13

14a

14b

15

16a

16b

17

18

7   M.S. Steven and Howard. Howard
moves forward, *camera panning
right with him.* Mary comes *into
frame from right* and Howard
guides her to her seat on the
sofa.
Howard is now in left foreground
*back to camera, which is shooting
down* to Mary, now seated. Howard
walks *off right. Camera moves in*
to Mary and rests.   Howard's
hands can be seen in background,
handling the drinks.

Howard :
Sit down, I'll get you a drink.

Mary :
A small one.

Howard : (off, to Steven, off)
Well, as I was about to say when
Mary came in—I think the most
striking thing about the German
people is their pathetic faith in
themselves.

8   M.S. Steven as he sits down.

Steven : (to Howard, off)   2 14
Why do you call it pathetic ?

9   M.C.S. Mary.   Howard's hands
can be seen in background.

Howard : (off, to Steven, off)   9 3
The belief of the muscular in
their own strength is always
pathetic, don't you think ?

10   C.S. Theatre programme on little
table, lying in front of a cigarette
box. Mary's hand moves forward
to open the box. Just as she is
taking a cigarette out, her hand
stops.

4 7

3 6

11   B.C.U. Mary.

12   C.S. Howard looking down to-   *Howard :* (to Mary, off)   2 7
wards Mary, off.   Ice ?

13   M.C.S. Mary. She is about to get   *Howard :* (off)   5 10
up. Howard's hands can be seen   Don't get up.
in background handling the drinks:
they motion Mary to stay seated.

14   M.S. Howard *from above. Camera   24 4
pans with him* as he walks around
sofa until Mary is brought *into
frame* as Howard offers her a
drink.   Mary stares up at him
but does not move.   Howard   *Howard :*
places the glass on the table,   Here.
on top of the theatre programme,
camera panning with his hand.

15   M.S. Steven looking puzzled.   3 9

16   F.S. Howard and Mary, Steven in   61 8
right foreground *back to camera.*
Howard, cigarette case in hand,
walks a little towards Steven and
stops.

Howard :
Personally, Stratton, I think
there is a fault in the Teutonic
mind, which shows up whenever they have access to great
power—sort of romantic hysteria—

94

He takes a cigarette out of his case and walks a little farther towards Steven.

—well,—perhaps not romantic, but hysteria anyway,—
—which seems to convert them from a collection of sober, intelligent, rather sentimental individuals, into a dangerous mob—

Howard walks past Steven to the left, turns and faces Mary and Steven in turn as he speaks.

—a mob which can believe a big enough lie isn't a lie at all, but the truth.

Howard lights his cigarette.

Mary :
Steven, it's getting late.

Steven gets up.

Howard :
Oh, let him finish his drink.

Mary gets up.

Mary :
Steven, will you go now.
Howard :
Aren't you losing your head, dear ?
Steven :
What is it, Mary ?
Mary :
Howard knows we weren't at the theatre.

17 M.C.S. Howard and Steven, who is *back to camera right.*

3

18 M.C.S. Steven and Howard, who is *back to camera left.*

Steven :
I see—
—I am sorry you had to find out this way but I think you had better know the truth.

The film presents Howard as an understanding, courteous man who has tried to be reasonable about his wife's affair for some time. When, however, he finally finds out that Mary has been meeting Steven secretly, he lays this trap with the theatre programme for them. Characteristically, he wants to avoid a vulgar row and to stage a coolly calculated show-down. The manners of all the three characters remain perfectly under control—there is no shouting or directly expressed anger. Instead, Howard, keeping quite calm and completely in charge of the situation, manages by a series of oblique remarks to enjoy a protracted cat-and-mouse game with Stephen and Mary. The aim of this sequence is to express through dialogue and action the deep hostility underlying the smooth and controlled behaviour of the three characters.

The passage starts in a casual, matter-of-fact manner, with Howard asking a series of seemingly innocent questions. Actually —as the audience knows—they are carefully and precisely calculated to drive Mary into a corner where she must confess her lie.

To all Howard's references to the theatre, Mary gives short evasive answers and changes the subject.

This evasiveness on her part is stressed by her actions : in *1*, after saying briefly, " Yes, fine," she turns and walks away to the gramophone ; in *2*, she gives another short evasive retort and moves away towards the bowl of flowers to change the subject ; in *4*, she is beginning to suspect that Howard may " know " and answers abstractedly, without moving ; with shot *6*, her reply is now almost hostile and she nervously walks out of frame—no longer attempting to change the subject : this time, her movement is simply an undisguised evasion.

The handling of these four shots of Mary implies the gradual change in her attitude ; at first she thinks she can merely evade Howard's questions and get away from the embarrassing situation. Later (*4*) she begins to suspect Howard's persistence. And finally, though the conversation is still quite natural—Steven suspects nothing yet—she moves away impatiently (*6*) and we know that she is beginning to suspect Howard's knowledge.

The actors' movements at every point strengthen the potentially hostile mood. Howard is perfectly—too perfectly—at ease : he mixes drinks, lights Steven's cigarette and appears generally quite amiable. Mary meanwhile walks nervously from one place to another, stops, walks off again ; then, as Howard asks about the restaurant, she draws his attention from Steven to herself by noisily closing the lid of the gramophone. She has her answer ready and is obviously afraid of Steven being caught off guard and giving the game away.

Then, in *3*, Howard walks away from camera, hands in pockets ; he turns to hide his smile, and the audience, knowing about his previous visit to the theatre, is aware of what the smile signifies.

With the close shot of Mary (*6*) we are given the first clue that the show-down is imminent.

Then in *7*, Howard quite deliberately guides Mary to the seat from which she will be able to see the programme. The action of this shot is so designed as to emphasize Howard's deliberate guidance : the camera moves with him as he converges with Mary and with unnecessary courtesy leads her to her seat ; the camera tracks in to Mary, and Howard's hands can be seen in the background handling the drinks.

In the following shots of Mary (*9–13*) Howard's hands can still be seen in the background—relaxed and casual as he handles the drinks, in contrast with Mary's stiff posture—a sort of symbol of Howard's calculated scheming.

Howard knows that Mary must now sooner or later see the programme and he quite deliberately changes the subject. His words at this point—" pathetic faith in themselves ", " belief of the muscular in their own strength "—become plainly an indirect allusion to Steven, and Mary (9) begins to sense their real meaning.

Then comes the climax with Mary suddenly seeing the programme : her quick realisation is expressed in the slight halting movement of her hand and her reaction is shown in a very big close-up. Both these shots (10 and 11) constitute the culmination of Howard's cat-and-mouse game with Mary and are shown in silence.

Howard, however, is still in control of the situation : he expected this to happen and knows how to take advantage of the situation. His quick ironic jab—" Ice ? "—clinches his victory with a calculated sneer. The timing of the shots has been most important here : there has been no dialogue over 10 and 11 and the pause has allowed Mary's reaction to come over ; it makes the cut to Howard appear rather abrupt and the shot (12) is left on the screen only long enough to allow the audience to register Howard's expression. This handling gives the shot the effect of a final sharp stab.

Now that Mary knows, Howard still has to ram home his advantage : he motions to her with his hands (seen behind Mary in 13) to sit down and conveys the impression of complete power over Mary's actions—as though pulling the strings of a marionette.

We know that the game is now over. The quick cutting stops and a long-lasting shot with no dialogue (14) is allowed to carry the full tension of the situation. The camera has followed Howard round the table and finishes up over his shoulder, shooting down on to Mary to stress Howard's advantage ; then, to clinch the point, he forcefully thumps down the glass in front of Mary in a sort of " that's that " gesture.

Having scored his victory over Mary, Howard starts all over again by launching an attack on the unsuspecting Steven. After it has been established that Steven is still in the dark about what is going on (15), Howard is shown setting about his new victim. He walks slowly towards Steven, takes a cigarette out of his case, talks on ironically and lights his cigarette. He is perfectly at ease pacing about while Mary and Steven, acutely uncomfortable, remain still in their seats as if under Howard's spell. The shot goes

97

on for a very long time, and the full implications of the situation are slowly, painfully conveyed.

During this time, Steven is still puzzled by what has been happening and sits rigidly still. Then Mary tells him that Howard knows of their evening out and the two hostile close shots of Steven and Howard (17–18) convey that the game is definitely over.

All the visual points we have mentioned so far have been concerned with the placing of actors and the direction of their movements. In addition, the camera is made to emphasise the points made in the acting. For instance, from shot 9 onwards, the camera is consistently shooting down towards Mary and up to Howard in order to emphasise that Mary is on the defensive. Again, the movement of the camera in 7 emphasises the way in which Howard deliberately *guides* Mary to the picked seat from which she will be able to see the theatre programme.

In the same way, the size of the images is not allowed to vary indiscriminately but follows a very purposeful editing pattern. While the scene is still casual and friendly (1–3) the action is played in long shot. Then as Mary begins to get suspicious of Howard's questions, the camera gets closer and closer to her (4 and 6). When Howard temporarily changes the subject and the tension drops for a while, the camera eases away from Mary (end of 7 and 9).

After this brief moment of false security, a big close-up suddenly bursts on to the screen at the moment of climax. In each case the closeness of the shots of Mary rigidly controls the state of dramatic tension. Similarly, as Howard starts off again with his new attack on Steven, the action again begins in long shot to allow the full contrast of Howard's easy pacing and Steven's and Mary's stillness to be felt. Then, when Steven comes to know, the two quick hostile close shots finally break down all the barriers of politeness.

In passing, it is interesting to note how the music has been used. At the beginning of the scene, we have been shown Mary walking over to the radiogram and switching it on. The tune is a sharp, raucous South American dance and although it is heard only very quietly, it underlines the mood of the situation without intruding in the action. The music is also purposely introduced for a particular effect a little after the quoted extract. When Howard is finally ready to have it out with Steven, he walks over to the radiogram and switches the music off. The sudden silence

—it is allowed to last a number of seconds with no one saying anything—builds up the tension to the point where Howard finally loses his temper and throws Steven out.

Of more general interest is the order in which events have been presented. There is practically no action or plot in the sequence which we did not know about before seeing it. Indeed, we have very deliberately been shown the theatre-programme being planted, and have, in effect, been warned of what is going to happen. The interest of the scene lies not in any surprising fact which is revealed but in the manner in which the characters react to the situation. If the spectator had not been aware of the programme on the table, he would have watched the scene—as Steven watches it—in bewilderment : the moment at which Mary first notices the pro-gramme would have come as a surprise and there would have been no suspense preceding it. Showing an incident in this seem-ingly reverse order is a commonly used device of presentation : the spectator is warned by some hint (in this case Howard placing the programme) of what is going to happen, and then has time and attention for the manner in which the characters will react to the situation.

Here, then, we have described what is after all a rather ordinary dramatic situation, which is transformed into an exciting sequence by the manner of the handling. Most of the visual manoeuvres (and a good deal of the dialogue) are, from the point of view of getting on with the story, quite unnecessary. But it is precisely this insistence on the small visual detail and the purposive editing which makes this into an effective sequence.

Obviously, the emphasis which is here given to the fine points of characterisation is not necessary or even desirable with every sequence. In many cases the editing of dialogue scenes simply turns out to be a question of presenting an actor—most often the box-office star—to best advantage. This is often largely a matter of showing only those pieces of an actor's performance in which he is at his most appealing, and letting the rest of the dialogue be carried by reaction shots or cut-aways. It may seem that this kind of editing is at best a commercial make-shift arrangement and normally, of course, it is. Yet, for instance, in some of the earlier sound films featuring Greta Garbo, this technique was developed into a fine art. In a film like *Queen Christina*—which *is* Garbo and nothing more—the editor's concern seems to have been to let all dramatic considerations go by the board and to concentrate solely on the most effective presentation of Garbo herself. The cutting is beautifully smooth : slowly, imperceptibly, the camera eases towards her in a progression of closer and closer shots. If a reaction shot is shown then it is usually to bridge the gap between one shot of the star and the next, more advantageous. In this way the editor certainly makes a substantial contribution to the final impressiveness of Garbo's performance which is, after all, the primary aim of the film.

Special considerations of this kind apart, the editor still needs to keep the closest watch on the actor's performances. By the negative means of simply cutting out the bad pieces, he can often make a mediocre performance appear quite good. In a more positive way, the editor can give a certain polish to a good performance which can greatly enhance its final effectiveness.

Omissions and adjustments of parts of an actor's performance are often necessary if it is felt that its pace is for some reason not exactly right. The lengthening of a pause or sharpening of a cue may make all the difference between a sloppy and a dramatically taut effect. The problem is not confined to dialogue scenes— precision of technique is always desirable—but here an additional difficulty is involved : the editor must respect the actor's performance. In an action scene, the exact timing of shots is very often left open to the editor and he can impose a pace on the sequence which he considers most fitting. In a passage of dialogue his problem is more complex because an actor sets his own pace in the playing. If the editor wishes to speed up the continuity, he can shorten the pauses between sentences, use cheat cuts and generally cut down all the footage not " anchored " by the dialogue. This is done very frequently, especially if the director has been uncertain in getting a suitable pace of performance from his actors on the floor. But interfering in an actor's performance can sometimes cause more harm than good. An experienced actor with a developed sense of timing may set his own pace during a scene which it is best to leave alone. To sharpen a cut here and there, in order to improve the overall pace of the sequence, may throw the natural rhythm of the playing out of gear. The moments preceding and following the actor's words are an integral part of his interpretation of the line, and to eliminate them may reduce the effect of the rendering.

This is an extremely difficult question to discuss in general terms since we are dealing with very small adjustments which are closely dependent on the precise nature of the actors' gestures. In practice, good examples of the respect with which editors treat expertly timed performances can be found in films featuring such experienced players as Katharine Hepburn, Bette Davis or Charlie Chaplin. Chaplin himself seems to rely almost entirely on his own faultless sense of timing and relegate the editor's job to that of a joiner of self-sufficient strips of film.

It is an odd phenomenon of contemporary film-making that while most films rely predominantly on spoken dialogue, dialogue scenes are on the whole made with much less care and imagination than is accorded to passages of action or description. In looking for a suitable example of dialogue editing to quote in this chapter, we had the greatest difficulty in finding a sequence which would stand comparison in inventiveness and visual eloquence with countless descriptive passages which could be quoted. Memorable dialogue passages, when re-examined, usually turn out to be scenes where the words have been brilliant and the visual treatment insignificant ; on the other hand, hundreds of dialogue scenes employing static medium shots, two-shots and close shots—especially close shots—can be found where the dialogue could be heard with closed eyes without appreciable loss of dramatic power.

5

COMEDY SEQUENCES

To theorise about laughter is a thankless task. A good joke, by its very incongruity, stubbornly eludes classification. Writers who have attempted to analyse the factors which go to make a comic situation have met with little success—analysing a joke tends to turn it sour. Fortunately, questions as to what makes one situation funny, and another not, do not concern us here. What we need to discuss is how, given a comic situation, it can be presented to get the biggest laugh. However good the original idea, a joke can be made or killed in the presentation.

Certain differences between the editing treatment of serious films and comedies immediately spring to mind. Whereas in a serious film the director generally sets out to give a sober, authentic rendering of a story, comedy may thrive in ludicrous, obviously distorted settings. The editor of a serious film must attempt to produce a smooth flow of images because a harsh, jerky continuity —unless used for a specific reason—tends to draw the spectator's attention away from the story and make unnecessary demands on his credulity. In a comedy, on the other hand, it is often not necessary to convince the spectator of anything ; it is only necessary to make him laugh. If this involves a harsh cut, a faulty piece of continuity or any other unrealistic distortion, then that may be all to the good. The funniest films are often those in which the editor has been absolutely ruthless in his disregard for reality and concentrated solely on extracting the maximum of humour out of every situation.

Since the advent of sound, film comedy has tended more and more to become the province of the gag-man. Comedians like Bob Hope or Danny Kaye, for instance, rely to a very large extent on purely verbal wit. They crack their jokes at a rate controlled entirely by their own sense of timing ; all the editor needs to do is to give the story a tempo in which the jokes can be effectively planted. In practice this means that the editor must keep the action going at a slick speed. The plots of these comedies are often little more than convenient frameworks upon which the comedian can build his jokes. If the film is not to become dull, the story points need only be sketched in very briefly so that the jokes follow each other in rapid succession.

Besides making the action develop with an appropriate swing, the editor must try to make allowances for the length of the audience's laughter reaction. A long laugh rewarding one joke may make the next inaudible. Yet, on balance, it is probably better to lose a few laughs by having them follow each other too fast than to miscalculate and to leave the gaps too long. It is better to have too many jokes than too few : not only do some of them inevitably misfire, but laughter is also to some extent conditioned by what has come before. A poorish joke, coming after a series of belly laughs when the audience is near hysteria, will get a good reception ; coming after a tedious bit of plot, it may not raise a titter.

The editor's job in this slick, wisecracking kind of comedy is the rather humble one of mounting the jokes. Only very rarely is he directly concerned in putting over the joke itself, and the better the actors' sense of timing, the smaller is the editor's contribution to the comic effect. In visual comedy, the exact opposite happens. Here, the director and editor are mainly in charge. There is, after all, only a very limited number of visual jokes— all more or less variations on the theme of a man getting hurt or in some way losing his dignity—and it is precisely in the presentation that they become funny. Hurling a custard-pie into someone's face, may, if badly shot and edited, be excruciatingly unfunny. Only through a careful consideration of what gives a situation its essential humour, and through shooting and editing the scene accordingly, does a slapstick situation become really effective.

David Lean has described how the oldest of old chestnuts might be treated.

Imagine two shots :
 1. *Laurel and Hardy running along a street in full-figure shot. After running for 15 seconds or so, Hardy slips and falls on the pavement.*
 2. *Close-up of banana skin lying on the pavement. After a few moments Hardy's foot comes into picture, treads on the skin and slips.*

Now where would you cut the close-up of the banana skin ? . . . The answer is nothing to do with a smooth cut . . . Looking at these two shots from a purely smooth cut point of view, it would seem that the best place to cut the close up of the banana skin would be the point at which the foot entered picture, carrying it on until halfway through the skid at which point one would cut back to the medium shot as Hardy crashes on to the pavement. Both cuts would be very smooth and the audience would laugh as Hardy fell, but they would not be getting the biggest laugh possible out of the scene.

The answer lies in a very old comedy maxim : *Tell them what you're going to do. Do it. Tell them you've done it.* In other words the scene should be cut like this :

1. *Medium-shot of Laurel and Hardy running along the street.*
2. *Close-up of banana skin lying on pavement.* (You have told your audience what you are going to do and they will start to laugh.)
3. *Medium-shot of Laurel and Hardy still running.* (The audience will laugh still more.) *Hold the shot on for several seconds of running before Hardy finally crashes to the pavement.* (The odds are that the audience will reward you with a belly laugh. Having told them what you are going to do, and having done it, how do you tell them you've done it ?)
4. *A close-up of Laurel making an inane gesture of despair.* (The audience will laugh again.)[1]

Why is it that the second, edited version will get so much greater response than the first ?

Pleasure and amusement at other people's (especially fat comedians') discomfort or loss of dignity seems to be a universal reaction. It is not the only source of humour but it is one potent one. Realising that the spectator will be amused by Hardy's misfortune, the editor deliberately sets out to stress Hardy's helplessness. Shot *2* is simply an announcement of what is going to happen : it puts the spectator, as it were, one jump ahead of the victim and gives him a feeling of amused superiority. Clearly, this foreknowledge makes Hardy look even sillier because the spectator is aware of the banana skin, while Hardy (*Poor fool !*) is not. This feeling of superiority sharpens the enjoyment of the joke and can therefore be further exploited : the few seconds of anticipation at the beginning of shot *3* give another opportunity to savour the joke to the full. After this, cutting to Laurel's inane gesture (*4*) evokes a sort of I-could-have-told-you-so reaction which is just what is needed. The continuity of shots, as David Lean stresses, is by no means ideal if we are thinking in terms of smooth cutting. The important thing in the three cuts is that they each make a separate humorous point in that each shows a new—and funnier—aspect of the same situation. The fact that the cuts may be visually slightly objectionable becomes irrelevant.

The editing of this incident can be considered as a working model of every banana-slipping, custard-pie-throwing joke that has ever been well made. It demonstrates a simple but highly

[1] Working for the Films. *Edited by Oswell Blakeston. Focal Press, 1947, p. 29. The quotation is from an article on* Film Direction *by David Lean.*

effective trick of presentation in its simplest form.   In practice the continuity may often be a good deal more complex, but the principle of showing the same joke in several different ways still applies.   Here is a finished example.

TOPPER RETURNS[1]
Extract from Reel 9

One of the Topper series of comedy films.   A rather slight but gruesome murder plot forms the background for the comedy. The scene is set in a creepy old country mansion full of trap doors and library shelves opening backwards into secret passages.   In the library there is a sort of Sweeny Todd chair, which can be tipped backwards through the floor, thereby hurling the occupant down a deep well under the house which communicates with the sea.

Mr. Topper (Roland Young),   a mild ineffectual man, unwillingly involved in the investigation, is trying, rather feebly, to find clues.   His wife (Billie Burke), a gentle, absent-minded lady, is quite unable to appreciate the gravity of the situation.   Eddie (Rochester), their negro servant, is thoroughly frightened by all the happenings.

			Ft.	fr.
1	Interior Library. Mr. Topper enters from left background and walks towards Mrs. Topper in right foreground. Eddie stands in left foreground.	Mrs. Topper : Well—where is she ? Mr. Topper : Wh—Where is who ?	9	3
2	M.C.S. Mr. and Mrs. Topper.	Mrs. Topper : You know perfectly well who I mean. That—that girl. Mr. Topper : But there wasn't any. Mrs. Topper : Oh yes there was. I heard you both in that room.	10	7
3	As in 1. Eddie walks towards chair and sits down. Mr. and Mrs. Topper are not looking at him.	Eddie : Pardon me, Mr. Topper, but it's getting kinda late, can't we settle this at home. Mrs. Topper : Edward, don't interrupt. Eddie : Yessum !	20	8
	Eddie sits down in the chair, it tips back and throws him down the well and then rights itself into position.	Just as chair is beginning to tip back : Mrs. Topper : Cosmo, I should think that after twenty years of married life, you wouldn't try to deceive me. Why, I remember our honeymoon in Atlantic City. You promised me you'd never look at another woman.		
4	Shot from top of well showing Eddie falling through space.	Eddie : Mr. To-o-o-opper !	1	15

[1] *Director : Roy del Ruth.   Editor : James Newcom.   United Artists, 1941.*

5	Eddie landing at the bottom of the well.	*Splash of water.*	4 10
6	Seal on bank, clapping his hind fins and barking with obvious joy.	*Seal barking.*	

We are now taken away for about 200 ft. from this scene to a sequence in which the handsome young hero fights with the masked murderer and ends by rescuing the heroine. Then back to the library.

7	M.C.S. Mr. and Mrs. Topper. Mr. Topper walks to the chair and sits down gingerly.	Mr. Topper : Clara, please—I've had a frightful night. Eddie : (off) Boss, wait !	6 2
8	M.S. Eddie, dripping wet, standing at library door. *Camera pans with him* as he runs towards Mr. and Mrs. Topper until they are all three *in frame.*	Eddie : Don't sit in that chair ! Whatever you do, don't sit in that chair. Mrs. Topper : Edward, WILL you stop interrupting ! (She looks at Eddie). —Why, you're all wet. Is it raining out ? Ah, but you haven't been out—	16 7
9	M.C.S. Mr. and Mrs. Topper.	—It can't be raining *in.* Well— if it has, it's all cleared up.	4 2
10	M.S. Eddie. *As in 8.* Mr. Topper goes to sit in the chair. Mr. Topper gets up.	Mr. Topper : Dear, I can't stand much more. Eddie : Oh, boss, that chair is deceptive, destructible and distrustworthy and this is the voice of experience. Mr. Topper : What ARE you talking about ?	13 2
11	M.S. Eddie.	Eddie : Boss, you sit in that chair and things happen. Quick.	3 4
12	M.C.S. Mr. and Mrs. Topper. *As in 9.*	Mr. Topper : Oh, don't talk nonsense. Eddie : (off) It ain't nonsense, it's serious—	4 15
13	M.L.S. of Mr. and Mrs. Topper and Eddie. Eddie walks to the chair, sits down. The chair tips back as before.	Eddie : —Look boss, I sat in that chair, just like this. Crossed my leg —just like this. Leaned back— just like this—Here I go again !	16 12
14	M.S. Mr. and Mrs. Topper looking down at the chair.	Mrs. Topper : But that's a SILLY way to leave the room. Why didn't he use the door ?	4 6
15	Eddie falling down well. *As in 4.*	Eddie : Mr. To-o-pper !	1 13
16	Eddie landing in water. *As in 5.*	*Splash of water.*	3 5
17	M.S. Mr. and Mrs. Topper.	Mrs. Topper : (quite unperturbed) Well, as I was saying . . .	

There is only one comic incident in the whole of this passage, yet it was necessary to quote it entire because the staging and editing of the business constitutes a highly elaborate build-up to the chair-toppling.

Mr. and Mrs. Topper are involved in a marital quarrel. (Mr. Topper has previously been involved in a rather compromising situation with another girl and Mrs. Topper is on her guard.) Thus while all the terrible things are happening to Eddie, the Toppers are too engrossed in their own troubles to take any notice : this forms an important part of the treatment, as we shall see later. Further, shot 2 has been specially used to establish that Mr. and Mrs. Topper are not in a position to see the treacherous chair. Both these points had to be established, otherwise the first accident would not make sense.

The actual toppling is presented as follows. In shot 3, Eddie walks towards the chair : the spectator knows what will happen if Eddie sits down and is therefore ready for the joke (cf. the banana-skin). Then, just as the chair begins to topple back, Mrs. Topper starts another totally irrelevant harangue about her husband's infidelity. For about nine feet, after the chair has toppled over, we are made to listen to Mrs. Topper, and only after she has finished do we cut back to Eddie falling down the well. In this way, the editor has made three jokes out of one.

The first laugh comes when it becomes clear that the chair will topple over ; the second, when we see Mrs. Topper blissfully unaware of what is happening ; and the third, as we cut back to the helpless and forgotten Eddie. Now, obviously, all pretence at realism has been thrown to the winds. An accurate cut would have taken us straight from the moment of toppling into shot 4. It would also have been considerably less funny.

After this incident there is a passage which from our point of view is irrelevant and then we are taken through the whole pro-cedure again. This time the spectator knows what is going to happen from the very beginning and the scene is made utterly farcical. (Note, for instance, the sheer lunacy of Mrs. Topper's remarks over 8 and 9, and the accelerated rate of cutting.) From the moment Eddie re-enters, up to the end of shot 13, it is quite obvious that the whole thing is going to happen again. Shot 13 carries the elaborate build-up to a ludicrous pitch and the actual incident is again cut as before : again, from the shot of the toppling chair we are not taken straight to the falling Eddie, but have to put up with the delay of shot 14. (Every time a comedian registers a double-take, he uses the same device.) As in the first case, three jokes are created out of one by the simple device of cutting away from the action at the crucial moment. Incidentally, Mrs. Topper's remark at this point gives the situation a new twist. We know that she did not see Eddie falling the first time and expect her, now that she *does* see him, to show some concern. What we hear instead is the remark : " But that's a *silly* way to leave the room . . . "

It is interesting to note that exactly the same comic situation and indeed exactly the same cycle of events has been shown twice, with only a minor variation. An even greater laugh follows the second showing. Repeating a joke in this way is, of course, a standard comedy device : if it was funny once, then it will be funny again. The second showing makes the victim look even more ridiculous and therefore produces an even bigger laugh.

Another striking instance of the humorous effect achieved by repetition is provided by shot 6. In a previous sequence, Eddie has already once found himself struggling in the water. On this occasion, we saw him repeatedly trying to climb on to the landing-stage ; every time he got a foothold, a seal waddled forward, with great glee applied his snout to Eddie's forehead and pushed him back into the sea. This episode took place some time earlier in the film and has since been briefly shown again every few minutes. Before Eddie finally manages to climb on to the bank, we have the impression that the game has been going on for a very long time. Later on, when we get the brief glimpse of the seal in shot 6, this is enough to suggest that the whole struggle is going to start all over again. There is no need to show the whole business in full : the seal is barking and happily clapping his flippers in anticipation of the game : the spectator can imagine the rest. The humorous effect is here created solely through the editing. By simply cutting in the shot of the seal at this particular point, it suddenly acquires a humorous meaning.

An incident akin to the above occurs in *Naked City*. There is a long scene towards the end of the film in which a number of cops are combing a quarter of New York in search of a murderer. Wearily they go into every house and shop, even stopping people in the street, asking everyone to identify a photograph of the wanted man. Then one of the men finds the criminal and the chase starts. In the midst of the excitement, we are suddenly shown an unexpected shot : an extremely weary looking policeman, still conscientiously questioning passers-by : " Lady, ever seen a man looks like this ? "

It was probably taken as part of the search sequence and subsequently rejected. By taking it out of its context and putting it into an unexpected place, it becomes funny.

A more carefully developed comedy effect was used in *The Set-up*, and occurs during an otherwise serious dramatisation of a boxing match. During the fight the editor constantly cuts away to familiar ring-side figures : a blind man, having the match described to him by a friend ; a gawky youth, shadow-boxing in unison with the boxers ; a refined middle-aged lady, mercilessly screaming " Kill him ! " ; and lastly, a fat man, unconcernedly eating. The fat man is introduced for a macabre sort of comic relief. In the first round we see him eating a hot dog ; in the second, sucking a lollipop ; in the third, eating peanuts ; and in the last round, drinking a lemonade. The humour of the situation springs from the fact that the fat man seems to be completely engrossed in the fight, yet somehow cannot bring himself to stop eating. But the effect, as presented, is better than this : after eating the hot dog, in the first round, we are given to understand that he is *still* eating in the second, *still* eating in the third, and finally washing all the food down with a drink. The implication is that he has been eating continuously and becomes more outrageous with every showing.

The last two quoted episodes are both essentially editor's jokes. The shot of the weary policeman in *Naked City* and the various shots of the fat man in *The Set-up* are not humorous in themselves. It is only through placing them into a special context that the editor has made them appear funny. In each case, the editor has introduced a shot against the mood of the story and thereby created a comic effect.

It may not be altogether useless if we attempt a tentative analysis of how these humorous effects are in fact achieved. Let us first look at a literary anecdote and see how it works.

A woman in widow's weeds was weeping upon a grave.

" Console yourself, madam," said a Sympathetic Stranger. "Heaven's mercies are infinite. There is another man somewhere, besides your husband, with whom you can still be happy."

" There was," she sobbed—" there was, but this is his grave."[1]

The principle of this anecdote is simply that a false inference

[1] Fantastic Fables *by Ambrose Bierce. Jonathan Cape, Travellers' Library, 1927 p. 244. The fable is quoted by Eisenstein in* The Film Sense *to illustrate the principle of montage.*

is created and then debunked. The phrasing suggests, at first, that the woman is mourning her husband : the reader feels a temporary sympathy for her and is unexpectedly—and comically—disillusioned. This is a very common comedy device. Shaggy-dog stories, for instance, all work in precisely this way.

The joke in *Naked City* is very similar. In the midst of the exciting chase, the shot of the weary policeman comes as an unexpected contradiction of what we have been made to expect. We are given to understand that the police are being faultlessly efficient in tracking down the criminal and are then suddenly shown one who is hopelessly out of touch with events. The unexpected contrast becomes funny. What is important from the editor's point of view is that the efficiency of the other policemen should have been well established before the joke is made, otherwise the shot will not come as a surprise. In other words, the editor must first convincingly evoke a false reaction before he can effectively surprise the audience.

There was a highly elaborate example of this kind of " debunking joke " in *The Third Man*, where Joseph Cotten is kidnapped by a sinister looking taxi-driver and conveyed to a mysterious castle : we assume that the abduction was planned by the ruthless black-marketeering gang and consequently fear the worst. Instead we see Cotten being cordially greeted by the representative of a literary society who asks him to address a meeting. (An almost exactly similar incident is used in Hitchcock's *Thirty-nine Steps*, where Robert Donat, running away from his pursuers, lands in the midst of a political meeting.) Here again, the joke is created through the carefully constructed build-up : the more sinister the kidnapping, the funnier will be the final pay-off.

The editing device employed in this episode is entirely different from the one employed in the banana-skin joke. While Hardy is running along the pavement, the editor shows us a glimpse of the banana-skin *before* Hardy has a chance of seeing it. Well before Hardy actually falls to the pavement, we already know what is going to happen. In *The Third Man* incident the editor proceeds in another way. Not only does he not tell us what is going to happen, but he deliberately misleads us. The two incidents are edited in sharply contrasting ways—in the first case the joke is made by *anticipating* it, in the second by making it come as a *surprise*.

In the first case, the incident is designed to make Hardy look silly. The joke is *against* Hardy and the fact that the spectator

110

anticipates his fall makes it even funnier. In *The Third Man* kidnapping, the joke is, as it were, on the audience. It is *we* who were gullible enough to believe that something terrible was going to happen and it is the surprise revelation—that the fuss was all about nothing—which makes the joke. In each case the director and editor have understood the source of the humour and edited the scene accordingly.

6

MONTAGE SEQUENCES

THE term *montage* has been loosely employed in so many different contexts as to need definition. It was used by early Russian directors as a synonym for *creative editing* and is still used in France to denote simply *cutting.* The term *montage sequence* as used in British and American studios means something more specific and limited : it refers to the quick impressionistic sequence of disconnected images, usually linked by dissolves, superimpositions or wipes, and used to convey passages of time, changes of place, or any other scenes of transition. It is with this last kind of sequence that we are here concerned.

The very pedigree of the word bears witness to the fact that the modern montage sequence owes its origin to early Russian experiments and was gradually evolved to its present form. The only thing it still has in common with early Russian films is that both use short, disconnected strips of film. But there the affinity ends : where the Russians conceived their films in terms of expressive shot juxtapositions, the montage sequence as commonly used to-day makes its points through the cumulative effect of series of images. Where the Russian sequences proceeded by steps like : shot A contrasts with shot B (the juxtaposition giving rise to a new concept), is further illuminated by shot C . . . etc., the modern montage sequence aims at saying : shot A *plus* shot B, *plus* shot C . . . *plus* shot X, when seen together, imply a transition of events from A to X. Since the aim of the modern montage sequence is to convey a series of facts which *together* will convey a state of transition, individual shot juxtapositions become un-important—even misleading—and are therefore largely ironed out by the use of dissolves.

All this is simply to point out that the similarity between Russian

112

montage and the modern montage sequence ends, once it has been admitted that both use strings of rapidly following shots. The modern montage sequence, as most commonly used, is merely a convenient way of presenting a series of facts which are necessary to the story but which have little emotional significance. It is used to convey facts which it would be cumbersome to show in full or which, though essential to the story, do not merit detailed treatment.

Take an example. Towards the end of Carol Reed's *The Third Man*, Major Calloway (Trevor Howard) has to try to convince Holly Martins (Joseph Cotten) that the police know Martins' friend Harry Lime (Orson Welles) to be guilty of various crimes. Martins is loth to believe this of his friend and Calloway therefore has to produce a great deal of evidence to prove his point. To let the audience know that Calloway does in fact produce this detailed evidence, it would have been necessary to show the evidence in full : this would have meant introducing a long, dramatically flat sequence just at a point when the story is reaching its climax. The difficulty was solved by making a short montage sequence with shots of finger-prints, documents, Lime's belongings, etc. In this way the audience was shown that Martins had in fact been convinced of his friend's guilt, while the pace of the action was only momentarily slowed down.

This example shows the kind of use the montage sequence is commonly put to in contemporary films and also points to its limitations. The sequence, like most montage sequences used to-day, is devoid of any emotional effect. It is necessary for the smooth development of the plot 'but is, in itself, emotionally neutral.

The actual details of editing montage sequences are generally left to the end of the production when it should be obvious exactly how much clarification is needed. The script-writer will often simply say something like : " Dissolve to scene 75 ; Montage showing country-wide effect of General Strike." It is then the editor's job to sketch in briefly what the writer has asked for. To do this, he must first decide on a small number of points he will wish to stress and then, using library shots or specially photographed material, assemble them into some sort of developing continuity. When editing his sequence, his main consideration must be to make it fast, while keeping each image on the screen just long enough to allow its content to come across. There must be a balance of subject-matter to ensure that the effect asked for—" the country-wide effects of the General Strike," in this case—is convincingly rendered. An over-insistence on one aspect of the theme—say on the fact that undergraduates helped to drive buses—may produce undesirable inferences and divert the spectator's attention from the main theme.

As for the mechanical details of editing montages, very little can profitably be said. Having established the highlights of the sequence, the editor merely has to produce a reasonably pleasant looking continuity. He may amuse himself by trying to arrange pictorially pleasing dissolves, superimpositions or wipes. Provided the continuity is clear, however, these small details of presentation become unimportant questions of personal taste.

Two things the editor must guard against. Firstly, a montage sequence operates, so to speak, on a different plane of reality from straight narrative. If it is to fulfil its practical function of unobtrusively filling certain gaps in the story, then it must do so quickly. A montage sequence which becomes unduly long un-necessarily interferes with the conviction of the rest of the narrative and thus destroys the effect it was made for.

Secondly, the montage sequence must be conceived as a whole. A continuous, more or less self-contained passage of music is generally used to bind the whole series of images together and to underline the rhythm of the passage of events. A badly planned montage with bits of realistic dialogue alternating with superim-posed general images can become a confusing affectation.

From what has been said so far, it should be obvious that the montage sequence employed for purely practical reasons of clari-fying the continuity should be used as sparingly as possible. The introduction of a quick impressionistic sequence in which the spectator is, as it were, asked to view the action from farther away, tends to interrupt the authenticity of the narrative because the spectator is suddenly made to view the story in an entirely different, less personal light.

The sudden switch from naturalistic narrative to montage was particularly common in war films made in this country and in America. Frequently, a montage implying an advance of troops, a mass landing or the launching of an offensive was introduced into a story dealing with a particular set of characters ; nearly always, there was a drop in dramatic tension as the story was taken from the personal to the general plane. A good instance is provided by Edward Dmytryk's *Back to Bataan* where the plot tells of a group of men engaged on a special mission ; when the operation is over, a montage sequence follows, employing shots of explosions and fighting, superimposed over a map of the battlefield and implying that a similar story is taking place all over the island. The sudden switch from the personal drama of the story to the journalistic montage does, no doubt, put the story into a larger context ; it also brings with it a chilling anticlimax.

For this reason, the pure continuity-link type of montage sequence has been increasingly falling into disfavour. Wherever possible, directors have in recent years tried to avoid the standard montage images—falling leaves, calendars, train-wheels, all well-worn *clichés* by now—and have tried to imply necessary transitions in more economical ways. The long unnecessary sequences of locomotives, wheels, rails, etc., used to convey a character from one place to another are usually quite superfluous : a hint that the character is just about to move, a dissolve and an establishing shot or remark at the destination is usually quite sufficient. Similarly, a passage of time—so often conveyed by flapping calendar-leaves—can often be conveyed quite simply through a trick of phrasing, a cut-away to another intermediate scene, or by simply changing the season or clothes of the characters in adjacent episodes.

If the purely utilitarian montage sequence has been used too frequently, then the script-planned montage which makes a dramatic impact has, if anything, been used too little. There have been hints in a number of films that the montage form can lead to remarkably interesting results when it is applied in an intelligent way. There is a whole range of dramatically auspicious situations to which montage is peculiarly suited or which cannot be conveyed by straight narrative. Here is a rather unorthodox example.

CITIZEN KANE[1]

A posthumous biography of a newspaper millionaire, Charles Foster Kane (Orson Welles). It begins with Kane's death, after which the editor of a " March of Time "-like newsreel sends out all his reporters to interview Kane's surviving friends. Thus we are taken from interview to interview, in each case the story told to the reporter being shown in flash-back. At the end of the film we are able to piece together Kane's whole life.

The extract quoted below is the flash-back of an interview with Jedediah Leyland (Joseph Cotten), Kane's oldest friend. He is telling the story of Kane's first marriage to Emily (Ruth Warrick), a niece of the President of the U.S.A.

(Bernstein, who is referred to in the dialogue, is the editor of Kane's newspaper " The Enquirer " and is decidedly not of Emily's social standing.)

[1] *Director : Orson Welles. Editor : Robert Wise. R.K.O., 1941.*

Leyland has been telling the reporter about various episodes in Kane's early life.

1	M.S. Leyland (now very old) sitting on hospital balcony in his dressing-gown. *Camera shooting over reporter's right shoulder.*

Leyland :
Well, after the first couple of months, she and Charley didn't see much of each other— except at breakfast.
It was a marriage—just like any other marriage.
Slow, romantic music begins.

43

Slow dissolve to :

2 L.S. Emily (Mrs. Kane) sitting at table. Kane walks in from left, places a plate in front of her, pretending to be a waiter. He bends down to kiss her on the forehead. *Camera is tracking slowly forward throughout the whole shot.*

Kane sits down in his chair at the end of the table, left.

Kane :
You're beautiful.
Emily :
Oh, I can't be.
Kane :
Yes, you are, you're very, very beautiful.
⌈*Emily :*
│ I've never been to six parties in
⎰ one night in all my life.
│ *Kane :*
⌊ *Extremely* beautiful.
Emily :
I've never even been up so late.
Kane :
It's a matter of habit.
Emily :
I wonder what the servants will think !
Kane :
They'll think we've enjoyed ourselves.
⌈*Emily :*
│ Dear—
│ *Kane :*
⎰ Haven't we ?
│ *Emily :*
│ —I don't see why you have to
⌊ go straight off to the newspaper.
Kane :
You never should have married a newspaper man—they're worse than sailors.

They are now in M.S. They look at each other for a moment in silence.

I absolutely adore you.

3 M.S. Emily.

Emily :
Oh, Charles, even newspaper men have to sleep.

4 15

4 M.S. Kane.

Kane :
I'll call Mr. Bernstein and have him put off my engagements until noon.

5 11

1

9a

2

9b

9c

3 (5, 7) 10 (12)

4 (6, 8) 11 (13)

117

5	M.S. Emily *as in* 3. She smiles, gratefully.		2 8
6	M.S. Kane *as in* 4.	Kane : What time is it ?	1 12
7	M.S. Emily *as in* 3.	*Emily :* Oh, I don't know—it's late.	4 8
8	M.S. Kane *as in* 4.	Kane : —It's early ! *Emily :* (She sighs.) Charles— (*She speaks the word in a slow, sleepy way, so that her sentence in shot 10 appears to follow on without interruption.*)	6 7
9	*Fast flick pan over some windows during which shot 8 fades out and shot 10 fades in.*	*Gay, fast music gets louder.*	1 4
10	M.S. Emily (in different clothes from preceding shot).	*Emily :* (cont. from 8 and 9) —do you know how long you kept me waiting last night—	6
11	M.S. Kane (in different clothes from preceding shot), lighting his pipe. (Slightly impatient.)	—while you went to the news-paper for a few minutes ?—	3 6
12	M.S. Emily *as in* 10.	—What do you DO on a news-paper in the middle of the night ? *Kane :* Emily—	2 1
13	M.S. Kane *as in* 11. He throws the match away.	—my *dear,* your only co-res-pondent is *The Enquirer.* *Emily :* Sometimes, I think—	9 5
14	*Fast flick pan as in 9, during which shot 13 fades out and shot 15 fades in.*	*Music gets louder ; fast, dramatic.*	2
15	M.S. Emily (in different clothes from preceding shot).	*Emily :* (contd. from 13 and 14) —I'd prefer a rival of flesh and blood. *Kane :* Oh, Emily—	1 10
16	M.S. Kane (in different clothes from preceding shot).	—I don't spend that much time on the newspaper.	3 11
17	M.S. Emily *as in* 15.	*Emily :* It isn't just the time. It's what you print ! Attacking—	5 11
18	M.S. Kane *as in* 16	—the President ! *Kane :* You mean Uncle John.	2 11

			Ft. fr.
19	M.S. Emily *as in* 15.	Emily : I mean the President of the United States. Kane : He's still Uncle John—	3 15
20	M.S. Kane *as in* 16.	—and he's still a well-meaning fathead who's letting a pack of high-pressure crooks run his administration. Emily : Charles !	7 12
21	M.S. Emily *as in* 15.	Kane : This whole oil scandal— Emily : He happens to be the President, Charles—not you !	5 3
22	M.S. Kane *as in* 16.	Kane : That's a mistake that will be corrected one of these days.	5 12
23	*Fast flick pan as in 9, during which shot 22 fades out and shot 24 fades in.*	Emily : Your Mr. Bernstein sent Junior the most incredible—	1 6
24	M.S. Emily (in different clothes from preceding shot).	*Slow, " foreboding " music getting louder.* Emily : (contd. from 23) —atrocity yesterday, Charles. I simply can't have it—	9 7
25	M.S. Kane (in different clothes from preceding shot) ; he is eating. He looks up from his food.	—in the nursery. Kane : Mr. Bernstein is apt to pay a visit to the nursery now and then.	9 8
26	M.S. Emily *as in* 24.	Emily : Does he HAVE to ?	2 8
27	M.S. Kane *as in* 25.	Kane : (very deliberately) Yes.	3 9
28	*Fast flick pan as in 9, during which shot 27 fades out and shot 29 fades in.*	Emily : (almost wailing) Really, Charles— *Music louder.*	2 2
29	M.S. Emily (in different clothes from preceding shot).	Emily : (contd. from 28) —people will think—	1 15
30	M.S. Kane (in different clothes from preceding shot).	Kane : (very gruffly) —what I tell them to think !	5 11
31	*Fast flick pan as in 9, during which shot 30 fades out and shot 32 fades in.*	*Calm but discordant music starts.*	2
32	M.S. Emily (in different clothes from preceding shot), looking at a newspaper. She glances up in Kane's direction and then back to the paper.	*Music continues.*	6 5

119

33   M.S. Kane (in different clothes   *Music continues.*   14 6
from preceding shot), reading a
newspaper. He glances up and
then down again.
Camera tracks slowly back bringing
Emily *into frame and continues
tracking back* until Kane and
Emily are seen in *L.S. as at the
beginning of shot* 2.

Slow dissolve to :

34   M.S. Leyland sitting on hospital
balcony in his dressing gown.   *After a pause :*
Reporter : (off)
Wasn't he ever in love with
her ?

The passage conveys the gradual breaking-up of a relationship. It is a flash-back of Leyland's account of Kane's first marriage : as such, the conception of the scenes underlines the sense of inexorable deterioration in Kane's relationship with his wife which Leyland implies in his account. The separate episodes are joined together to form a mounting pattern, and together make a self-contained sequence. Each short episode in itself (*9–14*, for instance) is of little significance : it is the gradually developing estrangement in the incidents—progressing from passionate love to cold hostility— which gives the passage its point.

Technically there are a number of points well worth attention. It was clearly the intention that the series should be more than a string of separate episodes : each incident should be implicit in the previous one. Hence the editing is devised to make the passage appear a unified whole. In each case, where there is a transition from one breakfast scene to another, the transition is carried out through a sort of flickering pan. This is in each case a switch from Emily to Kane, and is merely a variant on the constant to and fro cutting. More importantly, Emily's words are carried over each transition giving an impression of the continuous process of estrangement which is taking place.

At the same time the director has been at great pains to establish the quick transitions from scene to scene as concisely as possible. He has done this with all means available : the changing mood is conveyed through the dialogue which gets terser and more hostile throughout the passage ; the scenes get shorter and shorter, giving the impression that Kane is finding the breakfasts increasingly irksome ; the music, though continuous, subtly underlines the mood of each scene and rounds off the passage in low, discordant tones suggesting an atmosphere of suppressed, dormant rage ;

finally, the steady deterioration from admiration to hostility is most powerfully suggested by the acting.

Dialogue, rate of cutting, music and acting (and, incidentally, the costumes) have all been used to convey the precise state of the relationship in each episode. This precision has led to a striking economy. (Note, for instance, that the passages of time between adjacent breakfasts are implied by the merest hint : a flickering image lasting a second and a change of clothes.) In under 200 feet of film, an extremely intricate development has been conveyed with clarity and assurance.

This conciseness of presentation is obviously the result of thorough script preparation. (The very choice of breakfast as the setting for the conversations was an inspiration !) There is nothing fortuitous about the order and relation of the separate impressions —as is so often the case with the unscripted formula kind of montage —and the passage has been conceived as a complete entity already in the script.

Unlike the continuity-link montage, this passage has considerable dramatic power. The montage form is used because it happens to be the most fitting method of presentation. Indeed, it is difficult to see how the gradual change in the relationship between the two characters could have been so economically conveyed in another way. But having decided that the situation needs to be shown in a series of flashes, it was still necessary to provide a good dramatic reason for showing it in this way.

It might indeed be objected that the passage is artificial in its method of presentation and therefore does not carry the conviction of straight narrative. The objection would be valid if the passage were placed in the middle of a straightforward film. Actually, its framework is the flash-back of Leyland's reminiscences, and Leyland, it has been previously established, is giving a cynical, strongly biased account : the sequence is seen as if through a distorting mind. Thus although the treatment comes dangerously near to caricature, it is justified by the setting. There is a dramatic reason for showing the events in over-simplified montage form : Leyland, we are prepared to imagine, is describing Kane's marriage in a series of pointedly exaggerated impressions and that is the way we are ready to see it.

Similarly well founded montage sequences, which are quite different in mood, occur in such diverse films as *Pygmalion* and *On the Town*. We need only mention them briefly. In *Pygmalion*, there is a sequence in which Liza Doolittle (Wendy Hiller) starts on an intensive course of speech-training. Her bewilderment at the complexity and strangeness of her new surroundings is most forcefully expressed in the fast montage of gramophone records, recording instruments, metronomes and other paraphernalia. The sequence is, of course, utterly unreal, but it makes its point because we are seeing it through Eliza's confused eyes.

In the opening sequence of the musical *On the Town* we see three sailors, on twenty-four hours' shore leave, setting out to paint the town red. A montage sequence of the three sailors inspecting and dancing around the many sights of the town takes them from place to place while they are uninterruptedly singing the opening chorus " New York, New York, is a wonderful town ! " There can be no question of " realism " here. The fast, gay confusion of colourful images forms a fitting background for the opening song and most delightfully supports the *joie-de-vivre* of the whole film.

The three sequences from *Citizen Kane, Pygmalion* and *On the Town* show how the montage pattern can be used in a variety of dramatically effective ways. These have, if anything, been too little explored. In each case there is a valid dramatic reason why the spectator is suddenly asked to view the action in a different, more artificial way. In each case, in other words, the form of presentation is appropriate to the dramatic content. To decide that a particular series of facts is most conveniently told in short flashes is not enough : the dramatic content of the situation must also be in harmony with the montage form. Without this harmony of form and content, the montage sequence becomes at best a clumsy way out of continuity troubles, and at worst, an unjustifiable piece of trickery.

7

DOCUMENTARY REPORTAGE

" THE skill of the artist . . . [i.e., the director] . . . lies in the treatment of the story, guidance of the actors in speech and gesture, composition of the separate scenes within the picture-frame, movements of the cameras and the suitability of the settings ; in all of which he is assisted by dialogue writers, cameramen, art-directors, make-up experts, sound-recordists and the actors themselves, while the finished scenes are assembled in their right order by the editing department."[1] This is how Paul Rotha has summarised the nature of the creative work which goes into the production of the normal story-film. It is perhaps an over-simplification : the " treatment of the story " is a phrase which embraces many functions ; and the continuity of shots which the director has planned on the floor and which the editor interprets in the cutting room, may—and often does—entail a more positive attitude to editing than Rotha implies. But on the whole the picture is fair.

The maker of documentaries is concerned with a different set of values. His attitude to film making " proceeds from the belief that nothing photographed, or recorded on to celluloid, has meaning until it comes to the cutting-bench ; that the primary task of film creation lies in the physical and mental stimuli which can be produced by the factor of editing. The way in which the camera is used, its many movements and angles of vision in relation to the objects being photographed, the speed with which it reproduces actions and the very appearance of persons and things before it, are governed by the manner in which the editing is fulfilled."[2]

Here, then, one is dealing with an entirely different method of production, a method in which editing *is* the film. It is important

[1] Documentary Film *by Paul Rotha. Faber, 1936, p. 76.*
[2] Ibid., *p. 77.*

to realise that this difference of approach is not simply due to the caprice of one school of film-makers as opposed to another, but arises out of a fundamental difference of aims. A story-film—and this will have to serve as a working distinction between documentary and story-films—is concerned with the development of a *plot* ; the documentary film is concerned with the exposition of a *theme*. It is out of this fundamental difference of aims that the different production methods arise.

This distinction is necessarily rather vague. It is of course true that many films, quite distinctly " documentary " in flavour, have used a plot, and that many commercial story-films show a marked documentary influence. The distinction is one of total emphasis rather than of subject-matter alone. Thus *Nanook of the North* can be considered a documentary because its " plot " is merely a dramatised rendering of the film's theme, namely, the life of an Eskimo. On the other hand, a film like *Scott of the Antarctic* is a story-film : it is the adventure story of a set of characters with the setting in the Antarctic, not an essay in Antarctic exploration.

The absence of a plot is at once an advantage and a disadvantage to the documentary director. Many an indifferently made story-film can hold an audience simply by telling an intriguing story. An exciting plot can generate enough interest and suspense to compensate for shortcomings in the acting and presentation. The documentary does not have this advantage. Here the theme must be presented in a novel, stimulating way to hold an audience at all ; even if the theme itself is one in which the spectator might reasonably be expected to be interested, it is in the manner of the presentation, in the aptness and originality of the visual associations, and in the purposeful editing, that the film will gain its interest. In a documentary the theme is only the merest starting point, demanding interpretation. The film's merit will rest on the quality of the treatment, not in the spontaneous entertaining power of the theme itself. In many cases, the simplest themes have provided the starting point for the most successful documentaries.

What the documentary director loses in missing the suspense of a plot, he gains in his freedom to edit his films in an original and expressive way. He is not tied by the strict chronology of events laid down by a set story, but can present facets of his theme and alternations of mood in the order and tempo he chooses. He does not have his images anchored by a dialogue track, but can experiment with evocative uses of actual and commentative sound.

124

Most important, he has a greater freedom of interpretation than a story-film director, because it is the interpretation—the editing—that will bring life to his subject.

For this reason (and for the reason that documentary films are generally made on much lower budgets and therefore with smaller units) the documentary director is more completely in charge of production than is his story-film counterpart. The interpretation of a theme is so much a matter of fine personal judgments, that to spread the responsibility for writing, direction and editing between three separate individuals would be to impair the film's unity : it would, for example, be nonsensical to allot the editing of a documentary to an independently working editor —as is often done with story-films in Hollywood—for the acts of direction and editing are merely two stages of one creative process.

Thus the skill of the documentary director is essentially the skill of an editor. He must contrive to convey all the fine shades of meaning through the creative use of sound and by ensuring an eloquent flow of shot juxtapositions, for he has no actors through whom to express himself. More than with the fiction film, the editing process must begin long before the film reaches the cutting rooms.

Not until you come to cut do you realise the importance of correct analysis during camerawork and the essential need for preliminary observation. For unless your material has been understood from the inside, you cannot hope to bring it alive. No amount of cutting, short or otherwise, will give movement to shots in which movement does not already exist. No skill of cross-reference will add poetic imagery to your sequence if you have been unaware of your images during shooting. Your film is given life on the cutting-bench, but you cannot create life unless the necessary raw stuff is to hand. Cutting is not confined to the cutting-room alone. Cutting must be present all through the stages of production—script, photography and approach to natural material—finally to take concrete form as the sound is added.[1]

This need to obtain apt, incisive " raw stuff " before editing begins is demonstrated must forcefully in the production of the simplest form of documentary—the reportage film.

The aim of good film reportage is to convey the drama of natural events. At its simplest it is concerned solely with the presentation of natural happenings and does not set out to explore implications or to draw conclusions from its material. The method has been used in films like the monthly series of *This Modern Age* reviews, and is frequently applied when the aim is to spread

[1] Documentary Film *by Paul Rotha. Faber, 1936.*

information rather than to make specific propaganda. The facts alone are of interest and the director's task is to present them as authentically as possible.

At first sight nothing would appear to be simpler than to present an exciting event in an exciting way. Actually, as we shall see, to achieve a convincing impression of an actually observed scene, a most elaborate editing process may have to be brought into operation. An event which is dramatic when seen in real life does not necessarily remain so when recorded on to celluloid.

Take, for instance, a film of a football match. If the director takes a camera and shoots the whole of the match from the position of a spectator in the grandstand, the result is hardly likely to be very exciting. To get an effective film record, the director must cover various aspects of the game from different camera positions, in every case choosing the best set-up for any particular incident. He needs to select only the most significant moments of the game and then edit them in such a way as to convey the impression of more or less continuous play.

If, on the other hand, a director is asked to film an event like the launching of a rocket, he proceeds in an entirely different way. If he sets up his camera—however advantageously—and records only the moment of firing, his film will be flat and insignificant : the whole event will be over before the spectator has time to realise what is happening. In a case of this sort, a considerable build-up is needed : the director might photograph some of the activities leading up to the firing and might show the operator pulling the lever which will set the rocket off, before showing the firing itself. In one way or another, he might produce an atmosphere of expectancy for the culminating event and thereby extract the maximum excitement from the situation.

These two simple instances should serve to show in an elementary way how the director needs to distort and control the factor of time in order to make a natural event arresting and life-like. In the first case it is necessary to condense the duration of the game to a much shorter time than it would actually take to play ; in the second, the event has to be lengthened beyond its natural span of time. Although neither of these simple scenes requires any extraneous or specially rehearsed material, the use of only natural shots does not necessarily in itself make them appear real. It is precisely through the purposeful selection and editing of the natural material that a convincing and significant impression of reality can be achieved.

126

To make our point a little more definite, here is a short extract from a straightforward passage of reportage in which extremely economic shooting, allied to good editing, has produced a simple yet exciting sequence.

MERCHANT SEAMEN[1]

Extract from Reel 3

About merchant ship convoys during the war, how they steered their way through mine-fields and protected themselves against submarines. The characters are a group of sailors whose ship is sunk at the beginning of the film. The extract is part of the sinking of a submarine which attacked the new ship on which the group of sailors were working. ("Nipper," who is the junior member of the crew, is the gunnery expert.)

A U-boat is sighted and the captain has given instructions to man the guns. Men below are playing cards, a gramophone is playing. Shots of men hurrying to their guns on deck precede.

Round I

			Ft. fr.	
1	C.S. of gramophone playing.	Gramophone playing a military march.	1	6
2	"Nipper" runs into frame from the left and starts rotating the gun towards the submarine.	Gramophone music stops.	2	
3	A man comes up on deck carrying a shell. Control Officer walks *towards camera* and looks through his field-glasses towards the submarine.		3	10
4	L.S. Shadow of submarine in the sea, *within* OO *mask*, i.e. as if seen through binoculars.	Control Officer : Enemy in sight.	6	9
5	M.C.S. Control Officer peering through binoculars.	Control Officer : Bearing red 090.	2	10
6	"Nipper" turning gun as instructed.	"Nipper" : Bearing red 090.	3	
7	C.S. Gun base, as gun is turned to appropriate angle setting.	Control Officer : Train on periscope—	2	6
8	M.C.S. Control Officer looking through binoculars *as in 5.*	—range 010.	2	
9	M.C.S. Sight-setter and "Nipper" at the gun.	Sight-setter : Range 010.	1	9
10	C.U. "Nipper" sighting the gun.	"Nipper" : Trainer on. Control Officer : Deflection, 08 left.	2	

[1] *Director : J. B. Holmes. Editor : R. Q. McNaughton. Crown Film Unit, 1941.*

127

			Ft. fr.
11	M.C.S. "Nipper" and sight-setter *as in* 9.	*Sight-setter :* Deflection, 08 left.	2 7
12	C.S. The back of the gun.	Sights moving.	1 8
13	C.U. "Nipper" *as in* 10.	*"Nipper" :* Trainer on.	1 3
14	M.S. Gun-layer watching through sights.	*Gun-layer :* Gun-layer on.	1
15	C.U. Sight-setter.	*Sight-setter :* Set.	12
16	M.C.S. Control Officer with binoculars *as in* 5.	*Control Officer :* Control !	1 14
17	C.S. Breech of the gun. Hand comes *into frame* and snaps breech into position.		1
18	Gun from a little farther back.	*Breech worker :* Ready !	1 9
19	M.C.S. Control Officer. As in 5.	*Control Officer :* Shoot !	10
20	C.S. Sight-setter. As in 15.	*Sight-setter :* Fire !	10
21	M.C.S. Gun-layer watching through sights. *As in* 14.		9
22	Gun from the side, as it goes off and recoils. *As in* 18.	*Loud report.*	1 7
23	The sea. Shell strikes water in the distance.		3

Round II

24–29	The sequence leading up to the firing of the gun is now repeated, cut slightly faster ; it consists of large, static close-ups.		
30	The sea. Shell strikes water in the distance. *As in* 23.		2 9

Round III

31	Two men (the two seamen whom we met before, in the first and second reel) leaning over the side of the ship.	*First sailor :* (Digger) There he is, shooting again. There's no sub. around here ! *The firing of gun is heard in background.*	5 1

Round IV

32	*Closer shot* of the two men from the front.	*Second sailor :* Don't you be daft, Digger— there's a submarine there all right.	5 1
33	The sea. Another shot strikes the water. *As in* 23.	*Loud report of the gun.*	3 1

128

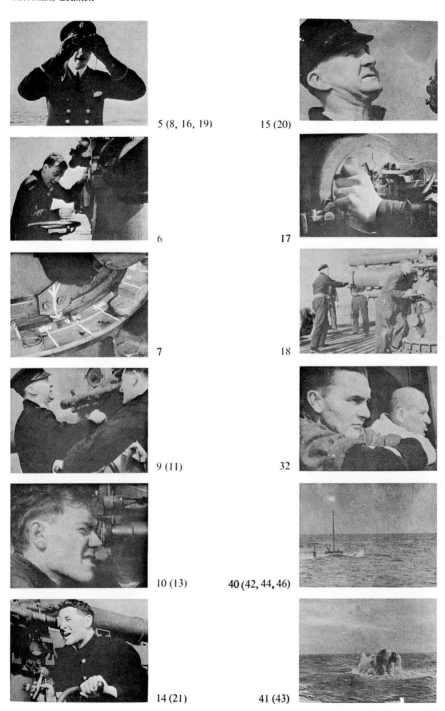

5 (8, 16, 19) 15 (20)

6 17

7 18

9 (11) 32

10 (13) **40** (42, 44, 46)

14 (21) 41 (43)

			Ft. fr.
34–38	Another sequence of shots preparatory to firing the gun. *Cut very fast ; mainly close shots of seamen's hands handling parts of the gun.*	*Various commands* (off).	7 13
39	Officers watching.	*Sight-setter :* (off) Fire !	2 1
40	L.S. Submarine surfacing.	*Loud explosion.*	1 5
41	L.S. Cone of water thrown up by the shell.	*Loud explosion.*	1
42	*As in* 40.	*Loud explosion.*	2
43	*As in* 41.	*Loud explosion.*	3
44	*As in* 40.	*Loud explosion.*	1
45	Explosion in distance.	*Loud explosion.*	1
46	*As in* 40.	*Loud explosion.*	1
47	*As in* 45.	*Loud explosion.*	2 9
48	Control Officer on right, other sailors on left.	*Control Officer :* Check, Check, Check. *Sight-setter :* Check, Check, Check.	2 15
49–50	Sailors moving about.	*Calm music starts.*	2 7
51	Control Officer *facing camera.*	*Control Officer :* Cease fire ! *Music continues.*	1 10

Merchant Seamen was made during the war and was designed to convince merchant sailors of the importance of learning gunnery as a means of defence against submarines. Intended to be viewed by experts, it was essential that the details of procedure should be faithfully rendered and that the " lesson " should not be too obviously planted. This meant, among other things, that the gun had to be shown firing several times before the submarine was hit —as, of course, would normally happen. Out of this necessity arises the overall editing pattern of the sequence.

The cycle of operations leading up to the firing is shown three times and implied twice more, before the submarine is finally hit. Having to show the action five times brought with it another problem : clearly, to be effective, the shooting drill must be quickly and efficiently carried out and must therefore be shown swiftly in the film. On the other hand, for dramatic reasons, the pace of the sequence as a whole has to increase towards the climax. This difficulty was overcome by showing the five operations not only at a different pace but in a completely different manner.

130

Round I. In shots *3–23* the first cycle of operations is shown. From the slow preceding scene we are suddenly plunged into the midst of battle. This abrupt change of cutting rate not only makes the dramatic point that an attack may come at the most unexpected moment, but also, by contrast with the previous scene, makes the first firing appear fast and efficient. The whole drill is now shown in full : all the commands leading up to the firing are heard clearly, each command coming from the person in picture.

As we have already remarked in connection with action scenes, the first essential in making a passage of this kind exciting is that the spectator should know exactly what is going on. The whole drill is therefore shown step by step first, in order to acquaint the spectator with the exact procedure ; although a single viewing will not at first explain the whole process to him, the spectator will accept it as genuine because it proceeds by apparently authentic steps.

In order to convey something of the quick, staccato rhythm of the manœuvre, the cuts are timed to a definite pattern. Each cut takes place a fraction of a second—a frame or two—*before* the appropriate character has finished his last word. For instance in *4*, the cut to *5* is timed just before the Control Officer has finished the word " sight " and we are taken straight to the next person in the chain of action. This timing is maintained right through the sequence.

In one or two places (*7, 12*, for example), a character's words are allowed to flow over into the next shot showing the effect of his actions. In these cases, the cut is timed on the last word of a phrase —in shot *11*, for example, on the word " left."

In addition to giving the sequence a definite rhythm of this kind, the tempo of cutting quite deliberately increases towards the climax. This is done by cutting down the moments preceding a character's words, making them get shorter and shorter up to shot *15*.

16 and *17* then provide a short pause while everything is ready for the firing, and *18, 19* and *20* are cut as short as possible : the words " Ready ! " " Shoot ! " " Fire ! " follow each other without pause and the images are in each case left on the screen only long enough to accommodate the sound-track of the words.

Shot *23* is left on the screen long enough to give the sensation of anxious watching. Coming after a period of extremely quick cutting, the three feet of shot *23* appear to last quite an appreciable time.

Round II. In *24–29* a second cycle of operations is shown. The spectator should know now how the drill is carried out and does

131

not need to be shown the complete procedure again. An abbreviated version of the drill is given again, but this time we do not start from the beginning.

The cut-away to the sea (23) makes it perfectly acceptable that when we cut back to the seamen, they are already halfway through their preliminary drill. The visual emphasis of this round is on the personal reactions of the seamen (shown mostly in rather static close shots) and most of the shots are not of speaking characters; it is therefore possible to give the sequence of commands as quickly as desired. Again (as with shot 23), shot 30 is longish in duration and conveys the anxious seconds of waiting before the shell strikes water.

Rounds III and *IV*. At this point we cut away to two subsidiary characters who are outside the main action. Digger, a disgruntled Australian, has been shown in earlier parts of the film to be extremely sceptical about the effectiveness of small guns and his remarks here are merely a further side-light on the " message " of the film. At the same time, cutting away from the main action provides an opportunity to imply in the sound-track that while these two men are talking, two more shells have been fired ; the shots of the two men are slow and relatively long, and make the firing of two more shells in this short time believable. Lastly, the scene, by slowing down the tempo of the sequence, strengthens the feverishly fast effect of the final round (34–38) which leads up to the sinking of the submarine. It is the calm moment before the final burst of activity which makes the climax more effective by contrast.

Round V. Shot 39 (like 23 and 30) provides the moment of expectancy while the shell is travelling through the air.

Then, with tremendous pace, the cycle of commands is repeated in 34–39 ; this time, close shots of hands speedily manipulating the gun are shown, and the total impression is of quick, frantic activity and movement. The commands are heard " off " and are given as fast as possible.

After one further cut-away to some onlookers on the ship, the submarine is briefly shown surfacing—the shot is left on the screen only long enough to let the spectator know what is happening and is quickly followed by the explosion itself. With the explosion dying down, the pace suddenly relaxes (by comparison with 40–46, shots 47–49 appear slow and leisurely) and the calm music takes over.

Looking at the passage as a whole, it becomes quite obvious

that considerable liberties have been taken with the tempo of the five operations. We see a process, which is in practice the same every time, in five different ways and at five different speeds, yet the final effect is one of complete authenticity. More than this, it conveys an excitement which is of the same kind as might be experienced in a similar situation in real life ; it is not the artificial, studio-made suspense of a last-minute rescue but that of a genuinely thrilling natural event. Telescoping, contracting and rearranging the material has merely brought out the full excitement of the scene in a way in which the spectator can most readily appreciate it. It is precisely through the purposive control of pace that the editor has achieved the impression of reality.

The explosion which ends the above sequence is not a real record of a submarine being blown up ; actually the submarine shot was taken at a different time altogether and merely shows a vessel coming up to the surface. The editor was therefore faced with the problem of conveying the impression of an explosion without having a shot of it. The result may not be ideal but it certainly gives the appearance of being authentic.

A great deal of the effect is achieved through the careful build-up. The whole sequence has been leading up to this point and the spectator is expecting something to happen. The observers who are on board (39) are shown for the first time ; they are anxiously looking out to sea and the shot serves as a warning to the spectator that something is just about to happen. Then we are briefly shown the submarine surfacing which creates the impression that it is in fact involved in the explosion which follows.

The explosion itself is conveyed by the rapid intercutting of frames of the submarine and of a cone of water thrown up by a depth-charge. A chaotic, bursting image is created by the alternating frames because the conning-tower of the submarine is on the left side of the picture and the cone of water is on the right. Almost before the spectator has time to realise what is happening, the whole screen is filled with a tremendous upsurge of water (actually a closer shot of a depth-charge exploding in the sea) which he takes to be the effect of the explosion. The effect is strongly reinforced by the sound of the explosion, heard for the first time.

It is by no means implied that this editing is ideal or that it should be taken as an example of the way to construct scenes of this kind. Yet the explosion, as here conveyed, is effective, and appears convincing in spite of the fact that no actual shot of an exploding submarine was used.

In passing, it is perhaps worth noting that Pudovkin has described a similar passage from his own experience :

I wished to show a terrific explosion. In order to render the effect of this explosion with absolute faithfulness, I caused a great mass of dynamite to be buried in the earth, had it blasted, and shot it. The explosion was veritably colossal—but filmically it was nothing. On the screen it was merely a slow, lifeless movement. Later, after much trial and experiment, I managed to edit the explosion with all the effect I required—moreover without using a single piece of the scene I had just taken. I took a *flammenwerfer* that belched forth clouds of smoke. In order to give the effect of the crash I cut in short flashes of magnesium flare, in rhythmic alternation of light and dark. Into the middle of this I cut a shot of a river taken some time before, that seemed to me appropriate owing to its special tones of light and shade. Thus gradually arose before me the visual effect I required. The bomb explosion was at last upon the screen, but in reality, its elements comprised everything imaginable except a real explosion.[1]

Why, it may be asked, is it necessary to distort the tempo of natural events, or even to use purely artificial means—as Pudovkin showed—to achieve an effect of reality ? The answer is at least twofold.

Firstly, successful reportage must be concerned with showing only the most significant aspects of an event ; it does not deal in absolute, literal reporting. Secondly—and this is why Pudovkin's edited explosion was more effective than the record of the real one —a natural event has a " feel " of its own, it evokes a certain emotional reaction which it is the film-maker's job to capture and which may be the clue to authenticity of presentation even if the details are not exactly right. The impression of cool yet hurried efficiency which is a feature of the firing sequence from *Merchant Seamen* is expressed in film terms by rapid cutting ; the changing emotional tension as the submarine gets nearer to the surface and brings the moment of danger closer, must in a film be expressed through the editing—through the variations of tempo and the constant shifting of emphasis. Clearly, these emotional overtones are not implicit in the uncut film and are only brought out on the cutting bench.

[1] Film Technique *by V. I. Pudovkin. Newnes, 1933, p. xvi.*

8

IMAGINATIVE DOCUMENTARY

FILM reportage of the kind we have just discussed touches mainly upon the surface appearance of events ; like a responsibly written newspaper report, it selects the most important facets of a given situation and presents them fairly. Straightforward film reporting does not strive for any deep aesthetic insight : it bears a similar relation to genuinely creative documentary as a newspaper article bears to an imaginative passage of prose or poetry.

The high esteem in which documentary films as a *genre* are generally held, is due mainly to the films which have probed beneath the surface of mere observation and have tried to convey something of the emotional overtones and significance of natural themes. Though their aims may have been widely different, the films of Dovzhenko, Flaherty, Ivens and Wright spring to mind immediately as examples of this more profound approach to reality. In this account we are not concerned with the purpose for which the films of these four widely differing directors were made, but with the aesthetic problems underlying their production. Thus, for instance, Flaherty's aim in making *Louisiana Story* was obviously quite different from Ivens' in *Spanish Earth*, yet the purely aesthetic problems of producing an imaginatively satisfying continuity are essentially similar.

Replace the fairy-tale of *Louisiana Story* with real-life drama ;[1] replace the alligator with real bullets ; replace the racoon with young loyalist soldiers of Joris Ivens' *The Spanish Earth* : a comparison of problems can then emerge. At the end of the alligator-racoon sequence, the director was free to choose whether the racoon should live or die. At the end of *The Spanish Earth* there was no soldier to be reunited with his mother and friends : he was killed. It was not the script which called for his death but a real, life-size bullet. The director could not re-shoot all the foregoing events, nor could he arrange for shooting sufficient material to cover the editing for the imposed change in ending. Thus the direction and editing had to remain flexible throughout

[1] *Notes by Helen van Dongen.*

the production in order to cope with the problems imposed by the actual events. But once the story-line was fixed, the essential editing problems in the two instances remain parallel.

For reasons of compactness, we shall limit our account of the editing of imaginative documentaries to the work of Robert Flaherty : his films have been most widely seen, and are in some ways the most consistently representative of the *genre*. In restricting our field in this way, it is of course not implied that Flaherty is the only exponent, or even that he is the only one of major interest.

An imaginative interpretation of a natural event must, above all, preserve something of the spontaneity of the event itself. Well aware of this necessity, Flaherty planned the continuity of his films only in the very vaguest form in the script. He used a rough, flexible story-outline to give shape and unity to his whole film, but employed nothing even vaguely resembling a shooting script. The details, and in many cases the larger outlines of continuity, were solely determined by the nature and quality of material which had been shot and were not worked out before reaching the editing bench.

For *Louisiana Story*[1] we did not have a shooting script indicating what individual scenes to shoot or where to place them in the final story. Instead we had a visually and cinematically written script, the main aim being that the story be readable. For instance Flaherty wrote the opening sequence as follows :

" We are deep in the Bayou Country of Lower Louisiana. It is the high-water time of the year—the country is half drowned. We move through a forest of bearded trees. There are wild fowl everywhere, in flight and swimming on the water. We are spellbound by all this wild life and the mystery of the wilderness that lies ahead . . ."

To cover this sequence an enormous amount of miscellaneous material was shot, not only when going out to make shots for this specific sequence, but all during the shooting period, whenever something was sighted that might eventually be used to express the atmosphere and geography of the country. (200,000 ft. of material were shot for the film which was in the end 8,000 ft. long.) Almost anything could cover this theme and almost anything was actually shot. Like everything living in the swamp, our images grew abundantly. We had scenes of alligators sitting on their nests, slithering through the water, basking in the sun or rearing their ugly heads from a mud-patch in the swamp-forest ; strange and magnificent birds perched on tree-tops or sitting on branches sticking out of the lily-pond ; snakes sliding up trees, lotus-leaves reflected in the clear water, dewdrops on the leaves, little flies skimming the water, a spider spinning its web, spanish moss dangling from huge oak trees, fishes, rabbits, fawns or skunks, and others too numerous to mention.

Such a great quantity and variety of material, all temporarily filed under

[1] *Notes by Helen van Dongen.*

the heading " scenes for introduction "—all of it covering the theme " atmosphere of the swamp and forest "—of course presents its own difficulties in editing. At the first screening all this material looks incoherent. Where, in this welter, is the main theme that must be developed ?

The editor had no precise shooting script to follow which told him : " We open with a close-up of a lotus-leaf silhouetted against the water, followed by a shot of an alligator climbing upon a raft . . . " Instead, there was only a general description of the locale and of the atmosphere and feeling which should be expressed (" We are spellbound by all the wild life and the mystery of the wilderness which lies ahead . . . ").

The editor has to discover and disclose the director's design and use as further guides :

(1) the indication that he has to portray a mysterious wilderness as yet untouched by civilisation ;

(2) that he has to portray this in a lyrical mood to conform to the style and balance of rhythm in the rest of the film and that this wilderness has to be seen through the magic eyes of a twelve-year-old boy (the editor has to watch that this particular sequence does not unfold like an epic or become a glorified travelogue) ;

(3) though each shot already possesses the inherent qualities of the mysterious wilderness, each shot in itself is still neutral in content and remains so until it is brought into proper relationship to another shot—when it will at once become alive and acquire a deeper meaning ;

(4) last but not least : the screening and discussions with the director.

The dominant factor in the selection and continuity of the scenes should be their emotional content, their inner meaning. Once the desired feeling and atmosphere are conveyed throughout the sequence and a balance and unity have been achieved between form and content, the metric and rhythmic values will take care of themselves.

Here is how the opening sequence looked, when finished :

LOUISIANA STORY[1]

The opening sequence

The film is " an account of certain adventures of a Cajun (Acadian) boy who lives in the marshlands of Petit Anse Bayou in Louisiana."

			Ft.
1	After a *very slow fade in (eight feet)* during which the *camera pans upwards slowly* we open on an enormous lotus-leaf undulating slowly. The leaf itself and some mud-patches form black reflections in the water-surface in which also bright white clouds are reflected. Tiny bugs skim over the water-surface.	*Music begins.*	13
2	L.S. Black, silhouette-like form of an alligator swimming very slowly. Again clear white clouds are reflected in the water.		11

[1] *Director : Robert Flaherty. Editor and Associate Producer : Helen van Dongen. Robert Flaherty Productions, 1948.*

137

		Ft.
3	The surface of the water with reflections of several lotus-leaves and branches with a bird on it. *Camera pans upward,* revealing what we have seen before in the reflections.	8
4	The surface of the lily-pond, lotus-leaves here and there in the water. An alligator crawls slowly on a cypress-log.	12
5	*C.U.* Lotus-leaf, the shadow of unseen branches on it. In the foreground of the leaf : dew-drops.	2
6	*C.U.* Dewdrop on the lotus-leaf.	3
7	*M.L.S.* Magnificent bird, perched on the branch of a tree.	8
8	*L.S.* of the forest in the swamp. The trunks of trees are standing in the dark water, silvery spanish moss dangles from the branches. (*Shot from a floating raft which moved slowly along, while the camera itself pans very slowly in the opposite direction, thus creating an almost three-dimensional effect.*) *After approximately 25 feet we discover from very far behind the trees a little boy paddling his pirogue.* He disappears and re-appears again far behind the enormous trees in the foreground.	72
9	Forest, low-hanging spanish moss in the foreground. *Camera moves farther in* through the moss, as if passing through a Japanese screen.	17
10	*C.U.* Swirl in the water-surface caused by the boy's paddle *off-screen.*	6
11	*M.C.S.* Boy in his canoe, *back to camera.* He is proceeding cautiously, stopping at times, looking around.	Commentator : His name is Alexander—Napoleon—Ulysses—Latour. Mermaids—their hair is green he says—swim up these waters from the sea. He's seen their bubbles—often.	41
12	*C.U.* Bubbles coming up to the surface, disturbing the tiny little leaves.		10
13	The boy bends low to pass underneath the low-hanging spanish moss. He paddles away from camera.	And werewolves, with long noses and big red eyes,	15

			Ft
14	Forest. The boy is very small in the midst of the huge oak-trees. He paddles forward *towards camera*.	come to dance on moonless nights.	12.
15	The boy now closer, paddling from right to left and *out of frame*.		13
16	Some trees, surrounded by water. The sunlight here penetrates the forest and reflects in the water. The slight movement of the water projects the sunlight in turn against the trees.		6
17	The water surface and over-hanging branches, reflected in the sunlight.		5
18	A fish gliding along just below the surface of the water.		4
19	M.S. Boy in his canoe, bending very low to pass underneath the spanish moss and moving aside an enormous lotus-leaf.		15
20	C.U. Alligator slowly raising his head.		9
21	M.S. Boy, holding the canoe with his paddle. He looks around but does not see the alligator *off-screen*.		13
22	The dark surface of the swamp-water. Nothing is visible but some reflections of tree-trunks.		5
23	M.L.S. Boy, partly hidden by the branches, moving away.		9
24	L.S. Boy in his pirogue, travelling slowly *away from camera*.		7
25	C.U. Snake wriggling along on the water-surface, *away from camera*.		7
26	M.S. Boy in pirogue, *facing camera*. He looks around, listens and touches the little salt-bag at his waist.	*Music stops.* *Commentator :* He'd never dream of being without this little bag of salt at his waist,	13
27	C.U. Bubbles coming up, disturb-ing the water surface.		5
28	*As in 26.* Boy looks inside his shirt.	and the little something he carries inside his shirt.	37
29	The boy smiles and starts paddling *towards camera*.	*Music starts with a new theme :* the " boy's theme."	33
30	C.S. Racoon on a tree.	*Music louder.*	

139

The sequence[1] is the slow beginning of a tale, a lyrical introduction to the beauties of the bayou-country and the mysteries of the swamp which lie ahead. Robert Flaherty's approach is a poetic, lingering one, admiring one object, then looking around and beyond it. Our surroundings are undisturbed by the hum-drum of civilisation and the editing is kept in harmony with these surroundings, free from the agitation of quickly changing scenes or intercuts.

Look for instance as a specific example at scene 8. For seventy feet, in one continuous shot, we glide through the swamp-water, discover the boy and follow him from far. Had this long scene been intercut with other detailed scenery, however beautiful, the feeling of complete tranquillity, the mystery and poetic atmosphere inherent in the image itself, would have been destroyed.

The introduction sets the pattern at the start with images of details. A leaf, strange and beautiful in form, a bird we do not see in our everyday life, the shadows of feathery branches, the silhouette of an alligator, a dewdrop glistening in the sunlight—together they form a pictorial narrative and indicate a strange and mysterious country. Only *after* we have seen these details is it revealed that we are in a forest, itself mysterious, for it is in the midst of a swamp. The huge oak trees have beards of silvery spanish moss hanging low. And then, almost unnoticed at first, we discover afar a human form, a little boy paddling his canoe through the silent waters.

This boy comes to us imbued with the mystery of the birds or the lotus-flower. We do not find it strange that his name is Alexander—Napoleon—Ulysses—Latour, for it is in keeping with grandiose and imposing surroundings. When we bend low with him, to pass underneath the spanish moss—as if parting a Japanese curtain—we penetrate farther into a fairyland and we accept readily that he believes in mermaids and carries charms to defend himself against werewolves and other unseen enemies of his imaginary world.

This ready conception and complete absorption of atmosphere is the result of the juxtaposition of shots. Had we, for instance, opened the sequence with the long continuous scene of the bearded forest (as an *orientation* scene of the locale in which the tale was set) we would have no preparation to understand and appreciate its charms and mysteries. The scene in that case would have represented nothing but a forest with a boy paddling through it. Had the details followed this scene they would have been mere images along the boy's course through the forest. In the continuity which we follow in the film we are emotionally prepared to appreciate the qualities of the forest. The preceding details, their mysterious quality and beauty, have awakened our curiosity and induce us to follow the boy eagerly and participate in his discoveries.

The choice of these scenes and their continuity was not decided upon *a priori*. Within the scope of the concept of the sequence their selection and continuity was determined by several factors :

(1) *the subject-matter of each scene* ;

(2) *the spatial movement* of each image, which is not a dominant but operates alongside other factors. It is secondary in importance but cannot be ignored ;

(3) *the tonal value*. By this I mean the colour of a scene, its nuances within the range of black and white. In combination with other factors this colour can set or sustain an atmosphere. (For instance : a brilliant shot can represent simply the middle of the day, or it could represent a happy day. Brilliant combined with silvery reflections can create a magical atmosphere. Grey could be simply approaching night or a cloudy day with approaching rain. Grey could also be used emotionally to warn of impending disaster) ;

(4) *the emotional content* which is the important and dominant factor.

[1] *Notes by Helen van Dongen.*

140

It is important to remember that all of these factors have to be seen, judged and used *in conjunction* with each other, for it is the *collective* estimate of all these elements, of all these appeals which eventually will result in a successful juxtaposition of scenes.

To show the relative importance of each factor and the complexity of reasoning between each scene, let us analyse for example the first two scenes of the introduction. Paying attention for the moment *only* to *spatial movement* :

After a very slow fade in (eight feet) during which the camera panned upward slowly, the scene opens up on an enormous lotus leaf undulating lazily. Behind the leaf there is an almost imperceptible motion in the water caused by little bugs skimming the surface. In scene *2* we see an alligator swim slowly, making lazy ripples in the water-surface.

Analysing *only the movements* in both scenes we find that the upward slow pan of the camera in the first scene coincides with the slow movement of the undulating leaf, which in turn is in accordance with the lazy movements of the alligator in shot *2*. An almost imperceptible sense of *direction* is created because in the first shot the leaf itself cups slightly towards the right and also bends over in the same direction, which is also the direction in which the alligator is swimming. The slight rippling in the water in shot *1* is continued in shot *2*.

Bringing the *mechanical* continuity so much to the foreground without mentioning the other factors gives it a significance out of all proportion. Actually these movements may be hardly noticeable in the film ; nevertheless they are part of the general appeal of the continuity of these two shots and they are part of the atmosphere and emotional content.

Examining the *tonal value*, we find that both shots have that silhouette-like quality, brilliant white in the reflected clouds, deep black in the reflected mud-patches. In one scene we have the black reflection of the lotus leaf, in the next the black form of the alligator. Both scenes indicate a brilliant, sunny day in beautiful surroundings. By itself this would mean nothing were it not so intimately connected with the other factors.

The *emotional content* in turn is a composite impression created through the subject-matter, the photographic quality and composition within the frame, the slow and lazy movements, the brilliant sunlight, the reflections and silhouette-like atmosphere. Each shot *by itself* records no more than a fixed event, fact or movement, and has a limited association. It is only when read in their present juxtaposition that these single associations, now combined, form a new concept. All these factors create a feeling of unreality. These two shots together indicate the indolence of the sub-tropics with the aura of mystery and magic which will be developed in the following scenes.

Let us go back a little to the breakdown of factors which led to the continuity of the first two scenes. Before any assembly is done, these two scenes might find themselves at widely separated places within the reels the editor is working with. The final continuity is the result of a long period of shifting scenes, now in one combination, then in another, until first some, then more, impose their own combination upon you. When in their right combination the scenes start speaking. The closer one comes to the final correct continuity the more the editor is able to read his scenes. Once the final continuity is reached one can read or analyse step by step all the factors which caused two or more images to demand to be in a certain continuity. The other way around seems to me to be impossible—unless everything, from the very first conception of the idea, is calculated beforehand.

Before going on to discuss Helen van Dongen's account of the editing of this passage, we must say something about the broad underlying intention of the film as a whole. Flaherty is not here concerned with making an instructional film : he uses natural material, of course, but only as a means of expressing an emotional atmosphere. The actual subject-matter of his shots matters only in as far as it reinforces and throws fresh light on a prevailing mood. The facts of the locale are used as the merest starting point through which the emotional climate of the scene can be expressed. What matters about the opening shot of the film, for instance, is the feeling of tranquillity which it conveys, not the fact that it happens to be a lotus-leaf. A different shot—of a sleeping animal, a gently swaying branch, or a shaft of sunlight on the bank— might have served equally well if it conveyed a similar emotional meaning.

This fundamental artistic aim—to express the feeling and atmosphere rather than simply the facts of a situation—is strongly reflected in the nature of the editing. The account given by Helen van Dongen bears little resemblance to our previous analyses. In the reportage and fiction-film sequences which we have discussed earlier, the shots derive most of their significance from their subject-matter and acting, and the editor's main job is to create smooth, dramatically effective shot-to-shot transitions. Here, however, we are concerned with an entirely different set of values.

The subject-matter is of secondary importance and there is no direct continuity of action from image to image. Accordingly, very little has been said about the mechanical transitions : each cut brings with it a further strengthening or slight modification of the prevailing mood, without revealing any new facts essential to the continuity. That being so, the predominant need is for a shot-to-shot balance of feeling and the purely mechanical transitions become of secondary importance.

Similarly, where the story-film editor deliberately sets out to give his passage a tempo appropriate to its dramatic content, Helen van Dongen hardly mentions individual problems of timing. Here, only very few shots carry essential factual information and the editor is not tied to keeping any one image on the screen longer than the mood of his piece requires.

If this involves the editor in using an unusually long-lasting shot, then there is nothing to prevent him from doing so. Shot 8, for instance, in the opening sequence, in which a new character is introduced, is left on the screen for fully seventy feet. Showing the boy for the first time in the course of this long-lasting shot,

142

makes it appear as if we were discovering just another wonderful thing in the forest—much in the same way as we discovered an alligator or a bird, earlier on. Had the boy been introduced for the first time by a cut, his presence would have been felt as something extraneous to the forest, and would have broken the emotional pattern which has been built up so far. (This is not to imply that correct timing and smoothness are unimportant. They are necessary in the same way as it is necessary to a painter to be a good draughtsman. Timing and smoothness form an essential pre-requisite of a creative editing construction without in themselves being a primary aesthetic factor.)

Questions of timing and smoothness having been relegated to a position of relatively subsidiary importance, we are left with two main creative processes in the editing of imaginative passages of this kind.

Firstly, there is the task of selecting the material. From the practical side, this is a job requiring a lot of hard work and a good memory ; it is, moreover, the prime creative process and as such requires a high degree of experience, ability to assess the fine shades of meaning inherent in a shot, and the judgment of an artist. In general, all that is worth noting here is that the various shots selected which will convey a certain shade of feeling when edited, do not necessarily reflect that particular feeling individually. The whole complex atmosphere of the opening sequence of *Louisiana Story* is conveyed by such emotionally varied images as the still close-ups of flowers and birds, calm yet menacing shots of the alligator, and swift electrifying glimpses of a water snake. Individually, these shots convey at best only a minute fraction of the overall feeling ; in juxtaposition they convey the whole awe-inspiring, magic-yet-real atmosphere of the forest.

Further than this, there is little that can profitably be said. Here, one is discussing factors which are so closely dependent on the individual aesthetic judgment of the artist as to make any hard-and-fast theoretical discussion useless and indeed meaningless.

The second task, which is of the profoundest importance once the preliminary selection has been made, is the organisation of the shots into a series of expressive shot juxtapositions. A bird, a glistening drop of water and a glimpse of sunlight can be used to convey a particular atmosphere, but in what order, and in what relationship to each other ? A series of images all reinforcing each others' mood (as in the first half dozen shots quoted) may be ideal in one place ; a sharply contrasting juxtaposition (as in

143

24, 25 and *26*) may be best in another   How crucially important the order of the shots can be in conveying a particular meaning is suggested by Helen van Dongen's remark that a rearrangement of scenes—using an opening image of the forest as an establishing shot—could have made this sequence into a sort of travelogue. Again, we are reduced to saying that the order of shots must be closely conditioned by the required atmosphere. Beyond that, the points of detail must remain the decisions of the individual artist.

The slow opening sequence which we have just quoted contains little plot, little essential information which *had* to be conveyed : the editor did not have to keep to any fixed continuity of events and was able to concentrate solely on the selection of the most evocative images. To show that the method is by no means limited to lyrical passages of natural scenery, let us look at another sequence from the same film in which the editor *had* to convey the atmosphere of a set of fixed operations.

LOUISIANA STORY

Extract from Reel 4

The passage quoted shows the oil drilling for the first time in the film. The process consists of the following stages : a length of steel pipe, with a drilling mechanism (the " bit ") screwed to its bottom end, is sunk into the ground and only its top end left protruding above ground level. A new pipe-length is swung into position by the Derrick-man standing at the top of the (over 100-ft. high) tower ; the bottom end of the new pipe-length is placed into the protruding end of the first one and the two ends are firmly screwed together by means of tightening chains and a torsion device called a monkey-wrench. When the two pipe-lengths are firmly screwed together, a weight is lowered from the top of the tower which pushes the assembled pipes into the ground and again leaves the top end of the upper-most pipe-length exposed above ground level. The process is now repeated for a great number of times until the required depth is reached. After this, the whole length of piping is steadily rotated by a motor and left in the ground for many hours : it is this rotating action which does the drilling. The " Roughnecks " place the pipe-lengths into position and operate the chains. They work at ground level.

The Derrick-man stands at the top of the tower : his job is to swing new pipe-lengths into position and to fix them to the weight which will push them down into the ground.

The " Driller " controls the movement of the monkey-wrench and the ascending and descending action of the weight. He is in charge of the operations.

The long sequence is, for purposes of analysis, broken down into six groups, only the last three groups being given in full.

	Ft.
Group A	160
Dusk. The bit at the bottom of the pipe-lengths is being changed. A new bit is attached and we are shown the Driller manipulating his levers as the pipe-lengths are	

Group A (continued)
sunk into the ground. The emphasis is on shots of work done at
ground level. These are inter-cut
with night shots of passing oil
barges and with glimpses of the
boy approaching the derrick in
the canoe. The sound of the derrick contrasts with the calm
accompanying the shots of the boy,
over which only the quiet per-
sistent heart-beat of the drilling
can be heard.

Group B
Dusk. The operations on the   180
derrick are shown in long shots :
some from the outside, with the
swinging pipe-lengths glistening
in the dark ; some from ground
level, shooting up towards the
top of the tower ; some from the
top of the tower, shooting towards the base of the derrick.
These are inter-cut with shots of
the boy approaching the derrick
in his canoe. As the sequence
progresses, the sound of the
derrick can be heard louder and
louder over the shots of the boy,
indicating that he is getting nearer.

Group C
Night. The boy arrives on the   100
derrick. He looks around ginger-
ly. We see various images of the
operations as through the boy's
eyes. The Driller spots him and
asks him to come and sit beside
the controls to get a better view.

Group D

1   From close, the back and arm of   *Very loud noise of machinery*   9
    one Roughneck holding the next   *throughout the sequence.*
    pipe-length. When the two pipe-
    lengths fall into each other with a
    thump, back and arm recede and
    another arm swings *into frame*,
    throwing the heavy chain around
    the pipe. Through *off-screen*
    manipulations the chain is
    tightened and the first arm
    appears again, ready for the next
    move.

2   M.S. Driller pushing the pedal ;   9½
    the chain appears *in frame from the
    right*, very much in the fore-
    ground, slashing back and forth,
    then it almost imperceptibly
    slackens.

A1

A2

B1

B2

B3

D1

D2

D3

D4

D5

D6

D7

D8

D9

D10

D11

D12

D13

4

D20a

E24

5

D20b

F25

6

D20c

F26

7

E21

F27

8

E22

F28

9

E23

F29

3   M.C.S. Roughneck unwinding the
     chain from the pipe-length, barely
     missing the end of it, his features
     all twisted.

4   M.C.S. Driller looking upward, his   1½
     hand ready on the lever.

5   *Shooting upward* towards the top   2½
     of the derrick ; the block with
     the dangling pipe is coming down-
     ward. When a third down, the
     downward movement is continued
     In :

6   M.L.S. Driller and the boy to-   3
     gether. Both follow the downward
     moving pipe-length with head and
     eyes, the driller to measure the
     pressure on his brake, the boy
     out of wonderment.

7   *Shooting up towards* descending   2½
     pipe-lengths.

8   *Shooting from ground level* : pre-   5½
     vious downward movement is
     picked up in the further descend-
     ing pipe-length. The downward
     movement ends in the final
     settling of the pipe-length in the
     well. An arm and two hands
     appear to unfasten the grip.

9   M.S. Boy, looking sideways at the   1½
     Driller, then up towards the
     rising block *off-screen*. The cable
     is winding behind the boy.

10   *Shooting up towards* the block as   5½
     it continues rising and halts near
     the Derrick-man.

11   M.S. Driller first looking upward,   4
     then quickly downward as if to
     check that everything is function-
     ing properly, then looking quickly
     upward again.

12   M.S. Roughneck, only his back and   8
     arm are visible, both quivering
     with the effort. The chain wound
     around the pipe stands out
     clearly. As soon as the Rough-
     neck has managed to bring the
     two pipe-lengths upwards, the
     chain is thrown upwards, then
     tightens.

13   C.U. Driller. By his body-move-   14½
     ments we know that he is pushing
     the pedal which tightens the
     chain. The chain comes slashing

148

Group D (continued) Ft.
into the foreground, then *the camera pans over* to the boy, rope and chain continue to slash in the foreground. The boy by now looks uncomfortable and while the chain continues to slash, his expression changes to fear.

14   C.S. Twisted features of the Roughneck, trying to hold on to the chain for further tightening.   2½

15   M.S. Driller who continues the tightening. The chain slashes brutally, the boy contorts his features even more and pulls up his shoulder and arm to protect his face.   4½

16   C.S. Roughneck, while he tries to unwind the chain. (The " danger " emanating from the boy's twisted features in the previous shot is continued here.)   2

17   C.S. Pipe-length sliding down through the hole of the stop.   8

18   M.C.S. Driller. His eyes follow the descending pipe-length off-screen, his hands ready on the brake.   2

19   C.S. " Stop " settling down. A thigh and knee bend *into frame* and hands reach to unfasten the grip, while the camera already *starts to pan upward.*   6

20   M.S. Driller. *The upward movement of the camera in the previous shot is caught* in the upward looking movement of the Driller ; then *the camera pans to the right* revealing the boy also looking upward. Behind the boy, the cable is unwinding. The boy quickly looks to the Driller off-screen, then up again ; then the camera pans down. Simultaneously the arm of the Driller and the handle of the brake move downward thus appearing *in frame.* When *camera comes to rest* the hand, and brake move upward again, revealing the boy's feet, toes wriggling excitedly.   22

Group E
21   *From slightly farther back than before,* we see the two pipe-lengths already fitted together. The Roughneck throws the chain around the pipe while the other one swings the monkey-wrench into position.   55

149

Group E (continued)

22   *M.S. Driller, starting the chain-pulling.* $9\frac{1}{2}$

23   *Continuation of shot* 21. While one Roughneck is intently watching the chain to grasp it quickly before it slips, the big monkey-wrench is moving back and forth in the foreground, screwing the two pipe-lengths together.   *Screeching noise of the machinery coming to a stop.* $13\frac{1}{2}$

24   *M.L.S.* of the two Roughnecks holding on for all they are worth, one to the chain, the other one to the pipes, the monkey-wrench still slashing in the foreground.   *Stillness.* $11\frac{1}{2}$

Group F

25   " Curtain-raiser " on the whole operation. In the foreground the monkey-wrench is slung low by the two Roughnecks, thus revealing in the background the Driller and the boy. The Driller moves his lever up, turns a valve and the pipe-length sinks down into the well. The hand of one Roughneck comes into the foreground, ready to grasp the grip. The boy looks in all directions and the pipe-length continues to move downward.   13

26   *M.S.* Driller. He pushes the brake farther down and then, bending in the direction of the boy, smiles at him. $4\frac{1}{2}$

27   *C.U.* Roughneck, his features still somewhat twisted, though not as much as before.   1

28   *M.S.* Driller still smiling at the boy off-screen.   4

29   A similar, total-curtain-view *as shot* 25. As the pipe-length moves down it reveals the boy again, now sitting in a far more relaxed position, on his legs and feet. $13\frac{1}{2}$

30   *M.S.* Driller and the boy. The Driller looks upward and the boy, now with a smile on his face, also looks up. The cable unwinds behind him. The boy points to something above and talks to the Driller, who answers him, but through the din we cannot hear what they say. $3\frac{1}{2}$

	Group F (continued)	Ft
31	C.U. shooting upward ; block descending slowly and unevenly without anything attached to it. It finally comes to a stop.	14½
32	M.S. Driller and the boy. The Driller points upward, the boy smiles at him and then looks up too. Then the Driller secures everything tightly at his machine, signifying the end of this particular operation.	10½
33	L.S. Derrick-man climbing down the ladder outside the steel girders.	15

In sequences like this,[1] one cannot neglect the undeniable logic in the chronology of the operation. Chaos and confusion during the technical process will bewilder the audience and prevent it from perceiving the inner meaning. But it is not the chronology which is most important, nor the purely formalistic movements of the all-powerful machine, however impressive, which should come to the foreground. These mechanical elements should be subjugated to the emotional content.

What is the total emotional impact you want to convey and how can you break it down into separate elements ?

In the oil-drilling sequence, the first one is a negative one, but of great importance. The sequence should never become didactic. We are not making a teaching film and there is no place for a purely technical explanation. Instead it should be the " observation of men and machine at work."

The positive elements are :

(1) *Admiration* for the skill of these men and for what they can do with their machines. The extraordinary co-ordination between the movements of the men and the movements of the machine. As it is, their movements and actions often resemble a sort of super-ballet.

(2) *Danger*—the slightest slip from one of these men will end in disaster. For example, if the Roughneck who handles the chain will miss by a split-second, one or the other might be decapitated by the slashing chain.

(3) *Awe*, from the boy whose only previous contact with technology has been his rusty rifle and an occasional glimpse of a motor-boat passing his father's shack.

(4) *Excitement and Magic*. The machine and men at work observed through the wondering eyes of the boy who accepts this complex machinery with the same confidence as he accepts the magic of his own half real, half imaginary world.

How does one go about choosing the scenes to portray all these elements, either separately or combined ?

The continuity of the scenes is not entirely built on the *external* nature of the separate images, nor on a technical detail or a specific rhythmic-spatial movement. Instead it is based on the total impression or " feeling " of the shots, which in turn is a result of all the elements inherent in each shot. Behind its general indication, one shot may have the dominant " Danger," another the dominant " Awe," still another " Magic " or " Human strength and skill." Each image may possess either a single one of these dominants or several others in any given combination. These dominant elements, plus the external nature of the shot, plus its combined emotional content, plus the sound, are

[1] *Notes by Helen van Dongen.*

151

regarded as equal units, and function as elements of equal significance in the choice of shots and their continuity.

Because a collective calculation of *all* the shots' appeals is used in making the continuity of the oil-drilling sequence, it is impossible to dissect a part of the sequence, scene by scene. The original thought process cannot be traced in purely rhythmic or external observations. Nor can the sequence be analysed abstractly—out of context with what precedes and follows. Aside from the afore-mentioned factors, its content and composition were also determined by previous appearances of the derrick and influenced in turn the form of later sequences in which the derrick appears.

As we are on the derrick in the midst of the operation, a certain atmosphere is already established, the foundation for which has been laid and then developed throughout the preceding sequences. To explain the quality of this atmosphere we will have to go back a little.

We see the derrick for the first time in the film when it suddenly appears against the horizon, far away, moving slowly. The music interrupts the boy's theme and changes to a majestic chorale. Neither the boy nor the audience knows yet what it is, but it is something new, something strange. A note of suspense is still lingering in the air because slightly earlier, strange people and a strange, tractor-like machine, which could ride on the water as well as on land, have been invading the marshes. When they left, all that remained was a stake sticking up from the bayou-waters. No one knew exactly what it was (actually it is the precise spot chosen by the oil-prospectors for drilling, and it is here that the approaching derrick will settle down).

As the derrick comes nearer we are only shown some beautiful details such as the web-like structure of the steel girders, the general activity of the tugboats pushing and pulling the structure, and the flotsam gathering on the water. Finally we concentrate on the stake and the reflection of the derrick in the water, leaving our thoughts with these last two images. A promise is given.

In the following sequence we approach the derrick cautiously with and through the boy. The derrick has now settled over the stake which is no longer visible. Huge steamclouds are billowing up the steel girders and for the first time we hear the throbbing of the powerful pumps, the heartbeat of the derrick. (Whenever the derrick is functioning in the film, this heartbeat is heard. It is the identification of the living derrick. When this heartbeat suddenly falters and then fails in a later sequence we are immediately aware of impending disaster.)

Instead of being shown immediately the operation of the derrick, we are introduced to some of the men on the derrick, men who make friends with a little boy whom they meet perchance. Through their questions, where he lives and how he caught that big fish, their human qualities are unfolded and we, through the boy, become friends with the men.

No premature exposition of the derrick's functions has been imposed upon us, nor are these functions hidden from us : through the boy we are invited to come aboard and, through the boy, we decline the invitation for the time being.

The introduction of the human qualities of the Driller and the Boilerman are important here. They set the stage for a feeling of familiarity and trust.

When we are actually *on* the derrick for the first time, we are merely observers. In the first group of scenes (Group A) we are shown the changing of the bit. The old, used one is taken off and replaced by a new and sharp one. This is intercut with scenes of passing oil-barges and scenes of the boy in his canoe on his way to the derrick. We are also shown the Driller who pushes a lever, which causes the bit and the attached pipe-length to sink

152

slowly down into the well. At this point, the simple operation is still broken down into many different shots (so that in the film it takes longer than in reality) but it makes you familiar with a spatial movement : that these pipe-lengths are continuously sunk deeper into the well.

Through the intercuts from the derrick to the barges and to the boy, we are able to make the slow transition from dusk to night. They also serve to emphasise the extreme contrast between the mechanised derrick and the rustic atmosphere of the bayous so far removed from modern mechanisation. This contrast is brought even more to the foreground through the rather abrupt, almost ruthless change in sound, from very loud to very soft. This atmosphere, of something highly mechanised happening in the midst of a mysterious wilderness, lingers on subconsciously during the rest of the entire sequence.

In the next group of scenes (Group B) the boy approaches the derrick more and more. Intercut with his approach, we find ourselves sometimes *outside* the derrick seeing the enormous pipe-lengths swing, the block going up and down, or the Derrick-man bending over precariously. Sometimes we find ourselves *inside* the derrick (the boy remaining on the outside) and are allowed to look upon the operation from entirely different angles.

In the outside shots it is the huge steel tower, glimmering like a lighted Christmas tree at night, or the dangling, almost fluid pipes and the phantas-magorial rising and falling movements of the block which impress us. The interior scenes give us an impression of tremendous height. The elements Fantastic, Awe and Danger are already present and will be emphasised in later sequences. We do not know much about the operation yet, but we have seen sufficient to realise that *men* regulate all these movements.

In the next group of images (Group C) the boy has arrived on the derrick. Remaining in the background at first, he turns his head, first in one direction, then in another, overwhelmed and awed with the variety of strange things he sees happening around him. Then he is invited to come on over and he comes forward.

The element of Awe, begun in the previous sequence, is now confirmed in the boy, but we are also taken another step ahead. The accent of the scenes, intercut with the looking boy, is on the *men* and the variety of *things they do*. No attempt is made to give a didactic analysis of the operation. Each shot shows a specific detail : the sum total is, not exact knowledge of the technical operation but a first insight into the abilities of these men. The human element has been pushed to the foreground. The phantasmagorial movements observed in Group B are regulated by the manifold manipulations of the Driller, his sureness and accuracy in applying the brake and pulling the chain, by the split-second readiness of the two Roughnecks and the Derrick-man. This is no rude awakening from a magic world to a world of reality. On the contrary, our astonishment and admiration increase when we see these men at work.

In the next group of scenes (Group D) the boy has taken his place on the lazy-bench next to the Driller and finds himself in dangerously close proximity to the operation. In this group of scenes we become, always through the boy, deeper and deeper involved in the magic of human skill, strength and co-ordination which are necessary to make this derrick operate. What an almost superhuman strength it demands is brought to the foreground most par-ticularly through the quivering back and arm of the Roughneck in shots *1* and *12* and simultaneously heard through the unearthly thump on the sound-track. One is amazed. How can *one* person carry such tremendous weight ? The force with which the chain is thrown resounds in a loud, crystal-clear clatter.

But it is not abruptly and exclusively in these two shots that Strength is introduced, nor does it abruptly end with the last frame of scene *1* or *12*. It is carried over and absorbed again into the other elements—only to come to the foreground again later—or it is indicated through the sound (heard with other images) as an element of equal significance.

The Danger element, still present after its introduction in Group B, is brought to the foreground again, especially in the continuity of scenes *13-14-15-16*. The concentrated and calculated actions of the Driller pushing the pedal which tightens the chain, in combination with the twisted features of the Roughneck watching and trying to hold the chain, show the danger clearly ; should the chain slip, someone might be decapitated. The fear of the boy is shown in his face, *continued* in the twisted features of the chain-thrower in the following scene, and continued again in the next shot of the boy, who finally puts up an arm and hand to protect his face.

The element Excitement more or less dominates shot *6*, showing the boy and the Driller together, the boy following intently the downward moving pipe-length, but it is quickly replaced by the element Danger ; excitement coming to the foreground again in shot *20* from when on it retains prominence, although always accompanied by one of several other elements.

" Co-ordination and skill " come particularly to the foreground in scene *11* of the Driller. Co-ordination in movement between the two Roughnecks in shot *12* and again in the continuity of shots *14-15-16-17-18-19*. The catching of the heavy pipe-length, seemingly in the nick of time, the almost vicious chain-throwing (as if to keep the demon within bounds), the swinging into place of the heavy monkey-wrench, all timed to a split-second—as aerial acrobats catch their trapezes, so difficult, yet so graceful. This human skill and co-ordination is carried over in the shots which only show the machine function, but when the block moves up we know that this is only possible because the *men will it so*. The sum total of the combined elements forces you to accept that these men are the masters of this machine.

The deep black, surrounding the derrick, reminds us that immediately outside there is the mysterious semi-wilderness, itself untouched by the mechanisation which surrounds us.

The next four scenes (Group E) again form a unit in which " Force and power " are dominant. We see the operation from slightly farther back than heretofore. A combined effort of both, men and machine, is shown : in the image, through the two Roughnecks who are holding on for all they are worth, one to the chain, the other one to the pipe ; on the sound-track, through an acceleration of terrific noise.

" Excitement " is here too, because we look upon all this through the wondering eyes of the boy who is no longer scared.

In the final group (Group F), " Magic " and " Excitement " are the two most important elements. In shot *25*, we see for the first time the boy, all the men and the complete operation, *all in one scene*, showing us the entity of the total which we are now emotionally ready to understand. It is as if a rising curtain revealed all that might have been partly hidden before, the excitement of the combined effort, strength and skill, and the wonderment of the boy experiencing all this.

We will smile happily with the Driller in shot *26* and *28* and are as excited as the boy in shot *30*. We have a feeling of accomplishment and satisfaction when the block comes down to a rest in shot *31*.

Had the total views *25* and *29* been put at the beginning of the drilling-sequence to *explain* to the audience how it is done they would have had at the most an educational value. It would have been impossible to discover so early in the procedure the emotional elements which these shots contain.

Successful images such as shots *25* and *29* could be referred to as prize shots. Until they find their final place, they are used almost anywhere because one *wants* to use them. They have a tremendous quality in themselves but it is very hard to discover immediately what exactly it is. One tries them here and one tries them there, but only when one finds their right juxtaposition do they become alive and acquire their deeper meaning.

So far little has been said about the sound-track. Mentioning what is heard on the track during a specific shot is misleading and does not explain the function and significance of the track as a whole—as an integral part of the sequence. The track was not added as a simple accompaniment, nor was it needed as a lift to inadequate images. If you take the track away from the drilling-sequence you will find that the picture by itself is already eloquent. The elements Danger, Magic, etc., are already inherent in the image-composition. But something is missing : the element of sound.

The composition of the drilling sequence as a whole was conceived from the very beginning *with the sound as an element of equal significance.* The same breakdown of elements I used for the selection and continuity of images was applied to the sound. These elements do not necessarily come to the foreground in the track and in the image *at the same time.* Picture and track, to a certain degree, have a composition of their own but when combined they form a new entity. Thus the track becomes not only an harmonious complement but an integral, inseparable part of the picture as well. Picture and track are so closely fused together that each one functions through the other. There is no separation of *I see* in the image and *I hear* on the track. Instead, there is the *I feel, I experience,* through the grand-total of picture and track combined.

Though the track gives the impression that it is constantly an actual sound of the image, speaking strictly technically, it is not. Many details in the drilling operation happen simultaneously, and while the image shows one detail, the track may :

(1) sound the same detail,

(2) sound the same detail *plus* (in the mixed track) sound another detail, happening simultaneously, or

(3) occupy itself exclusively with another, off-screen detail.

Usually when close-up sound-effects are heard in this sequence, another, more general noise is heard simultaneously, representing the total effect of noise heard on a derrick in operation. Sometimes this general and other secondary noises are pushed quite far into the background. In this way one sound standing out in the midst of sudden silence, is more ear-shattering than the combined din of many noises. (See for instance the clattering of the chain around the pipes.) This brake applied to the quantity of sound during increased activity on the screen intensifies the emotional impact.

Finally, one word of summing up. One cannot start with an exclusive theoretical or intellectual reasoning, saying for instance : between scenes *1* and *2*, I will think *this*, or between scenes *2* and *3 that.* A lot of fumbling must go on before you reach the point where the sequence conveys the desired emotional effect. Nor should too much attention be paid to the mechanical transitions from scene to scene : these play only a comparatively minor part in the composition and unity. What makes a sequence emotionally convincing is an imaginative selection of shots and a clear development of the thought-process underlying the continuity.

9

THE DOCUMENTARY FILM OF IDEAS

THE brief analyses of sequences from Eisenstein's *October* in the first chapter give a clue to the way a silent film director set about the task of expressing ideas in the film medium. Although Eisenstein's silent films all had a rudimentary story to tell, it was the speculations arising out of the plots which seem to have interested him most and which remain the films' most notable feature. Eisenstein repeatedly allowed himself (in *October* and *Old and New*) screen time for, as it were, intellectual cadenzas for which he had to evolve his own system of film montage. He assembled series of physically unconnected images and linked them according to their intellectual content : he built sequences not so much about an event or a piece of action as about an idea. One of the difficulties of this approach, as we have already seen, was that the intellectual passages were undramatic and were therefore not easily assimilated into a film narrative.

Eisenstein himself was aware that the montage of ideas was a difficult and in many ways inadequate method of expression. He wrote in 1928 : " The tasks of theme and story grow more complicated every day ; attempts to solve these by methods of ' visual ' montage alone either lead to unresolved problems or force the director to resort to fanciful montage structures, arousing the fearsome eventuality of meaninglessness and reactionary decadence."[1] As a result, he welcomed the advent of sound, claiming that, used contrapuntally—" treated as a new montage element (as a factor divorced from the visual image) "—sound would enrich the expressiveness of his montage methods. Unfortunately, the change of policy in the Russian film industry which was initiated in the early 'thirties and the fact that Eisenstein was never allowed

[1] Film Form *by Sergei Eisenstein. Dobson, 1951, p. 257. The quotation is from* " A Statement," *written in August, 1928, and signed by Eisenstein, Pudovkin and Alexandrov.*

156

to finish *Que Viva Mexico!* have meant that his theory was left to others to put into practice.

One of the most successful films to assimilate Eisenstein's theory was Basil Wright's *Song of Ceylon*. Before going on to discuss its use of the element of sound, let us look at an excerpt.

The excerpt from Reel 3 of *Song of Ceylon*[1] is quoted below in order to illustrate the function of editing on a dialectical plus emotional basis, where both the juxtaposition of image to image, and the relation of cutting to an elaborately edited sound-track, are conceived as part of a central idea or mood, and not in terms of normal continuity. *The reel should not be considered without reference to its fellows* : it is part of a logical progression which makes up the whole film. It contains, moreover, echoes from Reels 1 and 2 and in turn provides echoes (both in sound and picture) to Reel 4. Bearing this in mind, it is possible to break down the continuity into its main elements.

First : What does it set out to say ? Broadly speaking, it says (or implies) that there is a powerful impact of Western machines, methods and commerce on the life of Ceylon ; that this impact, for all its apparent surface significance, may not be as deep as it seems ; and that the benefits of Western civilisation may be less than they are commonly supposed to be.

Second : How does it set out to say it ? By bringing together completely incongruous elements in picture and sound. It is only by the principles of montage employed that the incongruous elements become congruous and then only when they *unfold in sequence*.

It is not easy to choose a brief excerpt for analysis because the reel depends on the continuity of visual-cum-sound effect. Wherever one breaks off, one is leaving things in the air. However, here is a brief passage from the opening of the reel.

SONG OF CEYLON

Extract from Reel 3

After the title, *Voices of Commerce*, we hear the whistle and puffing of a locomotive which begins before the fade-in. The fade-in reveals that the camera is on a train travelling through the jungle. There are several shots. We pass a woman walking beside the railway track ; then a small station. A slow dissolve takes us to a shot of an elephant pushing against a tree, clearing the jungle. The sound of the locomotive gets slower and slower as the elephant continues pushing (the sound of the locomotive was produced artificially in the studio in order to get the exact speed to coincide with the elephant's movements). The train has nearly come to a standstill when its sound is drowned by the splintering and creaking of the tree as it is uprooted and tilts over. The tree crashes ; as it hits the ground, there is the stroke of an enormous gong (a recurring *motif*), the vibrations of which continue over the subsequent shot—the elephant and his *mahout* towering over the prostrate tree.

Almost at once a voice comes in briskly : " New clearings, new roads, new buildings, new communications, new developments of natural resources . . . " Meanwhile, the scene changes to a procession of elephants breasting a steep hill in single file, each carrying a block of granite. Their trumpetings (the sound was purposely produced artificially in the studio) are cross-cut with the sound of the clatter of typewriters.

The scene dissolves to a long shot of a boy coming through a coconut grove towards camera ; we hear three different voices, inter-cut rapidly

[1] *Notes by Basil Wright.*

with each other, all dictating business letters. These are so timed that when the boy gets to the foot of the tree he is just about to climb and raises his hands in prayer to the god of the tree, the three voices repeat, one after the other, " Yours faithfully . . . " The boy starts to climb the tree and now the sound is the music which, in Reel 2, was used with the villagers praying to the priest. This is drowned almost at once . . .

This short excerpt, incomplete and approximately described though it is, should be sufficient to give an impression of the technique employed. The juxtaposition of sound and picture is such that the two unrelated factors produce an entirely new quality which neither has on its own. There is in many instances no physical connection between them but the simultaneous impact of sound-track and images—the boy praying and the business man dictating " Yours faithfully," for example—produces overtones of meaning which, if perhaps not fully comprehended, are nevertheless felt by the spectator. There is no simple continuity of action in the editing (much less in the sound) : the effect of continuity is achieved through a continuous flow of ideas and emotion.

Although *Song of Ceylon* itself has an emotional quality rare in any film, it is as well to consider how far its method is universally applicable. The objections to Eisenstein's films can be equally raised here. Much of the meaning of *Song of Ceylon* remains elusive on first viewing—a fact which is as much due to the complexity of the theme as to the director's way of expressing it. Certainly, it requires a trained sensibility on the part of the spectator if it is to be fully grasped. While this is in no way an adverse criticism of its montage methods, it makes it unlikely that they will be extensively emulated by many other film-makers : minority films of this kind have, unfortunately, come to be a rare luxury.

But a further, more important question suggests itself in connection with Wright's use of a sound track which operates independently of the picture. How widely is the method applicable ?

The theme of *Song of Ceylon* is the essential duality of life in Ceylon : on the one side the Western influence ; on the other, the traditional behaviour and life of the Sinhalese. The theme itself is, in this sense, peculiarly well suited to the treatment. Wright uses—not altogether consistently—the sound and picture to evoke respectively the two different aspects of life in Ceylon. Throughout Reel 3 we are shown in the picture the routine of native life in Ceylon and in the sound-track the sounds associated with the Europeans who control it—as if unseen forces were guiding the natives' lives. It is only by making the rhythm of the sound-track conform to the rhythm of the images that a kind

158

of physical unity is preserved. (The most obvious instance of this is the timing of the sound of the locomotive which is artificially made to harmonise with the rhythm of movements in the picture—i.e., the elephant pushing against the tree.) Bearing in mind the special circumstances of the theme of *Song of Ceylon*, one may conclude that the highly complex montage method employed in Reel 3 is only of a limited application, and that a more conservative approach to film continuity (such as the film employs in other sequences) is of more general use.

Here, for instance, is another continuity, quite clearly expressing a complex of ideas (and emotions), but which uses a simpler editing scheme.

DIARY FOR TIMOTHY[1]

Excerpt from Reel 3

An imaginative film essay about the war and its impact on the lives of ordinary people in Britain. The whole film is presented in the form of a diary recorded for a child born late in the war. The commentary (written by E. M. Forster and spoken by Michael Redgrave) introduces the various events as if addressing the child.

After a shot of the baby, Timothy, the commentator introduces various activities taking place up and down the country, finishing with a land-mine being exploded on a beach.

Dissolve to :

			Ft.
1	Leafless branches in the crown of a tree. *Camera tilts down* to reveal a man raking autumn leaves in a London park.	*Commentator :* But suppose you went up to London. London in November looks a nice quiet place.	10
2	Men digging on an allotment. Autumn mist.	—But you'll find things are chancy here too ; and the bad mixed with the good.	$6\frac{1}{2}$
3	The top of the Haymarket Theatre, displaying a large notice " Hamlet."	—You never know what's coming. *Voice of Grave-digger slowly fades in :* *Grave-digger :* I came to't that day that our last king Hamlet overcame Fortinbras.	$7\frac{1}{2}$
4	Inside the theatre. Hamlet and Grave-digger on stage.	*Hamlet :* How long is that since ? *Grave-digger :* Cannot you tell that ? Every fool can tell that ; it was the very day that young Hamlet was born ;	$10\frac{1}{2}$

[1] *Director : Humphrey Jennings. Editor : Alan Osbiston. Crown Film Unit, 1945.*

5   L.S. Stage from the back of the theatre.

he that is mad, and sent into England.
Hamlet :
   Ay, marry ; why was he sent into England ?
Grave-digger :
   Why, because he was mad : he shall recover his wits there ; or, if he do not, it's no great matter there.
Laughter.

181⁄2

---

6   Canteen.   M.S.   Man sitting at table and talking over a cup of tea.

Laughter dies away.
Man :
   Well, if this is the launching-site and that's the objective—two hundred miles between—and they launch one of those gadgets from here, rising at an angle of 45 degrees, to a height of 60 miles ; it travels at 300 m.p.h.—

36

---

7   Canteen. *Camera a little farther back* to include the men he is talking to.

—How long does it take to reach the objective ?   D'you know ?

11

---

8   M.S. Hamlet on stage.

Hamlet :
   Nay, I know not.
Grave-digger :
   A pestilence on him for a mad rogue ! a' poured a flagon of Rhenish on my head once. This same skull, sir, was Yorick's skull, the king's jester.
Hamlet :
   This ?
Grave-digger :
   E'en that.
Hamlet :
   Let me see—Alas, poor Yorick !

34

---

9   Canteen. *As in 7.*
An explosion rocks the house. The man's cup is upset. A commotion starts.

Man :
   Had to walk all the way home.
A loud explosion is heard.

17

---

10   C.S. Hamlet, skull in hand.

Hamlet :
   Here hung those lips that I have kissed I know not how oft. Where be your gibes now ? your gambols ? your song ? your flashes of merriment, that were wont to set the table on a roar ? Now get you to my lady's chamber, and tell her, let her paint an inch thick, to this favour she must come ; make her laugh at that.

47

---

11   Exterior.   Men clearing rubble after the explosion.

It is not easy to analyse in detail the niceties of idea and emotion conveyed by this passage. A sequence of this kind is made by the director to express the complex of thoughts and feelings in the manner it does, precisely because the same effect cannot be achieved in any other way : verbal description is therefore bound to fall short of capturing the complete meaning. The inter-weaving pattern of the continuity creates an effect which is not to be described in words, for the final impact on the spectator is more complex than the mere reception of two parallel events : the construction and timing of the images fuse the two events in the spectator's mind in a manner only possible in the cinema. The passage, in other words, is so purely cinematic that a description of the way it achieves its effect cannot begin to describe the effect itself. Bearing this in mind, we can merely analyse the form of the presentation without doing justice to the content.

Diary for Timothy sets out to portray and assess the various forces at play in war-time Britain, and a part of the intention of cross-cutting the stage performance of Hamlet with the scene in the canteen is to convey the simple fact that the two events occur simultaneously : side by side with the spirit of war-time Britain (manifested, in this case, by the man's ingenuous interest in the mechanics of destruction and apparent indifference to the actual physical danger) went a marked revival of interest in the arts. Jennings' intention in presenting the scenes in this way is, presumably, to suggest that the two things are not entirely unconnected.

But beside this surface connection, there is a deeper level of contact between the two streams of action. The Grave-digger's reference to England (" Why was he sent into England ? " " Why, because he was mad ; he shall recover his wits there ") is, one feels, a comment on the scene in the canteen.

Again, Hamlet's lines in shot *10* provide a poignant commentary on the events of shots *9* and *11* : the director's subtly nostalgic feeling towards the scene in the canteen—and, by implication, to the whole period—is made to reach the spectator in Hamlet's words.

To stress the unity of emotion between the two streams of action, the cuts are sometimes made to coincide with straight verbal links. For instance, the phrasing of the lines in shot *7* (". . . D'you know ? ") is such that Hamlet appears to be answering the question in shot *8*.

Similarly, the cut from *8* to *9* (" Alas, poor Yorick ! " . . . " Had to walk all the way home ") creates a verbal continuity with exactly the kind of affectionately ironic overtone which characterises the whole of the film.

The unity between the two actions is further emphasised by smoothing over all the transitions between them. This is done either through the verbal links we have already mentioned or by making an actual sound carry over the cut : (see the laughter over *5-6*, the sound of explosion over *9–10*). In this way the two scenes are knit together so closely as to come over to the spectator as a complex but homogeneous continuity. In contrast with the Eisenstein approach to editing, the cuts do not so much make points themselves ; they switch the argument about and keep it going at different levels.

Clearly, the continuity of *Diary for Timothy* exemplifies an entirely different approach to the film of ideas from that employed in *Song of Ceylon*. The effects are not achieved by the collision of shot with shot, but through a deliberately smooth continuity. The sound is not physically independent of the picture. It is, instead, in each case the sound of the scene being played on the screen and the effect is achieved by inter-cutting the scenes themselves. But this is not a completely representative instance of Jennings' usual technique, for, in addition to actual sounds, Jennings employed a commentary in most of his films. *Family Portrait*, for instance, his last film, which is a personal essay on the genius of the British people, has a commentary throughout. Here Jennings is dealing with highly complex ideas which it would have been impossible to convey in pictures alone. His commentary does not so much describe what is happening on the screen, as speculate on the significance and ramifications of the images. It leads, in a sense, just as much a life of its own as does Wright's sound-track, but it does so in words. Unexpected visual associations—for which Jennings had a particular talent—which would be all but meaningless without comment are given point by a hint from the commentator. The words and images interweave, now the one, now the other becoming the dominant.

What Jennings seems to have realised was that, to express ideas of a certain complexity, it is not possible to rely on pictures alone. If an idea is to be raised, then it must be done in the first instance in words. He seems to have been well aware of Eisenstein's " fanciful montage structures arousing the fearsome eventuality of meaninglessness," and therefore guided his audience by using an economical and highly suggestive commentary. The point really is that Jennings' commentaries are always suggestive, never descriptive. The few words preceding the passage we have quoted—and they are not a particularly good example—do not explain what is happening ; they set the key, so to speak, to the kind of thinking the spectator will be expected to do in the next few moments. Jennings' commentaries almost invariably deal with universals while his images deal with particulars. This is perhaps most spectacularly borne out in *Words for Battle*, where quotations from the English poets are heard while scenes of everyday life in war-time Britain are shown on the screen.

It is likely that if the intellectual film essay is to develop in the future, it will have to do so along the lines used by Jennings rather than those envisaged by Eisenstein. The kind of abrupt, shock-packed continuity which Eisenstein's " intellectual montage " inevitably entails is entirely out of tune with the current tradition of film-making. Moreover, there is a marked difference in level between Eisenstein's and Jennings' films. (This is no disparagement of Eisenstein's films which were designed to appeal to a broader, less sophisticated audience, although even to that, parts of *October* and *Old and New* proved unacceptable.) The long montage in *October* ridiculing religious ceremonies or the repetitive passage suggesting Kerensky's vanity, manages to convey only relatively simple ideas. Jennings' films work at an altogether higher level, yet they have a direct, easily assimilated appeal. For the film of ideas which is to be commercially possible, Jennings' synthesis of simplified montage effects and suggestive commentary seems to offer an ideal solution.

10

THE DOCUMENTARY AND THE USE OF SOUND

THE short sound continuity from *Song of Ceylon* which we have examined makes scarcely any use of actual sounds. Basil Wright uses his sound-track to throw oblique comment on his images rather than to add a further realistic dimension to his presentation : actual sounds, therefore, are irrelevant to his purpose.

Another instance of a similar use of commentative sound occurs in Pare Lorentz's *The Plough that Broke the Plains*. A sequence examining the state of American agriculture during the 1914–1918 war shows a series of shots of the countryside with farmers working on the land. Behind this we hear a military march, the steps of marching soldiers, gunfire and a commentary spoken as if on a parade ground. Partly, of course, this implies that the steady, regular routine of the farmer's year goes on while soldiers are fighting at the front. But there is an additional overtone of meaning: the continuity suggests that war-time farming had assumed something of the urgency and controlled discipline of an army. These sentiments are not directly expressed in the commentary : the comment provided by the contrast in the rhythm and content of the sound and images in itself conveys the desired effect.

Since similar experiments are comparatively rare in fiction films, the use of commentative sound in ways akin to those described has become one of the most noted features of documentary film-making. British documentary directors of the thirties gave serious attention to the ways the sound-track could be employed to enrich a film's final appeal ; as far as an imaginative use of sound is concerned, they pursued an altogether more adventurous policy than their studio colleagues. Part of the reason for this may have been simple necessity. Financial considerations often made it impossible—even where it would have been otherwise desirable— to take sound equipment up and down the country. Further, as Rotha pointed out, " Sound-trucks are . . . large and cumbersome

164

objects. They attract attention, disturb the natural character of the material being shot and upset the intimacy which the documentalist tries to create between himself and his subject."[1] Thus the temptation to make do with a straightforward track of actual sounds in many cases did not even arise.

A more important reason for the wide experimenting with commentative sound lies in the nature of documentary film-making itself. The visual continuity of documentaries is often necessarily rather fragmentary because physically unconnected images are being edited into a continuous sequence. In cases of this sort the use of actual sound not only presents insuperable technical difficulties, but also serves no useful purpose.

Sequences employing simpler visual continuities, on the other hand, can often be made to gain immensely from actual sounds. In a film dealing with human situations and designed to evoke an emotional response from the spectator, the creation of mood remains one of the main problems. The counterpart of this difficulty in a story-film lies to a considerable extent in the director's ability to guide his actors in speech and gestures : this, of course, is an entirely different problem. The documentary director does not normally work through dramatised incidents and must therefore convey mood in other ways. It is here that actual sounds can be of the greatest value. Synchronous and non-synchronous sounds can come into play.

The skill in fitting effects to a picture is partly, of course, finding a sound-track which effectively matches the picture or action appearing on the screen and arranging it so that the two appear synchronous. But a more interesting sidelight on this process is achieving an effect by laying, not the sound represented by what is seen on the screen, but by what may be happening just round the corner—out of range of the camera. For instance, to cover an empty street in the early morning in Manchester we might use the characteristic sound of hooves of dray horses clip-clopping along the cobbled street. It is quite extraordinary how a very dull shot on the screen is somehow brought to life by this sort of technique.[2]

In making *Listen to Britain*, Humphrey Jennings set himself the task of re-creating the atmosphere of war-time London, primarily through the characteristic sounds associated with the time. That he succeeded most brilliantly in doing so is testimony not only to his skill, but also evidence of the great emotional power of actual sounds. A detailed analysis of the sound-track of *Listen to Britain* would be almost impossible. For one thing, the

[1] Documentary Film *by Paul Rotha. Faber, 1936, p. 208.*
[2] Sound and the Documentary Film *by Ken Cameron. Pitman, 1947, p. 8.*

sound effects are too complex and depend for their effect too closely on the precise quality of the sounds themselves. For another, the emotional effect of sounds on the spectator is less direct than that of images and is therefore less readily described. As Ken Cameron has pointed out, " the effect [of sound] on the emotions depends more upon the association of ideas than upon . . . the sound itself. For example, the sound of an anti-aircraft gun and shells in the sky may be just what they represent and nothing more to an audience in Chicago. To an audience which has lived in London throughout the war they will conjure up ideas which are anything but commonplace."[1] The reader must therefore go to see (and hear) *Listen to Britain* if he is to get a clear idea of the way Jennings creates his effects.

To achieve the desired tempo and rhythm of presentation, the fiction-film director directs his scenes at the varying speeds appropriate, and subsequently sees to it that the rhythm of his direction is reinforced in the editing. In a documentary, individual shots—often of inanimate objects—tend to have no inherent rhythm of their own which the editor can work to. The shots are given a rhythmic value only when they come to be edited. (We have already seen in the excerpt from *Merchant Seamen* how a shot of the calm ocean can be effortlessly placed in a sequence of great speed and excitement.) Sound—actual or commentative—can play a most important role in this process of controlling the pace and rhythm of the originally inert shots. Here is a well-known example in which commentative sounds only are used.

NIGHT MAIL[2]

Extract from Reel 3

An imaginative documentary showing how night mail trains convey mail from London to the north of Scotland.
    The extract is from a sequence showing the train's journey through Scotland. Two slow panning shots of the mountain scenery through which the train is travelling just before daybreak, precede.

		Ft. fr.
Mountain scenery. Nearer dawn. *Camera pans slowly to reveal a train coming up through the valley.*	*Wind.* Commentator (Voice A) : This is the night mail crossing the border, Bringing the cheque and the postal order, Letters for the rich, letters for the poor,	24

[1] Ibid., *p. 8.*
[2] *Directors : Basil Wright, Harry Watt. Editor : R. Q. McNaughton. Sound Direction : Cavalcanti, W. H. Auden, Benjamin Britten. G.P.O. Film Unit, 1935.*

Slow rhythmic music fades in very gently.

2	L.S. Train coming across the valley.	The shop at the corner and the girl next door, Pulling up Beattock, a steady climb— The gradient's against her but she's on time. *Over the last line of commentary music is turned sharply up.*	11	
3	M.S. Stoker and driver shovelling coal into the boiler.	*Music continues : harsh, rhythmic ; as if in time with the sound of engine pistons.*	9	7
4	C.S. Boiler gate as shovel of coal enters.	*Music continues.*	6	
5	M.S. Stoker and driver. *As in 3.*	*Music continues.*	3	6
6	C.S. Hands on handle of shovel as they swing forward.	*Music continues.*	1	14
7	C.S. Engine driver looking on.	*Music continues.*	3	3
8	Front of engine, as seen from driver's cabin.	*Music fades down.* Past cotton grass and moorland boulder,	3	8
9	L.S. Train. *Tracking shot,* keeping train locomotive just *in frame to the left.*	Shovelling white steam over her shoulder, Snorting noisily as she passes Silent miles of wind-bent grasses ; Birds turn their heads—	12	3
10	C.S. Locomotive wheels.	—as she approaches, Stare from the bushes—	2	12
11	Passing trees, as seen from moving train.	—at her blank-faced coaches ;	1	12
12	Front of locomotive ; from left side of driver's cabin as the train goes under a bridge.	Sheepdogs cannot turn her course They slumber on with paws across ;	7	14
13	Looking over engine driver's cabin. *Camera facing* in direction of train's movement.	In the farm she passes no one wakes But a jug in the bedroom gently shakes. *Tempo of music slows down to long calm phrases.*	10	10
14	*Slow panning shot* of clouds at dawn.	*Music continues calm.* Dawn freshens—	12	2
15	C.S. Driver as he lifts his cap and wipes his brow with a handkerchief.	—the climb is done. *Music continues calm to end of shot 20.*	5	7

167

			Ft.	fr.
16	*Dissolve to :* Engine driver's panel. *Camera pans to left* to take in scenery as train speeds by.	Commentator (*Voice B*) : Down towards Glasgow she descends Towards the steam tugs, yelping down the glade of cranes Towards the fields of apparatus,	15	5
17	*Dissolve to :* L.S. Furnaces and chimneys.	—the furnaces, Set on the dark plain like gigantic chessmen.	6	6
18	*Dissolve to :* L.S. Valley with hills in background.	All Scotland waits for her ;	5	14
19	*Dissolve to :* Cottage in the valley.	In the dark glens beside the pale-green sea-lochs,	3	11
20	*Dissolve to :* Valley with hills in background.	Men long for news.	3	8
21	*C.S.* Wheels of engines ; fast rhythmic motion of pistons.	Commentator (*Voice A*) : Letters of thanks, letters from banks ; Letters of joy from the girl and boy . . .	4	5

The sequence[1] was the only part of the film which was not fully scripted before production began : its necessity had been agreed on at an earlier stage, but its actual shape was not evolved until the rest of the film was already in rough-cut. Some of the shooting had been done (speculatively) on location, but a few extra shots had to be obtained after Auden's verses had been agreed on. In general, it may be said that the editing tempo and the pictorial juxtapositions were largely determined by the previous composition of words and music ; (though this is rather a dangerous statement to make, since the whole job was a to-and-fro synthesis of effort involving Watt, Auden, McNaughton, Britten, Cavalcanti and myself : it would perhaps be better to say that the whole sequence resulted from a simultaneous group effort in terms of music track, word track and pictorial material). We were not working entirely in the dark, since we had the experiment of *Coal Face* on which to base our work.

The order of procedure was something like this : 1. The commentary was discussed, written and recorded : while recording voice A, a visual metronome was used to ensure a regular beat in the reading of the rhythmic passages ; 2. The picture was cut to fit in with the recorded words ; 3. Britten composed the score after seeing the above and recorded the music while listening to the words through ear-phones ; 4. The picture and words were slightly re-edited to fit in with the music.

The excerpt quoted consists of four separate phases, each with its own *motif* :

(1) Shots *1–13* : "*The gradient's against her.*" The theme of

[1] *Notes by Basil Wright.*

the images in this part is the effort and strain of the train making its uphill journey : each image contributes to this effect. Throughout, a definite and constant beat—as if keeping time with the straining movement of the pistons—is maintained.

Over shots *1* and *2* this rhythm is established by the commentary. The images show the train with its regular puffs of smoke emerging from the funnel, and are therefore easily linked in the spectator's mind with the rhythm of the words : thus the two opening shots—which establish the new sequence—can be left on the screen for a relatively long time without losing their rhythmic quality.

The following shots *3–7* do not contain any pronounced beat of their own. Here, therefore, the beat is produced by accelerating the rate of cutting and by the more strongly dominating musical phrases.

In *8–13* the commentary takes over again and its beat is, this time, further reinforced by the cutting.

(2) Shots *13–15* : "*The Climb is done.*" This is a transition passage showing the relaxation coming after the long climb. A visual clue is provided to this by *15*, where the engine driver pauses to wipe his brow and to take a short breather. But the main impression of relaxation of effort is conveyed by the breaking up of the rhythm which was established in the previous part. The line " Dawn freshens. The Climb is done." has no regular beat and the music becomes calm : the sense of strain of the opening shots is gently slackened.

(3) Shots *15–20* : " *All Scotland waits for her.*" This is a short descriptive passage. Any sort of beat which might be produced by cuts is consciously suppressed by linking all the shots through dissolves ; the naturally spoken blank verse becomes straightforward description and temporarily diverts attention from the train. The tempo is calm, contemplative, expectant.

(4) Shot *21* : " *Letters . . . Letters . . . Letters . . .* " Abruptly, the tempo is changed. After the slow, meandering passage, a cut takes us sharply to a shot of the fast-revolving wheels and the brisk staccato commentary starts up. The train, we are made to understand, after its struggle uphill and its relaxed progress at the summit, is now freewheeling down into the valley.

The passage from *Night Mail* was chosen for analysis because it makes use of almost every kind of sound device available to the recordist. It demonstrates the degree of complexity which may be necessary in a sound track to achieve a complete effect.

It is interesting to note, moreover, that in this instance the rhythmic variations in the passage (which are controlled by the sound) *explain* the sense of the sequence : the quick, accelerating rhythm in shot *21* and onwards, for instance, in itself conveys to the audience that the train is free-wheeling downhill—the fact is not established visually or in the commentary. The control of rhythm is here the decisive factor in making film sense of the images.

The order of procedure which was adopted—editing the visuals *after* the sound-track—is, of course, the reverse of the usual. Here, it has obvious advantages : the passage depends in the first instance on establishing a rhythm and it was therefore easier to " anchor " the beat (i.e., record the sound-track) before finally settling the visual continuity. This is not to say that the method is always preferable to the more normal routine : each problem and each individual director must choose his procedure on the merits of the individual case. But the fact that it is perfectly reasonable to compose the sound-track before the picture in imaginative documentaries of this sort shows that here the sound has become more than a mere adjunct to the picture : the two are of equal and complementary importance.

Documentary film-making is, to-day, more and more tending towards the straight propaganda film : sponsors usually insist on a clearly stated " message." This, unfortunately, means that more and more directors are coming to rely on the commentary to carry the substance of their films : the images remain useful only to illustrate or to clarify certain concepts which are more readily demonstrated in pictures than in words. The result is, at best, a pleasantly illustrated government pamphlet or an ingeniously contrived commercial brochure with pictures. From an aesthetic point of view, however, these films are valueless—as perhaps in some cases they are meant to be.

This does seem to be a waste of good opportunity. Documentary directors are in a uniquely favourable position to experiment with the use of their sound-tracks. To throw away this chance by using a continuous—however beautifully written—descriptive commentary is to waste one of the modern film's main and yet only partially explored assets—imaginative sound.

11

EDUCATIONAL FILMS

THE aim of the documentary or story-film editor is the creation of mood, the dramatisation of events. To the editor of educational films, these considerations are largely irrelevant. The purpose of his films is to teach and his aims must be clarity, logical exposition and a correct assessment of the audience's receptivity.

The editing of educational films is largely determined at the script stage. A logical flow of ideas and the correct placing of emphasis on the important facets of the exposition must be worked out in the script if the final result is to be satisfactory. More than with any other kind of film, it is necessary to make each point with the utmost precision and this cannot be done unless the aim is clear throughout the production process. With the script written, the continuity is further sharpened by judicious direction—in the placing of the camera, in the use of camera movement to link two ideas, and so on. If the script and shooting have been intelligently handled, the work left over to be done on the editing bench then usually only consists of assembling the shots in script order and timing them to fit the commentary. No purpose will be served here, however, if we consider scripting, directing and editing as three separate functions, for they are all part of the same process of exposition. No amount of brilliant shooting and editing can convey clearly an idea which has been inadequately analysed in the script.

The general aim of the editor of educational films should be smoothness of presentation. One shot must follow smoothly after another if the audience is not to be confused. A story-film editor can sometimes deliberately use a harsh cut or a surprise effect to give the audience a jolt ; this is almost certainly unwise in a teaching film, because it is *intended* to create a momentary confusion and will divert the spectator's attention away from the argument.

It must be stated at the outset that there is a distinction between instructional and teaching films. It is a difference of aims corresponding to the differing functions of the instructor and the teacher. An instructional film is concerned with drills, manipulative skills and rules of handling : whether it is made for apprentices in a particular craft or for a general audience, the order of scenes is more or less fixed by the actual procedure adopted in practice. The editing problem is to convey the nature and order of events as clearly, yet as concisely, as possible. A teaching film, on the other hand, deals with less tangible material : its topics range from the most general ideas or theories to expositions of complex principles in science or aesthetics. Logical inference takes the place of continuity of action and the editing problem is therefore completely different.

The first canon in the making of instructional films is to avoid any confusion in the mind of the spectator about the relation of each shot to what precedes and follows. Something easily recognisable in each shot must carry the eye forward to the next. This means in practice that every change of view (i.e., every cut) should be motivated by a deliberate action or camera movement. Failing all else, the pointing finger may have to be used before a cut to provide a suitable movement carrying the attention forward. Normally, however, a natural piece of action—an upward glance from a character, for instance, taking us naturally with a cut to a shot of an aeroplane—is preferable, because it makes the change of view more inevitable. Alternatively, the same effect may be achieved by panning or tracking the camera until a piece of mechanism singled out for attention is in the centre of the frame ; after this, cutting to a close shot of the mechanism makes a logical piece of continuity while establishing beforehand the geographical position of the detail in relation to the whole.

In working with diagrams or models, these conventions are still valid—a principle often ignored by animators. Diagrams should, as a rule, not be used unless there is no other way of explaining a point with equal clarity. When diagrams *are* used, it is most important to make exactly clear what they refer to, and which portion of the previous picture they are showing in detail. This is accomplished most simply by the matched dissolve, but numerous other simple continuity devices are possible. Models are used in the same way ; they are particularly useful in the

172

exposition of the inside workings of machinery which can normally not be photographed. Many instructional films have used the device of introducing a sectional model of a piece of equipment at the appropriate stage in the argument (by matching its position on the screen with the position of the actual apparatus in the previous shot), and then dismantling the sectional model piece by piece. The camera is not moved so that bit by bit the " works " of the model are made visible, while the relation of each part to the whole is kept clear. This is only a simple example, but it shows the kind of continuity which must be aimed at when complete clarity of exposition is desired.

To illustrate how an instructional film can be made visually clear by using the continuity devices which we have briefly noted above, let us look at a sequence from a film which uses no commentary but attempts to clarify an intricate process in pictures alone.

CASTING IN STEEL AT WILSON'S FORGE[1]

Extract from Reel 2

> Part I *(Making a Mould) shows the various processes concerned in preparing moulds for mine-tub wheels. It ends showing a line of moulds ready for the molten steel.* Part II, *quoted here, shows the preparation of the steel, and* Part III *(Pouring and Finishing) shows how the molten steel is poured into the previously prepared moulds.*
> *The film is silent throughout.*

TITLE : Part II : Melting and Converting

		Ft.
	Fade in	
1	Exterior Foundry. M.S. Base of Cupola. Ladle on crane-hook standing under spout of cupola. One of the furnacemen is unplugging the tap-hole with an iron tapping bar.	24
2	C.S. Spout. *Shooting across top of ladle.* Furnaceman moves away. A long-handled " pricker " is pushed in from out of picture and finishes unplugging the tap-hole. Molten iron runs down into the ladle.	23
3	M.S. Base of Cupola. *As in* 1. The molten metal running into the ladle. A " tap-hole rammer " *comes into picture* and is rested on the cross-bar of the ladle. It has a plug of clay pressed on to the end.	9
4	C.S. Spout. *As in* 2. The ladle is now nearly full of molten metal. The rammer is pushed in and twisted until the flow of metal stops.	12
5	M.S. Base of Cupola. *As in* 3. The rammer is withdrawn and the furnaceman comes into picture. He skims off the slag from the top of the ladle. His mate *comes in past camera* and takes up his position at one side of the ladle.	20
6	M.S. Furnaceman. He throws the slag on the ground, *camera panning,* where it is " killed " by throwing a spadeful of floor-sand on it. *Camera pans back to previous position.*	17
7	M.S. Base of Cupola. *As in* 5. The furnaceman finishes skimming and throws down his spoon.	4

[1] *Director and Editor : R. K. Neilson Baxter. Basic Film Unit for Ministry of Education, 1947.*

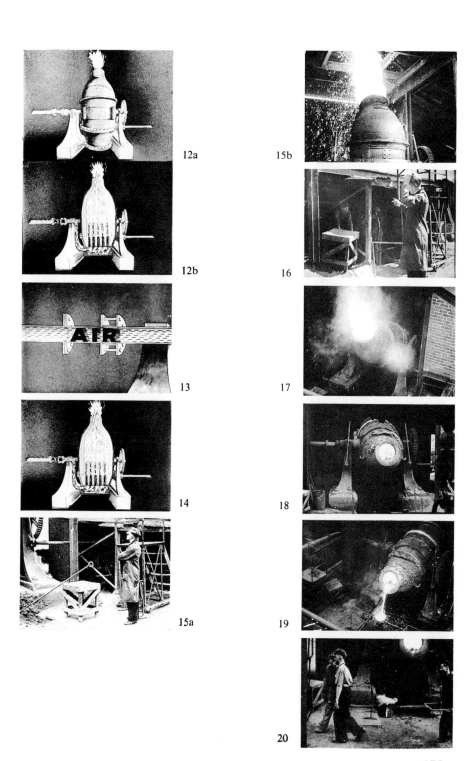

12a

12b

13

14

15a

15b

16

17

18

19

20

8   *F.S.* Bessemer Converter, from behind ladle. The converter is in its   30
horizontal position. Ladle is lifted (by the crane, out of picture) and
swung across to the mouth of the converter. The furnaceman and his
mate go up on rostrums at either side and the ladle is passed up to them.
Furnaceman starts to turn control-wheel.

9   *M.S. side angle,* Bessemer Converter. Furnaceman turns control-wheel   36
and contents of ladle pour into converter.

10   *F.S.* Bessemer Converter. *As in* 8. Contents of ladle finish pouring into   28
converter and it is swung away upside down. Furnaceman and mate
come down from their rostrum and wheel them out.

11   *L.S. high angle,* Bessemer Converter. It starts to turn up from the   44
horizontal and, as it does so, starts to '' blow.'' Fumes rise from the
top as the impurities start to burn off. Sparks of molten metal fly out.
Dissolve to :

12   *Diagram. F.S.* Bessemer Converter. *Approximately as in previous scene.*   18
After a few feet, exterior of converter *dissolves away* so that it appears in
cross-section This shows the air entering from the duct at the side and
passing up through the tuyeres into the molten metal. Fumes and flames
rise from the surface of the metal.

13   *Diagram. C.S.* Air Duct. To establish the word '' Air.''   10

14   *Diagram. F.S.* Bessemer Converter. *As in* 11. Animation as before.   16
Fade out.
Fade in.

15   Exterior Foundry. *M.S.* Chemist, looking up out of picture. *Camera*   16
pans to top of converter. A long flame is shooting up from the top of it.

16   *M.S.* Chemist. He pulls off his goggles and signs to the men in the winch-   10
house. They begin to turn the winch.

17   *L.S. high angle,* Bessemer Converter. It turns down from the vertical   22
towards the horizontal position.

18   *F.S.* Bessemer Converter, looking into the mouth of it, stationary, in the   8
horizontal position. Blowing has ceased.

19   *L.S. high angle,* Bessemer Converter. Two foundrymen move in with   31
small ladle. They place ladle on rails below converter mouth. Converter
tilts slightly and metal pours from it into ladle. The furnaceman pushes
back any slag in the lip of the converter mouth to let the metal pour
easily, and the foundrymen move away to avoid the splashes. When the
ladle is full, the converter tips up again, the two foundrymen move back
and a third one puts an anti-glare cover on top of the ladle.

20   *M.S.* Bessemer Converter. *As in* 18. Third foundryman placing cover on   18
ladle. He places a cross-bar under the left-hand end of the carrying bar
and the three men lift the ladle and carry it into the foundry.
Fade out.

The first shot establishes the position of the apparatus. The camera is placed to show the exact position of the cupola-spout (down which the metal will flow) relative to the ladle (which will receive the metal). We see in the background that a furnaceman is doing something to the tap-hole of the cupola ; this leads to the second shot where the tap-hole is shown from the front. The two shots are clearly linked because we see the same pieces of apparatus and the same furnaceman. The head-on view of the cupola-spout (*2*) shows that the long tap-hole rammer is in fact opening the tap-hole and causes the steel to pour into the ladle.

In actual practice, it takes some considerable time for the ladle to fill up with molten metal but there is obviously no point in showing the whole process here. The camera set up in *3* makes it impossible for us to see how full the ladle is, so that when we cut back to *4* we are readily prepared to believe that the ladle is now full, although we have seen in a few seconds a process which might take several minutes.

The position of the rammer acts as a visual link between *4* and *5* and we now see (*5*) that the furnaceman is skimming something off the top of the molten metal.

His action is continued in *6* where the camera movement emphasises how the slag is " killed."

The camera pans back to the furnaceman and his action is taken up in *7* which indicates that the process is now over.

Shot *8* is the beginning of the second manipulation of pouring the iron from the ladle into the converter. The camera is set at a slight side angle to show exactly how the ladle and converter are placed relative to each other. The crane which carries the ladle is not considered of any particular importance and is left out of the picture.

Shot *9* continues the turning movement started in the previous shot ; here the camera set-up again ensures that we see clearly what is happening ; *10* continues the action to show how the ladle is removed.

We are now left with the converter in the centre of the frame (end of shot *10*) and we cut to *11*, enabling us to get a better view of the turning movement.

At this stage it is necessary to show what goes on inside the converter and this must be shown by diagram. A matched dissolve introduces this so that there can be no doubt about what it refers to. The diagram then changes to a sectional view, and since it is important to establish the fact that air is being driven through the converter, a close view of the inlet pipe (*13*) is shown.

The diagram sequence is shown at some length because the process of converting goes on for a considerable time. Similarly, the fade which follows makes it clear that there is a passage of time between *14* and *15*.

The camera movement in *15* shows that the chemist is looking at the top of the converter.

In *16*, we see by his gesture that he judges the process to have finished, and the men begin to turn the winch.

The effect of their turning appears in the next shot (*17*) and in *18* the head-on view of the converter establishes that the blowing has finally ceased.

177

The pouring of the metal is now viewed from a new camera set-up to reveal the action to best advantage (*19*), and the movement of placing the cover over the small ladle is continued in *20* to take us smoothly to the last shot.

This rather tedious detailed description of the editing of a complete passage has been given here in order to show how *every* cut is motivated by a deliberate piece of action or a camera movement. Complete clarification of each step is the primary necessity of an instructional film and it has seemed pertinent to analyse a sequence in detail to show how it is done. In addition, it is worth noting that the director has been at great pains to use as few camera set-ups as possible in order not to complicate the issue ; the first seven shots, for instance, are edited from shots taken from only three set-ups.

This excerpt from *Casting in Steel at Wilson's Forge* presents the problem of instructional film-making at its simplest. The film was intended for a general audience and there was no need to show the processes in any great detail. The subject is, moreover, fairly simple, and could be presented by following the order of operations adopted in practice. Not all subjects are as simple as this. Many points of detail may have to be shown repeatedly from different viewpoints in order to make them perfectly clear and in such cases a commentary will be essential to let the audience know exactly which stage of operations they are asked to view more than once.

A commentary is, of course, extremely valuable in any event. A hint from the commentator can draw the spectator's attention straight to the point and can keep the flow of thought in the desired channel. But it should never be used to convey something the visuals can convey better or to cover up mistakes in the shooting. As any instructor will testify, a practical demonstration is more convincing than complex verbal explanation. With instructional films a simple, lucid flow of visuals, such as we have described above, must always be the primary aim.

The techniques employed in the making of teaching films are much more numerous. The nature of the subjects and the audiences for which the films are designed are so varied as to make a uniform approach impossible. What, however, in general distinguishes the editing problems of teaching and instructional films is the nature of the film continuity. In teaching films the continuity can no longer

178

arise out of a continuity of action, but out of a continuity and development of ideas. It may, for instance, be desirable to illustrate a general principle by a series of physically unconnected examples. In a case of this sort, there can be little visual continuity from shot to shot and the normal considerations of continuous action editing will become irrelevant. The editor can do no more than produce the least objectionable visual continuity and time the commentary in such a way as to make the cutting appear smooth. But the problem is not as great as it sounds, because, if the ideas follow each other in a logical progression, the development of the argument will draw attention away from any slight imperfections in the mechanical continuity of the images.

If the script has been thoroughly worked out before shooting, and the director has shot the material intelligently, the editor's task is the comparatively simple one of timing the shots. On some occasions, the editor may suggest simple alterations to the intended continuity—if, for instance, shots which were to follow each other are discordant in tone, or the action of one shot directs the eye away from the point of interest in the next ; more frequently, it may happen that an unexpected visual inference is created by a particular shot juxtaposition and it may then become capable of a wrong interpretation. (An effect akin to this was demonstrated on one occasion while showing *Hydraulics* to a school class. One of the first questions asked after the showing was, " What keeps an aeroplane in the air ? " The introduction of a shot of aircraft in flight, to make a point in the argument, had somehow turned several of the viewers' attention away from the hydraulics principle on to something with which the film was not concerned.) Obviously, in a case of this kind, the editing must be reconsidered.

Although it is true that the motion picture can be used to relate a set of normally unrelated phenomena to illustrate a central theme, the greatest care must be taken in the editing not to let any one of the single phenomena become so important as to take away the attention from the whole principle.

Since the ideas presented in teaching films are often extremely complex, and since it is in the nature of these films not to rely on any visual continuity, it is almost always necessary to add a commentary. The commentary is written at the script stage and finally amended to fit in with the timing of the visuals. It is the editor's task to fit the words of the commentary to the images in such a way that they reach the audience at exactly the right moment. As we shall see in the example quoted below, the correct timing of words and picture is a most important factor in achieving a concise and completely clear result.

On the other hand, it is generally not advisable to have the commentary going on all the time ; pauses not only allow the audience to take in what the images are conveying, but also give the opportunity to let the lesson sink in. The function of the commentary is primarily to keep the audience thinking in the right direction ; it is *not* to tell the audience what they can very well see on the screen.

In the example quoted below, the commentary is continuously employed to make the audience draw certain conclusions from the visuals ; although it never describes the picture, it gives each shot a meaning in its context, by discussing the general principle which is being illustrated.

HYDRAULICS[1]

Extract from Reel I

The sequence quoted here is the introductory passage explaining the basic properties of liquids on which the principle of hydraulics rests:

(1) *That liquids change their shape.*

(2) *That liquids are almost completely inelastic.*

The rest of the film shows applications of these principles.

			Ft.
1	*High angle L.S.* sea. Waves breaking on rocks.	Commentator : Liquids change their shapes easily.—	14
2	*Shooting* at sea level. A large wave comes *towards camera and completely fills screen.*	—They take their shape from—	7
3	*C.S.* Basin, with water running into it. Hands come *into frame* and turn off the taps.	—solids. Water running into a basin, takes the shape of a basin—	8
4	*C.S.* Water surface in basin. Two hands come *into frame* and start washing.	—and closes tightly round a hand plunged into it.	10
5	*C.S.* Jug full of beer and a glass beside it. A hand comes *into frame* and lifts the jug, *camera tilting up* with the hand. The jug is tilted and *camera follows* the stream of beer down to the glass which is filling up.	Beer in a jug is the shape of the jug or of the glass into which it is poured.	21
6	Hose-pipe. *Camera moves along* the pipe to reveal a man spraying the wheel of a lorry.	Because a liquid can be made to take the shape of a pipe, it can be led from one place to another.	9

[1] *Director : Ralph Elton. Editor : R. K. Neilson-Baxter. Petroleum Film Board, 1941*

180

		Ft.
7	C.S. Man's hand spraying the wheel.	4
8	L.S. Three boys on the bank of a stream, under a bridge. One dives into the stream and then another.	8
	Solids, then, appear to be—	
9	M.S. Boy swimming.	—the masters of liquids.	$1\frac{1}{2}$
10	M.S. Two boys swimming. They get to the bank and beckon to someone.	5
11	High angle L.S. Man diving into water from a springboard, and doing a belly-flop.	4
	Splash of water. But liquids—	
12	M.S. Boy on bridge, highly amused.	—are not elastic.	2
13	C.S. Man rubbing his stomach after his dive.	5
	Dissolve to :		
14	F.S. Winchester quart bottle filling up with water.	Fill a bottle with liquid, right up to the cork.	12
15	C.S. Top of full bottle with cork in. A hand comes into frame and vainly tries to push cork down.	The cork cannot be pushed down into the bottle.	13
16	M.S. Man turning lever attached to pressure pipe leading through cork into the bottle.	If we try to compress liquid into a bottle—	4
17	C.S. Lever being turned.	—the liquid will not give	5
18	C.S. pressure pipe. Camera pans down the pipe up to cork in top of bottle.		$4\frac{1}{2}$
19	As in 17, lever being turned gently.	What does give—	3
20	As in 18. Bottle explodes.	—is the bottle. Sound of splintering glass.	

Little purpose will be served by analysing this sequence shot by shot, because it is simple and straightforward. We can content ourselves with a few comments :

The sequence begins slowly—shots *1* and *2* are rather long in duration ; this is done to give the audience time to settle down and be ready for the argument. The waves are shown (shots *1* and *2*) partly to convey the power of liquids in motion—which is discussed later in the film—and partly to make the first point in the argument, namely that water has no shape of its own.

Mention in the commentary of a new point is always made to coincide exactly with its first introduction in the visuals. The operative word " solids " is introduced at the exact moment when shot *3* begins ; similarly, " *But liquids are not elastic* " coincides exactly with the belly-flop (*11–13*).

Shots *3* and *4* introduce two facets of a new idea : shot *3*, that liquids take their shape from solids, and shot *4*, that liquids give way to solids. The two ideas follow logically because there is a visual connection between them, namely the basin of water.

The camera movement in shot *5* emphasises the point that water changes its shape in accordance with the shape of the container in which it is kept. If the operation had been shown in a static set-up, with both jug and glass in the same shot, the concept of the change of shape would have been conveyed much less forcefully. Similarly in shot *6*.

The dissolve after shot *13* is used to indicate the change in the approach : from the everyday example of the man's " dive," we are now taken to check the empirically reached conclusion by a laboratory test. The dissolve also allows for the laugh which might follow shot *13*.

The commentary is needed over shots *14* and *15* because the audience might not otherwise know what conclusion to draw from the visuals.

The sequence *16–20* may seem superfluous because the whole experiment could have been shown in one shot. Cutting the passage in the way it is cut, however, adds authenticity and conviction. Shots *17* and *18* show how the pressure is conveyed from the man's hand turning the lever to the bottle ; shot *19* is simply a touch of showmanship—a moment of slight suspense implying that two opposing forces are acting against each other and one of them must give—and makes the explosion, when it comes, more effective.

Note the pauses in the commentary (over *8, 10, 13–14*) intended to give the commentary time to sink in.

These are all small points of editing technique, designed to make the passage as clear as possible. The overall structure of the sequence is designed to the same end. The first idea—" liquids change their shape "—is conveyed by a series of simple everyday examples (*1–10*) ; shots *8–10* are rather indifferently effective examples of " solids being masters of liquids," but they lead naturally on to the dive which introduces the second idea. The point here is that the fact that water is inelastic may be new to an audience and must be introduced forcefully. Shots *8–11* thus serve as a build-up to the striking illustration of the inelasticity of water (shots *12–13*) and therefore make it doubly effective. At the same time the idea has been introduced naturally, with no discontinuity in the argument. With this point made, it only remains to ram it home by repeating it with two more examples (*14–15* and *16–20*).

It may be objected that we have said altogether too much about this sequence, that the details we have discussed are all small, unimportant points. But it is precisely through this minute accuracy of presentation that a teaching film achieves its effect. It is most important that *every* point should be made clear : if the presentation slurs over only a small portion of the argument, the spectator *may* still be able to understand the whole film, but conciseness and complete conviction will be lost.

Something should here be said about the timing of shots. The aim should be to strike a balance between not leaving enough time and making the film difficult to follow, and giving too much and making it dull. The danger of making a teaching film dull is a very real one : as a subject develops it tends to get more complex and the cutting rate must be reduced. The film, in exact contrast with the usual story-film practice, may then tend to get slower towards the end, a difficulty which can generally not be avoided. Further than this it is impossible to generalise : correct timing is largely a matter of experience and close observation of the results of previous films.

12

NEWSREELS

THE makers of newsreels are the cinema's equivalent of journalists and reporters. Twice weekly they produce a pictorial presentation of current events and send it out on time. The material must be slick, interesting, and represent a balanced selection of the news ; more than that, the newsreel must entertain.

News events which make big headlines in the morning papers do not necessarily make good newsreel material. The abdication of a king, a political speech, or a murder case do not make a good *visual* story : they are interesting to read about in the newspapers because they are " news," because the reader is hearing about them for the first time. The newsreel does not have this advantage : the events shown will, by the time they reach the cinema, be stale news. They must therefore present subjects which do not primarily depend for their appeal on the element of surprise. Newsreel material must be visually interesting and must be presented with that touch of showmanship which can make even slightly stale news appear rather exciting.

Sidelights on the news and personal details of the events already reported in the press, rather than facts alone, make for a good newsreel. In presenting an international conference of statesmen, for instance, it may interest the public to see the smiles on the diplomats' faces as they shake hands ; it will probably interest them less to hear what the diplomats have said, and anyway, those interested will have read it in the papers. A newsreel of Ascot may devote as much footage to the fashions as to the race itself, because the audience, if at all interested, will know the winner of the race but may not have seen the ladies wearing the latest creations. It is in this selection of significant details—" the human angle "—that the newsreel producer's skill lies.

The newsreel producer's first job is to select from the week's news those events which he considers most interesting and most suitable for visual presentation. Anything from one to ten different items are shown in each reel and they must be carefully balanced to interest the largest proportion of spectators. Having chosen his topics, the producer must get together his unit—cameraman, editor, script-writer and sound-crew—and discuss with them the way in which the selected item is to be tackled. (In a newsreel unit the man in charge is generally referred to as the *Editor*, and the man who does the actual assembling in the cutting room, the *Cutter*. We will use the term *Producer* for the former and *Editor* for the latter—the appropriate titles which would be used in any other unit—in order to maintain a consistent terminology throughout this book.)

A newsreel must be planned as accurately as possible in advance to save time and footage, and to ensure that the whole unit is working for the same effects. If the planning is not done beforehand the cameraman may come back with the wrong, or at any rate inadequate, material ; the editor will have to compromise by producing a makeshift continuity from the material available ; time—a most important factor—will be wasted, and the opportunity for getting the best material will have gone. You cannot send a man out to get retakes of the Grand National. In practice, of course, the producer will try to gather around him a team of experienced cameramen who can visualise the complete story while they are shooting. Material which is not designed to fit anywhere in particular will often fit nowhere at all.

From the moment the negative arrives in the cutting rooms, the predominant consideration is speed. Some of the things newsreel technicians do in an effort to save time would appear outrageous to any other film technician. The rushes are seen and subsequently cut in negative form, partly to save time and partly to save printing costs on the footage which will not be used. They are seen by the producer and editor who decide roughly how much footage will be devoted to the item, and the negative then goes to the cutting room to be edited.

The editor's main job is to produce a reasonably smooth continuity and to place emphasis on the points which need it. He will decide how much time he wishes to devote to showing his audience the Ascot fashions, how long he need spend over his joke about the bookies, and how much he will leave for the race itself. Often he does not have time to concentrate on making smooth transitions from one shot of the action to the next, and will use the cut-away to give an appearance of smoothness. He knows that the audience will see his reel in conjunction with what one can only describe by story-film standards as a highly aggressive sound track, which in many cases will carry the visuals with such a sweep as to make any lack of smoothness almost imperceptible.

Finally, the editor must give shape to his story. He is bound naturally by the chronology of events from which he cannot deviate far. He must see to it that each situation is established as economically as possible, and that the main event receives a proper dramatic build-up. In the space of seven or eight minutes the audience will have to see half a dozen separate and unrelated incidents, and the transitions from one to the next will have to be quickly established. The title is, of course, a considerable help here, but the editor will generally leave the opening of an episode devoid of any important action, to give the commentator time to prepare the audience for what is to follow. Having established his opening, the editor must construct his sequence in such a way as to make it develop into a climax. There is, for instance, nothing particularly interesting in seeing one horse crossing a finishing line in front of a lot of others unless we have seen the preceding struggle to win. A great number of the newsreels one sees are dull precisely because of the lack of this kind of showmanship.

With the visuals edited, the sound editor's job is to select and lay the music and effects tracks. Where there is any significant sound to be recorded, a sound camera will generally be sent out to do it. (Since a smooth continuity of sound is more important than a high degree of realism, only one sound camera is sent out to record the effects.) Where there is no particularly interesting sound, an event will be shot silent, and the sound editor will add such effects as are necessary from the sound library. There is generally no need for meticulously realistic effects, since, when the commentary comes to be added, it will probably be found that most of the effects have to be re-recorded at low volume in order not to smother the commentator's words.

Music plays a comparatively subsidiary rôle in the newsreel. With the short time at his disposal, the sound editor can do little more than choose a piece of accompanying atmosphere music from his library and fit it to the visuals. He will have in his library a large selection of recorded pieces which he will keep catalogued under rough headings like " slow, mourning," " wild, African " or " light sports march." From these he will choose the most appropriate piece and lay the track in synchronisation with the picture. He may find that he needs a particularly strong ending and will lay his track so that the finale of the recorded track coincides with the

186

climax of the sequence. It is normally easiest to change from one track to another when the volume of the music is low, that is, at a time when the commentator is speaking.

Sometimes as many as half a dozen tracks may be used in turn in a single news item in order to stress the changing moods. The function of music in a newsreel is such that it makes this rough and ready preparation—even if it could be avoided—perfectly suitable. The music is there to establish and strengthen the prevailing mood of the piece and to keep the track live while the commentator is not speaking. Since sudden variations in the volume of the sound track are rather disconcerting to an audience, it is most important that the dubbing editor should be able to cross-fade from the dialogue to the music track at any time and the music track must therefore be laid for the whole reel.

The commentary, which is being written while the tracks are being laid, informs the audience of what is going on and interprets the picture in the way the producer wishes it. This is necessary since newsreel material often has little visual continuity. Indeed, newsreels lean more heavily on the commentary than other types of film. More than any other factor, the mood and urgency of the commentator's voice will set the key to the audience's reaction, and needs to be spoken with a wide range of variations in the delivery. As long as the voice keeps going, the impression is conveyed that a lot is happening on the screen at a great pace ; it has a spell-binding effect in that it does not allow the audience to relax.

Finally, the script written, the commentator speaks his lines from a closed booth from which the screen is visible and his voice is dubbed together with the music and effects tracks without ever being recorded on a separate track. Since this is so, the main principle of dubbing the sound tracks in a newsreel is fairly simple : when the commentary is being spoken the music is faded down, and when the commentary stops the music and effects are turned up.

Now let us look at the finished product.

ITEM FROM A PATHÉ NEWSREEL[1]

Pathé Credit Title.		Ft. fr.
Cut to :	Music starts.	9 10
I Crowd in front of grandstand.		
Title superimposed :	Music changes to rousing, brassy	
" Doncaster.	march.	
Thousands see St. Leger		
classic."	Music fades down and changes to	
Title fades.	light sporty tunes.	

[1] Editor : N. Roper. Pathé Newsreel, 1950.

187

			Ft.	fr.
2	L.S. *High angle* on to dense crowd facing camera.	Commentator : Ascot weather greets the season's last classic, the St. Leger—	6	15
3	L.S. Crowds wandering about in front of grandstand.	—Britain's oldest and richest race. Sweltering thousands—	4	9
4	M.S. Young lady spectator looking at race-card and then chatting to neighbours.	—pack Doncaster's course. The crowd's big talking point—	4	12
5	M.S. Jockey Johnny Longden talking to his wife.	—is how America's Johnny Longden will do in this—	5	4
6	C.S. Johnny Longden.	—his first big race in England.	3	8
7	L.S. High angle on to crowd ; racecourse in background.	Music gets louder.	5	12
8	C.S. Bookie.	Music continues.	3	3
9	M.S. Punters inspecting their race-cards.	Music fades down.	2	8
10	L.S. Race board being hoisted up.	Commentator : For the first time in many years, the year's Derby winner is not—	4	1
11	L.S. *High angle* on to course.	—in the Leger field, and not even race-goer Number One, the Aga Khan—	5	6
12	M.C.S. Aga Khan.	—quite knows what to make of it. Champion jockey Gordon Richards, several times the Leger winner—	6	5
13	L.S. Gordon Richards as he walks *towards camera into C.S.* and then *past camera right.*	—carries much of the public's money, but any one of the sixteen entries can scoop the prize. With Royal Forest—	10	
14	L.S. *High angle* on to the paddock where horses are being paraded.	—out of it, Gordon is up on Krakatao—	3	6
15	F.S. Horse No. 15 being led across right to left.	—while his American opposite number—	2	13
16	M.S. Johnny Longden being helped into the saddle.	—Johnny Longden mounts Mon Chatelain.	3	11
17	L.S. Johnny Longden riding *towards camera. Camera tilts down* and stops with his leg in *centre of frame.*	Note his typical American style : the short stirrup. Music gets louder.	5	14
18	C.S. Johnny Longden's leg, his foot in stirrup.	Music continues.	4	5
19	L.S. Crowd ; *shooting across* grandstand.	Music continues.	3	4

20	*L.S.* Horses on course getting ready for the start.	*Music continues.*	3 6
21	*C.S.* Spectators watching through binoculars.	*Music continues.*	4 12
22	*L.S.* Horses coming up to the starting gate ; they start and *camera pans left* as horses run into the distance left.	*Music fades down and changes to a fast tune with a gallop rhythm.* Crowd shout : " They're off." *Commentator :* Away ! On a mile and three-quarter race for the season's biggest prize. Royal Empire, Musidora and Lone Eagle head the field as they race out into the country.—	22 2
23	*C.S.* Princess Royal watching through binoculars.	—The Princess Royal closely follows the race's progress—	3 1
24	*L.S.* Bunch of horses running right to left. *Camera tracks along course keeping leading bunch in frame.*	—as the field passes the three-quarter mile post. Royal Empire still leads, Lone Eagle is pressing hard with Mildmay II and Musidora well placed. *Music gets louder.*	18 7
25	*M.C.S.* Spectator.	*Music continues.*	2 3
26	*L.S.* Horses coming towards camera, rails on the right. They go round the bend and *as they approach the camera, it pans with them to right* as horses move *across* screen left to right.	*Commentator :* (now more urgent) Rounding the bend it's still Royal Empire in the lead, but only just. Lone Eagle No. 15 making up ground and slowly jockey Bill Carr forces his mount ahead. Lone Eagle now makes the running, but with only a furlong to go, the lead changes again !—	19 10
27	*M.S.* Aga Khan.	—Ridgewood pushes ahead and jockey—	3
28	*L.S. High angle* on to horses running left to right. *Camera pans right* to show winner crossing the finishing line.	—Michael Beary races away from the field to romp home winner by *three lengths*— Dust Devil, the Aga Khan's choice, second.	13 12
29	*M.C.S.* Aga Khan.	*Music still low, changes again to light " sporty " tune.* Ridgewood's success is a triumph for that veteran	4 5
30	*L.S. High angle* Michael Beary being led into the winner's enclosure. *Camera pans slowly left with him* until he dismounts.	—among jockeys — Michael Beary ; he keeps his age a secret but the knowing ones say that he is—	8 3
31	*C.S.* Head of the winning horse	—half a century older than his mount. Only one bookie is complaining.—	7 3
32	*L.S. High angle* on to bookie paying out money.	—With the winning odds at 100 to 7, the joke is on the punters again.	6 2
33	*L.S.* Crowd.	*Music fades down.*	5 9
34	*Title of next news-item.*		

The first four shots of this sequence simply establish the situation and give the commentator time to prepare the audience for what is to follow. The music, which was loud and rousing over the title—to make the audience look up—is now faded down under the commentary, and changes to a light background tune to harmonise with the feeling of a pleasant afternoon's racing.

With the shots of Johnny Longden (5, 6), the first detail is brought in. The presence of America's champion jockey is of interest to racing enthusiasts and, moreover, serves to establish that the race has not yet begun, since the jockey is still in his street clothes.

The scene is now set : it has been established that we are on a race-course, that the race has not yet begun, and we have been introduced to a personality whom we shall later see in action.

In shot 7, we are shown the course for the first time which tells us that the race is soon to begin.

With the raising of the race-board, (10), we are one stage nearer and instinctively look towards the course (11).

The Aga Khan—a picturesque personality who is always news—Gordon Richards and Johnny Longden are now shown in short flashes (12–18) but the story is progressing because the scene of the action is now the paddock, with the riders getting ready.

An interesting point in Johnny Longden's style is noticed (18), and we see now why it was useful to draw attention to his presence earlier : if the audience had not seen him before, a long digression would now be necessary, which would be out of place just as the race is about to begin.

Shot 20 takes us one stage nearer, with the horses already on the course. The cut-in of the crowd (19), was necessary to indicate the passage of time while the horses file out of the paddock and reach the course.

Similarly, we cut away to the crowd again (21), to create a smooth transition to the shot of the horses starting the race (22). These two shots of the crowd (19, 21) also convey something of the atmosphere of anticipation before the race, and add to the effect of suddenly released excitement when the race begins.

For the same reason there has been no commentary over the last few shots ; when the voice starts again with a sudden " Away !" the feeling of built-up tension and sudden beginning of the event is conveyed with greater force than could have been achieved if the commentary had been going on throughout.

The race is shown in only four shots (22, 24, 26, 28), all much longer in duration than anything that we have seen before. The race is now on and there is plenty of action in the shots themselves ;

there is no longer any need to cut them up into short lengths to create a lively flow of images. They are, after all, the *raison d'être* of the whole sequence, so they can be shown at length. The commentary is helping to create excitement : the commentator is speaking his lines quickly and excitedly. The music has changed to a fast galloping rhythm and when it takes over from the commentary (over shot *25*) it adds to the action by emphasising the rhythm of the horses' movement.

The four action shots are linked through bridging shots of the crowd and individual spectators (*23, 25, 27*) because it is necessary to imply the passage of time between the shots of various stages of the race. In shot *24*, for instance, the action is moving from right to left, while in shot *26* it is in the opposite direction. A physically ugly cut would result from joining the two together, so the transition is made smooth via the Aga Khan (*25*).

Under the commentary (over shot *29*), the music changes again to a more peaceful theme. The race is now over, the winning jockey and horse are shown and, after the joke about bookies, the sequence finishes with the crowd dispersing.

This example is perhaps one of the most obvious newsreel stories. Yet it presents the problems which are typical of almost any simple newsreel item. The whole sequence is carefully constructed by presenting seemingly haphazard shots on a race-course, and building them up into a complete incident. The fact that the shot of the Aga Khan (*12*) was taken three races before the St. Leger does not matter ; nor does it matter that the race being shown is not the first of the meeting and that, in fact, a great deal happens between the arrival of the jockeys (*5, 6*) and the race itself. The main consideration is to keep the story going as fast as possible: a careful examination of this sequence shows that everything is designed to this end.

Hardly anything of interest actually *happens* before the beginning of the race : to make it appear arresting, no shot is left on the screen for more than six seconds, most shots only for two or three. Again, the constant cutting away from the main action is, as we have already remarked, designed to make for smoothness ; but it is also right as a piece of film-making, because the cut-away— always a very short insert—gives the whole piece a staccato rhythm which helps to keep the sequence fast and exciting. The sound track is kept continually " live " and blares away at a much higher volume than is normal in any other type of film. The commentary, besides describing and interpreting the picture, conveys immense urgency through the pace of the delivery.

The sequence of the St. Leger which we have quoted is a representative example of a news event which contains considerable excitement in itself. Not all stories are quite as simple as this. It may happen that the producer wishes to feature an event which does not contain a clear-cut plot, and which therefore must be presented in a more subjective way. The main event may be simple and short, and therefore insufficient to carry a whole item. In such a case the producer's problem is to collect associated material which, when shown in conjunction with the main event, will build it up into an interesting news item. Basically, this is the same problem as is faced by the director of the more factual kind of documentary : to convey a not particularly interesting fact in the most entertaining way.

Take an example. Some time ago, there appeared in the press a story of a Welsh building contractor who had hired a helicopter to transport cement up to an inaccessible region on a Welsh mountain-side, where he was repairing the crack in a dam—not a particularly strong story. The main point of interest was the presence of the helicopter, but it so happened that there had been a number of helicopter stories in recent editions of the newsreels and their news value was diminishing. To get over this difficulty, the producer sent out his cameraman with detailed instructions to build a story around the main event. It was to deal with the reason for the use of the helicopter and its contribution in an everyday job, rather than with the newness and wonder of the flight itself. Shots were accordingly taken of the Welsh mountain and the utter desolation of the region ; of someone wearily walking up the narrow footpath and the steepness of the path ; of a shepherd—miles away from inhabited areas—looking in amazement at the flight ; of cracks in the dam ; and finally, shots of the contractor discussing the job on hand with his men.

All these were then edited into a sequence together with the shots of the helicopter dropping the bags of cement on the mountain-side without landing. A continuous story was built to give meaning and significance to the whole operation ; the commentary was written to underline this, and the audience was presented with an interesting news event containing a beginning, a plot and a build-up to the main event.

Finally, we must mention a rather different type of newsreel. It seems likely that if the newsreel is to survive the competition of the more up-to-date television news service, newsreel-makers will have to adapt their style of presentation to create a rather different level of appeal for their product. A more interpretive approach to news events than the simple reporting technique which is now predominantly employed will have to be developed.

At present, with the shortage of screen time available, there is little enough time to present all the news, much less elaborate and interpret it. Only on rare occasions, when a famous man dies or when some past event is being commemorated, does the newsreel producer prepare an interpretive symposium of past events. For that purpose, each unit is continually building up a comprehensive library of news material, from which any item may be found at a moment's notice. The problems confronting an editor in a venture of this kind are, however, similar to those met by the makers of compilation and documentary films, and we have dealt with these in other chapters.

Comparing the roles of the newsreel and story-film editor, we find that the difference in their contributions to a film arises out of the different conditions under which they work, and out of a difference of aims.

The newsreel editor works with a given length of footage to which he cannot add, because there are no retakes. He has no time to prepare a rough cut and to have another look at his material after discussion with his associates. His main assets are his own speed of judgment, the ability to improvise and cover up the deficiencies of his material : that is to say, a thorough knowledge of editing *technique*. He has little scope for artistic interpretation because the newsreel does not need it. In this sense the documentary or story-film editor's job is more difficult : it requires a subtler understanding and interpretation of the shades of meaning in the uncut shots, *as well as* presupposing a knowledge of editing technique. To say this is not to belittle the difficulty and importance of the newsreel editor's work ; it is simply to point to a difference in function.

Just as we do not expect to find the beautiful simile or poetic image in the columns of the morning papers, so we do not find a subtle aesthetic interpretation of events in a newsreel. The editing is designed to present interesting essentials and such sidelights on the news as will make the story faster and more exciting—often much more so than the actual event being presented. To see, for instance, a boxing contest with its long periods of preparation and inactivity, and to compare it to the excitement of a well presented fight in a newsreel, is to acknowledge the effectiveness of an editing technique perfectly suited to its purpose.

13

THE COMPILATION FILM

> It is my belief[1] (and some day I mean to conduct the experiment), that given at random, say half a dozen shots of different nature and subject, there are any number of possible combinations of the six that, with the right twist of commentary, could make film sense.

THE maker of compilation films extends this hypothetical experiment into a practical method of film production. Working with newsreel and allied material which has not been scripted or shot for the purpose for which the compiler will use it, he is able to make films with a smooth, logically developing continuity. Without the advantages of a planned shooting script—without directed performances from actors, properly interrelating shots, etc.—the compiler's sole assets are his skill as an editor and his ability to exploit the remarkable suggestive power of spoken commentary.

The production of compilations is made possible by the systematic preservation of newsreel and documentary footage which now forms an accepted part of the work of most newsreel companies and national film archives. The earliest examples of newsreel compilations were produced in this country from diverse material covering the 1914–1918 war, and the potentialities of the method have been widely realised in many countries since. The Russian director Dziga Vertov experimented in the *genre* as early as 1923 (*Kine Truth, Kine Calendar*) and followed his early experiments with more ambitious ventures in the early days of sound, in *Enthusiasm* (1931) and *Three Songs about Lenin* (1934). The Americans have developed their own vigorous polemical style of compilation, beginning with such early successes as Louis de Rochemont's *Cry of the World* (1932) and Seldes and Ullman's *This is America* (1933) and reaching a peak of achievement in the *March of Time* films and Frank Capra's war-time *Why We Fight* series. The Germans

[1] *Notes by Peter Baylis.*

194

used the compilation method to produce such powerful propaganda documents as *Baptism of Fire* (1940) and *Victory in the West* (1941).

The success of these films bears witness to the immense potentialities of the compilation film as a means of dramatising first-hand historical records. In competent and scrupulous hands, the unrehearsed, spontaneously shot material can be dramatised and edited into faithful renderings of past events. But it must be stressed that the authenticity of the original material does not necessarily guarantee that the final impression of the film will be a truthful one. In the process of dramatising the newsreel shots by editing and commentary, the more or less inert shots can be twisted into new meanings ; the method can be used to falsify historical events because it is in the process of selection and editing that the shots acquire most of their significance.

A striking instance of the possibility of abusing the compilation method is afforded by some of the Nazi propaganda films. *Victory in the West*, for instance, uses a number of shots which were also used in the third of Capra's *Why We Fight* films, *Divide and Conquer* (1943). While the commentary gloats over the unfortunate victims, shots of fleeing French refugees are made in the first film to symbolise the total victory of the German army ; the identical shots are used in *Divide and Conquer* in the course of a compassionate account of the fall of France. If the compilation film is to give an authentic view of its subject, the proviso that the makers approach their subject honestly is a most urgent one.

The scope of films made by compilation is necessarily limited by the material available : it is not, of course, possible to compile fiction films which trace the fates of particular groups of characters. On the other hand, films of the type Baylis calls " broad canvas " documentaries can be made as, among others, the makers of *The True Glory* and *Desert Victory* have shown. These films gave a comprehensive picture of highly complex themes and must be compared in intention with scripted documentary films dealing with similar subjects.

To discuss compilation is to discuss the " broad-canvas " documentary as a whole.[1] Whether the material is sought after and found, or scripted and shot, is really beside the main point. By sheer accident of method, the compiled film leads to a fundamental editing technique—fundamental ever since the early days of cinema—the art of telling a story with pictures and telling it, not as a story of a tiny group of individuals, but of individuals in a community or as a nation.

[1] *Notes by Peter Baylis.*

195

The compiler's first task is to view all available material and make a selection of the shots which are likely to be useful. While gathering his material, he should have a rough idea of the overall shape of the film, if he is to avoid being swamped by thousands of feet of superfluous material which will make his final task more difficult and incur unnecessarily high printing costs.

After overall selection,[1] each shot has to be carefully assessed and its exact cinematic content determined. At first reading this may seem a little peculiar —after all, is not the cinematic content of a shot of a house merely—a house ? Well, the cinematic content may be merely a house, but on the other hand it may be a symbol of opulence or of poverty depending on the state of repair or scale of the house. The cinematic content may not fundamentally be that of a house at all but merely the depiction of a season—governed by whether the house be shot in snow or sunshine. This is an absurdly simple case but it will serve to state the principle involved. The deeper the cinematic content of a shot lies, the more difficult it is to perceive, and the more difficult, there-fore, does it become for the editor to place it in its correct position. In com-piling historical films I have known such shots " roam " over the whole length of production—for while fully aware that these shots " have something," I have been at a loss for some time to discover exactly *what* that something was.

In the end, like the last piece of the jig-saw puzzle, each shot drops neatly into the exact position where its cinematic content can most effectively make itself felt. The analogy with a jig-saw puzzle, incidentally, always strikes me forcibly when working on such films, because, providing the editor has made his choice wisely in the first place, it is often quite astounding to find what little material there is left over.

This problem of fitting a shot into a context where its cinematic content will be most effective is the crucial problem faced by the compiler. The meaning of a shot is always considerably affected by its context and can often be bent to convey the impression desired from it. For instance, if the shot of the house we have men-tioned were to be shown in the course of an attack on the luxury and wastefulness of the rich, the house would quite naturally symbolise opulence and probably evoke resentment in an audience ; if, on the other hand, it were shown as an example of a particular style of architecture, preceded and followed by other examples, then the emotional meaning given to the shot in the previous sequence would never arise.

Yet in making use of this principle the greatest care must be exercised. The fact that a shot of a house acquires some of its significance from its context, does not mean that *any* shot would serve equally well. If a clear, incisive effect is to be achieved, the most suitable shot must be selected. No doubt, a series of shots which roughly fit into a sequence thanks to their subject alone,

[1] *Notes by Peter Baylis.*

could, with a suitable commentary, be given some sort of meaning. But it is in the precision of selecting exactly the *right* shot that the compiler's skill lies. A shot of a house which in itself symbolises opulence will fit into a passage condemning the idle rich much better than a shot which merely acquires its significance from the context, because the " opulent " house will *give* something to the overall effect, whereas the other merely takes its meaning by an association of ideas.

When the editor has made his overall selection he must try to assemble his material roughly in the right order. Once this is done, the script-writer is called in and the rest of the production must be carried out in close collaboration with him. The compilation film leans very heavily for its mood on what the commentator says, on the inflection of his voice and the pace of his delivery. Only the closest collaboration between writer and editor can lead to an incisive result. For instance, a series of luxurious looking houses could, as we have seen, be used as an attack against the rich. Equally, with a little stretch of the imagination, the images *could* be used to justify " the Good Old Days " when the wealthy had a certain grace and dignity which went with their very real responsibilities. The emotional response of an audience would in each case be completely different.

But it is wrong to conclude that the same set of images would make both sequences equally effective, for the visuals must have some sort of emotional significance of their own which cannot work equally well both ways. Thus, although the commentator's words are crucial in bringing about the desired reaction, they cannot do this incisively, if they are not perfectly in key with the visuals. We shall see how this works out in practice a little later.

A further reason for the close co-operation between editor and writer is the *technical* help which the writer can sometimes give to the editor. The control of time-continuity and adjustment of tempo, which are accomplished to some extent by the careful timing of dissolves and fades in the story film, can here be conveyed by the simplest hint from the commentator.

Continuity in the visual sense of the story film is practically non-existent in compilations.[1] Merely by stating in the commentary " and the following Christmas," one can, in effect, cut to next Christmas. The dissolve or fade used for time continuity is in most cases quite unnecessary. Often in dealing with historical material of insufficient footage or quality with which to make opticals, I have been forced to do without—only to find in the long run that

[1] *Notes by Peter Baylis.*

the dissolve or fade would have been a waste anyway. In such work the time-scale of the story-film simply does not exist, and often a trick of phrasing or a turn of speech can convert a meaningless group of shots into a smooth effective sequence.

At this stage of production there must necessarily be a great deal of to and fro adjustment between the requirements of the visuals and the commentator's intentions. The two must be fitted to each other as closely as possible before the commentary is recorded. The script-writer sees the roughly assembled sequence and it suggests a way of commentating it : a character is conceived. Keeping a very close watch on the images, the writer then prepares the commentary. Finer points which have developed in the writing are met by inclusion of extra material, trimming of existing shots and rearrangement of the continuity to tighten the complete effect. When this is done, the commentary is recorded and the visuals are again trimmed to fit it exactly. This final stage is largely a matter of taking a few frames off here and adding a few frames in another place ; it is, as we shall see in the examples quoted below, a most important operation.

Here is a sequence showing how the compilation technique is applied to a simple descriptive passage.

THE PEACEFUL YEARS[1]

Extract from Reel 2

A compilation of newsreel material covering events between the two wars. The extract quoted is preceded by shots of the turbulent events taking place in Russia, Italy and Germany round about 1921. The key commentary (by Emlyn Williams) is, both in content and delivery, formal but sympathetic. By contrast, the Cockney (James Hayter) is down-to-earth.

			Ft. fr.
1	F.S. Speaker standing on platform right, addressing a large crowd in Trafalgar Square. *Camera pans slowly left* across a large mass of people listening.	*Crowd voices.* *Key Commentator :* And in victorious Britain, economic events were proving that in modern war victor *and* vanquished suffer alike. *Commentator :* (Cockney) Plenty of people had the answers—of course. The trouble was they were all different. Higher wages !—	27 12
2	L.S. Another speaker left, addressing large meeting.	—Lower wages ! Longer hours !—	3 14

[1] *Producer and Editor : Peter Baylis. Writer : Jack Howells. Associated British Pathé, 1948.*

198

		Ft.	fr.
3	*High angle L.S.* Crowd pushing. Two men in foreground holding a banner.	—Shorter hours ! The only thing you could take as certain was—	5	4
4	Railway yard completely deserted.	—strikes. All the trains stopped. *Crowd voices fade out.*	6	1
5	*L.S.* People standing about in front of railway station. A man, hands in pockets, walks slowly right to left.	*Low music begins.* People waited outside the stations for hours.—	6	10
6	*L.S.* Bus. A queue of people stretches away to left. *Camera tracks slowly left* along the enormous queue. Taxis pass *in front of camera.*	—As for the buses, you couldn't get on *them* for love or money— I tried both. Yes, they had a nice line in queues even in those days.—	23	12
7	*C.S.* Sandwich-board man carrying airline advertisement placard.	—Of course they invited you to go by aeroplane.—	4	9
8	*F.S.* Motor-car with aeroplane in background. Three men get out of car and straightaway board the plane. A dog jumps in after them.	—But aeroplanes weren't much good to me—by the looks of them, they weren't much good to anybody ! Anyway, I never wanted to go farther than Brixton.—	16	9
9	Back of lorry. Policeman helping people to get on.	—And then, to crown it all, the buses stopped—	6	9
10	*F.S.* Lorry full of people.	—and we had to ride in lorries.	3	
11	*F.S.* Back of lorry, people mounting steps up to it.	The wind blew—	2	6
12	*F.S.* Back of lorry starting to move away from camera. Golders Green station in background.	—from Golders Green right up the Old Kent Road.	6	1
13	*L.S.* Docks deserted. *Camera pans slowly left.*	Then up at Liverpool, the dockers came out.	8	4
14	*L.S.* People standing in front of boarded-up shops. Horse and cab pass *in front of camera.*	The shops were all boarded up and the Government called in the Army.	6	10
15	*F.S.* Two soldiers, *back to camera,* facing a crowd of people.	Things began to look very nasty.	6	9
16	*L.S.* Tanks and military vehicles. Two soldiers leaning over railing waiting *in foreground, back to camera.*	Even *without* strikes, there were enough people doing nothing. *On the cue "* . . . *doing nothing," music rises to a sudden crescendo.*	6	8
17	*Large title :* 1,750,000 Unemployed.			

The shots of this sequence are more or less homogeneous in character, which makes the editing comparatively simple ; they show various aspects of the scene up and down the country and

199

are edited so as to convey something of the atmosphere of the time. The opening three shots immediately establish that men are out of work. The first shot is rather long and might have served for this purpose, but *2* and *3* are included for a definite reason.

After I had written the commentary[1] it struck us that "*Higher Wages Lower Wages—Longer Hours, Shorter Hours*" needed shots for balance, and these were included ; they were then cut to a definite rhythm. The cutting of the first three shots went something like this : "*Higher Wages*" goes on the tail end of shot *1*; we then cut to shot *2* on the words "*Lower Wages*" ; "*Longer Hours*" goes on the end of shot *2* ; and again, we cut to shot *3* on "*Shorter Hours.*" This may seem elementary but close attention to all such detail makes all the difference between messy presentation and a clear, slightly stylised continuity.

This is a simple example of the intimate co-operation between writer and editor which is essential for a precise effect. The timing of the shots here gives a great deal of extra power to the words by punctuating them, as it were, with cuts. The same precision of presentation is achieved throughout the passage by exactly synchronising the visuals with the appropriate words of commentary. The seemingly effortless continuity is achieved through the casual sounding descriptive commentary which hides a great deal of the editorial and writing skill.

Besides describing facts for the audience, the spoken words do something more. They create character : the events are presented through the mind of a Cockney observer who very clearly betrays his attitude to the situation.

A straight commentary[2] rubbing in the obvious depression of the shots would have been dull, and, to me, untruthful ; one important factor would have been missing—the cheerful, good-natured courage of ordinary people in crises of this kind. We felt that the Cockney commentary supplied this. For instance, the aeroplane advertisements on the sandwich boards and the aeroplane itself (*7* and *8*) were apparently diverse material in that they did not fit into a transport strike. (They were probably shot after the strike was settled anyway !) But together, they represented a phenomenon of the year and we wanted to use them. We could, of course, have made the material stand simply for aviation progress, but that would not have fitted. So we used the shots to represent an ordinary man's ironic point of view in a crisis— " Of course, they invited you to go by air. But aeroplanes weren't much good to me "—and rounded it off with the Cockney's natural defence mechanism— his sense of humour : " By the looks of them, they weren't much good to anybody."

The whole of this passage leads up to the question of unemployment at the time, and the problem arose how to make the audience aware of the fact most forcefully. In the event, the dramatic announcement—1,750,000 *UNEMPLOYED*—was cued in by a

[1] *Notes by Jack Howells.*
[2] *Notes by Jack Howells.*

200

casually spoken line and the sudden crescendo of music. The abrupt cut to the title and the sound build-up makes this much more forceful than it would have appeared if the words had been declaimed in the commentary.

This simple descriptive passage presents comparatively small editing problems. The aim is to present a smooth, natural continuity and to give it an emotional significance through the interplay of visuals and commentary. More complex effects can be achieved in compilation films by giving a sequence a sort of " plot " which produces its own drama.

THE PEACEFUL YEARS[1]
Extract from Reel 4

The sequence quoted is preceded by shots of the Clyde, Jarrow and South Wales, where unemployment was at its worst in 1931, and of a mass demonstration. The commentary in each case is in the local accent. In contrast, James Hayter picks up in Cockney.

			Ft. fr.
1	F.S. Door of 10 Downing Street.	Noise of crowd dies down. Commentator : (Cockney) At No. 10—	6
2	L.S. Five Cabinet Ministers descending steps into the garden.	—everything in the garden looked lovely.	6 3
3	L.S. Group of Ministers in the garden. They offer each other cigars and chat happily.	The new Government was made up of Socialists and Tories together. Wonderful sight—we'd tried 'em separately—	10 15
4	M.S. Ramsay MacDonald smoking and chatting to some others.	—the only thing left was to mix 'em up. And they called the mixture—	6 3
5	Group of Ministers sitting for their photographs.	—a *National* government. Mark you, a lot of us weren't very clear *what* a National government was !	9 8
6	L.S. shooting down on to platform where Baldwin is addressing a meeting.	*Baldwin :* (voice reverberating through the hall) A National Government—is a great ideal . . . *As Baldwin continues, his voice gives way to Gracie Fields singing " I'm Looking on the Bright Side . . . "*	
7	A short sequence of people enjoying themselves on the beach at Brighton, etc., begins.		

[1] *Producer and Editor : Peter Baylis. Writer : Jack Howells   Associated British-Pathé, 1948.*

201

The ease and effectiveness of the two ironic twists given to this short passage hide a great deal of editing skill. Since it is perfectly obvious what the passage is intended to mean, it will be most useful to see how this seemingly effortless effect was achieved.

An editor brought me[1] the news that he had just found a synchronised speech with Baldwin addressing an audience. I heard it and decided that it had something. There was a pompous intonation in the way he started : "A National government is a great ideal . . . " I saw ironically funny possibilities if it were cued in at the proper moment. So I worked backwards, as it were, and then towards it, like this :

(1) A Scot comments dourly on conditions on the Clyde.

(2) A woman's voice picks up—bitterly dry—over Jarrow.

(3) A Welshman picks up with philosophic Welsh humour over South Wales and ends up by saying : " The chaps started to march to London. Why not ? They had nothing else to do ! The time I went we got as far as Hyde Park—and that was as far as we did get ! " (Shots of marchers in Hyde Park which also brought us filmically to London.) " We found the government had resigned."

(4) After this, we cut to the passage quoted above.

The point I am making is that this gag needed a considerable build-up, but this build-up presented something worth showing in its own right too. We were able to cut from the cue—" Mark you, a lot of us weren't very clear what a National government was ! "—straight to Baldwin's opening sentence. The effect was threefold : one, it emphasised Baldwin's words ; two, it gave an indirect comment on Baldwin himself ; and, three, it gave a smooth and amusing continuity.

When we had got Baldwin speaking from the platform, we found that our next shots (for other reasons) had to be open-air, happy, out-of-door shots. If we had cut straight from Baldwin to the open air, the effect would have been inadvertently that Baldwin was responsible for all this outdoor happiness. We frankly didn't think so. That was the first difficulty. The second difficulty was that Baldwin's speech was delivered indoors at night while the following shots were out of doors and sunny ; a cut therefore would not have been very happy.

In cases of this sort experience tells us not to scrap the idea but to look around for some other way out ; often, if we find it, the effect will be all the better for the difficulties involved. So, in this case, it struck me that the song " Looking on the Bright Side " might effectively bridge the gap between night and day—whilst also having symbolical overtones. That was stage one. But when I brooded on the lyric, I was overjoyed to find that when laid back over Baldwin speaking (as it had to be for mechanical reasons) there were delicious satirical overtones. Witness : Baldwin posturing and Gracie Fields singing, " sticking out my chest, hoping for the best, looking on the Bright Side of Life." Even if the audience did not get the finer points of the satire, the song was still doing its major job of bridging the gap between night and day.

There are two examples in this extract of the use of colloquial commentary which are perhaps worth noting. It is a golden rule for me in *all* commentary writing, that the metaphor or figure of speech should, where possible, spring from the visuals. For example, how dull and unnecessary it would be to say

[1] *Notes by Jack Howells.*

over shot *2* : "*But the government seemed quite unconcerned.*" How much better to say, since the Ministers are enjoying themselves in a garden and as a Cockney would say anyway : "*At No.* 10, *everything in the garden looked lovely.*" This may sound elementary in retrospect, but is not so obvious at the time. Similarly, the commentator used the word "mixture"—which, visually, shot *4* was—in a rather unconventional way.

There is no visual continuity between the three shots which make the point in this sequence. The scene changes effortlessly from the garden in Downing Street (in daytime) to a meeting addressed by Baldwin (indoors at night), and again to the beach at Brighton (outside on a sunny day) by virtue of the merest hints in the commentary : the phrase "Looking on the Bright Side," by being overlaid over the end of the public meeting, quite naturally bridges the gap between night and day. Similarly a simple statement links shots *12* and *13* in the first quoted passage and takes us smoothly from Golders Green to Liverpool. These are only two examples, but a careful examination of both passages shows that each transition is clarified in the commentary in some such way.

The extremely important part played by the commentary in the two excerpts quoted is not typical of all compilation films. *The Peaceful Years* covers a great variety of events, linked, in many instances, only by historical accident. To establish unity between this diverse material it was necessary to guide the spectator continually by the spoken words. Where a compilation film has a more unified theme, however, it may prove possible—and cinematically more effective—to let the pictures speak for themselves. The following excerpt from *The World is Rich* makes the point.

THE WORLD IS RICH[1]

Excerpt from Reel I

A film surveying the world food situation, compiled from material drawn from hundreds of documentary, travel, newsreel and instructional films and in some instances supplemented by specially shot material. The excerpt is from the opening of the film.

		Ft.
	Fade in :	
1	Overhead shot of a vast field of wheat, the ears swaying gently in the breeze.	Music starts.	17
	Dissolve to :	
2	L.S. A large herd of cattle being driven slowly through a plain, away from camera.		9

[1] *Director and Editor : Paul Rotha. Associate Director and Editor : Michael Orrom. Script : Arthur Calder-Marshall. Films of Fact, Ltd., for Central Office of Information, 1947.*

		Ft.
	Dissolve to :	
3	*L.S.* A combine harvester moving *towards camera. Camera pans slowly left* to reveal a row of combine harvesters moving in parallel with the first.	12
4	*Overhead shot* of a cattle yard. The whole screen is filled with large, healthy-looking bullocks jostling each other.	4
5	*C.S.* A large, circular fishing net being raised out of the sea, bulging over with fish. *Camera pans left* with the net as it swings on to a boat.	5
6	*C.S.* A pig trough into which swill is being poured. Two pigs' snouts can be seen greedily attacking the food.	5
7	*C.S.* A native African worker picking a large corn cob.	3
8	*C.S.* A basket swelling over with grapes. *Camera tilts up* as woman swings the basket on to her back.	3
9	*C.S.* An African picking large fruits off a tree.	4
10	*Overhead M.S.* of three fat, healthy bullocks lying in a field.	3½
11	*Overhead L.S.* A modern circular cowshed, highly mechanised and clean. The cows are being electrically milked, attendants are standing by.	6
12	*M.S.* A chef carrying a steaming dish past shelves laden with food.	6
13	*M.S.* A pastrycook placing two large pies on to a wooden tray standing at the door of a large oven.	2½
14	A slaughter house. The steaming carcasses are being stripped of their skin.	2½
15	*As in* 13.	3½
16	An expensive restaurant. Two waiters, their trays laden with food, pass each other between tables.	5½
17	*M.S.* A diner licking his lips as a waiter heaps food on to his plate.	7½

204

18	*C.U.* Another diner. *Camera moves down* to his plate, *pans across* to another plate, then *tilts up* to another eater enjoying his food.	10
19	*C.S.* A roast chicken. A knife *enters frame* and starts cutting into the breast.	4
	Commentator (A) : Yes—	
20	*C.S.* A plate of pudding. *Camera tilts up* showing a woman eating, her mouth a little too full.	
	—it's a rich world.	7½
21	*M.S.* A young girl in dressing gown, luxuriating on a divan, reading a fashion paper. Without looking up, she takes a chocolate from a nearby box and starts munching it.	8
22	*C.S.* A wine glass. The top of a champagne bottle *comes into frame from left* and starts pouring wine into the glass.	3
	Commentator (B) : So rich that some people have more than they want.	
	Dissolve to :	
23	*C.S.* A garbage bin. *Shooting from above* as the lid is removed and a plateful of food is scraped into it.	5½
24	*F.S.* A dairyman, pouring a full churn of milk down a drain.	3
25	*C.S.* The drain, as the milk pours down it.	6½
	But what about the rest ?	
	Dissolve to :	
26	*L.S.* A vast wind-blown field. The wind is sweeping the top-soil away in little eddying clouds.	12
27	*L.S.* A starved, solitary bullock, roaming slowly across a dry deserted field.	5
28	*Overhead shot* of three peasants picking a few stray ears of corn.	6
	Commentator (C) : One in every three people living on the earth to-day—	
29	*M.L.S.* An aged woman bending over a dust-bin, trying to pick out something to eat.	6
	—is threatened with death from hunger or—	
30	An Indian street. A young Indian comes out into the street from a house. He throws a parcel of scrap food on to the pavement. Immediately a group of children pounce on it.	5½
	—the diseases that travel in the track of famine.	

205

31	*Closer shot* of the children. They scramble for the food and each retires in turn with his small piece. One small boy remains *in frame* : he picks up a small parcel of stale food and avidly bites into it.	

32 An Indian crowd. Everyone is holding dishes above his head, appealing for food.   4

33 *F.S.* An old starving Indian woman, gesticulating with her hands, appealing for food.   *Commentator (D) :*   5
                                        Why ?

34 *Overhead shot.* A large Indian   What is the reason for it ?   8
   crowd on a hunger demonstration.

Fade out.

The makers of *The World is Rich* viewed (and cross-indexed for reference) some 800,000 feet of film in search of the right material. Some impression of the variety of material they have drawn on is given by the sources of the first few shots : *1, 6* and *8* are from an American documentary, *Harvest for Tomorrow* ; *2* and *3* are from Flaherty's *The Land* ; *4, 12, 13, 15, 16* from a *March of Time* film ; *7* from a *Colonial Film Unit* documentary ; *11* and *14* from *Minnesota Document* ; *17–23* were specially shot.

The criterion of selection was, in each case, that every shot should make its impact directly, without the aid of words. Each image must make a strong impression when seen on its own and communicate its point without any shade of ambiguity. In shot *1*, for example, the whole screen is filled with a vast view of ripe wheat : the shot is taken from above and the sky-line (which might have given the image a kind of picturesque landscape significance) does not at first appear in the frame. In the same way, every subsequent shot is chosen for the same quality of making an immediate and forceful impression. The directness of the impact of the whole passage thus depends on each shot making its contribution to the total effect : none of the shots take their meaning only from an association of ideas.

The whole excerpt quoted is a prologue to a film essay on the world food situation and concisely states the two sides of the problem which are investigated in detail in later reels. It will be noticed that though the commentary occasionally makes a small point to strengthen an effect, each new aspect of the theme is in the first place established visually.

The first fourteen shots establish in visual terms what the title of the film implies—that the world is rich. Here, not only the choice of individual images but also the rhythm and order of their assembly has been made to underline the desired effect. The passage shows in turn the cultivation, preparation and consumption of food, in each case stressing the lush, plentiful quality of good living. The three opening shots are left on the screen for a relatively long time and are linked by slow dissolves : the opening thus acquires a leisurely, peaceful quality which is precisely what is wanted.

The exact cutting points of the subsequent shots (*4–11*) cannot be theoretically justified by analysis. In each case, the image is left on the screen long enough to make its point and cut at the moment the editor judges that it is made. This necessarily remains a question for personal judgment. But it should be recalled that the shots being assembled have already been pre-selected with a view to each shot's inherent rhythmic quality. The tempo of the opening shots is slow, exploring, contemplative, and each shot is made to reflect this. A shot of a herd of cattle being driven at speed across a plain (such as one has seen in action films like *Red River* or *The Overlanders*) might, for instance, have served to make the same point as shot *4*. But the quick activity within these shots would have been out of keeping with the overall tempo of the sequence.

A comparison between shots *10* and *11* reveals another factor which governs the timing of this diverse material. Where a shot is static and makes its impression immediately, it need be left on the screen for only a relatively short time (see *10*) ; where a general panoramic view is given of a complex activity (*11*), more time is needed to allow the shot's impact to reach the audience. To an editor working with material which was not in the first place shot for his use, this problem of finding the right length for a shot may sometimes present technical difficulties. Shot *32*, for example, as it was used in its original form, was too short for the present film and had to be step-printed to the needed length to make it comprehensible.

Shots *12–15* take up a new aspect of the theme—the preparation of food. The stress is on the efficiency and cleanliness of proper handling of raw food-stuffs. *13* and *15* are cut to the rhythmic movements in the shot to strengthen the impression of mechanical efficiency of large-scale catering.

The next group of shots (*16–22*) goes on to the next logical step in the argument—the consumption of food. On shot *19*, as the knife cuts into the breast of the roast chicken, the commentator affirms the impression already given by the visuals—" Yes—it's a rich world." From this point onward the images undergo a gradual and subtle change. An impression of the greed of a minority is slowly conveyed : by the time *21* appears, the impression of good living which can be derived from this rich world is tinted with an impression of the self-indulgence of a particular section of society. The spectator is subtly introduced to the next step in the argument.

The shot of the wine-glass (*22*) dissolves into a similarly composed shot of the top of a garbage bin (*23*). The smooth, at first imperceptible transition links the two ideas represented by the two images in the spectator's mind : he concludes that waste is the inevitable result of badly planned food distribution. The three shots symbolising the wastage of food take the " the-world-is-rich " theme to its extreme conclusion and the spectator is now ready to see the other side of the problem.

The other side of the problem is the poverty and starvation of " one in every three people living on the earth to-day." To show this, the shots have again been selected for the directness of their impact. The vast wind-blown field (*26*), the starving cattle (*27*), the woman picking scraps from a dust-bin (*29*), all make different appeals on the same central issue. And the single, personal appeal of the images is strengthened and put into perspective by the commentary's explanation of the extent of the problem. The sequence ends, having through the contrast of well-being and starvation posed the problem, by asking why the problem exists. Here, the commentary's rhetorical question is immensely strengthened by the bewildered, questioning gestures of the starving people in the last three shots.

This forceful and seemingly effortless interaction of word and picture hides a great deal of planning and co-operation between the editor and the writer. The joint effect of sound and visuals—which is nowhere one of mere repetition—can often give the images overtones of meaning which alone they did not possess. Here, the intimate and painstaking collaboration between writer and director becomes a crucial operation. In the passage we have quoted, the commentary is mainly employed to punctuate the various phrases of the argument and, where necessary, to strengthen contrasts. The question spoken over *25* sharpens the effect of the juxtaposition of the sequences on wealth and poverty by warning

208

the spectator of the impending contrast. The transition from *25* to *26* is given point by the words.

Apart from this timing of the words to the content of the images, finer points of timing are again subject to the editor's conception of the overall rhythmic pattern of the passage. It is noticeable that, whenever a cut interrupts a continuous sentence, it is made to coincide with a natural break in the rhythm of the words, usually at the end of a clause.

A further dimension is given to the impact ot the images by the use of music. Clifton Parker's score stresses and interprets the various themes as the film progresses : the scenes of luxury are accompanied by a " Black Market Blues," which is later picked up and expanded ; a " starvation " theme, used first over the last part of the quoted excerpt, recurs throughout the picture. In this way, the music ensures the flow of the film's argument and helps to maintain an emotional unity which might sometimes become obscured in the diversity of the compiled material.

SECTION 3

PRINCIPLES OF EDITING

14

EDITING THE PICTURE

General

. . . if I am in the middle of a scene of action, I shall find my attention and with it my glance, attracted now in this direction and now in that. I may suddenly turn a street corner to find a small urchin, thinking himself unobserved, carefully aiming a fragment of rubble at a particularly tempting window. As he throws it, *my eyes instinctively and instantly turn to the window* to see if he hits it. Immediately after *they turn back to the boy again* to see what he does next. Perhaps he has just caught sight of me and grins derisively ; then, he looks past me, his expression changes, and he bolts off as fast as his short legs will carry him. *I look behind me* to discover that a policeman has just turned the corner . . .

The fundamental psychological justification of editing as a method of representing the physical world around us lies in the fact that it reproduces this mental process described above in which one visual image follows another as our attention is drawn to this point and to that in our surroundings. In so far as the film is photographic and reproduces movement, it can give us a life-like semblance of what we see.; in so far as it employs editing, it can exactly reproduce the *manner* in which we normally see it.[1]

IN this passage, Ernest Lindgren suggests a theoretical justification for editing. He shows that cutting a film is not only the most convenient but also the psychologically correct method of transferring attention from one image to another. The mind is, as it were, continually " cutting " from one picture to the next, and therefore accepts a filmic representation of reality through abrupt changes of view as a proper rendering of observed experience.

This theoretical argument must, however, be applied with caution. In the incident quoted, all the images seen by the observer are viewed from a roughly stationary position : the image is changed in each case by the observer altering the direction of his view without appreciably changing his position in the street. In assembling a film, an editor is often called upon to make cuts which are not strictly comparable to these conditions. He may have to cut from a shot of an object to a closer or more distant shot of the same object—i.e., to cut from a mid-shot to a close-up

[1] The Art of the Film *by Ernest Lindgren. Allen & Unwin, 1948, p. 54. My italics.*

213

or a long shot. In a case of this sort the cut instantaneously changes the *position* of the observer, a manœuvre which in real life is physically impossible. Yet when an editor cuts from a medium shot to a close-up he is not taking an unwarrantable liberty : he is merely interpreting a mental process different from the one we have discussed so far.

An example should clarify the point. I have, a few feet to my right, a bookshelf full of books. If I decide to turn my head to look at it, I can see a vague general impression of the shelf and all the books on it. Then, as my eye travels along one of the rows, my attention is suddenly caught by one specific book, a volume with a red cover. My eyes focus on this as I try to decipher its title from a distance : I am no longer consciously aware of the general mass of books—it is now a particular *one* which holds my whole attention. After a while I manage to read the title and my gaze reverts back to my desk. During the whole of this period, three separate images have been significant for me : first, the general impression of the whole shelf ; then, a detail of the previous impression, namely, the one red book ; and third, the independent image of my desk to which I subsequently return my attention.

In transferring this scene to the screen, it is not sufficient to show the general impression—in this case a shot of the whole shelf— and let the spectator pick out any detail he chooses : the specific detail must be artificially brought to his attention. At the dramatically appropriate moment, the editor must cut from the general view of the whole shelf to a close shot of the chosen red volume. In doing this, he is not reproducing the physical conditions which obtain when I experience the scene : he is interpreting the mental process by which I see it. A spectator watching the film will immediately identify this method of presentation as a psychologically accurate one, and will accept the cut to the close shot without becoming conscious of the device.

In the first case, using Lindgren's example, we have found a justification for cuts which change the direction of the camera's view but leave it fixed in one position. In the second case, we have justified cuts where the camera's position relative to an object, but not its direction of view, is altered.

This, however, does not exhaust all the possibilities. On a great many occasions it is necessary to cut to a shot taken both from a different position *and* facing in a different direction from its predecessor. In assembling a dialogue scene, for instance, an editor often cuts from one close shot to another. From a shot of B taken over A's shoulder, he cuts to a reverse angle : to a shot of A taken over B's shoulder. In doing so, he is changing the direction of view as well as the position from which the picture is taken. Clearly, there can be no analogous experience in real life. No simple theoretical justification of such cuts is possible by comparing the film treatment with normal experience.

When a director sets out to film a story, he is normally not concerned with showing it as an exact record of one person's experience. Instead, he interprets events, shows them in the way he considers dramatically most appropriate. When making a dialogue scene, to take the example already mentioned, he does not attempt to show it through the eyes of one of the characters on the screen : that would mean keeping the camera still, showing all the time only the close shot of the opposite actor. Nor does he try to show it through the eyes of an impartial observer physically present at the scene : that would mean that he could only cut to shots which were all taken from a fixed camera position. Instead, the director's aim is to give an *ideal* picture of the scene, in each case placing his camera in such a position that it records most effectively the particular piece of action or detail which is dramatically significant. He becomes, as it were, a ubiquitous observer, giving the audience at each moment of the action the best possible viewpoint. He selects the images which he considers most telling, irrespective of the fact that no single individual could view a scene in this way in real life.

In doing this, the director does no more than exercise his elementary right as an artist : namely, to select from a given situation particular aspects which he considers significant and to present them in the manner he feels to be most useful to his purpose. Thus if we can find no parallel in actual experience for certain editing devices, it is simply because the editor and director do not want to reproduce the physical world as one normally sees it. A spectator, moreover, does not expect to see a film unfold like an episode of real life—any more than he expects a novel to read like a diary. He accepts the film-maker's right to select and emphasise, to show a piece of action in a way which is obviously more suitable to dramatic presentation than is our normal perception.

This is as far as a theoretical justification of editing can take us. In so far as the editor changes images abruptly, he is reproducing the normal mental mechanism by which we alter our attention from object to object in real life. This justifies the mechanical process of cutting. In so far as he accomplishes particular changes of view which are not comparable to outside experience, he exercises the right of selection which we accept from an artist.

Constructing a lucid continuity : smoothness

Before the final continuity of a sequence is arrived at, the editor normally takes his material through two distinct stages. First, he assembles a rough cut in which the order of shots makes film sense and the transitions are mechanically smooth. Second, he approaches the material again to refine the continuity of the rough cut in such a way that it becomes dramatically as well as physically appropriate. Some writers have divided these two functions, calling the first *cutting* and the second *editing*, but the terms are, in common usage, applied interchangeably so that the distinction is likely to confuse rather than to clarify the issue. Nevertheless, we will find it convenient to consider the two phases of the work separately because they present somewhat different problems.

The main purpose of assembling a rough cut is to work out a continuity which will be understandable and smooth. We have used the word *smooth* as applied to a cut several times and it is now time to say a little more about it. Making a smooth cut means joining two shots in such a way that the transition does not create a noticeable jerk and the spectator's illusion of seeing a continuous piece of action is not interrupted. If, to take an absurdly simple example, we cut from a long shot of an actor standing by a mantelpiece straight to a medium shot of the same actor reclining in an arm-chair, the transition will obviously be unacceptable : a spectator seeing it will immediately become aware that he is not viewing a continuous piece of action and the illusion will be broken.

This simple instance shows that the process of smooth cutting is subject to certain mechanical principles. These we shall attempt to state below. But as will be seen later, all the " rules " of smooth cutting are subject to the much wider discipline of the *dramatic*, as opposed to the *mechanical* demands of the continuity, so that they are not to be taken as binding or universally valid.

Matching Consecutive Actions

The most elementary requirement of a smooth continuity is that the actions of two consecutive shots of a single scene should match. While the film is still on the floor, the director—aided by

216

the continuity girl—sees to it that if a scene is shot from more than one angle, the background and positions of the players remain the same in each take. Clearly, if a long shot of a room showed a fire burning in a hearth, and the following mid-shot revealed the grate empty, then a cut from the one to the other would create a false impression. Keeping the set background constant throughout a series of shots is, however, a comparatively simple matter.

A more difficult aspect of the same problem is to keep the action and movement shown in consecutive shots accurately continuous. If an actor starts a movement—say he is half way through opening a door—in one shot, then that movement must be continued in the next from the precise moment it was left. If the editor cuts the two strips of film together in such a way that a part of the action is duplicated in the two shots the effect will appear unnatural. Equally, if he skips a piece of action—say he cuts from the shot where the door is half open to another where it is already closed— there will be a noticeable jump in the continuity and the cut will not be smooth.

The matching of actions in two consecutive shots is a comparatively simple matter for the experienced editor, and even for the novice it is only a question of experimenting until a satisfactory cutting point is reached. More difficult, and also more open to opinion, is the problem of where in the course of a particular piece of movement the cut should be made.

Take an example. A man is sitting at a table on which stands a glass of wine. He leans forward, picks up the glass with his right hand, brings it to his lips and drinks. Let us assume—as shown in *Figure 1*—that this simple scene has been covered from three different angles and consider the various ways in which the editor could cut from one to another.

If the intention is to cut from long to medium shot, the editor could do one of two things. He could let the action start in long shot, and then at some point during the downward (or upward) movement of the man's arm cut to the matching mid-shot. Alternatively, he could wait for the point when the hand grasps the glass, and time the cut in such a way that the *whole* of the upward movement appears in the second shot. Without being dogmatic about the point, we can say that it is normally preferable to use the second method. By showing one specific movement in long shot and the other in mid-shot, the cut does not interrupt a continuous flowing movement, but is, so to speak, punctuating the whole

Figure I. The three main angles : close-up, medium shot and long shot. How to cut from one to another is discussed in the text.

action at the moment of rest. The impression created is that two distinct phases of the movement are seen in two distinct ways : the flow of movement is not interrupted until it has of its own accord momentarily come to a stop.

An alternative moment of rest occurs when the actor is just about to start his movement, and this provides a third and possibly the best cutting point. Just before the actor starts his forward movement, his facial expression—a glance downward, possibly— will register his intention. If the cut is made precisely at this point— i.e., just *before* the hand begins to move—it will be smooth, because it will coincide with the moment of change from rest to activity. Before the cut, the actor will be sitting still : then, as he registers his intention of moving his hand, the spectator will anticipate what is about to happen and will be ready to see the effect of the resolution in another shot.

This last timing of the cut is particularly apt in the case where the transition is to be from close-up to mid-shot. At the moment the actor begins his forward movement, the spectator will *want* to see the effect and will therefore welcome the cut from close to

218

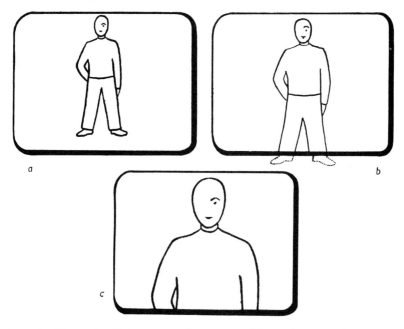

Figure 2. There is insufficient contrast between *a* and *b* to make a smooth cut ; a cut from *a* to *c* makes a distinct contrast.

medium shot. The cut will, in fact, merely be altering the size of the image in such a way that the entire action of picking up the glass (which the close-up cannot show) becomes visible.

If the reverse is required, that is to say if a cut from mid-shot to close-up is needed, then there is again a good case for cutting *during* a movement. Most of the action could be shown in the medium shot and the cut to the close-up delayed until the point in the man's upward movement at which the hand is just entering frame. In such a case, the editor must, of course, match the action of the two shots. The cut will be effective because it will, so to speak, be cueing the hand into the close-up. There is a pictorial reason for the cut because it comes at the precise moment at which the close-up begins to contain all the significant action.

Thus it appears that a cut which is made on the end or beginning of a movement, or a cut which is necessary to accommodate a piece of action not visible in the previous set-up, is usually preferable to a cut which fortuitously interrupts a continuous movement. But it must be emphatically stressed that this is not *always* so. We are here only concerned with describing the various mechanical

219

possibilities without, for the moment, considering which is dramatically most apt.

Extent of Change in Image Size and Angle

Figure 2 shows a possible progression from a full shot to two alternative closer shots. It will be seen that the difference in size between *a* and *b* is very small, and that the pictorial composition of the two shots is almost the same. As a result a cut from *a* to *b* will be unsatisfactory. The spectator will witness only a very slight change in the image, and will be momentarily irritated by what will appear to him as a small but clearly perceptible shift. There will be insufficient contrast between the succeeding images to make the transition smooth. A cut from *a* to *c*, on the other hand, makes a quite distinct contrast : the composition of the two pictures is entirely different and there is no longer any question of a small shift in cutting from one to the other. The cut will therefore be smooth.

A similar example is provided by *Figure 3*. Here again, the cut from *a* to *b* brings about too small a change in image size to make it mechanically satisfactory ; if a cut to a closer shot is desired, then it must be to a *considerably* closer image, such as is illustrated in *c*.

Apart from this mechanical reason, there is another consideration which in both cases makes the cut from *a* to *b* unacceptable. Every cut—this much we can insist on—should make a point. There must be a reason for transferring the spectator's attention from one image to another. In the case of cutting from *a* to *b* the change is so small that the dramatic point the editor is trying to make is, apparently, not really worth making. No appreciable dramatic purpose can be served by cutting from a full shot (*Figure 2a*) to a slightly closer image which is cut off at ankle level (*Figure 2b*). The spectator will sense that nothing significant is being said by the cut and will therefore not accept it without irritation.

What is true of changes in image *size* is equally true of changes of *angle* permissible between two consecutive shots. *Figure 4* shows a plan of camera set-ups in a transition from medium to close shot. In the diagram, a character stands facing the camera, in front of a rigid object on the set, say a standard lamp. From the first camera set-up we are asked to cut to a close-up. A cut from *I* to *IIa* brings on the screen a close-up in which the lamp is still in the same position relative to the character as it was in the

220

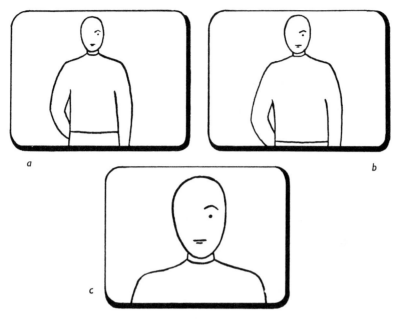

Figure 3.   A cut from *a* to *b* has too small a change in image size ; the cut needs to be to a considerably closer image as in *c*.

medium shot. The cut is therefore acceptable because it is showing the same picture as its predecessor, only closer to. If, on the other hand, the close shot is taken from the camera position *IIb*, where the angle of shooting has been slightly changed, the resulting image will be as shown in the diagram : the standard lamp is now in a different position relative to the actor. As a result, the spectator will get the impression that the lamp has suddenly and inexplicably shifted to the left. The position of the actor's head is in both cases in the centre of the frame, but the background in *IIb* seems to have moved. (In practice, the effect might be cheated by moving the lamp.) Thus the spectator will momentarily become aware of the change and the cut will not be smooth.

If the editor wants, for some reason, to cut to a close shot which *is* taken from a different angle, then the angle change must be made considerably more marked. A position where the camera has been moved through 90 degrees will produce an image entirely different from the mid-shot and will therefore not create momentary confusion. The actor's face will be clearly seen in profile instead of head-on, and the spectator will therefore not expect to see the background in the same position relative to the head.

221

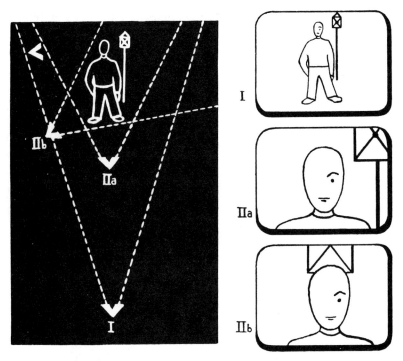

Figure 4. IIa faces in the same direction as *I*. *IIb* makes a slight change. The same angle or a marked change is to be preferred.

Preserving a Sense of Direction

In discussing the battle scenes from *Birth of a Nation*, we noticed that Griffith took the greatest care to show each opposing side always facing in a fixed direction. By doing so he was able to preserve a lucid continuity because the spectator came to recognise that one side was advancing from left to right, the other firing from right to left. Wherever two opposing forces are shown on the screen and a sense of contact between them is to be established, then this clear directional continuity must be preserved. We have already seen in the extracts analysed in the previous section how close shots of two characters in dialogue scenes are made alternately to face left and right (e.g., *17* and *18* in the extract from *The Passionate Friends* on p. 93 and the whole series of alternating close shots in the montage passage from *Citizen Kane*, on p. 117).

In practice, the problem of making adjacent close shots face in opposite directions is illustrated by *Figure 5.* Shot *I* establishes that the characters *A* and *B* are facing each other. Where two

222

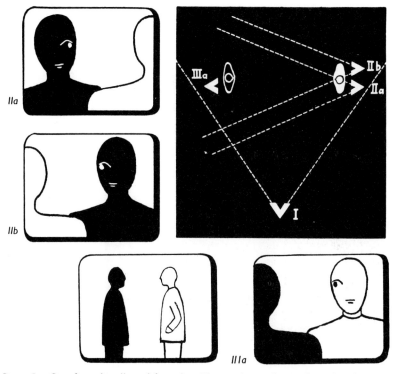

Figure 5. Cuts from *I* to *IIa* and from *I* to *IIIa* are clear ; the cut from *I* to *IIb* would not be clear.

close shots, each taken over the opposing character's shoulder, are desired, the question of where to place the camera arises. If camera set-up *IIa* is used, *B* will still be facing left to right as he was in the medium shot. The cut will therefore be clear. If *IIb* is used, the close shot will show *B* facing from right to left. This will *not* make a clear transition, because the direction of the actor's glance will have been reversed. Similarly, the same argument applies to the close-up of *A* : this must be taken from *IIIa* as shown in the diagram. A clear practical example of this procedure is provided by the sequence of three shots from *Topper Returns* quoted on p. 87. Here the two close shots are taken from so close that the opposing actor's shoulder is not visible, but it will be seen that each actor is facing in the same direction in the close shots and the medium shot.

The necessity for preserving a clear sense of direction is not limited merely to the placing of the camera. Where actors move

223

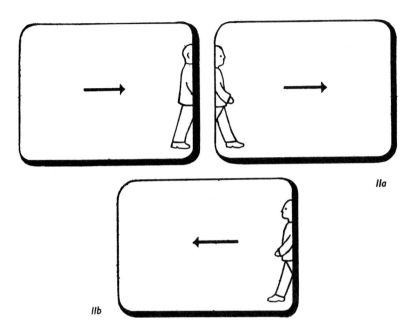

Figure 6. A cut from *I* to *IIa* maintains the same direction of view ; a cut from *I* to *IIb* reverses it and is confusing.

in and out of frame, a similar consistency in the direction of their movements must be preserved. *Figure 6* shows an example. If the actor walks out of frame to the right, it will be perfectly acceptable if he enters the next shot from the left : i.e., if we cut from *I* to *IIa.* On the other hand, to cut to *IIb* would not be acceptable because it would imply that the actor instantaneously and without reason turned through 180 degrees. If, owing to the demands of the story, it is desired that the actor should turn around in the course of his walk, then the moment at which he turns must be *shown* (or in some way implied). *Figure 7* illustrates the point. In *a* he is walking from left to right and out of frame ; in *b* we see that he turns back ; and in *c* we are therefore prepared to see him re-enter frame from the right. To leave shot *b* out, however, would confuse the spectator because he would not expect to see the action travelling right to left, and would be surprised to see the actor re-enter from the right hand side.

All these simple rules are to be taken with a certain amount of caution. In the normal way, it is almost certainly better to cut the scenes as we have indicated, but, as we shall see later, there may be

224

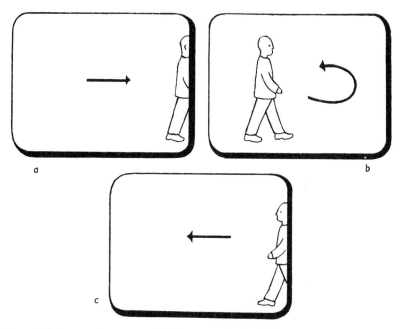

Figure 7. If the actor does reverse his direction, this should be shown as in *b* ; a direct cut from *a* to *c* would be unacceptable.

exceptions when the rules need to be modified to convey certain dramatic effects.

Preserving a Clear Continuity

Several other points, besides keeping a clear sense of direction, must be kept in mind if a lucid continuity is to result. In general, it is true to say that a sequence which introduces a new locale should start by establishing the topographical relationship between the players and the background. After this, the various close shots, in which individual characters and objects are singled out for closer inspection, will be seen by the spectator as part of the larger surroundings which have already been shown. There are, however, many exceptions to this procedure. Sometimes a director will deliberately *start* a sequence on a close shot of a detail and only later reveal it in relation to the larger setting. The opening sequence from *Louisiana Story* (p. 137) is a case in point. But it should be noticed that the purpose of this treatment was to create an aura of mystery about the swamp-forest ; it was not to give a continuous, developing piece of " plot." Even where a sequence starts

225

on a detail, it is important that the whole setting should be shown at some stage.

Taking this principle a little further down the scale, we see that, if a big close-up is used, it should be preceded by an image which shows the detail in its setting : i.e., by a shot in which the same object is seen from farther away.

In the same way, if there is a new development of some sort in the scene, which alters the situation shown in the establishing shot, then the scene must be re-established. If a new character walks into a room it is essential to show him coming in and placing himself relative to the other characters before any close shot can be introduced. The whole of the sequence from *The Passionate Friends* (p. 90) provides an instructive example in this respect. Just preceding the extract quoted we have seen Howard and Steven talking to each other, and the scene was played in a series of close shots. As Mary enters, the whole scene is re-established. Shot *1* quite clearly shows Mary entering and takes her to a definite position in the room. After this, when the close shots come on the screen, we know exactly where each character is positioned. Each time one of the actors begins to move, the camera goes a little farther back to show his movement. Again, towards the end of the passage, when Howard begins to talk to Steven, we start with a shot which re-establishes the situation so that the new grouping of the actors is clearly explained.

Matching Tone

While the cameraman is shooting the film, he takes care to maintain a constant photographic quality throughout the whole of his work. When the editor comes to cut the material he must guard against joining two shots in which the key of the lighting is noticeably different. The sheer physical difference in the light and shade values of the two shots will draw the spectator's attention to the transition and result in a harsh cut.

With the cameraman constantly in control of the lighting and the grading of the prints, this problem of matching shots according to their tone is generally not great. In a documentary or compilation film, where the material has often been shot by several cameramen working separately, it becomes much more acute. Equally, the editing of colour films sometimes presents great difficulties in matching the colour values in adjacent shots. This is, however, primarily a problem for the art director, cameraman and colour expert and is in most cases outside the editor's control.

226

Making Sound Flow Over a Cut

It is often possible to improve a cut which is mechanically not smooth by letting sound flow over it. This is discussed in the next chapter.

So far we have dealt only with negative considerations : we have merely described the editing mistakes which must be avoided if a mechanically smooth and physically lucid continuity is to be achieved. We must now turn our attention to more positive problems, to see how a dramatically apt continuity can be evolved.

We have insisted that, whenever a cut is made, there must be a good reason for it : to transfer attention, however smoothly, from one image to another, when the previous image would have answered equally well, can serve no useful purpose. To say this is not merely to state an empty rule : making a cut for a specific dramatic reason may often become a simple matter of necessity, for unless it makes a point a cut is often found to be unsmooth. If, for instance, we cut from a mid-shot to a close-up of a character, there may be no mechanical reason why it should not be acceptable. If the cut marks an important dramatic development it will, in fact, usually be effective. Yet the same cut in a different context may become harsh and unacceptable. If we were to cut to a big close-up just as the actor was saying, " I'll have two lumps of sugar, please," the cut would be emphasising a dramatically insignificant gesture and would appear meaningless to a spectator. It would, in other words, not be a smooth cut.

Thus, although the mechanical rules of cutting must be kept in mind, the decisive consideration at the junction of any two shots must be that the transition should be motivated by dramatic necessity. A continuity of shots in which each cut is dramatically useful will often appear smooth even if the mechanical matching is imperfect.

Take an example. A man is sitting in an arm-chair. He has put a cigarette in his mouth and is searching his pockets for matches. It is clear that he cannot find them. He glances around the room and suddenly a look of recognition comes over his face : he gets up and walks to the other end of the room, where a box of matches is lying on a table. There are two entirely different ways in which this scene could be cut. The whole action in the chair could be played in one shot and cut to another matching shot which takes up the actor's movement and pans with him as he walks to the table. The cut would be mechanically smooth and the action would be clear.

Now let us look at an alternative way of editing the scene. The first shot could be shown as before. Then, when the actor recognises something off screen and is just about to get up, we cut to what he sees, namely a shot of the matches lying on the table. The shot of the matches is now held until the actor walks into frame and we see him pick them up. At the moment the actor looks up, the spectator *wants* to see what it is that has caught his eye. At this moment there is a motive for cutting : the cut makes a point because it identifies the *reason* for the actor's movement. In the first method of cutting the scene the cut made no point : no idea was carried across it—the joining of the shots was a simple physical necessity which could have no significance for the spectator. In the second case, the cut made a point : the first shot *caused* the second, and the continuity was therefore more incisive.

In comparing these two methods of cutting a scene, it would be wrong to insist that every cut should be motivated in the way we described in the second example. There are obviously a great number of cases—such as when a character has to be taken from one room to another—where it is physically necessary to shoot the scene in two separate takes and simply join them to form a continuous movement. One can, of course, not make a hard and fast rule. What does seem clear is that a series of dramatically apt cuts is generally to be preferred : it keeps the audience thinking and reacting continuously and never allows the presentation to become a passive record.

There is, moreover, a further advantage to be gained from editing the scene in the second way. Say, for example, it takes the actor ten steps to cross the room and reach the matches. In the first case, where the whole movement has to be shown, all the ten footsteps must be seen if the continuity is not to become jerky. In the second case the man's walk is not shown at all. From the moment at which we imply that he is about to rise, we cut to the matches. Then after a very short time of holding shot *2* on the screen, the actor can be allowed to enter frame. The spectator, interested only in the sequence of significant events, will not notice any physical inaccuracy. The editor is able to reduce the screen time of the scene by simply cutting out the interval during which the actor is crossing the room. In other words, he is able to edit the scene in such a way that the significant events are shown in full and the physical movement is unobtrusively cut down to a minimum.

In cases where a character has to be conveyed from one place to another between two consecutive scenes, this principle of implying the unnecessary intervals can be carried a stage further. For instance : *A* is shown talking to *B* in the street just outside the apartment house at which he lives. We see him taking leave of his companion, and the script demands that the next scene should take place between *A* and his wife, in his third floor flat. Now if the transition from the first scene to the second were to be shot strictly as it would happen in real life, it would be necessary to show *A* entering the house, pushing the button to call the lift, waiting for the lift to descend, stepping into the lift, ascending to the third floor, getting out, walking up to the door of his flat, and opening the door. Only after all this could the second scene commence. Unless there is some dramatic point to be made in the course of the journey, this is clearly an unnecessary waste of time. The time gap between the scene in the street and the scene in the flat must in some way be bridged.

Several ways suggest themselves. As the two men are seen parting in the street, the camera could stay on *B* and let *A* walk out of frame, obviously towards his house. Then, after *B* had been held on the screen for a little time, a cut could take us straight up to *A* as he was entering his flat. The period of time during which *B* was held on the screen would be sufficient to imply that *A* had meanwhile had time to ascend to the third floor.

Alternatively, it would be possible to cut the scene in another way. As the two men are parting, *A* might say something to the effect that his wife is waiting for him at home. The line of dialogue would justify a cut straight to the interior of the flat where the wife is waiting. After a very brief period it would be permissible to cut to the inside of the flat door and show *A* entering. The spectator will not mind seeing *A* entering the flat a few seconds after he was seen in the street : it will appear to him that the short time in which the shot of the wife was held on screen was sufficient to let *A* ascend to the third floor. It will be seen that the physical continuity is wrong, yet because the order of events is dramatically significant, this does not matter. From the street scene where the wife's name is mentioned, the logical cut is to a shot of the wife herself. From the shot of the wife waiting for her husband, the logical cut is to a shot of *A* entering.

In each case the idea of the scene is carried over into the next and the dramatic continuity is strong enough to make the spectator ignore the physical inaccuracies.

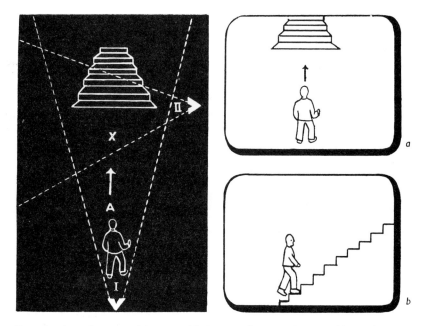

Figure 8. A cut from *a* to *b* is acceptable because the action is ostensibly continuous, although a portion of the movement is omitted.

The ability to shorten (or lengthen) the screen duration of an event is a most important factor in the editor's control of pace. In the cases we have mentioned, the shortening of an interval is brought about by implying that the piece of action is taking place off screen. But this principle of condensing real time can often be carried a stage further. It is sometimes possible to join two shots in such a way that the action is ostensibly continuous, yet, in fact, a portion of the movement has been omitted.

Say, for instance, an actor is seen running away from camera towards an ascending flight of steps. The camera is behind the actor and it is intended that as he reaches the steps we should cut to another closer shot facing across the flight which will show him jumping on to the first step (*Figure 8*, shots *a* and *b*). Now, strictly speaking, the two shots should be matched : the point in the action at which the first is cut should be taken up by the second.

In practice, this may not always be necessary. In the course of the first shot there may come a point when the spectator will begin to realise that since the actor is running towards the flight, he will jump up the first two or three steps when he actually gets there. In such a case, it may on some occasions be acceptable to cut to

230

shot *b* a few feet before the actor has reached the bottom of the steps in shot *a* : say, at the point at which the actor has reached position " x " marked in the diagram. The fact that the cut is mechanically wrong does not matter unless the spectator can notice the error, and the chances are that it will pass unnoticed. The idea " he is going to jump " is planted in the first shot and the actual leap is shown in the second. The impetus of the idea is so strong that it makes the mechanical discrepancy appear unimportant. In case this example appears a little too fanciful, here are two similar instances quoted by Sidney Cole from his own experience :

In *They Came to a City*[1] . . . we had a scene in which Frances Rowe having decided, not surprisingly, to go back to the city instead of returning to Bournemouth with her mother to console her declining years, says " Good-bye" and goes, leaving the mother (Mabel Terry-Lewis) in tears. The emotional climax of the sequence is a shot in which Miss Terry-Lewis moves away from the camera and recedes, a lonely and defeated figure, into the distance.

The problem that confronted us when editing was that, because of the physical nature of the set, there had, for reasons of continuity, to be another shot between that of Miss Terry-Lewis in tears and the long shot in which she made her final exit. In the first shot, she was standing inside the base of a tower ; in the last shot she had already emerged from the tower and descended the two steps that led up to it. It was clear, therefore, that the second or middle shot was one in which she emerged from the tower and descended those two steps. Nothing could be simpler, as a piece of physical continuity. Unfortunately, from the point of view of dramatic tension and carry-over of emotion, this second shot was redundant.

Michael Truman, the editor, and myself were stymied. We could eliminate the offending shot and dissolve or wipe from shot *1* to shot *3*. But that would almost certainly be as destructive of dramatic effect, since optical transitions of this kind invariably suggest changes of time or place to the audience. It would, in any event, look untidy to the professional eye. There was no other shot that we could place between shot *1* and shot *3* with any sort of logical or emotional justification. So we took our courage—and our scissors—firmly in our hands, removed the offending shot, and made a physically smooth cut from shot *1* to shot *3*. Topographically speaking, we had jumped our character from inside the base of the tower to a position twelve yards distant, ignoring such details as a doorway and two steps on the way ! Dramatically we had preserved the emotional rhythm of the scene.

I have not had one comment from professionals or laymen about this cut. Music was flowing over it, which probably helped its acceptance. But I think that in similar circumstances such a cut would be acceptable even without any sound at all.

The final sequence [of *My Learned Friend*] shows Will Hay and Claude Hulbert trapped in the clock-chamber of Big Ben by a demented Mervyn Johns, who proceeds to pursue them with a beefeater's halberd. In desperation, Will and Claude try the nearest door they see, walk through and only realise as they come to the edge of a parapet and see traffic hundreds of feet below them that they are out on the ledge running around the base of the clock-face of Big Ben.

[1] Film Editing *by Sidney Cole. British Film Institute Pamphlet, 1944.*

Now the effectiveness of this gag depends on the audience realising where Will and Claude are before they do themselves. The sequence of angles was designed to help this. From a mid-shot inside the tower in which they go through the door, the cut was to an enormous long-shot outside, showing the whole top of the Big Ben tower, with the two tiny figures of Will and Claude getting to the parapet. The next shot necessarily had to be close enough to show their reaction to what the audience already knew, thus topping off the gag.

The difficulty was this. We had to let them go through the door in the *inside* shot, to make clear what they were doing. Once we did this, the point at which in strict continuity we could pick them up in the outside long-shot left so few feet of that shot before we had to cut to a third shot, that the action it contained had insufficient time to register. I suggested to the editor that, without altering either of the shots on either side of it, he should make the long-shot of a length sufficient to enable it to be seen. " But that means I'll have to repeat the action," he said. " Precisely," was my reply. " You've taken them through the door in mid-shot ; nevertheless, start your cut of the long shot with the door *closed* and repeat all the action of opening the door and coming through." He did this and found that by this repetition he gave time for the audience to adjust their eye to the extreme change in size of shot ; and this adjustment was complete at just about the point in the long-shot where it was in exact continuity with the inside mid-shot.

These two examples throw light on the whole problem of smooth cutting. In the first passage a portion of the action is omitted ; in the second, a movement is partially duplicated. (The second device is relatively common in comedies.) Yet both passages are smooth because the continuity of ideas is forceful and clear. The conclusion we must draw from this is that mechanical smoothness is only a secondary factor in good editing. A smooth flow of ideas from shot to shot, that is to say a series of purposeful juxtapositions, is the primary requirement. There is sometimes a tendency in modern film studios for the editor to be so preoccupied with the mechanical details of presentation that much of the positive value of editing is lost in the process. This is the result of an entirely misplaced professional pride. Smooth cutting is not an end in itself; it is merely one of the means to a dramatically significant continuity.

Timing

The ability to lengthen or shorten the duration of an event in bringing it to the screen gives the director and editor a highly sensitive instrument for the control of timing. We have seen how unimportant intervals can be bridged and how certain actions can be shown on the screen happening much faster than they do in real life. But the control of timing which the film-maker gains through editing can be used for more positive purposes than the mere cutting down of unnecessary intervals. It enables him to present a series of consecutive events in such a way that each new development is revealed at the dramatically appropriate moment. This applies to the spacing of events within the whole story as well as to the timing of individual cuts.

In order to get a clear picture of the full advantages which are derived from the purposive timing of cuts, it may be useful to consider two passages from a film which did not employ cutting at all : by assessing the loss in dramatic effectiveness which is incurred by discarding the factor of editing, we should be able to get a clear picture of its real value.

Two short extracts from Alfred Hitchcock's film *Rope* are given below. The film was an experiment in which the director attempted to construct a continuity entirely without cuts : the action was kept moving by means of a continuously moving camera.

(1) Two young college students, Brandon (John Dall) and Phillip (Farley Granger), have killed their fellow-student, David Kentley. Out of sheer bravado, they plan a party on the night of the murder to which they invite their old schoolmaster, Rupert Cadell (James Stewart), and the murdered boy's parents. Throughout most of the party, the boys succeed in hiding from their visitors the fact that they have seen David on the same night : they pretend to have invited him and feign surprise at his lateness. Rupert notices their strange nervous behaviour and begins to become suspicious. Then, as he is ready to depart, he goes to fetch his hat from the maid and accidentally finds the first material clue to the boys' guilt.

In a mid-shot of Rupert and the maid we see her handing him a hat from the cupboard. Rupert absent-mindedly puts it on : it is the wrong hat, for it is obviously too small for him. He takes it off, lowers it down in front of him (*la*) and suddenly notices something inside. As Rupert holds the hat in front of him, the camera slowly moves in to a close shot (*lb*), and reveals that there are initials inside the hat—the initials of the murdered boy. (In order to let the camera pick out this detail it was necessary for Rupert to tilt the hat to one side and wait for a period of about three and a half seconds (5 feet of film) while the camera was moving in.) Then, when enough time has been given to the audience to identify the initials, the camera slowly moves up to show Rupert's expression (*lc*) as he suddenly realises what has happened.

(2) Toward the end of the same film, Rupert has returned to the boys' flat to question them about David's disappearance. He has in his pocket the rope with which he suspects the boys strangled their friend, and is now ready to force them to confess.

Rupert is standing with his back to the two boys. The camera is holding a close shot of his pocket : we see him take the rope from it (*2a*). He is talking obliquely about a murder, not referring to the details of the scene, but in a tone which makes it clear that he knows what has happened. Suddenly he turns around to face the boys, holding the rope in front of him (*2b*)—giving the final proof that he knows who murdered David. While he goes on speaking, the camera slowly pans away to the right, recording in its path first the corner of the room (*2c*), then a neon sign visible outside the window (*2d*), and then finally reaching the reaction shot of the boys (*2e*). It takes the camera 10 feet to reach the boys and a further 5 feet to come to rest on them.

Both these extracts show how the timing of effects is dulled by the inability to use cuts. In the first passage, there is a simple instance of how an effect can be wasted through bad timing. At the moment we see Rupert pausing to identify something inside the hat, the dramatically important image becomes what he sees. In the course of a normal film, the editor would at this point cut straight to a close-up of the initials, thereby giving the impression of showing the reason for Rupert's hesitation. The first image gives a dramatic motive for showing the second and the continuity would therefore be clear and incisive. In the way the scene has been managed, there is a dramatically meaningless interval between the time Rupert sees the initials and the close-up. The camera movement does not contribute to the effect, it merely delays it by a meaningless—and psychologically inappropriate—device. What matters in the scene is the shot of Rupert (i.e., the image seen before the camera starts moving) and the close-up of the initials (i.e., the image seen at the end of the movement). No purpose can be served by making a camera movement intervene between the two.

Similarly, when the close-up has been on the screen long enough to let the spectator identify the initials, the next significant event is Rupert's reaction. In a normal film, a cut would have taken us from the one to the other : a clear dramatic cause-and-effect relationship would have resulted. The slow retreating of the camera merely blunts the effect.

A similar process can be observed in the second example. At the precise moment that Rupert turns around, the two boys know that they have been found out. The next significant event is their reaction. If the film had been normally edited, the editor would at this point have cut to the reaction shot (*2e*) so that the spectator could immediately see the effect of the previous image. The image *2b* poses, as it were, the dramatic question " How will they react?" and *2e* answers it : the most effective continuity is therefore to cut straight from the one to the other. As it is done here, there is a considerable interval between seeing the rope and the boys' reaction.

It may be objected that this delaying of the reaction shot was intentional, that the director wanted to keep the spectator in suspense by not revealing *2e* immediately. This would, of course, be a perfectly justifiable interpretation of the scene. But even if this was the intention, it is questionable whether the delay has been achieved in the most effective way. After the camera begins its panning movement, it reveals on its travels a series of objects which are completely irrelevant to the situation. The image of the neon light outside—in itself a picturesque but utterly insignifi-

234

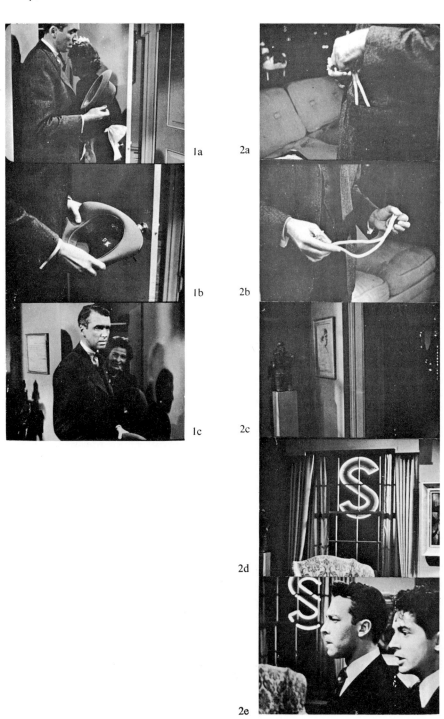

1a

2a

1b

2b

1c

2c

2d

2e

cant detail—does nothing to reinforce the tension. The delay in the reaction is brought about by showing the audience something that has nothing to do with the story : the dramatic conflict is momentarily side-tracked.

If the director had not been bound to this particular formula of presentation, he could have delayed the reaction equally well by cutting. He could have left the shot of Rupert on the screen for as long as he felt necessary : the cut to the boys' reaction could then have been made at the point when the director felt that the suspense had been held long enough. The advantage of this method of editing the scene is that the spectator would all the time be watching something on the screen that is part of the conflict. Holding the shot of Rupert would not have decreased the suspense to be derived from delaying the reaction : on the contrary it would have increased it, because the spectator would all the time have been watching images relevant to the cat-and-mouse game being enacted on the screen.

In making a comparison between the continuity of *Rope* and that of a normally edited film, several points emerge. It must be obvious that, had the two scenes been edited, the dramatic effects would have been achieved more incisively. The exact moment at which the image of the two boys' reaction should be seen could have been selected—after some experiment on the cutting bench, if necessary —and then carried into practice ; the precise moment at which it becomes important that the spectator should see the initials inside the hat could have been *chosen* and then used. The editor could have timed the effects to best advantage without being hampered by any of the physical complications of long camera movements. If the scene had been shot from the requisite number of camera angles, he would have been able to do this with complete freedom. Where a general lack of dramatic precision is the overall impression created by *Rope*, a precise, dramatically taut continuity could have been achieved.

The effect on the total impact of a film made in this way can be imagined. The five feet of camera movement which the camera takes to burrow into the hat is a complete waste of screen time. If this loss of time is multiplied by the number of times it must occur in the course of a complete film, one gets a picture of the overall loss of pace which must result.

Apart from the problem of timing individual cuts, the question of correctly timing an entire event in relation to the rest of the sequence can become extremely important. In the chapter on editing

236

comedy sequences, we have discussed how in some instances a joke can be achieved by anticipating it—by forestalling the actor who is later to find himself on the receiving end of a custard pie ; or, in other cases, by surprising the audience—having a joke " on " the spectator. In the sequence from *Topper Returns* the joke is timed to appear a good deal after it was first established that it would occur, and it is precisely this seemingly reversed way of showing the events that has produced the comic effect. In the passage quoted from *The Third Man*, the timing procedure was the exact opposite and a different kind of comic effect was achieved.

A similar choice is open in more serious dramatic scenes. In the passage from *The Passionate Friends* the spectator knows long before it actually happens that Mary will discover the programme. A feeling of suspense is created by delaying her reaction and finally showing it after the passage has gradually worked up to a climax. The order of events is precisely analogous to that employed in the *Topper Returns* example.

The alternative method of introducing an important event is to let it come as a surprise to the spectator. Here is an example.

GREAT EXPECTATIONS[1]

Extract from Reel 1

The opening of the film. It is preceded only by a shot of the leaves of a book over which the commentator establishes the little boy in shot 1 to be Pip.

			Ft. fr.
1	Exterior Thames Estuary. Sunset. V.L.S. of a small boy—Pip—running left to right along the bank of the Estuary. *Camera tracks and pans with Pip as he runs round a bend in the pathway and comes towards camera.* A gibbet is built on the edge of the path, *camera right,* and Pip glances up at it as he passes—he continues running and moves *out of picture camera right.*	The wind is making a high-pitched, ghostly whistling noise.	38

Dissolve to :

2	Exterior Churchyard. M.S. Pip. He is carrying a bunch of holly in his right hand. He climbs over a broken stone wall and *camera pans right* with him as he walks past the tombstones and old graves in the churchyard. *Camera continues panning* as he makes his way towards one of the tombstones and kneels in front of it—he is now in *M.L.S.*	Wind continues.	31

[1] *Director : David Lean. Editor : Jack Harris. Cineguild, 1946.*

237

			Ft. fr
3	M.S. of Pip kneeling at the foot of the grave. He pulls up an old rose bush which he throws aside, pats down the earth again and then places his bunch of holly at the head of the grave near the engraved tombstone.	Wind continues. Crackling of branches.	21 5
4	M.C.S. Pip kneeling near the tombstone. He looks round nervously *towards camera.*	Wind gets louder.	10 11
5	L.S. *from Pip's eyeline* of the leafless branches of a tree. The wind is blowing them and to Pip they look like bony hands clutching at him.	Wind and crackling of branches.	6 3
6	M.C.S. Pip looking round *as in* 4.		5 9
7	M.S. of the trunk of an old tree *from Pip's eyeline.* It looks very sinister and to him like a distorted human body.	Crackling of branches.	4 10
8	M.S. Pip. He jumps up from the grave and runs away right to left towards the stone wall. *Camera pans with him, then becomes static as he runs towards camera* and into the arms of a large, dirty, uncouth and horrible-looking man. From his clothes and shackles it is obvious that he is an escaped convict.	Pip screams loudly.	6 12
9	C.S. Pip. His mouth is open as he screams, but a large, dirty hand is clapped over it, silencing him.		1 11
10	C.S. of the Convict. His face is dirty and scowling, his hair is closely cut. He leers down at Pip.	Convict : Keep still, you little devil, or I'll cut your throat.	3 9

Shot *1* is mainly an establishing shot of the locale, but its atmospheric value is tremendous.[1] The lighting is propitious—neither day nor night—and the sinister quality of the scenery is heightened by the presence of the gibbet. The distance gives the effect of loneliness to the small figure of the boy.

Next (2), we see Pip entering the churchyard : we see his features for the first time and our suspicion that he is frightened is confirmed. The whole scene is still sinister but a little more grotesque—the camera is keeping to Pip's height, making the gravestones look a little larger than life.

During all this time we have heard the wind : it is howling and whistling with a haunting, high-pitched note. Towards the end of shot *3*, a new sound is suddenly heard. Strange rustling and creaks are introduced for the first time.

[1] *Notes by Jack Harris.*

1a

1b

2

3

4

5

6

7

8a

8b

9

10

We cut to a closer shot of Pip (4) as he looks up from the grave. His look suddenly freezes as he notices what we see in shot 5—a large, creaking tree with branches like weird limbs stretching towards him, shot from a low angle as if seen through the eyes of a child.

Again, we cut back to Pip (6) and again (7) are shown an even more hideous image of another tree : this time the trunk looks like some horrible mutilated body.

The boy and we can stand no more of this and it is a distinct relief to see that the boy is running away from this ghost-like, supernaturally frightening atmosphere. When he has gained some speed in his run and is well on his way to escape from the cemetery, suddenly we see that he has run into something horrible—horrible and alive. Before we can see any more, Pip starts to scream and we see him doing so in close-up.

Only after this do we see for the first time what the boy has run into—a large, horrible man ; then for the first time he speaks, with a voice like a rasp.

The whole of this passage was planned in cuts before it was shot, although the director did, of course, shoot a certain amount of cover. The most difficult thing to get over by photography was the sudden appearance of the convict. The effect was finally obtained by panning with the boy until he runs straight into the stationary convict.

The difficulty in the editing was to decide on the exact frame up to which to leave the panning shot on the screen and to cut to the boy screaming. The effect aimed at was to leave the shot on the screen sufficiently long to let the audience see that the boy had run into a man—and not a very nice man, at that—but not sufficiently long to get a good look and be able to decide that he was after all something recognisably human. As a matter of interest, there are fourteen frames from the time the convict appears to the close-up of Pip. The sound of Pip's scream starts four frames before the cut, at just the precise moment that the apparition is taken away from the audience's sight.

Here, then, is an instance where the intention was to take the audience by surprise, to introduce a new fact through a shock. It will be seen that, to do this, it is not enough to let the surprising fact merely appear in the course of the narrative : the shock must be planned from some way back. First, an atmosphere of mystery is conveyed, a danger is established. Then, just as a rather frightening image (shot 7) has been shown, Pip starts to run away : we are just ready to feel relieved when the really frightening image appears. It takes us unawares, just at the moment when the tension was beginning to slacken. The director and editor have deliberately contrived to make the spectator believe that the danger is over, and then caught him on the rebound.

If the director's intention had been to give suspense to the sequence, he would have had to edit it differently. He would have shown us a shot of Magwitch watching Pip and would therefore have warned us of what was about to happen. The surprise would have come to the boy. The audience's emotional reaction would have been the suspense of waiting for the moment it happened.

240

What is worth noting here is that, whether the effect comes after the spectator has been prewarned, or whether it comes as a shock, it must be planned from some way back. If suspense is aimed at, the spectator must first be shown what to wait for. If a shock is intended, the prewarning must be, so to speak, negative : the spectator must be deliberately led away from the significant event before it can come to him as a surprise.

The choice between anticipating a climax and bringing it on as a surprise arises on a more routine level every time an editor cuts to a close shot. The question arises when a particularly startling event is just about to occur—say a character is just about to take poison—whether to cut to the close-up *at* or *before* the crucial moment. If the cut to the close-up occurs some time *before* the actor swallows the poison, then the very fact that a close-up has come on the screen will make the spectator anticipate a climax and feel suspense for it to happen. Alternatively, if the cut to the close-up coincides with the moment the lips touch the glass, it will come as a surprise. In the example we have just quoted, the editor, after giving the spectator a shock, chose to hold back the really frightening image for a further fourteen frames, thereby adding a momentary uncertainty and suspense before the final revelation.

Pace : Rhythm

In our analysis of the final chase sequence from *Naked City* we saw how the director and editor contrived to vary the state of tension by continually altering the rate of cutting. By various mechanical means they controlled the speed of the passage of events and thereby the degree of excitement evoked by the scene. We must now turn our attention to the different mechanical means of controlling pace which are at the editor's disposal.

The variation of pace is significant only in so far as it quickens or dulls the spectator's interest in what he sees on the screen. In any discussion of it, it is therefore important to distinguish between the pace created mechanically—by simply making the images come on the screen at a faster rate—and the pace generated by the inherent interest of the story. A sequence can be at once fast-moving and dull—witness the chase at the end of almost any second-rate Western ; or it can be slow-moving and tense— witness some of the famous Hitchcock suspense scenes. However quickly the passage of events at the climax of *Naked City* had been presented, however urgent the sound accompaniment, its impact on the spectator would have been much less if the dramatic conflict had not been previously convincingly established.

A superficial impression of fast, exciting action can often be created simply by cutting a sequence at great speed. Making images follow one another faster and faster in itself produces an effect of increased excitement and can be used to strengthen the story's interest. But it is important that this speeding up of the cutting should be carried out with the closest attention to the content of the shots. In attempting to increase the rate of cutting, it is useless to look at the absolute lengths of the shots and then arbitrarily reduce them. A sequence composed of shots each about five feet long can, under certain circumstances, appear much slower than another sequence employing strips of film twice this length. Each image tells its own story and must therefore be considered individually. One image will convey all its meaning in a short space of time, another will take longer : this must be taken into account if the increased rate of cutting is not to lead to obscurity. For even if a sequence is to stimulate the spectator's interest primarily through the increase in pace, it is still necessary that each shot should remain on the screen long enough to be intelligible.

For instance, if the director wishes to show an insert of a letter on the screen, the length of time for which he will have to hold it obviously depends on the amount of writing the letter contains. There is a definite length of time which allows the average spectator to read all the words. To hold the shot for a shorter time than this means withholding part of its information ; keeping it on the screen longer means boring sections of the audience while they wait for the next shot. An image of an actor running from one place to another must be shown in full if its complete meaning is to reach the audience. To cut away from it before the actor has reached his destination, because it happens to be desirable that the sequence be cut faster, will mean that part of the shot's information is withheld from the spectator. On the other hand, an insert of a static object—say a close-up of the revolver in the killer's hand—merely establishes that the killer is, in fact, holding a revolver : a few seconds will suffice to allow this shot to convey all its meaning.

Similarly, where a long shot of a piece of action must usually be left on the screen for a considerable interval of time to let the spectator identify the action, a close shot makes a much more direct appeal and is more quickly comprehensible. Thus—and we are here talking in much too general terms to suggest any definite

242

rules—it will normally be permissible to hold the close shot for a shorter time than the long shot.

Having considered the content of each shot and the size of its image, there is a further factor to be taken into account : the context. A shot which introduces an unexpected fact to the audience must be left on the screen longer than one which merely reintroduces something familiar. We shall have more to say about this later. Meanwhile, all we can suggest is that each shot, in order to be intelligible and to convey all its meaning, must be held on the screen for a certain minimum length of time. That minimum is determined in each case by the size of the image, its content and amount of movement within it, and the context. It is not, of course, implied that this " critical " length of a shot can be precisely calculated, or even that it should be, were that possible. The point is that when an editor is assembling a sequence with a view to giving it an extremely fast tempo, he must bear in mind the particular characteristics of each shot.

Cutting down shots to their minimum length is not, however, the only method of creating an impression of speed. When a sustained impression of rapid action is desired, it is often better to achieve this through *varying* the pace rather than by keeping to a constant maximum rate. In the passage we have quoted from *Merchant Seamen* we saw that although the whole sequence is concerned with an extremely rapid series of operations, the pace of presentation is continually varied. The fast passages are deliberately punctuated by slower ones, and this very variation accentuates the impression of speed. If the whole passage had been edited at the rate employed at the climax, the constant maximum speed would soon have become monotonous. The effect of urgency which is conveyed to the spectator depends on the contrast with what has preceded : the *acceleration* of tempo evokes a much greater feeling of fast activity than would a constant maximum rate of cutting. To see this principle at work, we need only look again at the opening of the *Once a Jolly Swagman* excerpt and the two quite artificial changes of tempo in the excerpt from *Brighton Rock*.

The effect which the rate of cutting has on the spectator is further governed by the nature of the shot juxtapositions. Commonly the passages in which the very fastest cutting is employed are sequences in which two parallel streams of action are cross-cut. Here the spectator comes to recognise the pattern of the continuity and *expects* the cut from pursuer to pursued. Each cut makes a point which the spectator can immediately take in and the cutting can therefore be made extremely rapid. In another passage where the cuts take us to new, widely divergent images, each shot must be left on the screen for a considerably longer interval in order to allow the spectator enough time to get accustomed to each new image. The long shot of Will Hay and Claude Hulbert on the Big Ben tower in *My Learned Friend* (p. 231) is an interesting example of this. The size of the image is very considerably changed by the cut so that the long shot needs to be left on the screen for some time to let the spectator get used to it.

Positive use can sometimes be made of this principle, as is illustrated by the passage from *Once a Jolly Swagman*. Here we saw how the editor deliberately switched to various different images of a single piece of continuous action. As a result the spectator was kept continually on the alert and received the impression that the sequence was progressing at great speed.

The problem of maintaining an appropriate pace in the presentation does not end here. Besides controlling the rate of cutting within a sequence, the editor must also evolve suitably timed transitions from one scene to the next. In practice, this presents a choice between joining two consecutive scenes by a cut, a dissolve, or a fade.

The most usual way of joining two consecutive sequences is by means of a dissolve. The artificial pictorial effect creates a discontinuity which clearly separates the adjacent scenes. Through years of usage, moreover, the dissolve has come to be commonly associated with a passage of time. If therefore, the editor wants to imply that the second scene is taking place some time after the first, he will introduce the second scene through a dissolve. Equally, a flash-back, which takes the story back in time, is commonly introduced and terminated in a dissolve : provided that the time interval is clearly brought out in the action—by changing the characters' appearance, the locale, or the time of year in the adjacent scenes—the spectator will have no difficulty in following the story.

To use a dissolve merely to bridge a passage of time between two consecutive pieces of action is, however, not always desirable. In the previous section we discussed the case where a scene taking place in the street outside an apartment house is to be followed by a further scene in the third floor flat of one of the characters. We saw that a phrase of dialogue could effectively link the two scenes in such a way that a cut from the one to the other would make the transition acceptable. In a different set of circumstances the two scenes could have been linked through a dissolve and the transition would, of course, have been equally smooth.

244

Dramatically, however, the two transitions would be somewhat different. Joining two scenes by means of a dissolve introduces a discontinuity ; it creates the impression that one scene has finished and another is beginning. If the scenes are linked by a cut in the way we previously suggested, this break in the action does not become apparent. The sequence appears to be continuous and the dramatic flow is not interrupted. It is of course not possible to say which of the two methods is preferable in the case we have quoted without taking into account which of the two possible dramatic effects is more suitable to the story. But it is worth noting that the automatic use of dissolves to bridge *any* two sequences, which is so common in contemporary films, often leads to inappropriate continuity effects. The dramatic pause which is implied by a dissolve is by no means always desirable when one scene happens to be giving way to another.

This alternative method of joining sequences by a dramatically motivated cut is well illustrated by the flash-backs in David Lean's *The Passionate Friends.* On two occasions (one is discussed on p. 271) he uses a cut to take the action into and later out of flash-back. This gives the impression that the scene in the flash-back forms a dramatically continuous part of a longer sequence ; isolating the content of the flash-back through two dissolves would merely have broken up this sense of continuous development.

The choice between making a transition through a dissolve or a cut is further subject to the requirements of pace. In the film *The World and his Wife* (in U.S.A., *State of the Union*), for instance, Frank Capra (said to supervise closely the editing of his films) frequently makes his scene transitions by cuts. On several occasions he cuts away from an uproarious slapstick sequence just after the crowning joke has been made. While the spectator is still laughing, he is already plunged—through a straight cut—into the next sequence. The impression created is one of tremendous pace : the spectator's interest is never allowed to flag for a moment.

Dissolves can sometimes be used for a more positive purpose than we have described. It is sometimes possible to make the few moments in which the two images are left on the screen together hold a specific dramatic significance. The dissolve into flash-back in the passage we have quoted from *Citizen Kane* (see p. 115) in which the image of Leyland, knowingly shaking his head, is replaced by images of Kane and his wife, carries an obvious dramatic inference.

The use of fades is a more specialised matter. A fade expresses a more pronounced pause in the continuity : it breaks the narrative flow and seals off the action which preceded from the action that follows. Where this is the intention, fades can often be highly effective. Some film-makers, on the other hand, hold that fades should not be used at all, on the grounds that a blank screen is a meaningless thing to show to an audience. There is no point in taking sides on this issue. All that need be said is that a fade, when properly used, can sometimes produce a necessary pause for reflection and give the audience a moment to absorb a dramatic climax. It may thus, if properly timed, be deliberately used to exploit a dramatic carry-over to the following scene.

Other optical devices are sometimes employed to join consecutive scenes. A wipe may sometimes be used instead of a dissolve and an iris may on occasion introduce or close a shot in a more telling way than a fade. The use of these special optical devices is, however, at present rather out of fashion. This is not to say that they may not, at some time in the future, again pass into common usage. The choice between them is largely a matter of currently accepted convention : at present, film-makers seem to prefer the pictorially less artificial effects, namely fades rather than iris shots, dissolves rather than wipes.

So far we have discussed the question of timing of cuts in relation to individual dramatic effects and in relation to the larger requirement of the overall pace of the sequence. We must now turn to the less easily definable factor of film rhythm which imposes a further discipline on the editor's timing.

The problem of cutting shots in a suitable rhythmic relationship is a matter of small, hardly perceptible variations in length : it is difficult to discuss in general terms because the precise shortening or lengthening of each shot depends so closely on its content, and because the importance of correct rhythmical assembly can only be appreciated on viewing a sizable length of film. Further, where a faulty or jerky rhythm has been imposed on a scene, the effect will usually be clearly felt ; where a sound rhythm has been achieved, the effect will appear natural—as if no effort of timing had been involved.

In an earlier part of this chapter we tried to discuss the relative merits of cutting during a movement or at a point of rest. We said that the cut which is timed to coincide with a moment of rest in the action is usually preferable. We are skating on very thin ice here, for the problem of rhythmical cutting is very much open to individual preference. Nevertheless, the reason why we preferred the cut at a moment of rest should now emerge.

The editor should, as we have already said, always strive to preserve the rhythm of the actors' performances. If he introduces cuts in the middle of the actors' movements, he is imposing visual interruptions which do not coincide with the rhythm of the acting. Let us look again at the example we have used before. The movement of the actor leaning forward and picking up his glass of wine takes place in two stages : a forward movement and a backward movement. At the end and beginning of each, there is a moment of rest. Now if the cut coincides with a moment of rest, it is reinforcing the rhythm of the actor's performance. If, on the other hand, it occurs *during* a movement, then it is imposing an externally contrived rhythm on the action.

It is difficult to say precisely why this cutting to the rhythm of the action is so important. Part of the reason is possibly that the cuts are made smoother by being, as it were, visually motivated. But whatever the reason, the practical effect is usually perfectly clear. A carelessly edited sequence, in which the cuts break up the rhythm of the action within the shots, has an untidy, unprofessional appearance which is only too easily recognisable.

The danger of imposing a false rhythm on the action arises also in another way. We have already noted, in the chapter on dialogue scenes, that it is sometimes possible to cut down the intervals between consecutive lines of dialogue and thereby increase the pace of the presentation. This, however, is a rather dangerous practice. The good actor, with a highly developed sense of timing, uses the pauses between lines for a specific reason, and to tamper with his interpretation is often to reduce its effect. What is true of dialogue scenes is equally true of any other scene. The director controls the playing of a scene on the floor at such a pace and with such variations in tempo as he feels to be most appropriate. It is really here that the essential rhythm of the action should be determined. The editor can give it a certain polish, can refine the continuity so as to bring out the highlights, yet the rhythm of the playing, that is to say the rhythm of the actions *within* the shots, will assert itself. There can be little point in cutting out a few frames here and there to accelerate a sequence, if the scene itself is played at a slow tempo.

It is important that we should not give the impression that the creation of an appropriate rhythm is merely a negative concern, something that will come of its own accord provided the actors' timing is respected by the editor. Certain passages where the action is to be told primarily in pictures may sometimes be covered by the director from a large number of angles with a view to creating a special artificial rhythm in the cutting room.

In Howard Hawks' *Red River*, for instance, there is an early passage in which a group of men are just about to start on a long trek across thousands of miles of territory to take their cattle to market. The scene is at dawn and we see—in a long, very slow panning shot—the huge herds of cattle restlessly waiting in their enclosures. The atmosphere is calm and expectant. Then the leader of the expedition gives the word that it is time to set off. The news is passed on and suddenly a large close-up of one of the cow-hands comes on to the screen : his horse rears and the man's face moves across the screen as he shouts " Yippee ! " About a dozen similar shots of the other men follow in rapid succession. After this we cut to another long shot, taken from behind the now advancing horde of cattle, as they slowly start off on their weary trek. The music-track comes in with a traditional theme and the journey has begun. It is difficult to describe in words the precise effect of this passage, for it depends so closely on the timing. The rapidly following series of close-ups acts visually as a sort of clarion call into action : it forms a kind of symphonic opening to the long trek. This is achieved through breaking up the slow monotonous rhythm of the long shots with the dozen or so close-ups. The emotional overtones produced are certainly not inherent in the unedited material : they are produced by the entirely artificial rhythmic pattern which the editor has created.

Selection of shots

If one were trying to formulate a comprehensive theory of editing, one might proceed along the following lines. One might take a simple dramatic situation and list the various possible ways of selecting the most fitting images to express it. Any such theoretical analysis would need to take into account the part played in the sequence by the acting, the lighting, the dialogue, the sets, the sound and the music. An analysis of the editing problems alone would be of little value, because a given passage acted by two different players, lit by two different cameramen, or using slightly different lines of dialogue, might have to be differently cut in each case. Thus a consideration of the problems of selection would involve a detailed analysis of the respective functions of all the other creative elements of film production. It is for this reason that we have made

248

our exposition of the excerpts in Section II embrace the problems faced on the floor—that is, the problem of choosing appropriate images—as well as those faced in the cutting room. In this way it is hoped that most of the problems of selection have been at least raised in the practical examples. In the examples we have chosen, however, the selection of shots was largely designed to reinforce the effectiveness of the dialogue and the acting.

It now remains for us to look at some less typical examples in which the actual choice of images is the crucial creative process. In these, the very acts of selecting the shots and their subsequent juxtaposition are designed to convey emotions and ideas which are not capable of any other form of expression. We are, in fact, dealing with passages of pure cinema in which the editing pattern *is* the film.

THE QUEEN OF SPADES[1]

Extract from Reel 8

St. Petersburg, 1806. Herman (Anton Walbrook), a poor but ambitious officer in the Engineers, has got to know that the Countess Ranyevskaya knows the magic secret of how to win at cards and determines to obtain the secret from her. To gain this end, he courts the Countess's young ward, Lizaveta, in order to get access to the Countess's house.

In a previous sequence, Lizaveta and the Countess—supporting herself with a stick and wearing a long fur cape which rustles as she walks—have been to the opera. Herman has managed to see Lizaveta alone for a few minutes during the performance and arranged to visit the Countess's house. When, later that night, Herman confronts the Countess alone in her bedroom, the Countess dies of the shock of being reminded of her evil past and Herman returns to his quarters without the secret.

			Ft.	fr.
1	C.S. Herman reading book which can be seen. It is : "The Dead Shall Give Up Their Secrets." He drinks. *Camera tracks back and pans down to C.S. of Herman's hand putting down glass. He picks up bottle and fills glass. Camera cranes up as he raises bottle to show Herman in M.C.S. He puts bottle down.*	Music starts. Herman : (whispering) "The Dead Shall Give Up Their Secrets." Music fades.		39	8
	Dissolve to :				
2	C.S. Herman lying asleep. He opens his eyes and looks round, trying to locate the tapping.	*Tapping.*		24	3
3	C.S. Curtains with shadows moving on them.			4	4

[1] *Director : Thorold Dickinson. Editor : Hazel Wilkinson. Screenplay : Rodney Ackland and Arthur Boys, from the story by Pushkin. World Screenplays, 1948.*

249

4	M.C.S. Herman's back. He moves towards window and swiftly opens curtains and windows.	*Tapping.*	28 2
5	M.S. Herman. He leans out of window, then closes it and turns back into room looking puzzled ; he moves forward a step, then stops, listening ; then moves *out of shot.*	*Tapping.* *A sharp banging noise at irregular intervals.*	43 11
6	M.C.S. Herman at door, listening. He opens door suddenly, to see who is outside. The Corridor is empty : a door is banging.	*Banging.*	17 7
7	M.C.S. Herman looking at door.	*Tapping stick.*	10 2
8	L.S. empty corridor. *Camera pans* to show Herman standing there watching. He draws curtains, shuts door and leans against it. He moves *out of shot,* door blows open and curtain blows up into room.	*Tapping stick and dress rustling* *Door slams.* *Strong gale.* *(Continues to shot 19)*	31 15
9	M.C.S. Herman staring with gale blowing in room.		2 1
10	Table with bottle and glass. Table is set *at an angle.*		1 5
11	Dust blowing out of grate.		1 1
12	Standard lamp falling over.		1
13	Lamp in centre of room swinging round and round. Curtains in background.		2 3
14	Bed, with maps blowing off wall		1 2
15	Maps blowing off wall.		1 8
16	Table with bottle falls over.		1 8
17	Lamp swinging round and curtains blowing.		3
18	Window. *Camera moves back* as maps and papers are blown against the window. Curtains flap wildly.		9 3
19	M.S. Herman in middle of room with lamp swinging over his head. Curtain blows down *in front of camera.*	*Wind stops.*	5 7
20	M.S. Herman back to camera. He moves slowly back. Curtain is now still.		6 8
21	M.L.S. Herman. He looks round the disordered room and walks slowly backwards. *Camera starts*		124 7

250

" Lady from Shanghai "

tracking in. He hears the stick and retreats to window. *Camera moves into C.S. as he sits down on the sill.* He closes his eyes as noise of Countess's dress and stick gets louder and louder.	*Tapping stick and dress rustling*
	Stick and dress sound ceases.
	Wind blows.
Herman looks up.	Countess's voice : I am commanded to grant your request . . . three . . . seven . . . ace . . . I forgive you my death on condition that you marry my ward, Lizaveta
He closes his eyes again.	Ivanovna.
	Stick and dress rustling die away.
Herman opens his eyes and looks round the room. *Camera pans up to sword hanging on wall.*	

The sequence is significant from our point of view for the manner in which the director has chosen to convey the state of mind of his character. The whole passage, right up to the end of shot *20*, is an elaborate preparation for the visitation which occurs in *21*. A series of separate images of individually hardly significant details (especially *10–18*) is composed into a sequence. When shown in their present context, the details add up to evoke a sense of the presence of some uncontrollable supernatural threat. It is important to note that, although the shots are viewed from increasingly grotesque angles, each separate image would convey only a minute fraction of this highly complex total effect. It is the cumulative result of the whole series of details, seen in the carefully contrived progression, which gives the sequence its powerful appeal.

An entirely different kind of editing composition is exemplified by the following excerpt.

LADY FROM SHANGHAI[1]

Extract from Reel 2

O'Hara (Orson Welles), a tough, sentimental Irish sailor, gets involved in a fight on behalf of Mrs. Bannister (Rita Hayworth) under circumstances which he suspects were phoney and pre-arranged by her. Mrs. Bannister asks O'Hara to join her and her husband on a pleasure cruise on her husband's yacht. O'Hara refuses. Next day, Mr. Bannister (Everett Sloane), a cripple, who is " the greatest living criminal lawyer," seeks out O'Hara at a sailors' employment exchange, but O'Hara again refuses to join the cruise. O'Hara and Bannister and some sailors then sit down to a drink, at the end of which Bannister pretends to get drunk and collapses.

The Narrator is O'Hara himself, telling the whole story.

[1] *Director : Orson Welles. Editor : Viola Lawrence. Columbia, 1948.*

252

" Tobacco Road "

1

3

2

4

5

6

			Ft. fr.
1	*Dissolve to :* Exterior harbour. A motor boat is travelling *across screen right to left.*	*O'Hara :* (off, narrating) Naturally, someone had to take Mr. Bannister home. I told my-self—	15
2	*Dissolve to :* Motor boat coming *towards camera.*	—I could not leave a helpless man lying in a saloon. Well, it was me that was unconscious—	8
3	*Dissolve to :* Motor boat travelling *across screen* as it passes between two moored boats.	—and he were exactly as help-less as a sleeping rattlesnake.	7
4	*M.C.S.* Dachshund, paws up on side of boat, barking fiercely.	*Loud yapping bark of dog.*	3 2
5	*M.C.S.* Mrs. Bannister looking down.	*Mr. Bannister :* (off) It's nice of you, Michael—	3
6	*Shooting over side of yacht.* A sailor and O'Hara are lifting Bannister from the motor boat into the yacht. Mrs. Bannister in right foreground *back to camera,* hands in pockets, looking on.	*Barking of dog fades out.* *Bannister :* —to be so nice to me when I was *so* drunk.	

The effect aimed at here can perhaps best be appreciated if we imagine the sequence without shot *4*. Without it, the passage is simple : a sailor helping a drunken man aboard ship. With it, a note of warning is sounded : Michael, as we discover later, is being led into a trap. Mrs. Bannister's impassiveness is made more noticeable by contrast with shot *4* and some of the raw ferocity of the dog's yapping is unconsciously transferred by the spectator on to her seemingly disinterested expression. (A precisely analogous device was used by Orson Welles in a sequence near the end of *Citizen Kane* with an image of a screeching parakeet.)

The effect is achieved in this case by means which are external to the story. The dachshund appears in only one further shot in the film and is of no further significance in the plot. Shot *4* is merely used as a suddenly illuminating cross-reference which gives—through the implied contrast—a dramatic meaning to the scene which it would otherwise not have.

Whether the effect in this particular case " comes off " must remain a matter of personal taste : it is perhaps a little too showy a device for so simple a context. Nevertheless it should be sufficient to establish that a straightforward visual contrast of this kind can sometimes be used to great effect.

Another kind of editing composition—and one can hardly imagine an example more different from *Lady from Shanghai*—is illustrated by the sequence of shots from the closing episode of John Ford's *Tobacco Road* (see stills on p. 253). Jeeter (Charley

Grapewin) and Ada (Elizabeth Patterson), after being evicted from their home, are seen slowly and sadly making their way to the poor farm. The sequence forms the end of their story and Ford has contrived to give a slow lingering impression of this tragic climax. All the six images say, in effect, the same thing, and it is this reiteration—as the figures get progressively smaller and more isolated—which gives the passage its emotional power.

The three passages we have quoted can be taken to illustrate three different kinds of editing composition : the first, depending on the cumulative effect of a series of unconnected images ; the second achieving an effect by a direct contrast ; and the third, by reiterating a single theme. But to do this is merely to attach artificial labels to fundamentally similar processes. In each case the director's intention is to make the dramatic points in the images alone : it is the act of selecting the images which comes to constitute the important creative step and must therefore obviously be varied for different dramatic needs. Our extracts from *Queen of Spades*, *Lady from Shanghai* and *Tobacco Road* can equally well be taken as particular evidence of the great variety and elasticity of visual editing patterns. Whichever way one looks at it must depend on whether one approaches the art of film editing theoretically or in the empirical way more congenial to most artists. Either way, the three extracts must make one realise the wonderful eloquence of passages depending only on the basic attributes of the film medium : the selection and editing of exciting images.

15

SOUND EDITING

General

IN the previous chapter we have justified the procedure of cutting from one view of a scene to another, on the grounds that we constantly register similar sharp changes of attention in ordinary life. As I look up from the book I am reading to see who has just entered the room, I change my attention abruptly from the book to the door. My eyes momentarily register the objects intermediate between my book and the door, but I do not become conscious of them because I am not interested in seeing anything but the book before turning my head, and the door after I have turned it. From these observed facts we have drawn the conclusion that the proper way to accomplish a change of view in a film is normally the cut rather than the pan.

The mode in which we register sounds is somewhat different. Unlike the eye, the ear is sensitive to stimuli reaching it from *any direction*, provided that the stimulus is strong enough. We can hear many different sounds coming from various directions, all at the same time. When a new sound comes within our audible range, it does not displace the others, but becomes part of the total sound which we can hear. Cutting from one sound-track to another would therefore be an artificial way of conveying natural sound and would tend to nullify the additional element of realism which sound brings to films. Clearly, then, a different approach is needed.

To develop a closer analogy between sound and visuals, let us first examine the mechanism of vision. The eye, as we have already said, is unselective in that it sees everything in its field of vision. But it does not see everything with equal clarity. As I am writing at my desk, and concentrating on the paper on which I am writing, there are within my field of vision a number of objects—an ash-tray, an india-rubber, my left hand—of which I am not consciously aware. Not till a physical movement or a conscious mental effort makes me change my attention to one of these surrounding objects, will I become fully aware of them. If, for argument's sake, some silent hand were to start scribbling something at the top of my page, I would immediately become conscious of the *movement* and instinctively look up. The moving hand would then become my new centre of attention. This is the reason a director will commonly try to keep his action near the centre of the picture frame, thereby ensuring that the rest of the cinematic field of vision (i.e., the screen) is disposed more or less symmetrically around the main point of attention.

A similar effect can be observed in depth. If I am standing at a cross-roads looking at a sign-post, all the scenery in the background will be in my field of vision, but it will be out of focus and I will not be conscious of it until something—the sudden ascent of a bird, for example—causes me to re-focus my eyes to a more distant point. This is why a cameraman photographing a scene will normally try to hold focus only for a limited range of distances from the camera, thereby automatically focusing for the spectator and drawing attention to the intended objects. The background will then be out of focus, which is as it would be if we were actually observing the scene.

The normal mechanism by which we react to sound is somewhat similar. Going on around me at this moment are a number of sounds—the ticking of an alarm-clock, the wireless playing next door—of which I am not aware unless I specifically set my mind to hearing them. In the same way as I was unaware of the landscape in the distance behind the sign-post, I am now unaware of the ticking of the clock. Indeed, it is a perfectly common experience not to be aware of any sounds at all, when one is concentrating on something else. If, on the other hand, the alarm-clock were suddenly to start ringing, my attention would be involuntarily drawn away by the sudden *change* in the quality and volume of the sound, just as the sudden *movement* of the bird drew my attention away from the sign-post.

If sound is to provide a realistic accompaniment to the picture in a film, the mechanism of normal hearing which we have outlined must be taken into account on the sound-track. It is not necessary to make an objective recording of all the sounds which would accompany the visuals in life. Just as I am not aware of the ticking of the clock when I am thinking of something else, so the spectator does not mind (he does not even notice) if there is a clock on the screen which does not tick, provided there is action on the screen to absorb his attention. In other words, only sounds which have a particular significance need to be recorded.

But there is a limit to which this principle can normally be carried. If two characters are seen sitting in a moving car and talking to each other, it is advisable to let the audience hear the whirr of the engine to establish that the action is taking place in a genuine car. If the sound of the engine were absent when we cut to the car for the first time the audience would immediately be conscious that there was something wrong. When the two characters start to talk, however, it is no longer necessary to hear the engine noise, since the conversation is more interesting ; accordingly the engine noise can now be faded down. To do this is not in any way to take liberties with the scene as it would naturally be experienced ; in a similar situation in real life, the noise of the car becomes utterly unimportant and we cease to be aware of it. Yet it is not possible to cut from the track of the car to the dialogue track, because, as we have seen, the mind is sensitive to sudden changes in sound ; the cut would draw attention to the change and would consequently appear unnatural. Instead, the sound of the engine should be gradually faded down and can then be kept at the lowest audible volume.

This simple example will serve to establish the different nature of the filmic treatment of sound and visuals. Changes in the general level and quality of sound—as opposed to isolated sounds like words—have to be accomplished by a sort of audible dissolve or fade rather than by a simple cut. Since changes in sound of the kind discussed above must in a film be recorded as actual changes corresponding to a subconscious mental process, they must be accomplished gradually in order not to disturb the audience. The technical method of recording a number of separate sound-tracks and then re-recording them at varying volumes has been evolved to make these gradual transitions possible, under conditions where the sound-engineer is in complete control of the volume of each individual track.

So far, we have only discussed sounds which arise from sources visible on the screen, that is to say, synchronous sounds. Our ears, however, receive sounds coming from all around us, irrespective of the direction of our field of vision : in our normal experience we are conscious of a large number of sounds which arise from sources we cannot see. These non-synchronous sounds have to be recorded on to the sound-track side by side with synchronous sounds, if a faithful overall effect is desired. More than this, we shall find that non-synchronous sounds are in a sense the more important of the two. If I am walking uphill and see a car coming downhill towards me, the fact that I can also hear the engine of the car will not add anything new to my awareness of the outside world. If, on the other hand, another car is coming uphill from behind me, I shall *hear* it before I *see* it. In this case, the noise will have brought to my attention something I did not know before, namely, that a car is going to pass. Here, a non-synchronous sound is clearly of greater significance than a synchronous one.

The subconscious mental process by which we select for our attention particular noises from the total sound going on around us, and shut out others from our consciousness, largely operates in favour of non-synchronous sounds. Pudovkin gives an example to illustrate this.

. . . in actual life, you, the reader, may suddenly hear a cry for help ; you see only a window, you then look out and at first see nothing but the moving traffic. But *you do not hear the sound natural to these cars and buses* ; instead you hear still only the cry that first startled you. At last you find with your eyes the point from which the sound came : there is a crowd, and someone is lifting an injured man, *who is now quiet*. But, now watching the man, you become aware of the din of the traffic passing, and in the midst of its noise there gradually grows the piercing signal of the ambulance. At this your attention is caught by the clothes of the injured man : his suit is like that of your brother, who, you now recall, was due to visit you at two o'clock. In the tremendous tension that follows, the anxiety and uncertainty whether this possibly dying man may not indeed be your brother himself, *all sound ceases* and there exists for your perception a total silence. Can it be two o'clock ? You look at the clock and at the same time you can hear its ticking. *This is the first synchronised movement* of an image and its caused sound since first you heard the cry.[1]

It may be objected that the incident Pudovkin cites is an in-genious example specially contrived to make a point in the argument. Nevertheless it should be sufficient to show that it is a common experience not to be aware of synchronous sounds— I am normally not aware of the scratching sound of my pen as I am writing—while non-synchronous sounds tend to be drawn to our attention because they tell us something we were not previously aware of, something, moreover, that we *want* to hear.

It should now become clear why we have digressed for so long. If a director is to make a creative use of the sound-track, he must bear in mind the general principles which we have discussed above. Yet strict adherence to observed experience can lead, at best, only

[1] Film Technique *by V. I. Pudovkin. Newnes, 1933, pp. 157–8.*

to a faithful re-creation of actuality. Where, then, does the director's and sound editor's freedom of interpretation come in ?

As with images, so with sound, the director must give his own interpretation of an event ; he normally does not wish to show a scene in the humdrum fashion of everyday life, but—keeping within the limits imposed by credibility—tries to give the most effective dramatic rendering. With this in mind, he can take considerable liberties with the sound-track without drawing attention to the technique employed.

Again consider the clock, visible on the screen : we have already said that, provided the action is interesting enough, the ticking of the clock *need* not be heard. On the other hand, it *may* be. If the director wishes to convey something of the state of mind of a character, anxiously awaiting news of some vital point in the story, the ticking of the clock will add to the atmosphere of suspense. For other reasons, the director might have used the ticking at the opening of the scene and faded it out later ; or he could have used any number of non-synchronous sounds, either singly or simultaneously, in conjunction with the ticking. A wide choice of sounds is in fact available to him, making possible the dramatisation of natural sounds.

The skilful use of sound does not only entail the addition of the most effective sound-track to a previously conceived picture. It implies that the picture must be conceived, not independently, but in terms of possible sound associations. Fritz Lang's *You Only Live Once* contains a simple example of this, though many others could be cited : a girl (Sylvia Sidney) is waiting alone in her room, sitting on a piano-stool with her back to an open piano ; she knows that her husband (Henry Fonda) is due to be hanged at eleven o'clock. As the clock reaches the appointed time, she rises from the stool and accidentally puts her hand on the open keyboard ; a dull, ugly discord is heard against the silence and conveys something of the cruel finality of her loss. For this particular effect the visual action had to be conceived so as to give rise naturally to the desired sound effect. The choice of the mill as the locale of the robbery sequence in *Odd Man Out* (see below) is an example of the same process.

The choice of sound effects rests with the director and the sound editor ; clearly, the earlier in the production process that the full sequence is planned, the better the results are likely to be. The sound editor, however, has another most important task, once the decisions are made : the recording of the tracks. Knowing the dramatic requirements of his sequence, he must try to record effects of appropriate *quality*. A scene may, for instance, require the sound of the hooter of a car. It is not enough for the editor to get any track of a hooter from his library and lay it over the picture. He will have to decide the exact significance of the sound in the scene and prepare a track accordingly. Here are three possible scenes in which the hooter of a car might be needed :

(1) As part of the general background noise of traffic.

(2) In a comedy scene where a little boy has climbed on to the seat of his father's car and insists on repeatedly using the hooter, much to the annoyance of his parents.

(3) As the final desperate warning from a driver just about to run over a child.

It is extremely difficult to describe in words the fine differences in sound quality, even if they are easily recognisable when heard. Still, we can say that in the first case a low, irregular, intermittently long and short hooting sound could be used ; in the second case, the sounds could be made long and loud, with a shrill, insistent quality which would be particularly annoying ; in the third case, a single short, rather high-pitched, piercing sound might convey the imminent danger most effectively ; in each case the sound would be perfectly credible, but through its quality add something to the dramatic force of the scene.

Analysis of a sound track

In the last few chapters, dealing primarily with the visual editing of films, we have often noticed how the tempo and rhythm and to some extent the volume of the sound-track affects the overall pace of a sequence. Before discussing this aspect of sound editing in general terms, let us look at a sequence from *Odd Man Out* and see how it works out in practice.

ODD MAN OUT[1]

Extract from Reel 2

Johnny McQueen (James Mason), the leader of an illegal revolutionary organisation, has for six months been hiding in a friend's house. He has planned to raid a local mill to steal money for the organisation's funds. Having been shut up in a house for six months, he is overcome by a spell of dizziness during the raid and his momentary indecision leads to failure. Pat, who drives the car, Nolan and Murphy are Johnny's assistants on the raid.

Before the sequence quoted below, we have seen Pat picking up Johnny, Nolan and Murphy, and driving them to the mill.

[1] *Director : Carol Reed. Editor : Fergus McDonell. Sound Editor : Harry Miller. A Two Cities Film, 1946.*

1–2	Johnny, Nolan and Murphy get out of the car and walk up the steps to the mill office building.	Footsteps and chimes of the city clock.	9
3	Shooting through the glass door of the office building as the three men enter.	The city clock completes its chime before striking the hour. The swishing of the swing doors as the men enter the building. The low pulsating noise from the mill begins.	11
4–5	Nolan, Murphy and Johnny walking along the passages inside the building, in both shots towards camera.	Hollow sound of men's footsteps getting louder throughout the two shots. Mill beat in background.	24
6–17	The three men enter the accounts office, draw their revolvers and make all the clerks sit still ; Johnny goes over to the open safe, takes wads of bank-notes out and places them in his brief-case. There is a glass partition in background behind which mill-girls are working. Throughout the sequence, Nolan is watching the clerks and directing them away from the partition ; as he does so, he makes little whistling noises. Very few words are spoken.	The mill beat is heard at a higher volume than before. All the incidental noises of banknotes rustling, footsteps, etc., are heard distinctly. There is hardly any dialogue, but we can hear Nolan's little whistling directions—" Pst, Pst, Shh . . ."	75
18	Pat, outside, waiting in the car. He looks out of picture.	Mill beat stops. A girl's laugh is heard. Ticking over of the car engine and one quick revving up.	7
19	Shooting from Pat's eyeline: two people are walking up office steps. Camera pans on to alarm bell on front of building.	Faster and louder engine noise. Loud distinct footsteps of couple going up steps.	8
20	C.S. Pat, nervously looking about.	Horses' hoof-beats in the distance can be heard. A coalman cries : " Coalman ! " Car noise continues.	5
21	From Pat's eyeline ; horse-drawn coal cart slowly approaching camera. It draws up by the kerb opposite a shelter, thereby blocking Pat's exit route.	Horses' hoof-beats stop. Car engine continues.	3
22–24	Pat anxiously looking at coal-cart.	Car engine continues.	10
25–28	Inside accounts office. Johnny is putting the last bundles of notes into his brief-case ; the two other men edge round towards the door, ready to leave. Nolan gives a couple of warning whistles to his friends to hurry.	The mill beat as before. Rustling noise of Johnny fumbling with bank-notes and putting them into the case.	34

29	The three men leave through door and hurry down the corridoor, *away from camera.*	*The sound of the hurried footsteps of the three men heard over the pulsating beat of the mill is suddenly shattered by the starting of the loud, shrill alarm bell.*	15

30 The men hurrying down another corridor. Several people look up at them and half-heartedly shout after them to stop.

As in 29
Onlookers : (shouting)
    Stop, Stop ! Who are you anyway? Stop, I tell you . . . etc.

9

31–52 Nolan and Murphy run down the steps outside the office building. Johnny follows, but suddenly stops, feeling dizzy. Nolan and Pat shout to him to hurry. The cashier runs out of the door behind Johnny with a revolver and blocks Johnny's path down the steps. A fight begins in which the two men roll about on the ground. The cashier shoots Johnny in the shoulder. Johnny manages to draw his own gun and shoot the cashier. Nolan and Murphy rush out of the car to help Johnny.

Mill noise stops. Quality of alarm sound changes as the scene moves outside the building.
Pat, Nolan :
    Johnny ! Come on. Come on, Johnny . . . come on ! Mind yourself.
Cashier :
    Hold on, who are you ?
All the small incidental noises of the men rolling over and fighting are heard distinctly. A shot.

Another shot
Nolan :
    Get him into the car quick.
All through the sequence the alarm bell and the loud revving of the engine (Track A) can be heard.

50

53 C.S. Pat in driver's seat.

Pat :
    Get him in, man. Take his arm, will ye, quick.
Alarm bell and revving continues.

3

54 Murphy and Nolan assisting Johnny.

Alarm bell continues. Car revving up very loud (Track B). Footsteps of the men going towards the car.

6

55 M.S. Car. Murphy enters car which starts to move. Nolan follows and Johnny clambers on to the running-board with difficulty.

Alarm bell continues. Mounting high revving of car (Track C) as car makes a quick get-away.

6

56–64 Alternating shots of the street ahead and close-shots of Pat and Nolan as the car is driving away. Johnny is not properly in the car yet and Nolan and Murphy are trying to pull him in. The car passes between the coal-cart and the shelter with a swift turn and then Pat very sharply pulls it round a corner. Nolan and Murphy cannot get a grip on Johnny to pull him into the car.

High pitched car noise dies down a little. Over the close-shots of the interior, a " close-up " track of the car (Track D) is heard reverting to the less loud engine noise with the shots of the exterior of the car.
Murphy :
    Wait till we get him in.
Screeching of tyres : bump as car goes on to pavement. Very sharp skidding noise as car goes round corner (Track E).
Murphy :
    Mind out, he's slipping.

11

263

Ft.
1½

65   C.S. Johnny. He makes a vain attempt to grasp the hood of the car and falls backwards.

Car engine continues.
Nolan :
  Look out he's slipping.
Murphy :
  Don't let him go.

66   Camera *shooting from moving car pans* with Johnny as he falls out. He hits the ground and rolls over. Camera *holds him in centre of frame* as it moves away from him.

Car engine continues.
As Johnny hits the ground a loud dramatic chord of music suddenly swells up.

   7

67–69 Murphy and Nolan panic and shout to Pat to stop the car.

Music continues.
Car engine continues.
Nolan and Murphy shouting at Pat.

   5

70   Car drives *into picture* and stops in M.S. suddenly.

Music continues.
Sudden screeching of brakes. (*Car track F.*)

   2

71   M.C.S. Pat. Camera *pans left to centre* indicating that car is pulling up with a jerk. Pat turns to face Nolan and Murphy.

Music continues.
Screeching of brakes stops. There is silence but for the distant ringing of the alarm bell.
Pat :
  There you are now, the whole crowd of us will be lifted.

   4

72–92 The three men in the car argue but cannot decide what to do. They drive on, hoping to pick Johnny up round corner. After a while Johnny gets up and as he starts to run off a dog runs after him. He runs down a deserted street, past a small child and along a row of shelters ; he stops at one of the shelters.

Music continues.
Pat and Nolan and Murphy shout at each other.

As he rises loud barking of dog begins following him as he runs.

Music begins to fade.

  90

93   Interior shelter. Johnny, exhausted, enters shelter. He slowly staggers towards a bench flanking the right-hand wall. He rests his head on the wall for a moment. He lifts his head and slowly slumps off the bench to the ground. Camera *pans down* his arm and we see blood trickling down his hand.

Barking of dog dies away in distance. Music fades out.
Crunching of broken glass on the floor as he staggers along. Loud panting is heard.

Silence except for Johnny's slow breathing and the very distant sound of the alarm bell.

  45

Dissolve to :

The robbery sequence quoted here is presented realistically ; the men are shown as a set of ordinary, fallible human beings whose attempt to obtain money for their cause ends in tragedy. There is none of the improbability and glorification of ruthlessness that might have been present in a similar sequence in a gangster film. While this did not prevent the sequence from being exciting, it did preclude the use of obviously unnatural, larger-than-life effects in the sound and visuals, if the realism was to be sustained. Everywhere the sound is natural ; only through the variations of quality and the carefully worked out variations in the tempo and urgency of the track, does the sound contribute to the dramatic effect.

The few lines of dialogue which are spoken are never explanatory. They simply add to the effectiveness of the visuals. For instance, Pat's frantic exclamations to Johnny, hesitating on the steps, add to the urgency of the sequence without telling us anything that is not implicit in the images. In this sense, the dialogue track can be considered as one of the effects tracks : it does not anchor the visuals by conveying any important information, but adds to the total effect on a contributory rather than a primary level.

The story of the film covers twelve hours. From the time Johnny first leaves his hide-out, the chiming of the city clock is heard at intervals throughout the film. It emphasises that the whole action takes place in this comparatively short period and makes the audience aware of the slow, relentless passage of time leading up to Johnny's death. Introducing the chimes at the beginning of this sequence also conveys something of Johnny's feeling of isolation and strangeness on his first venture into the streets after several months' internment.

As the men enter the mill, we can hear the slow, dull, pulsating beat of the mill machinery. The track was recorded at an actual mill, where the quality of the sound was found to be most suitable for the particular dramatic purpose which will emerge later. A point to note is that, in writing the script, any office building might have been chosen for the location of the scene, but the mill was presumably selected at least partly for the possible sound associations.

As the three men approach the accounts office along the corridor (4–5), we can hear the hollow sound of footsteps over the background noise of the mill. The track of the footsteps was recorded from men walking over wooden boards. This gives the sound a significant quality which draws it to the attention of the audience while not being unusual enough to make one doubt its genuineness. As the men get nearer to their objective, the sound of their steps increases in volume—by the end of shot 5 it is unnaturally high—thereby building up the tension before the robbery.

At the beginning of shot 5, the men are actually farther away from

265

the camera than at the end of shot *4* and a strictly naturalistic sound-track might at this point have dropped slightly in volume. Actually, as we have seen, the opposite happens for the purpose of creating a build-up for the main event, which is the robbery itself. Here the director's conception of the sound is designed for a particular dramatic effect and ignores the requirements of natural sound perspective ; it provides a good example of the sort of deviations from realistic sound which are justifiable when the primary aim is to achieve a dramatic effect.

The action of the robbery (*6–17* and *25–28*) contains practically no dialogue ; it is a passage of intense urgency, and the mill beat which now acquires a special significance becomes louder. It conveys that the mill-hands, unaware of the robbery, are going on with their work, and emphasises the danger that at any moment one of the girls working behind the glass partition may look up and ring the alarm. At the same time the dull unhurried beat of the mill stresses the slow passage of time while the men are trying to get the money away. By dividing time, so to speak, into a series of mechanically following units, the rhythmic beat of the mill makes the sequence appear intolerably long-drawn-out, almost as if we were experiencing it through the mind of a member of the gang. All the small incidental noises of Johnny putting away the bank-notes and of people moving about are heard clearly, partly to emphasise Johnny's nervousness, partly to convey the panicky vigilance of the clerks in the office who are watching his every movement. Nolan's little whistling sounds enhance this effect.

The cut to Pat, anxiously waiting outside (*18–24*), maintains the tension at a different level. With his car motionless, he is impatiently waiting for his friends to come out. In contrast with Johnny, hurriedly trying to finish off his job, Pat has to wait for something to happen ; he becomes over-sensitive to his surroundings and suspicious of casual passers-by. Accordingly, the sound-track is made subjective. When he hears the faint, casual laughter of a girl going up the steps, he involuntarily put his foot down on the accelerator and looks round in the direction of the laughter (*19*). The quick revving of the engine (*18*) constitutes a sort of reassurance to himself that there will be no delay in the get-away ; it is the subconscious gesture of a man impatiently waiting for action. At the same time, the noises of the surroundings are heard at an exaggerated volume, since Pat, fearing that any passer-by might become suspicious of the car's running motor, is unusually sensitive to them.

266

In shot *20* we first hear the hoof-beats of the horses drawing the coal-cart and the cry " Coalman ! " The track of the hoof-beats was recorded in a street flanked by high buildings and has an ominous echoing quality.

As Pat looks round, he sees (*21*) that the coal-cart is blocking his exit route. With this danger established, we leave him (after *22–24*) in even greater anxiety, hearing only the steady (and therefore to him insignificant) noise of the car engine.

While the men are making their escape (*29–30*), the sound mounts in volume and urgency. A few seconds after they have left the accounts office, the sharp insistent sound of the alarm bell starts up. Here the track was again shot with a careful consideration for dramatic quality. As the scene moves to the outside of the building, the quality of the alarm changes and the sound of the mill stops. In the tense struggle between Johnny and the cashier, all the small incidental noises of the fight are heard. In the picture, the fight is unspectacular and is shown as a series of close views of the slow, grim struggle which requires the sound effect to make it convincing. At the same time, the loud revving of the car and the alarm bell maintain the tension.

As the car is making its get-away, the alarm sound recedes. The sound-track of the car is now extremely accurate : the fast ticking over of the car with occasional revving (A), the very fast revving up (B), the fast acceleration (C), the sound close-up accompanying the shots of the interior of the moving car (D), the screeching of tyres (E), and the screeching of the brakes (F), all have their separate tracks in order to make the total sound effect completely convincing. At the same time, the danger and terror of the situation are conveyed by the skidding of the car (E) and the high volume of the sound generally.

As Johnny falls out of the car (*66*), the music suddenly begins. This is the culminating event of the robbery sequence. Bearing in mind the construction of the film, everything up to this point has been only the setting of the situation. With this shot, however, the situation is posed and the long tragic search begins. Johnny's fall, therefore, has a significance beyond that of the culmination of an isolated exciting sequence : it is the motivating point of the whole film and as such its dramatic significance is conveyed by the sudden artificial entry of the music. Because music has been used sparingly up to this moment, its sudden entry makes a more precise and definite point than would have been possible with a continuous background score.

As Johnny rises to run away, he is followed by a barking dog ; its fierce yapping dramatically establishes the hunt which has, in effect, now begun. It follows Johnny as he runs down the deserted streets and its effect is reinforced by the quality of the music.

The rather long scene in the shelter (93) brings the sequence to an end. The first round of the chase is over, and Johnny has gained a momentary respite. The music stops and the tempo of the action is suddenly slowed down (shot 93 is much longer than any of the preceding shots). We see only Johnny, exhausted and in pain, wearily staggering into the shelter. The sharp crunching sounds of his steps on broken glass strengthen our awareness of Johnny's agony as he attempts to move into a safe position to rest. As he slumps on to the floor we hear his short, staccato breathing ; against this, only the very distant sound of the alarm bell tells us that, far from being over, the hunt has only just begun.

Here, then, we have seen how a sequence whose sound and visuals are planned in conjunction can gain in dramatic power from the sound track. The location of the mill, the presence of the dog, and the glass on the shelter floor are all visual points which are not essential to the story or could have been expressed in other ways ; only by their sound associations do they sharpen the complete effect. Johnny's run down the deserted streets, for instance, is not made appreciably more effective by our *seeing* a dog following him. On the other hand, we believe that a dog *may* have followed him and the incident provides the means to strengthen the scene through the fierce pursuing sound of the dog's barking.

Again, the *quality* of the sounds has been carefully selected for each track. No doubt any library shot of horses' hoof-beats would have served to establish the presence of the coal-cart as Pat is waiting for his friends (20). Giving the sound the special quality it has does more than this : the deliberate, echoing sound, which was in fact used, acquires in the context a sort of claustrophobic significance.

This insistence on the appropriate quality of sounds needs a little further comment. In the short scenes where the three men are approaching the accounts office (4–5), the sound of the footsteps has a peculiar hollow ring. The director and sound editor must have felt that, while having no special dramatic significance, the sound of the footsteps should nevertheless be made slightly unusual *in itself* in order to bring it nearer to the audience's attention. This was done for the specific purpose of allowing the slow mounting in volume of the steps to create a dramatic build-up for the robbery. But how far is it right to insist on significant sound quality in general?

In this connection, the composer Antony Hopkins has written of the sound-track of *The Queen of Spades*:

> . . . I have only to shut my eyes to be able to recapture instantly the sound of Edith Evans' huge stiff crinoline dragging across the marble floor of the Opera House, punctuated by the dry tapping of her stick. Now I do not think I am being harsh with Thorold Dickinson when I say that, had he not wanted to plant that sound in our minds so that it could be used later in the visitation scene, he might not have used that particular effect at all. Dame Edith would have limped across the hall, and even had the sound of her dress and stick been audible there would have been the usual rhubarbia claptrap in the background. Why? Such a sound is fascinating and exciting enough in itself: I had no idea, on first hearing it, that it was to be used again, yet it made that particular moment of the film arresting and beautiful.[1]

It is the phrase, "arresting and fascinating in itself," which needs to be considered. *Should* the sound-track of a film be arresting in itself? There is a danger that a sound-track which requires this special attention from an audience may become an intolerable nuisance. The spectator may be continually distracted by the peculiar quality of the sounds and, if these have no particular dramatic meaning, his wandering attention will result in a loss of dramatic impact. If, on the other hand, the sound quality is made significant in order to make a point in the story, then it is not only justifiable, but extremely valuable. The footsteps in *Odd Man Out* and the dragging sound of Edith Evans' crinoline in *The Queen of Spades* each make genuine dramatic points, which obviously justify the unusual quality of the sounds.

Sound and the editing of the picture

In the chapters on newsreel and documentary films editing, we have already noticed the importance of the sound track as a means of controlling pace. In newsreels the high speed of events is conveyed almost entirely through the tempo and urgency of the commentator's delivery, often working against the natural flow of the images. In our comments on sequences from story-films the power of the sound-track to slow down or accelerate the pace of the sequence has often been noticed. To get a closer view of *how* sound can govern tempo in practice, let us look at the sequence from *Odd Man Out* again.

In the scene of the robbery, we are shown the three men desperately working "against time." The visuals are accordingly

[1] Sight and Sound, *December, 1949.*

cut rapidly to convey the speed of the operation. Yet while they are hurrying, the men are acutely aware of the long time they are taking in completing this dangerous job, and the sound track with its casual rhythmic beat of mill machinery slows down the pace of the scene to convey something of their state of mind. When we are taken outside with Pat, the sound track becomes slow : the casual hoof-beats and deliberate footsteps convey something of the way Pat is experiencing what to him must seem an intolerably long period of waiting. When the men are making their get-away the track, for obvious reasons, becomes very fast indeed, much of the effect being achieved by the high volume of the sound. When Johnny finally slumps down in the shelter, time momentarily " stops." The sound slowly fades down and the regular breathing merely emphasises the slow, calm-after-the-storm feeling of the passage.

In many instances, sound can be used to act in opposition to the visuals, in quality or tempo. The robbery sequence in *Odd Man Out* achieves an atmosphere at once of frenzied hurry and tense leisureliness precisely through the contrasting tempo of sound and visuals. Here the tempo of the sound is used as a counterpoint to the visuals, not as a reinforcement. In the same way, the emotional quality of the sound has been used as a counterpoint to the mood of the picture. In the Launder-Gilliat film *Millions Like Us* there is a scene in which we are indirectly told that Patricia Roc's husband has been killed in combat. When we next see her, it is at a raucous workers' canteen concert party where everybody is having a wonderful time. While the camera singles out the girl and slowly tracks towards her, we hear nothing but the rowdy singing of the munitions workers around her and the scene gains greatly in effect by the contrast.

The use of this kind of sound-picture counterpoint needs to be employed with the greatest caution ; it can very easily lead to archness and artificiality if the contrast is conveyed too obviously.

The two examples we have cited should be sufficient to show that sound can often be used very successfully, not by giving it a mood which mirrors the mood of the images, but rather strengthens it by contrast. Again, the spectator should not be made aware of the conflict between sound and picture : if he is allowed to do so, he may have time to decide that the contrived situation of placing the grieving Patricia Roc in gay surroundings is rather an obvious, maudlin trick. Ideally, the spectator should not be given time to consider the sound and visuals independently ; he should receive the combined impact without becoming aware of the contrast.

It remains for us to say something of the part sound can play in the mechanics of editing. By using a continuous sound track, an apparently smooth continuity of images can sometimes be produced from a series of more or less disjointed scenes. A musical accompaniment will hold together a montage sequence and make it appear a unified whole. If the ear is receiving a reasonably smooth flow of sounds as one sequence gives way to another, the sound will tend to bind the two sequences together and make the transition acceptable. In the same way, sound can often be used over a single cut to make it appear physically smooth. Here is a hypothetical example.

The flowing of sound over a cut is one of the important features of sound films—especially of dialogue films. The completely parallel cut of sound and action should be the exception, rather than the rule. Let me make this quite clear with a simple example. When the hero says, as he too often does, " Can't you see what I'm trying to tell you ? I love you ! " if I cut away from the visual image of the hero, *and* from his sound track, at the same time, I have made a parallel cut. In practice, however, I almost certainly would not do this. My exact cutting point would of course depend on the particular context ; but to take my simple example at its simplest, I should probably cut after " trying to tell you " to the visual image of the heroine, letting the hero's declaration of love continue over this shot until the point at which I had to cut on the sound track to her hardly more inspired remark, " Oh, George ! "[1]

The overlapping of sound in dialogue sequences is often not only desirable for dramatic reasons, but also essential for smoothness ; it is often necessary to cut from a static shot of one actor to another, when there is no movement in the picture on which to make a visually smooth cut. In such an instance, an overlapping sound may solve the problem.

In some instances, a sharp sound, heard at the precise moment of the cut, may have the same effect. For example : it may be necessary to cut from a shot of a man leaving a room through a door to another shot of the same man shutting the door behind him as he enters the next room. It may be that the mechanical matching of movements is not perfect in the two shots, or that for some other reason it is difficult to make the cut smooth. If in such a case the cut is made at the point where the man bangs the door, and the sound of the bang is heard at the moment of the cut, then the spectator's attention will be momentarily shifted and he will find the cut perfectly smooth. A more controlled example of this commonly used device occurs in David Lean's *The Passionate*

[1] Film Editing *by Sidney Cole. British Film Institute Pamphlet, 1944.*

Friends. From a shot of Mary Justin (Ann Todd) sitting in a chauffeur-driven car, we are taken into a flash-back of her thoughts —somewhere miles away. Then, just before coming out of the flash-back, the skidding of wheels coming to rest is heard. With the sudden unexpected sound, a cut takes us back to Mary sitting in the car. Without the sound, this cut would have been rather obscure and therefore unsatisfactory. Here, however, the jarring noise gives the impression of suddenly bringing Mary's thoughts back to reality, and gives the abrupt break in continuity a dramatic meaning.

It is fitting that a book on film editing written to-day should end with a concrete example showing how, in a contemporary film, sound can be made an integral part of a continuity and how it can directly condition the editing pattern of a series of images. A historian of the future, looking back at the first two decades of the sound cinema, may well conclude that the element of sound had a retarding influence on the development of the cinema's visual eloquence. Pioneers of editing technique of the calibre of Griffith and Eisenstein have been slow in coming to the sound cinema—a fact which is perhaps due more to external causes (the high cost of sound films, for example) than to a lack of talent or some new limitation of the medium. Even the few original sound effects we have discussed in the last few pages seem to point to fertile new fields of experiment and achievement.

272

PART II
SECTION 4

THE FIFTIES AND SIXTIES

INTRODUCTION TO THE FOURTH SECTION
OF THE ENLARGED EDITION

IN the 15 years since it was first published, Karel Reisz's book on the technique of film editing has proved as successful as any textbook on cinema in the English language. Already it has achieved 13 reprints in English. In translation it has become the standard work on the subject in the Spanish, Czech, Polish and Russian languages.

After this long interval, the book clearly reflects the normal attitude of established film makers to cinema: that development as far as they are concerned stops now. Experiment is for the new-comer and the degree of success won by his new ideas determines his position among the established, who refresh themselves by studying his novel approach but rarely adopt his methods. The surviving members of the group of craftsmen and women from among whose experience the material of the book was drawn had no inkling of the innovations and changes ahead of them.

With the widening of the screen and the return to deep focus matching an increasing sophistication in film making and in audience reaction, cinema has developed so far and so rapidly during the intervening period that this work requires a new look. In ambitious fiction films the function of film editing is more and more being determined at the time of planning and shooting, and less and less in the subsequent assembly work in the cutting room.

The particular examination of genres in Mr. Reisz's work remains valid in so far as the genres survive. For example, the montage sequence dealt with at some length in *Section 2* is no longer obligatory in the fiction film, though it is not as yet entirely obsolete. However, a number of the general statements in *Section 1* and *Section 3* no longer reflect current thinking and pro-cesses.

275

With these ideas in mind, *Part II* (the new text in this work) has been written, in consultation with Karel Reisz, by Gavin Millar, a former student of the Slade School of Fine Art in University College London, as a report on work in progress rather than as a study of an historical development which has settled into a more or less definitive pattern.

But the problem remains. Too many books on cinema have been falsely updated by the mere attachment of additional chapters to an out-of-date work. Yet in the present case re-writing was impossible, since nearly thirty contributors to the original work were involved, scattered over many countries and some no longer living.

Our solution has been first to stress the dating of the two parts, for unless cinema remains stagnant (horrid thought) *Part II* will itself become out of date sooner rather than later. Second, to highlight in *Part I* those statements which I believe are no longer valid. Notes on these follow below.

On travelling about the world during the last fourteen years I have enjoyed a number of warm, personal references which my association with this work have brought me. I remember in 1953 seeing the jacket of this book decorating the wall of a cutting room in Herzlia, Israel. I remember, too, in 1959 a Japanese university professor greeting me in a crowded foyer in the Kremlin: we learn English, he explained, to read books like this.

The first paragraph of my introduction of 1952 is no longer valid: we are, it appears, at last to found a National Film School in Britain. I hope this new revised edition will prove as useful there as its predecessor has long been in the established film schools of the world.

The following notes refer to new paragraphs opening on the pages quoted.

to: pp. 35–6 (last and first paragraphs)
The somewhat grudging note in these two paragraphs is no longer appropriate. *October* is now recognised as a live political cartoon which only falls back on narrative when Eisenstein and Alexandrov no longer had time to be more inventive. *October* was one of the milch cows of the *nouvelle vague*.
Appeal to the active imagination cancels the need for " reason or explanation ". Dissolves waste time. The raising of the bridge is no " laboured effect ": it is a deliberate contrivance, a stretching of time like the Odessa Steps sequence in *Battleship Potemkin*.

to: p. 40 (last paragraph)
But what an experiment! And entirely comprehensible and worthy of study at more than one viewing like any evocative work or art. Cinema is now permitted its ambiguities: it seems to be coming of age.

to: p. 44 (first paragraph)
We have progressed far beyond these limits. Fifteen years ago the film was still tied to natural sound just as a trolley-bus is powerless out of contact with its overhead power-cable. The bus of cinema now has a four-wheel drive that lets it make its way over curious and unprecedented country, and wings, too, when real imagination comes into play. Synchronous realism is no longer a *sine qua non:* it even has to justify itself.

to: p. 45 (first paragraph)
Dissolves are rare enough nowadays to break the illusion and make the modern audience screen-conscious.

to: p. 46 (opening paragraph)
Quick, momentary flash-backs are now entirely acceptable, so long as they are logical. (I remember using them in 1954.) It was the tyranny of synchronous, natural sound that made these flashes disturbing.

to: p. 47 (second paragraph)
Emphasis. This paragraph is far too gentle. More and more the final shape of dramatic films is determined during and by the shooting and it is a poor film that can be assembled in any other way.

to: p. 48 (penultimate paragraph)
Nowadays smoothness is in the eye of the beholder. It is rhythm, composition, selection and timing that govern the flow of the film, not the succession of smooth cuts which was the aim of the early sound film enslaved to its synchronous, geographically realist sound track. The modern editor is the executant for the film-maker and no longer his equal on any self-respecting film.

to: p. 57 (second paragraph)
Thank heaven Capra's letter is a thing of the past and film-making is accepted as an integrated function from script to screen.

to: pp. 61–64 (special styles of editing)
This section is for us today bound to appear as archaic in its approach as Lewis Jacobs' book *The Rise of the American Film* (1939) had already begun to appear in 1953 and indeed as these present notes will be in fifteen years' time or less. Meanwhile, so long as *Part II* of this volume, written by Gavin Millar, remains valid, the reader is urged to turn to it for an assessment of current values.

to: p. 112 (Montage Sequences)
The then " modern " montage sequence was great fun for the editor, like the candenza for the pianist in a piano concerto. Sometimes an outside contractor such as Slavko Vorkapich would shoot and build up a montage sequence to specifications supplied by the scriptwriter, and the result would then be dropped into the edited film as a sorbet is inserted into the middle of an elaborate dinner. The idea was to provide a visual breather in the middle of the excessive amount of dialogue by which most stories were told on the screen. Nowadays the whole film can be adequately ventilated from beginning to end thanks to the increasing development of equipment.

to: pp. 216–7 (Smoothness)
Eisenstein told us nearly forty years ago that making a smooth cut is a wasted opportunity. Increasingly audiences are finding it entertaining to be forced to activate their imaginations rather than passively to expect a lifelike continuity of movement. One does not necessarily park one's mental faculties before buying a ticket. One may even come back and see the film again. As for the smooth cut, there are ways of cutting from a long shot of an actor

(or nowadays someone who is not an actor and is merely behaving) standing by a mantelpiece to a medium shot of the same person reclining in an armchair, and of making it entirely acceptable. Spectators are grateful for the omission of intervening action that would happen on the stage of a theatre. Hitchcock will never live down the boredom of *Rope* in which the action from start to finish appears to be wholly continuous.

to: p. 272 (final paragraph)
This final paragraph is a generous forerunner to *Part II*, now published for the first time. Anyone who belittles the value of *Part I* should remind himself that it has fertilised much of the development recorded in *Part II*. And so, we hope, ad infinitum.

Thorold Dickinson,
Slade School of Fine Art,
University College, London.

16

WIDESCREEN

General

" WIDESCREEN " as we now loosely term it, was certainly the first significant technical development of the fifties. It is a term applied to the variety of screen ratios devised to supersede the 1 : 1·33 rectangle which had been the average screen shape throughout the cinema's history. It describes the first and perhaps the best-known process, 20th-Century Fox's Cinemascope, as well as the numerous rival processes patented, under the stimulus of competition, by other companies, first in Hollywood, later throughout the world.

In the early fifties the rapid post-war decline in cinema attendances continued. The novel impact of widescreen was the industry's response to this economic threat. The old proportions of 1 : 1·33 were a convention deriving from the size of the Edison/Dixon Kinetoscope, strengthened by usage and the commercial requirement of uniformity. Attempts were frequently made to circumvent the limitations of the shape. One of the best-known early examples occurs in Griffith's *Intolerance*, where he masks the sides of the frame to strengthen the impression of height as a soldier falls from the walls of Babylon. Masking devices, especially the iris, were an early method of altering screen size in the interest of composition.

For a few years after the introduction of sound the frame became square to accommodate the sound track, but the former proportions were resumed when the height of the image was slightly reduced. Various proposals have been put forward over the years for the ideal dynamic screen shape, infinitely adaptable, always appropriate.

Despite the triple-screen method developed by Abel Gance no real advance towards a solution has been made. Truffaut's *Jules et Jim* (1961) uses masking devices freely and effectively, but they remain an expensive, awkward and still unaccepted form, and they

279

are still, of course, tied to the overall dimension of the normal wide screen.

The wide screen itself, for all practical purposes, was invented by the French professor Henri Chrétien as long ago as 1927. His method was to compress a wide picture, by means of an anamorphic[1] lens, on to normal 35 mm. film stock and to enlarge it once more in projection by use of a compensating lens. Nobody took any notice of his invention at the time.

But it was in Chrétien's Anamorphoscope that 20th-Century Fox now found what they were looking for. They revived it and christened the new process Cinemascope.

In fact Chrétien's invention had been used before. Claude Autant-Lara's film *Pour Construire Un Feu* (1929) was shot with the anamorphic lens.[2] Autant-Lara apparently constructed his screenplay so that alternate episodes—on separate reels—used the wide screen on one projector and the tall screen on the other. The idea has not been revived. Indeed, as we have pointed out, the process was ignored for twenty-five years, although the intervention of the war and the cost of equipping theatres for Cinemascope must certainly have been a hindrance to its acceptance.

But once having taken the plunge, Fox couldn't afford to forget it. The announcement was made that *The Robe* was to receive the accolade of being the first Cinemascope picture. Before the year was out (1953) most other big American companies had laid plans for their own widescreen processes and productions. The battle was on, and it was to have a major effect on film—and therefore on editing—techniques. The wide screen began to redefine the aesthetic of the cinema.

But not immediately. The process was launched by the company with enthusiasm and received by the critics with scorn. Much fun was had at the expense of rooms allegedly " the size of tennis-courts." A spate of bedroom dramas was playfully envisaged in which the screen would be more conveniently filled by horizontal than vertical actors.

In an enquiry conducted by *Sight and Sound* in 1955, several directors pointed out that the extension of the medium's tools was

---

[1] *There are suggestions that " anamorphotic " is a more correct usage, but this is the more current one.*

[2] *As noted by Thorold Dickinson in* Sight and Sound, *Spring' 1955, p. 210. Dickinson notes that Autant-Lara used a Gance-like technique in running two or three images side by side. He further suggests that with Vista-Vision, Autant-Lara could have " splashed images of all shapes and sizes all over the screen . . . for that matter, the way is now open." Well it may be, but as far as we know no-one in the intervening thirteen years has taken it.*

always welcome, but that since none was always apt, none should ever become obligatory. These were sentiments with which few could disagree, but it was more difficult to be clear about where the tool was apt. . . . The width of Cinemascope made it inappropriate to rhythmic cutting said Lewis Milestone. Jean Renoir claimed that it meant the death of the close-up. And in a rousing phrase Abel Gance condemned all processes which fell short of his (nonexistent) panacea, the variable screen or " polyvision, the cinematic language of tomorrow."

But in the Spring issue of *Sight and Sound* that year, Penelope Houston conceded that the " The Man That Got Away " sequence in George Cukor's *A Star Is Born* (1954) ended " with a shot so skilfully composed that it almost makes the Cinemascope screen seem defensible." Gradually the wide screen began to take its place. Credit must be given to Basil Wright for one of the earliest appreciations of the potentialities of the new process in a review of *The Robe* (1953):

You have to look at it differently, and when it is, successful, the difference is that of motion. In *The Robe*, certain scenes are successful because the motion is fitted to the area involved. This happens, roughly speaking, in two ways. The first is when the entire slit of the screen is filled with action, as in the staggering night shot, with a tracking camera, of four white horses galloping towards you. The second is when a complex series of actions balance within the long and narrow area before you. There is only one sequence in this film which sustains this complexity of action—the Crucifixion. Here can be seen in embryo all the possibilities of the system. The levels of perception involved are (a) the extreme long shots of Calvary and of the City of Jerusalem; (b) the watchers and the gambling soldiers; and (c) those on the three crosses. The interesting thing about this sequence is that the close-ups of the Greek slave watching Jesus are not off-balance as are most of the other close-ups in the film. The vast acres of space to the side of Victor Mature's contorted face are somehow filled (not visibly, but in context) by the wider images which precede and follow. The wide, low screen here works, and it works partly by editing and partly by an extraordinary piece of camera movement—a vertical crane shot from ground level to behind the shoulders of the Man on the Cross. There is a hint here—much more so than in the obvious scenes of pageantry, chase or combat—of real possibilities in this new and as yet recalcitrant aspect of the film medium.[1]

Wright's main points are worth reiterating: that the wide screen works well when filled with action; that a long and complex series of actions can be handled well if balanced skilfully within it; and that the close-up also is perfectly acceptable when sustained in context by the editing.

It was not to be expected that the potentialities of the wide

[1] Sight and Sound, *Jan.–March 1954, p. 143.*

screen would be immediately appreciated.[1] There is an analogy here with the silent cinema. When sound was introduced directors were at a loss to know how best to use it. In the same way wide-screen cinema suffered from the initial crude attempts to adapt all scenes, irrespective of their content, in the interests of spectacle. Increased size was felt to be appropriate to melodrama, in which emotions are larger than life. *River of No Return* (Dir. Otto Preminger, 1954) is a good example of the earliest demonstrations that widescreen could be used intelligently.

River of No Return

The story tells of a pioneer homesteader who comes to a frontier town to reclaim the small son he has earlier abandoned. He meets the town " chantoose," who has become his son's protectress. Her boyfriend robs and cheats the hero. She, the hero and his son, pursue the robber down-river on a raft, during which the girl falls in love with the hero. The robber is shot by the hero's son. The three survivors live happily ever after.

The film opens with a long travelling shot through the bustling frontier town at night. Preminger takes great pleasure in being able to pack the screen with incident. A multitude of activities proceed in the background while a little bit of plot concerning the boy is pursued in the foreground. In the middle distance a buggy full of good-time girls, entering the camp at a swift gallop, tips up and spills the girls out, skirts flying. The screen is big enough and clear enough for this kind of event to be almost thrown away, and yet to gain in power in some way by being noted but unobtrusive. In other words, the wide screen helps to avoid the overweighting of the importance of an event that isolating it in a separate shot often produces.

An example more integral to the plot was noted by another critic:

As Harry (the thief, boyfriend of the singer, Kay) lifts Kay from the raft, she drops the bundle which contains most of her " things " into the water. Kay's gradual loss of the physical tokens of her way of life has great symbolic significance. But Preminger is not over-impressed. The bundle simply floats away offscreen while Harry brings Kay ashore. It would be wrong to describe

[1] *However, as commercial interests in western countries found that Cinemascope films were beginning to attract back to the cinema the audiences that had been lost to television, a poor man's version was introduced which achieved a wider image with normal lenses by composing the image for an aspect ratio of 1:1·65 or even 1:1·85. This allowed the less ambitious cinema to cut down the height of its screen or slightly extend its width without having to cater for anamorphic lenses. At the same time it meant that old films and films from eastern countries were and indeed still are subjected to mutilation by cutting off the top and bottom of images composed in the traditional ratio of 1:1·33.*

this as understatement. The symbolism is in the event, not in the visual pattern, so the director presents the action clearly and leaves interpretation to the spectator.[1]

Again the point is made that a refusal to cut to a close-up of the bag results in a more discreet treatment of the events. It is the wide screen which creates this opportunity.

Preminger treads warily in the interiors however. In Kay's " cramped " dressing-room behind the bar, he seems at a loss to know quite how to fill the yawning spaces. A rope stretched across the scene and a blanket tossed over it relieves him of the obligation of finding action to fill the unwanted area. But the gesture has the tentative air of an expedient. There is a feeling, in some early widescreen pictures, of embarrassed apology. It soon disappeared as directors learnt to use the new width with boldness.

The characteristic of the wide screen, as we have hinted in this brief early example, is to be inclusive. The more detail you can clearly and naturally include in shot the less need will there be for you to draw attention to any of its parts in a separate closer shot. Since the cut is in a sense an artificial device which draws attention in turn to the form rather than the content, the fewer cuts there are the more " natural " and spontaneous the action will appear to be. The impression will be that the action has gained in objectivity since the film maker seems to have had less of a hand in it. It may be nothing more than a psychological trick, though it is true that each new set-up doesn't only draw attention to the mechanics of filming but is in itself an interpretative device. The appearance— or substance—of objectivity, whichever you prefer, that the wide screen encourages is akin to a current of feeling popular among film makers and audiences alike. Documentary truth-to-life has been a quality much admired, especially since the days of Neo-realism.

André Bazin

If any one man was responsible for popularising this feeling by his writing, it might be said to be André Bazin, the " philosopher " of the theory of authenticity and objectivity in screen editing. Bazin, towards the end of his life editor of the influential French periodical *Cahiers du Cinéma*, detected in his critical writings a tradition in the cinema which had remained unbroken from Stroheim to his own day. (He died in 1958.) He championed the type

---

[1] *V. F. Perkins*, Movie No. 2, *Sept. 1962, p. 18. Of the opening shot Perkins observes that " it ends when it ceases to provide the clearest view of the situation."*

of cinema in which the event was allowed to assume more importance than its presentation. He pointed to the dangers of manipulating reality by editing devices. He professed his mistrust of all that
the unscrupulous—or simply thoughtless—artist can add to the
image to distort reality. His heroes were Stroheim and Murnau.
To his mind the line of realism was continued through the thirties
by Renoir, who developed the long take, the travelling camera and
composition in depth. The tradition was continued in the U.S.A.
by Welles and Wyler and on the Continent by Rossellini and
Visconti, and later Antonioni.

Without going into too much detail about Bazin's theories we
may be able to summarise them by quoting two short passages
from his book *Qu'est-ce que le Cinéma?*:

> When the essence of an event is dependent on the simultaneous presence
> of two or more factors in the action, cutting is forbidden.[1]

And, as if in illustration of that proposition:

> The editing of Kuleshov (in the famous Mosjoukine experiment), of
> Eisenstein and of Gance didn't show the event: they made allusion to it.[2]

Bazin was a great champion of Flaherty. He spoke with
enthusiasm of the seal hunt in which Nanook, the hole in the ice,
and the seal are seen in the same shot. But he criticised Flaherty
for the sequence in *Louisiana Story* in which an artificial suspense is
built up by cutting as the crocodile chases the bird. There is one
shot in which the crocodile and the bird are both seen which, he
says, redeems the sequence.

Though Bazin, in this article, makes no explicit reference to
widescreen, then still in its earliest days, it can be seen that the end
he is proposing is particularly well served by that process. Widescreen, by its inclusiveness, helps the director to maintain a scenic
unity—if he wants to. In widescreen the bird and the crocodile
might have been more readily connected.

Thus it comes about that a critical movement of opinion towards
a certain type of cinema finds, by a mysterious accord, the technical
means suddenly available to its further achievement.

Beyond the concrete examples with which Bazin's piece is
illustrated, there are other considerations which the growing use
of the wide screen prompted. By a kind of analogy with the last
example, the width of the screen has been represented as an aid in

---

[1] *Montage Interdit. André Bazin,* Qu'est-ce que le Cinéma? *Vol. I, p. 127. Editions
du Cerf. 1958.* ·
[2] *L'Evolution du Langage, op. cit., p. 133.*

the quest for documentary truth: it is said to enable the director to reveal a much more " natural " swathe of real life on the screen. The fact that more people can be embraced by its relaxed dimensions encourages us, in certain circumstances, to believe that they can perhaps behave with more naturalness than they would inside the cramped confines of the small rectangle.

However tenuous these speculations are it is true to say that the wide screen has certain distinct advantages. Its width and clarity make it possible to unfold a scene of great complexity and length without losing sight of detail or overall shape, meanwhile preserving the intensity which is dissipated by cuts which are only mechanically necessary. The shape makes it possible to compose horizontally or diagonally in a new way. Correspondingly it is not an embarrassment when, in order to concentrate attention on a detail, an area of the screen is blocked off.

The following stills, with descriptive notes, are chosen to illustrate these points. It will be seen that in some respects the responsibility for " cutting " has shifted increasingly from the editor to the director; or, to look at it another way, in the more fluid widescreen films, the distinction between the directing and the editing process becomes harder to make.

Widescreen examples

The wide screen is particularly suited to diagonal or horizontal compositions. But it can be effectively reduced in width when necessary. The size of the screen is not a hindrance to the big close-up.

1   After the chicken-run. (*Rebel Without a Cause*. Dir. Nicholas Ray. 1955.) Jim (James Dean) and company line up on the cliff top over which Buzz has been carried to his death.

2   Rachel and Barabbas at the tomb of Christ. (*Barabbas*. Dir. Richard Fleischer. 1962.) The effect of this composition is not merely to reduce the screen size and concentrate attention on Rachel's face. By comparison the massiveness of Barabbas' back seems to threaten her and provoke our sympathy.

3   Charlie (Charles Aznavour) at the piano. (*Shoot the Pianist*. Dir. François Truffaut. 1960.)

Cutting widescreen images together: shots of different scale match satisfactorily.

4-7   Four consecutive shots from the final arena sequence of *Barabbas*. Torvald (Jack Palance), a sadistic gladiator, is about to be killed in combat by his intended victim, Barabbas. 4 *is a static C.U.*, 5 *is a wide, fast tracking-shot*. 6 *is its companion, a fast reverse tracking-shot*. 7 *is a static L.S.*
These shots might be the corollary of Basil Wright's proposition, quoted earlier, that different sizes of shot look all right on the wide screen if " sustained in context by the editing ". In this case the carefully-chosen balance of image size and movement builds up into a *tour de force* difficult to achieve

1

2

3

on the traditional 1:1.33 screen. 7 has a complex impact. 4 and 6 have built up tension and the tension is sustained by 7. But the sudden expansion of the image floods the tension with a strange excitement which is almost a sense of triumph. This is a very equivocal and uncomfortable feeling for the viewer since he is anxious that Torvald should *not* claim his victim. This ambivalence is central to the film's theme, which is, in part, a discussion of the seductive power of violence.

The width of the screen often helpfully accentuates qualities in the image which would barely be present on the traditional screen.

8   In the middle of the Tennessee River an old lady refuses to quit her island plantation which the Tennessee Valley Authority plans to flood in an irrigation scheme. The signpost is a laconic reminder of her resistance to the Authority. The power of the resistance it betokens is in inverse proportion to its size in the frame. (*Wild River*. Dir. Elia Kazan. 1960.)

The width of the screen can give added intensity to the placing of characters in the frame.

9, 10   At this point in *A Star is Born* (Dir. George Cukor, 1954), Norman Mayne, an ageing star (James Mason), and Vicki Lester, a rising young one (Judy Garland), come to the studio front office to announce their engagement. On either side of them are the studio head, Oliver Nile (Charles Bickford), and the publicity chief, Matt Libby (Jack Carson). Mayne's reputation with women gives them little hope for this liaison. They regard it as a threat to her career and therefore to the studio, too. The threat is expressed by the disposition of the people in the frame. The couple appear through the door at the back of the room and walk forward to stand flanked by the two studio men. They seem therefore to " split " the studio, in the persons of Nile and Libby. At the same time they are forced to announce their marriage within, as it were, the studio's embrace. It is a reminder that their relationship is still at the mercy of their careers.
This disposition of four people could naturally be contained on a smaller screen, but it seems clear that the wide screen gives, for instance, added intimacy to the closeness of the couple, and added menace to the two " outsiders," who remain immobile throughout the scene. When the couple leave once more through the door, centre (10), the space they have vacated between the two men becomes, if anything, more tense.

A combination of the moving camera, changes of scale, and the exploitation of the screen's full width, can achieve effects of unusual power or delicacy.

11–16   Six stills from two consecutive shots in *El Cid* (Dir. Anthony Mann, 1961). The wide screen here offers the " double close-up," so to speak, which is not simply the doubling-up of a single C.U. Chimene (Sophia Loren) and Queen Urraca (Geneviève Page) watch El Cid ride off to battle. They are suspicious of one another. The wide screen gives them virtually equal weight in the frame. But the current of hostility between them is mysteriously increased by the fact that they are almost exactly alongside one another and yet a certain distance apart, as they could hardly be on the smaller screen. The dissolve (12) takes us from Chimene's soft face to a hard and rocky landscape. The camera pans left downhill on to a file of soldiers working their way towards us (13). They are led by El Cid. They approach and pass (14, 15) and the camera pans left to right with them. Suddenly a sharp reverse tracking-shot forces a rock into the side of the frame and with it a scimitar, which grows to fill the screen. The Cid has been led into an ambush. The widescreen image augments the unexpectedness of the action by ensuring that it takes place almost, but not quite, outside our field of vision.

17–21   The stoning and death of Rachel (*Barabbas*). Rachel is accused by the Pharisees of preaching a false religion, and sentenced to be stoned to death. After her

287

4

5

6

7

8

9

10

11

12

13

14

15

16

290

17

18

19

20

21

291

death the mob streams away into the city and the camera rises, as if in distaste, to draw away in the opposite direction. But when Barabbas, Rachel's former lover, appears at right of frame, the camera pans and drops down again slowly, bringing the black smudge of Rachel's body delicately up the frame line. The effect is that, though Barabbas and Rachel are finally separated—by death and by the width of the whole screen—the movement and the positioning relate them closely. They seem to transfer the responsibility for her memory directly across the space to Barabbas. The width of the screen creates a kind of spatial tension new in the cinema. This is not to say that it is necessarily more powerful.

The wide screen encourages more complex patterns of plotting both laterally and in depth.

22   Judy (Natalie Wood) begins to be drawn to Jim (James Dean) (*Rebel Without a Cause*). He and her boy-friend Buzz (Corey Allen) are about to drive in the chicken-run in which the latter is killed. Meanwhile Plato (Sal Mineo), a lonely boy supported financially, but in no other way, by an absentee father, finds a friend and protector in Jim. He resents Judy's attraction to his new hero.

We have argued that, generally speaking, it is the virtue of the wide screen to allow greater complexity and density within the shot. This is particularly true of two types of image: one in which the original frame is greatly altered but not obliterated within the shot; another when two quite distinct but related activities are going on within it.

23, 24   Dancers in the wings at the charity show where Norman Mayne first encounters Esther Blodgett (later Vicki Lester) (*A Star is Born*). This Dégas-like composition in blues and greens is broken up when the drunken Mayne staggers through the scenery, spilling a flood of red light in his path (24). It acts as an image of the probable effect he will have on the girl he is about to meet. The picture area allows the director to design a significant piece of developing action within the shot while losing neither detail nor grasp of the overall image. On the smaller screen the impact of Mayne's irruption would almost certainly have to be caught in a separate shot, and the balance of the whole re-established in a third.

25   At Mayne's house, where he is showing the latest of his films to friends (*A Star is Born*). Oliver Nile escapes into the TV lounge. Here he is joined by Mayne who encourages him not to miss the start of the film. Nile protests that he wants to watch a boxing-match on TV, but it is clear that this is an excuse. He is forced to confess that he is worried about Mayne: the days of the big star are over, he says. Mayne is to be dropped by the studio. In this shot the oppositions are dramatically illustrated within the same frame. The screen on which Mayne's new film is about to begin is on the far right. Mayne is pouring himself a drink, the first of many.

There are some things the wide screen can do which no other shape of screen can. The ability to preserve "distance" between characters while keeping them both in C.U. is a positive wide-screen gain. We have seen a similar example in *El Cid* (11, 12), a shot which would have been possible though less effective on a smaller screen. Here is something which only the wide screen makes possible.

26   Oliver Nile and Vicki Lester are in her dressing-room (*A Star is Born*). She is pleading with Nile to find Mayne a job to prevent his further cracking-up.

22

23

24

25

> The way they both cling tenaciously to the edge of the frame seems to speak for the delicacy of her request and the delicacy of their feelings towards one another as old friends. It suggests concern on his part as well as tentativeness on hers, but on both sides an unwillingness to presume or intrude too much on the other.

The wide screen naturally has unique strength in horizontal compositions. The following examples show that the horizontal line need not be restricted in meaning.

27   Chuck Glover (Montgomery Clift) is the envoy whom the Tennessee Valley Authority has sent to the backward South to persuade the old woman to abandon her island (*Wild River*). The clean sweep of the bus's horizontal lines seems to imply that he has brought the forces of progress and modernity with him. (See note 8.)

28   This shot follows 27. It is what Chuck Glover sees. Horizontal lines do not necessarily lend themselves only to modernity—

29   —they can also mean lassitude and obstinacy. Glover greets Grandma Ella Garth (Jo van Fleet) and the household he is appointed to shift.

30   Naturally the house she lives in presents a different image to Grandma Garth from the one Glover sees. To her, the reassuring rectangles of her home represent security and the undeviating habits of a lifetime. They also in some way convey a sort of four-square honesty. But to this settled and ordered way of life Glover is a threat and an irritant. Like an invading insect he promises not only to traverse the window-pane, but to buzz in through the open door. The oppositions between these two people and their ways of life could be expressed with quite this flavour on no other shape of screen.

One further example from *A Star is Born* might be mentioned.

The wide screen lends itself particularly to expressions of equality or brotherhood or companionship, where the traditional squarer screen tends more readily to express rank, hierarchy, domination and subjugation. Take, for example, the song already referred to in *A Star is Born, The Man that Got Away,* sung by Vicki Lester (or Esther Blodgett as she then was). Norman Mayne has followed Esther to a little nightclub where she is rehearsing with her band. He waits quietly in the shadows while she sings this song. As the number draws to an end the camera pulls back from a close-shot of her gradually to include the whole band, who are arranged on either side of her. The effect is to stress that the bonds between her and the band are very strong. The widening out of the shot, which matches a musical movement, expresses this solidarity visually. (Mayne of course is about to offer her a screen test which will mean leaving them.)

Precisely this effect would be difficult to achieve on the squarer screen. In the latter case the reverse track would have sharpened and dramatised the perspectives and offered the following compositions. (i) Esther would have risen to the top of the frame and so dominated the band. (ii) She might have sunk to the bottom of the frame, with the opposite effect. Or (iii) she could have stayed in the centre but with the pointedly symbolic effect of appearing

26

27

28

29

30

like a sun with the members of the band as her rays—or in some way as the source of their energy. This may be a legitimate effect but it is a different one from that achieved on the wide screen where the flatter perspective seems to trace an extension of sympathy rather than lines of force. In any case the combination of widescreen and camera movement together, as in many of these examples, produce an effect which makes unnecessary the cut one might have looked for in the past.

17

CINÉMA-VÉRITÉ
AND THE DOCUMENTARY FILM
OF IDEAS

Cinéma-Vérité

In the cinema at present the camera has become a sort of god. You have a camera fixed on its tripod or crane, which is just like a heathen altar; about it are the high priests—the director, cameraman, assistants—who bring victims before the camera, like burnt offerings, and cast them into the flames. And the camera is there, immobile—or almost so—and when it does move it follows patterns ordained by the high priests, not by the victims.

Now I am trying to extend my old ideas, and to establish that the camera finally only has one right—that of recording what happens. That's all. I don't want the movements of the actors to be determined by the camera, but the movements of the camera to be determined by the actor . . . It is the cameraman's duty to make it possible for us to see a spectacle, rather than the duty of the spectacle to take place for the benefit of the camera.[1]

The taste which widescreen had fostered among film-makers—and presumably the public too—for allowing the action to develop as naturally and spontaneously as possible, with little interference, was well served by the widescreen processes. But the taste found more advanced expression in a different sort of cinema at the other end of the scale; a cinema whose style came soon to be known as cinéma-vérité, or spontaneous cinema, or direct cinema. The words describe a method of shooting and presenting material so as to preserve primarily the spontaneity and flavour of the real event. The editor in this situation is therefore under some constraint to preserve the unbroken flow of actuality. At first sight then, it would seem that his role would be reduced to that of a mere scene-joiner's. But that this is not so, some of the more successful cinéma-vérité films conclusively demonstrate.

There are many good reasons for the development of cinéma-vérité. One of the best is stated by Jean Renoir in the quotation

---

[1] *Jean Renoir interviewed by André Bazin in* France Observateur. *Translated in* Sight and Sound, *Winter 1958–59.*

above. The clumsiness and clutter with which the traditional cinema had surrounded itself—a huge camera, tracking rails, dollies, blimps, tripods, cranes—was intimidating and inhibiting, especially to non-professionals. Richard Leacock, a key figure in the development of cinéma-vérité, was involved in Flaherty's *Louisiana Story*, and he has noted that wherever synchronous dialogue was needed, the paraphernalia of equipment that was necessary quite changed the nature of the event they were recording. It was from those professionals interested in preserving accurately the raw event—sociologists, ethnographers—that a great part of the stimulus in the development of new equipment came. Jean Rouch, whose *Chronique d'un Eté* (1961), made in collaboration with the sociologist Edgar Morin, we shall discuss later, was primarily an ethnographer before he was a film-maker.

Another stimulus came from television. Here studio interviews were conducted live in front of electronic cameras and beamed direct to the public. They created an appetite for the same thing in situations which were normally beyond the reach of electronic cameras. The film camera, not bound to the studio, was encouraged to become as direct as in interview situations.

So lightweight film cameras were gradually developed alongside lightweight synchronous tape recorders of high quality. Finer 16 mm. stock capable of being blown up to 35 mm. without severe increase in grain was a help too. The equipment is easily carried by two-man crews able to move in and around their subject unobtrusively.

It is worth remembering that undirected realism has been one of the cinema's great attractions throughout its history. There was nothing new in the aim. If cinéma-vérité is different it is only because it is an extension of a movement present in the cinema from its beginnings. Even Lumière was making use of the natural fascination we have at watching ourselves doing perfectly ordinary things on a screen. It is still agreeable to watch natural events on the screen: to watch trains steaming in, workers leaving a factory, babies eating soup or gardeners hosing the lawn. But it wasn't long before Lumière was starting to tamper with the real event and introduce fiction. He makes the boy step on the gardener's hose. It is worth remembering too that Grierson's documentary movement of the thirties was dedicated to " *the creative treatment* of actuality." Flaherty's editor, Helen van Dongen, has revealed that Flaherty's attitude to his raw material—the life of Nanook, or of the Aran islanders—was anything but ethnographically respect-

298

ful. He wasn't above creating and staging " natural " situations for the camera to record where the real event might have taken weeks to film or even have been impossible to film. The result makes interesting film but may not be acceptable to an anthropologist.

Similarly the Neo-realist and Free Cinema movements, for example, although concerning themselves with themes and real-life situations quite different from those of the conventional feature film, were never at any stage content to make a straightforward record of real life. All attempts to film real life—from Lumière onward—have relied on the editing process to add an interpretation to actuality.

It is noticeable that most of the documentary movements in the cinema's history have been European in origin. But in the last ten years America has been active in this field, too. In Lionel Rogosin's film *On the Bowery* alcoholics play themselves in barely dramatised scenes. The action takes place entirely in the location of the title itself, the film is put together in such a way as to preserve as far as possible the spontaneity of the events filmed. In an attempt to get a similar spontaneity into a more dramatic context John Cassavetes' *Shadows* used actors in real locations, but without a formal script. Cassavetes' camera was at the mercy—more or less —of the actors' own development of their scene. But in the opinion of many, the more successful parts of the film are those most carefully worked out beforehand and directed with an editing plan in mind.

Editing plans form no part of the output of many of the New York Independents, a school of " spontaneous cinema " makers which grew up during the early sixties. They spoke of " a passionate obsession to capture life in its most free and spontaneous flight." Robert Frank and Alfred Leslie call their film *Pull My Daisy* " an accumulation of images rather than a selection " and this may be a token of a growing inclination to eschew the editing process altogether during the last ten years.

The power to select and order is a privilege dangerously dispensed with and it is the central issue in all discussion of improvised cinema or cinéma-vérité. The director never can do away with the editing process altogether, as we have repeatedly pointed out. What he can do in the way of denying himself the benefit of any of the editor's traditional technical resources is demonstrated by the films of Andy Warhol. *Sleep* shows a man asleep. An early version lasted eight hours. The only cuts are for reel changes. This is to place a very high degree of faith in the virtues of filmed

299

actuality, as do many of Warhol's other films showing natural activities at what seems unnatural length. If his aim is to abstract from the filmed event any possible taint of control, he has probably succeeded, for what it is worth.

More interesting examples of the apparently artless in direct cinema stem from a company calling itself Drew Associates. This comprised Robert Drew, a former *Life* magazine reporter, Richard Leacock, formerly cameraman to Flaherty on *Louisiana Story*, and Donald Pennebaker. Their films include *Primary* (about the Kennedy-Humphrey battle for election in Wisconsin in 1960), *Football* (in collaboration with Claude Fournier, about an inter-school football competition), *The Chair* (about the struggle to save a young negro from the electric chair) and *Jane* (a portrait of Jane Fonda on the opening night of a play which proved to be a flop). They use lightweight cameras synchronised to the recording apparatus by electronic watches accurate to a quarter of a second over twenty-four hours. Their films seem to be extensions of the eye. They seem to hook, as it were, an eye and an ear permanently on the shoulder of the subject, watching his actions, revealing his motives, fears and ambitions with an intent and comprehensive stare which should, one would think, be utterly objective and un-interpretative. On the contrary a hypnotic and persuasive view of the subject emerges, which however is often criticised (by Rouch among others) for its uncritical involvement.

This kind of film-making demands that editing decisions be made largely in the camera. The idea of film has moved a long way in its journey from Lumière through Griffith and the painstaking re-construction of reality in the camera by the Russians and Germans. We are now almost back with Lumière again, but it is a kind of Lumière filming which requires a great intuitive tact on the part of the director. So much so that it is virtually necessary for the director, cameraman and editor to be one and the same man. Albert and David Maysles, who produced the portrait of the show-man Joe Levine, *Showman*, have recognised this. Albert Maysles worked as Godard's cameraman on the Godard sketch in the portmanteau film *Paris Vu Par . . .* (1964). He said later that the logical extension of the kind of film Godard was making was that he, Godard, should become his own cameraman.

Chronique d'un Eté

The ethnographer Jean Rouch criticised the Drew-Leacock partnership as we have noted, for making of the weapon of cinéma-vérité an uncritical recording apparatus. Rouch and his associate, sociologist Edgar Morin, have eagerly embraced and developed the techniques of cinéma-vérité for primarily sociological reasons. The particular balance of non-interference and skilful compilation which they maintain is well illustrated by their film *Chronique d'un Eté*, which we shall look at in a moment.

Other film-makers have adapted the vérité techniques to didactic purposes in what we might call still, remembering Eisenstein, the cinema of ideas. We shall look also at Chris Marker's *Le Joli Mai*, and another example of didactic cinema, Georges Franju's *Hôtel des Invalides*—not a vérité film, but a forerunner with many instructive comparisons.

But first *Chronique d'un Eté*. Rouch and Morin set out without a thesis, but with a sociological aim: quite simply to ask people if they thought they were happy. They asked the question of people picked at random from the streets of Paris. After some progress they arranged meetings between chosen strangers, they filmed "follow-up" interviews, they even staged some settings. In a number of ways even before the cutting-room was reached they had shaped their material.

Rouch and Morin chose a girl to be a focal point. The girl, Marceline, is a Jewess who was in a concentration camp during the war. A number is tattooed on her arm, with half of the Star of David. She shows it to an African student who doesn't know what it is. She has had an unhappy love affair, and we are present at a meeting at which she and her ex-boyfriend discuss it with Morin. In other words there are a number of dramatic threads in the girl's life out of which an interesting enough pattern can be woven. Rouch and Morin seem to know the girl well. And yet at our first meeting with her they outline the course they think the story will take, and the things they want her to do. She reacts as though she hasn't heard anything about it before, which can hardly be true. If we are being told that the material is unrehearsed then we judge it on that basis. If it *is* rehearsed, then those parts of the subject's reaction which depend for their impact on surprise or confession are *ipso facto* invalid.

The problem of spontaneity and honesty comes to the fore with this film. The film allegedly puts itself in the hands of its subject totally. Rouch and Morin are, so to speak, at the mercy of their material in a new way. The subject of the film is the actions, reactions and opinions of the people in it, unacted upon, so far as it is possible, by the technique of filming them. The role of the editor, it seems, is being whittled even finer. But this isn't so. On the contrary, his position in this situation becomes even more crucial and the moral decisions he has to make ever more delicate.

Take a small example first. Early in the film we visit[1] the flat of a couple who describe the way they live. At one point while the woman is talking we cut to her man who gets up and crosses the room to wind up and set in motion an antique pianola. The camera follows him with perfect omniscience. On the track the woman's voice is saying that they like to save up their money so that they can " buy things to make life richer."

We wonder whether this shot was set up specifically to describe this phrase. Perhaps even the woman's phrase was rehearsed, too. If she had brought it out naturally in a pre-filming conversation would Rouch have been justified in asking her to repeat it for the camera? And did he perhaps ask the man to do that action in order to counterpoint the phrase? Is it right to design a piece of fake-spontaneity even with the most honourable intentions? The point is particularly acute here since what emerges is a slight preciousness about the couple. A vérité director has to be very careful not to misrepresent real people by his organisation of the shooting and editing. It must be admitted that the technical challenges in making vérité comprehensible sometimes lead the director/editor into making cuts—even at the shooting stage—which may be good cinema but poor vérité.

On the other hand, under the impact of this sort of film-making perhaps our ideas of what a film is will have to change. Some of the most remarkable effects are achieved in *Chronique d'un Eté* by circumstances entirely beyond the control of Rouch or Morin, and would have the same effect however they were presented and in whatever order.

Take, this time, the example of Angelo. Angelo is an ordinary working man doing a mechanical job in the Renault factory. We see him in a number of situations: getting up in the morning, going to work, coming home, practising judo, reading a book. Then we see him being introduced to an African boy, Landry, with whom he discusses living and working conditions in Paris. Later we discover that he has been victimised at work for taking part in the film. He quits his job. At the end of the film he goes on holiday in the south of France with Morin and his children.

[1] *We say " we visit the flat " since that is the effect the walking hand-held camera has. We shuffle in the door in much the same way as the cameraman does. The atmosphere is very well caught: it is clear that we are visiting strangers—an unusual film experience—and the desire to sink out of sight in a corner with a drink is strong.*

Angelo's life, one might fairly say, had been altered by the film. That fact affects the audience's attitude to the material. In this respect the function of cinema can be said to have undergone a curious development. But in other ways Angelo is not affected so much as revealed. We begin to put together the clues each episode has given us about Angelo. His mother, not his wife or his mistress, brings his morning coffee to him in bed and kisses him good morning. He is in his thirties probably. When he describes his workmates to Landry he eagerly grasps the opportunity of telling Landry, an outsider, that they are " pauvres types." He seems eager to make a bid for Landry's friendship and approval. They talk about inferiority complexes. Landry says he had one, but not any more. When he meets trouble, or racialism as it usually is in his case, he just walks away from it and ignores it. Angelo goes home to his solitary judo practice. We learn later that his foreman and bosses have been victimising him, taunting him, he says, about " going into films." They've heaped work on him. They obviously want to get rid of him he says. So he quits.

Certainly no charge of bias on the part of Rouch or Morin can be brought in this case. As we said, in a technical sense there are almost no editing decisions involved here at all, unless Rouch and Morin chose the situations with Machiavellian cunning. But they could hardly have meant Angelo to get the sack. And they didn't tell him in what terms to describe his workmates to Landry. The revelation of Angelo is achieved by the simple device of including the necessary scenes in the same film.

Chronique d'un Eté was clearly the kind of result one could have expected from contemporary currents in the cinema. It has as its aim not " truth " but the many truths out of which some picture of reality can be built. It confines its control to the choice of people and situations. It tries as little as possible to intrude on them, once chosen. The function of editing has taken on a new aspect.

Le Joli Mai[1]

The subjects of Chris Marker's film inquiries, or letters as he often calls them, are akin to Rouch's and Morin's, but the finished product is a highly personal, sophisticated piece of film, as much as it is a social document. He demonstrates that the film-maker need not abdicate in favour of the ethnographer or sociologist. In order to see how this works in practice, we shall take a look at a charac-

[1] *Director: Chris Marker. Editor: Eva Zora. Sofracima. 1962.*

teristic example of his work, *Le Joli Mai*, which provides thematic-ally an interesting comparison with *Chronique d'un Eté*.

Le Joli Mai was shot in Paris in the month of May, 1962. It sets out to give a realistic picture of the city and its inhabitants. It discusses their moods and preoccupations throughout that month.

Some of the principles of selection which have guided Marker might be mentioned here. He is a Marxist, and his interests are, as clearly seen in the film, in social conditions and how they are affected by government, big business and organised religion. The extract below follows on an introductory section about Paris's growth through history, which deals with the old city, the people who lived in it, the new city and its appearance, dominated by cars and huge blocks of new flats. The theme of the film might be best seen in a line of commentary:

If we dissect this many-faced crowd, we shall find that it is made up of a sum of solitudes.

			Ft. fr.	
I	L.S. from ground level of several blocks of high modern flats.	*Gentle piano music.* From the tops of its towers and its surrounding hills, Paris can see the Paris	12	
2	*Extreme L.S.* Panorama of Paris.	of the future rise on the same hills where St. Genevieve saw the bar-barians	7	
3	*Extreme L.S.* Panorama of Paris.	appear. Now the barbarians are here.	4	5
4	*Extreme L.S.* Aerial view of Seine and its bridges.	The metamorphosis which should have inspired an architectural festival has two guardian witches, anarchy and grim death.	14	
5	L.S. Classical group statue in fore-ground. Behind it an immense box-like modern block filling the screen.	One would like to see a New York—	6	12
6	M.S. Caryatids on an old building.	—tempered by the Seine.	2	4
7	M.C.S. As 6.	One does not.	2	4
8	L.S. *Pan off* intersection domin-ated by 19th-century buildings, across rooftops, and on to a narrow street in an old quarter filled with traffic and people. *Aerial view.*	Even if the nuances of solitude have two thousand windows, even if what is described as " project pathology " does not succeed in making us regret the former slums, we know at least—	21	
9	M.L.S. Closer view of a street very similar to 8, seen from the same angle. Also an *aerial view.*	—that there there was room for happiness.	9	

304

10 L.S. Several blocks of modern flats. The *camera tracks slowly back* down a narrow service road, with cars parked on both sides leaving only one lane in the middle. Some cars are having difficulty in parking.

And here we're not sure. 31

11 E.L.S. *Camera tracking left* along face of large modern block of flats, the flats filling the whole screen.

33

12 M.S. *Walking track moving left.* Unseen interviewer asks questions of a little girl accompanied by adults in street, and receives answers.

Music stops.
Int: What did you say?
Girl: What did I say?
Int: Yes, what did you say?
Girl: I said they were prehistoric.
Int: What are prehistoric?
Girl: The old walls.
Int: The walls?

13 C.S. *Crab left* over old wall to reveal in MLS an ancient courtyard, now a near-slum. *Title superimposed* (30 *mai aubervilliers*). As the *camera walks* into it an old man looking straight at us, walks out into the yard, and, moving to our right, washes his hands at a water barrel in the open air. The *camera pans round* with him, holding him, and the barrel, in a C.S. then *walks backward* up the yard, looking in the direction from which it has come. Two women neighbours are revealed as the shot widens. The *camera continues to pan right* across a wall in C.S. and across some shutters.

A new piece of music starts. The voice of what purports to be an estate agent reads: 67
  Here are twelve reasons which make the Kleber-Chaillot residence the most sought-after in Paris. First, the face of the building is of white Carrara marble. Second, the decoration and fountains in the entrance halls which cover the entire ground floor. There will be soft background music in the halls, which will also be heard in the elevators.

  Third, the ultra-rapid elevators are lined with stainless steel.
The voice fades. A new voice, the interviewer's, comes in over it. A new piece of music replaces the other, and soon fades.
Unseen Int.:
  Where did you learn to grow flowers—

14 *Track* in to woman in M.S. and then C.S. leaning out of ground floor window. The interviewer is off-screen throughout this scene. The *camera tilts down* below the woman to reveal a window-box perched on the wall under the window. It holds a few small flowers. *Camera tilts back up* to woman.

— to look after them? 50
Woman:
  Well I'm not sure. It just came naturally I suppose.
Int:
  But you must have learnt somewhere. Pansies are very difficult to grow.
Woman:
  I sow them in the garden then plant them out.
Int:
  You spend a lot of time on it?
Woman:
  No, not much.

Zoom in to C.U.

Int:
You do it in addition to your work?
Woman:
I'm out of work for the moment. Otherwise I do it at the week-end. Then of course I water them in the evening.
Int:
And when you are gardening—

15   M.S. Vase of flowers on garden wall. *Camera* immediately *pans right* and *tilts down* over tiny garden patch filled with miscellaneous, not altogether horticultural, objects.

—what do you think about? 15
(*off*).
Woman's voice:
I think it's pretty. I love flowers. Well, I was born in the country, but I've been here for a long time.

16   *Hand-held walking track* along garden fence. Oddly regular flowers seen poking sparsely up from patch of earth. Camera roams over them, *panning right again.*

Music begins. 28
Int. (*off*):
What do you think of plastic flowers?
Woman:
They're not so good as natural flowers. They're not as pretty.
Int:
Have you any plastic flowers?
Woman:
Yes, in the garden.
Int:
To give the impression they're all real?
Woman:
I've put them there for the moment till the others come up.

17   *Camera pans right* over garden patch again leaving behind a Yuri Gagarin plaque on a wall.

Int. (*off*): 10
What gave you the idea of growing flowers?
Woman:
Just an idea.

18   *Zoom in* to old glass-framed government warning notice, attached to wall.

6 11
Notice announces:
" Mesures de protection contre bombardements aériens."

19   *Walking track* towards high wall and gateway. Two men and a woman stand in the gateway watching. A peeling, barely legible, notice reads " Hotel Meuble." *Camera pans left* past them and points back down the way it came. A boy is standing in the road looking at the camera.

27

20   M.C.S. Handwritten notice in window. Notice reads: " Réunion Publique à 20h. 45. 'Le Chrétien et la soif de justice ' "

14

306

and underneath: " Vendredi 11 et 18 mai 'Cours de Lectures pour nord-africains.' " *Pan left* to see a man watching camera from the pavement some yards away.

21 *M.S.* Crates on waste ground. *Tilt up* to backs of old apartment buildings in *L.S.*

Music, which ends after 9 ft.
Natural location sound, continuing.

16

22 *C.S. Hand-held camera climbing stairs,* banister rail of staircase and gallery, *looking down* into courtyard of old block of flats.

18

23 *Walking track* along gallery above courtyard. Festooned with washing. *Tilt down* into yard to see man filling portable bathtub from yard tap. The shot ends with a *pan left* over washing in *C.U.*

27

24 *C.S.* Wall *panning left* into doorway in *M.S. tracking into C.U.* of door.

Int. (off):
Well, have you heard the good news?
Woman and interviewer's voices together on track, both unseen:
—good news—yes—heard the good news—etc.

5 10

25 *Walk in* to interviewee, Mme. Langlois, behind interviewer. *Camera holds* Mme. Langlois on her doorstep throughout this shot, sometimes pulling back to include the back of the interviewer, sometimes closing in to a tight shot of her alone. At one point, the *camera skirts round* behind the interviewer and comes up on his right-hand side so that Mme. Langlois' face at moments is half-hidden by the door-jamb. At the end of the shot, the *camera pans off left* into the roadway. Throughout the shot, the interviewer and Mme. Langlois talk continuously. The interviewer's voice is asking a question during the *pan off* into the roadway.

212

26 *M.C.S.* Mme. Langlois answering the interviewer's questions.

21

Many of Marker's characteristics can be seen to advantage in this section. The mixture of ingredients is perhaps the most characteristic of all: carefully composed dolly- or car-shots, with a strong formal appeal; hand-held work, including walking tracks, backwards, forwards and sideways; hand-held, marathon interviews; random street encounters; use of all and any graphic material including notices; acceptance of deliberate public participation; a synchronous and a wild track; and a constant intuitive flexibility responsive to hints in the interviewee's voice or behaviour.

The beginning of the extract consists of a series of agreeable but undramatic views, intended to carry a fairly concentrated and literate commentary. After the short irony of 6 and 7 we are lulled by the long, ranging pan (8) while we grapple with the thought. We are further lulled by the formal elegance of the tracking shots 10 and 11. The grid pattern of 11 covers the screen entirely and symmetrically and is offset by the passing flicker of thin saplings planted between the camera and the building.

Then suddenly shot 12 pitches us into a random street conversation with a little girl we know nothing about and have never seen before. The continuing leftward movement from the previous shot helps the cut. The conversation is self-explanatory, since we cut immediately afterwards to an old wall, which we are invited to assume is the wall in question.

The irony in 13 is in the contrast which the commentary makes with the images: the description of the luxury block with these crumbling quarters. The hand-held camera is made to accommodate here a shot lasting sixty-seven feet, starting in close-up on a wall, opening out suddenly to a depth of field of at least fifty feet, closing up again quite quickly to a two-shot, turning to shoot against the light and finishing with a rapid, in-focus, pan across a wall not more than four or five feet away at some points. It doesn't appear as though any supplementary lights were used. This kind of shooting demands a certain amount of give and take from the audience. It means that from time to time some areas of the picture will be unavoidably underexposed and some will flare. The advantages of flexibility and spontaneity which the methods bring surely outweigh these defects. The people in shot make no bones about looking at the camera, and Marker appears to encourage it, as why should he not, since we all know the camera is there. In this type of film-making the camera is, as we have already mentioned, liable to develop a personality of its own, since it stands in for the interviewer/spectator/director who is at the same time in control as well as being informed. The camera has lost omniscience, but has gained tact.

At the end of this shot, the interviewer's voice is mixed up over the "estate agent's," to prepare us for the woman in 14. The

308

operator doesn't lose the opportunity of tilting down to pick up the window-box and its flowers when the unseen interviewer mentions the pansies. It tilts back up in time to catch her next but one reply. In the exchange following, the camera zooms in to a close shot of her, but in this case to no particular advantage. We cut away from her almost immediately. With the hand-held camera and the autonomous operator, the temptation to alter the frame size constantly has to be resisted since the resultant restlessness is often more boring to the spectator than the imagined monotony of a static frame.[1] There will surely be no monotony if the words are interesting enough.

Shot *15* is a fair example of how to get out of one interview into another. It involves a certain amount of sleight-of-hand. The question appears to be asked to the woman we are still holding in shot *14*. But it is clear that the answer is in another voice. The interview may have been recorded without vision, simply on tape. It is tactful of Marker not to let us see this woman. The dangers of condescension in this kind of interviewing are lurking in the questions in *14*. " Where did you learn to cultivate flowers?" and " Do you spend a lot of time on it?"—of an absurdly tiny window-box. The danger is of transferring the scorn he feels for a social condition to its victim. It breaks almost too nakedly through the surface in this present exchange with the woman who plants plastic flowers. But if Marker's weakness is irony, his strength is compassion, which outweighs it. It does so, finally, here by virtue of two touching contrasts. When the woman says she was born in the country but she'd been there in the city a long time, the image of the cluttered garden, a travesty of the countryside and a sad place to be for any length of time, is enough to stifle absurdity. Secondly, it is clear that he finds the patent weakness (rationally) of the woman's reply—" Just an idea "—very moving.

Shot *18* is a strong irony. The notice must have been there over twenty years, which says something for the state of the property.

In shot *19* nothing happens. There is very little to read, no commentary and the music is rather boring. And it is twenty-seven feet long. But it conveys admirably an impression of the district; of what the two men think about it; and that Marker agrees with them. The camera again does one of those characteristic 180 degrees pans as if to say it doesn't wish to conceal anything.

[1] *Some cameraman/directors, carried away by the analogy between the film and music, treat an Eclair with a zoom lens as though it were a slide trombone.*

309

The interview with Mme. Langlois is, of course, the core of the sequence. The substance of it is that she has just been awarded a new house, two days before, by the housing committee. She had lived in the slum for years in tiny rooms with her husband, eight children and an adopted niece. She describes affectingly how the postman waited while she opened the letter with the good news, how she didn't tell her husband when he came home for his dinner at midday, but left the letter by his plate . . . and so on. Her joy is moving, and by one of those happy accidents by which cinéma-vérité justifies itself, the camera, at a particularly nice moment, has moved close to the wall so that Mme. Langlois' face is briefly half-hidden by the edge of the wall where it meets the door-jamb. The effect is of an inexplicable delicacy.

The long interview is certainly the heart of this film. In turn, Marker questions a men's outfitter, young boys in their first year in the stock exchange, a tyre mechanic who paints, an inventor, a young engaged couple, two consultant engineers, an African living in France, three young good-looking sisters, a communist Algerian boy living in Paris, an unseen woman prisoner. Because it is cinéma-vérité, no-one should expect it to be impartial. A strongly sympathetic attitude emerges to the workers, to strikers, to the African and the Algerian especially. A certain amount of polite disdain is felt for those who can't be bothered to take up political attitudes or inform themselves about the measures their government is taking.

Such close scrutiny of peoples' private lives and opinions might seem indefensible if it wasn't done with tact and honesty and here the editor has a great responsibility not to betray the material in any way. After all, the material brings its own special opportunities. When the African boy talks of the colonising missionaries his eyes glint in a way no actor's ever would. " They put me with the brothers," he says, meaning the religious brothers, and only the merest narrowing of the eyes on the word " frères " indicates the intensity of his feeling about it. He goes on: " I'd rather go to hell with my ancestors than go to heaven with I don't know who." In this case the operator has to know what kind of a face to stick to and what to leave. The camera rightly never leaves this boy's face. But the inventor, wild and wordy, elusive, equivocal, agreeable, vain, is transfixed for posterity by a large money spider which nonchalantly explores his shirt front before sauntering off down his sleeve. The camera follows it, fascinated.

There are many faces it would be wrong to quit if a nest of

spiders were manoeuvring on the shirt front. The maker of cinéma-vérité needs this kind of discretion. In cases like this the editing decisions are not so much the editor's or even the director's, but rather the operator's.

Being ready for the unexpected always pays dividends. While the two boys at the stock exchange are being interviewed, a voice from the crowd interrupts. The camera immediately swings to catch the speaker who is angrily saying: " What are you filming them for? You might as well ask two-year-old babies for their opinions." Swiftly a clapper board is swung in—it remains there in the finished film—the speaker composes himself to reply, and the reactionary in him dies instantly at the smell of greasepaint. He becomes reason itself, but too late—for him, not us.

There is a technical problem to be overcome in filming these long interviews. Even the French can't keep up a steady flow of informed and witty comment, and the time comes when the editor must chop something out. One customary practice is to cut to the listening interviewer, but Marker's interviewer is rarely seen. Where there has been a camera cut, the new take often starts on a detail. In one sequence, for example, we start on the hands of the person interviewed and tilt up into his face for the start of his answer, while the interviewer's question is laid over the beginning of the shot. Another device is, as we have seen with Mme. Langlois, to pan away at a certain point and cut back when you want. But at other times, when he just wants to chop out a section in the middle of a long conversation, Marker cuts in some perfectly irrelevant but charming cats—his trade mark; and accompanies it with a little harp music before going back to the original. At one point, when reference is made to people going about their daily jobs, four film directors are seen: Jean Rouch is seen sitting at a café table, Alain Resnais striding purposefully towards us, and so on. Once, instead of the cats, he cuts in a shot of passengers in the métro. The interviews themselves—diffuse, halting and gabbled by turns, sometimes inaudible—would have been found unacceptable not long ago, to say nothing of the devices used to link them.

When all is said and done though, anyone can make some sort of shot at filming an interview. What is it that makes Marker's films an experience on more than a sociological plane? The answer is, principally, editing: the power to arrange and shape the material, especially the power to follow one episode with another, and the power to counterpoint visuals with an intelligent and eloquent commentary, and to use sound and visuals in a synthesis which doesn't leave the one limply supporting the other. The Algerian boy describes how he was set upon by the police and beaten up in his room in front of his parents. He mentions the place—some old huts—they were living in at the time. Immediately we see similar huts on the screen—perhaps they are the very ones. The camera walks down the alleyway between them, stopping to peer at infants squatting in the sunlight. At the end of the alleyway a shadow strikes across the huts. We turn the corner into a dark passageway where black walls press in on us. On the track the boy's voice continues: after the police attack he had a nervous breakdown. There is no point, he goes on, in his going back to Algeria. All his family are dead.

The commentary, allied to carefully chosen and cut mute shots, is as much Marker's strength as his penetrating interviews. Indeed, it gives his films the flavour and the eloquence which, for example, Rouch and Morin's *Chronique d'un Eté* for all its honesty, lacks. The end of *Le Joli Mai* is a particularly good example.

LE JOLI MAI
Extract from Reel 6

In the shots preceding the extract, exteriors of a Paris prison accompany the voice of a woman prisoner who describes prison life. The last thing she has said in answer to the interviewer's question: " What's the worst thing about prison?" is " The other women."

		Commentary	Ft. fr.
1	M.L.S. Prison block exterior wall. *Fast pan right* along wall and across trees.	When prisoners think of the city, it is of these two wonders: doors which open—	15
2	*Fast motor-track* along long wide straight tree-lined road, looking up at the trees in silhouette. The shot is sombre and backlit. The trees, and a railway viaduct they give way to, are black and menacing.	—from the inside, and steps which go in straight lines. *Music begins—an eerie combination of very low* musique concrète *growls and high tinkling notes, perhaps of a harp.* During this month we have crossed Paris in a straight line— just as our journey could be made up of all those lines that prisoners cover in a circle from wall to wall.	37
3	Similar shot to 2, but more intimate and small scale. At the end of the shot the *camera is pointing straight into a low sun* which floods the lens and the roadway in front of it, on the word " phenomena."	We tried to look through the eyes of a prisoner on his first day of freedom when he himself tries to understand how these strange phenomena, free people, live.	16
4	As 3. A low sun points towards us.	We have met those people—	10

5	As 4. Continuing the *fast forward track* along dawn streets.	We have given them the biggest rôles in this film. Those who are able to question, to refuse, to undertake, to think, or simply to laugh.	12
6	As 4	They were not without contradictions or mistakes. But they persevered, even with their mistakes, and perhaps truth is not only the end but also a means. (*Pause*)	24
7	As 5		7
8	As 6	But there were others,	$4\frac{1}{2}$
9	As 7. Place de la Concorde.	a great number, who would amaze the prisoner, for their prison is inside	$10\frac{1}{2}$
10	M.C.S. Young lorry-driver's face in cab of lorry. (The following sequence of close shots is of people in the streets, candidly observed.)	themselves.	10
11	M.C.S. Businessman smoking, at wheel of car. Stares at camera. Drives off left out of frame.		10
12	M.S. Middle-aged woman shrugs.		3
13	M.C.S. Close-cropped man with thick neck.	Their faces we see—	3
14	M.S. Old woman walking right, obscured by another younger woman who turns and stares worriedly at the camera.	—every day. Do we need a screen to understand what would be obvious to any Martian just landed on the planet Earth? One would like to call out to them, to say—	11
15	M.S. Old man leaning forward looking out screen left, anxiously.	—what's bothering your faces? What invisible things can you see that dogs can see, and it frightens you?	17
16	M.S. Cross in cemetery.		1
17	M.S. Young man with moustache biting lip.	Is it the thought that your	7
18	M.C.S. The cross.	noblest deeds are mortal?	2 3
19	M.S. Elderly man turns, *camera pans down* to girl with head bowed on arm.		3 12
20	L.S. Twin tombstones, out of which two black stone arms reach to hold hands.		4

313

21	General view of cemetery.		4 8
22	M.C.S. An attractive girl.	Men have always known them-selves to be mortal, and have even found new ways of laughing and singing mortality. Is it because beauty is mortal that to love a human being is to love also his passing?	17
23	M.S. Statue in garden. Pigeons on stone basin of a fountain.	Men have invented a masculine for beauty which is called—	8
24	F.S. Statue of naked woman in public garden.	—art. It's sometimes a little erratic in its form—	5 12
25	Upper portions of two figurines. Focus pull reveals in background the painting of " St. George and the Dragon " by Uccello.	—but it is sometimes very beautiful.	$7\frac{1}{2}$
26	C.S. Uccello painting.		6
27	M.S. Gallery interior. On the walls, a painting; out of the window a view of domes and roofs.		$4\frac{1}{2}$
28	C.S. The painting.		9
29	B.C.U. Old lady, anxious face.	Then what's the matter?	8
30	C.U. Man smoking cigar.	You are in Paris, capital of a pros-perous country, in the midst of a world which is slowly recovering from those—	10
31	C.S. Woman's head. The back of another head goes through the frame on the cut, blotting out the image.	—hereditary evils, treasured like the family jewels, poverty, hunger, hate, logic. You are perhaps—	10
32	M.C.S. Back of girl's head. She is wearing a black head-scarf, blow-ing in the wind.	—opening the second greatest switchbox of human history since the discovery of fire. Are you afraid of ghosts? Is that it? Or is it that you think too much about yourselves? Or is it because with-out being aware of it, you think too much about others?	21
33	M.C.S. Man and tree trunk.	Perhaps you feel in a confused way that your fate is tied to the fate of others, that—	$4\frac{1}{2}$
34	M.S. Boy in glasses, putting back of hand up worriedly to stroke his face.	—happiness and unhappiness are two secret societies, so secret that you join without knowing—	12
35	M.C.S. Girl with white scarf.	—it, and that, without hearing it, you shelter within yourself this voice which says—	8

314

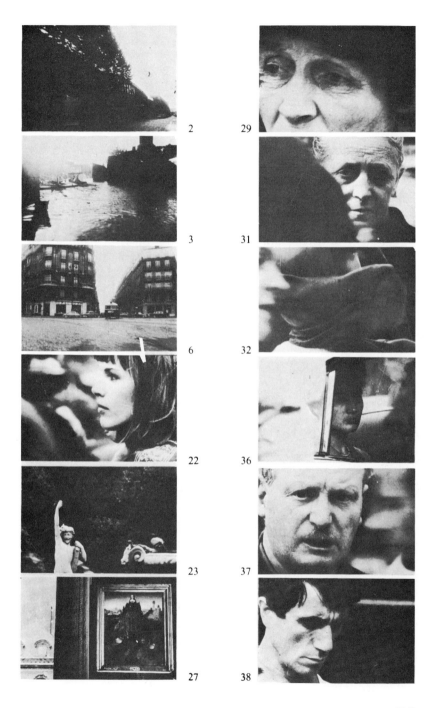

2

29

3

31

6

32

22

36

23

37

27

38

			Ft. fr
36	M.S. Girl in back of large car.	" As long as poverty exists you're not rich."	9
37	C.S. Middle-aged man staring hauntedly into the camera.	" As long as despair exists, you're not happy."	14
38	M.C.S. Young man looking down.	" As long as prisons exist, you're not free."	19 10

FADE

As a piece of film-with-commentary this can hardly be bettered. The thing to avoid in this kind of filming is over-loading the combination of image and words. Marker never makes the mistake of trying to " visualise " complex intellectual ideas. This is not to say that he concentrates only on simple ones. The commentary is the vehicle which states the proposition. It is the combination of the thought with the immediate sensuous impact of the image which produces the complexity that gives his films their flavour.

We don't, for example, immediately think of the metaphorical associations of dawn and rising sun in shots *1–9*. But the feeling of the fast, silent, spellbound tracking shots is appropriate to the wonder with which the newly-released prisoner—or perhaps the newly-landed Martian—would look at this new world. It helps us to look at it too with new eyes. Then again Marker doesn't make the mistake of trying to give too concrete expression to his verbal metaphors. " Happiness and unhappiness are two secret societies "—but although all we are looking at is a worried face, it is enough. There is nothing about the image except the natural mystery of the face. His hints of metaphor or simile are so delicate as to be hardly there. When the commentary asks the sad passers-by (*32*) " Are you afraid of ghosts?"—we are looking at the back of a young woman's head. She is wearing a black headscarf. When we hear the word " ghosts " the wind lifts her scarf softly, like a ghostly shroud.

We never have to make a forced connection between the words and the pictures. There is a progression in shots *1* to *9* which is independent of the words, though it reinforces them. The sequence starts with a blocked image—the prison wall—and we travel it seems along a deep dark tunnel in shots *2* and *3* until the sun begins to gleam through in *3* and *4*. At the same time, the streets widen out gradually until, by shot *9*, we are in the infinite spaces of the Place de la Concorde. The feeling is one of gradual liberation which is what the commentary is about. But then, strangely, we see that those free people outside the prison are in fact more imprisoned than any; imprisoned metaphorically like the lorry-driver in his cab, but really imprisoned in themselves. The commentary goes on, still watching passers-by with their private faces and secret worries, to inquire what is bothering them. Here Marker deals, with perfect freedom and with no embarrassment, with larger questions than the form usually permits: love, hate, death, life, beauty, art, freedom. Because he is direct about it, he gets away perfectly well with the simplicity of cutting in a tombstone to represent mortality, or a statue to represent art, or a pretty girl to represent beauty. The shots don't simply have an intellectual significance: they have an emotional one too and that is why they work.

The tombstone *is* grim, the statues and the pigeons *are* beautiful, and so is the girl. Marker doesn't make abstruse connections. Yet, with these simple elements, closely observed, tactfully put together, he creates a personal synthesis. His film is about freedom and love, and those are the qualities he makes it with.

Hôtel des Invalides

It may have become apparent during the last section that some at least of Marker's methods bear a strong resemblance to those of Eisenstein in his more didactic films. We suggest that what is different about Marker is the way in which he has adapted the methods of the didactic cinema primarily to personal rather than generalised expression; and secondly, blended this type of abstract, intellectual film making with long stretches of cinéma-vérité in which he is primarily at the mercy of the material.

Much the same methods—of conducting a discussion of ideas by referring to them in symbolic images—are used by Georges Franju in his film *Hôtel des Invalides*. He uses no cinéma-vérité at all but his film makes an interesting comparison with those of Eisenstein. Coming years after Eisenstein, when the method has become part of cinema language, he is able to use it with greater sophistication and complexity; so much so, indeed, as to question its very validity.

In order to support this rather baffling statement it may be as well to take a close look at an extract from the above film.

This short film was ostensibly a straight documentary account of the building which housed not only the tomb of Napoleon and a military museum, but also a number of war-wounded veterans. As the commentary sardonically remarks " Here the army has its museum," an old crippled soldier is wheeled across the square between the cannons. Irony in fact is the keynote of the film. We are left in no doubt that Franju considers the museum to war and its instruments an obscenity, and the hospital of old, shattered soldiers an unspeakable sadness. To die for one's country is not, to his mind, the summit of human happiness, and it is, to say the least, dishonest of the State to pretend that it is.

HOTEL DES INVALIDES[1]

Shots of war machinery in the courtyard precede this extract.
The footages are 16mm. footages, i.e., 40 frames to the foot.
Each foot lasts approximately 1½ seconds.

			Ft. fr.
1	Barrels of antique cannon standing up against the courtyard walls.		2 33
2	A *close shot* of a cannon. Quick dissolve to	*Voice of museum guide:* As we sing, Victory opened the barriers,	2 20
3	Painting of a cannon.	—victory of the Revolution decapitated Absolute Monarchy.	3 32
4	A tapestry insignia.	La République!	2 38
5	Statuette of an eagle. Smoke swirls round it.	*Bugles and drums play.* L'Empire! *Bugles and drums continue to shot 16.*	4 1
6	*Track left* along a line of flags— the " colours "—hanging close-packed above us.		17 2
7	Three groups of flags surrounding a mirror.	Take your hats off, gentlemen, before the colours.	2 35
8	*Track in* to a statue of a soldier on horseback, arms uplifted.	The statue known as " Long Live The Emperor," the work of Maître Richefeu.	5 0
9	*C.S.* Statue as in 8.		2 18
10	*B.C.U.* Statue as in 9.		1 9
11	Statuettes of soldiers.	The charge of the Grenadier Guards.	2 9
12	A statuette of Napoleon with a characteristic shadow.	The Emperor!	3 2
13	Napoleon's relics. *L.S.* (in the form of a bedroom).	Assorted souvenirs belonging to the Emperor.	3 0
14	Napoleon's bed.	His camp bed.	2 12
15	Napoleon's table.	His working-table and his First Consul's brief-case.	2 15
16	A stuffed horse and a dog.	His faithful dog and his horse.	3 0

[1] *Director: Georges Franju. Forces et Voix de France. 1952.*

318

17	*C.U.* Horse.	They are life size.	2 6
18	*C.U.* Dog.		1 33
19	Glass case with uniforms and clothing in it.	Napoleon the First died at St. Helena on	3 6
20	Death mask of the Emperor.	5th May 1821.	1 38
21	Painting of a battlefield.	His famous epic, still hovering over the battlefields, is illustrated in this canvas of the painter, Edouard Detail, which inspired the celebrated song "The Dream Passes."	7 4

      Superimposed Titles
      (Les soldats sont là-bas,   *Music starts.*
      Endormis sur la plaine.)   The soldiers are left behind, Asleep on the plain.

22   *Closer shot* of canvas.   1 25

      (Où le souffle du soir   Where the evening breeze
      Chante pour les bercer.)   Gently soothes their bodies.

23   *B.C.U.* Part of canvas.   4 3

      (La terre aux blés rasés   The earth from which the corn
      Parfume son haleine.   is reaped
      Le sentinelle au loin   Lends a sweet perfume to the air.
      Va d'un pas cadencé.)   The sentry in the distance
                                     Walks with measured step.

24   *C.U.* Different, more dramatic part of canvas.   2 7

      (Soudain, voici qu'au ciel   Suddenly, in the heavens
      Des cavaliers sans nombres   A host of warriors rides
      Illuminent d'éclairs   Illuminating the twilight with
      l'imprécise clarté)   their flashing swords,

25   *Pan off* canvas right to Napoleon's three-cornered hat.   And the little hat (i.e., Napoleon) seems to guide their shadows towards   3 19

26   *B.C.U.* Hat.   Immortality.   2 23

27   *Tracking shot* down the line of mounted model soldiers in uniform and on horseback.   See how they go! (Chorus) The Hussars! The Dragoons!   9 18

28   *M.C.S. Tracking* past horseman and large sword.   The Guards!   1 25

29   The *tracking shot* continues as in 27 closing in on two cavalrymen.   6 14

30   *M.S.* A cavalryman leaning intently forward in the saddle. Static.   They all salute   2 16

31   White bust of Napoleon amongst rows of men and horses.   the Emperor whose gaze is on them.   4 10
                                            Music stops. Piano takes up theme.

319

32   The wall of a room in the museum.
The guide's shadow moves across
it, followed by his party. An old   Ladies and gentlemen, if you'll
man with a heavy limp brings up   follow me, please.
the rear.

The music stops.

This sequence has obvious affinities with *October*, and particularly the passage detailed on pp. 33–5 of this book. Both of
them proceed by means of a list of isolated objects which have a
typical, sometimes emblematic, significance. In both of them, the
tone is ironical. But the difference in Franju is that the objects are
also present on the scene, and are themselves the subject of the
sequence. In Eisenstein they are alien references introduced for
their intellectual significance.

The objects illustrating the concept " For God " (*157–186*) in
October are an assembly which has nothing to do with Kerensky
or Kornilov. No more do the shots illustrating the concept " For
Country " (*189–199*). This barrage of images carries no more
impact than the few comparable shots in the Franju sequence.
See for example how in shot *4* a tapestry represents " La
République." Franju uses, in fact, the *inadequacy* of the emblem
as a way of properly representing the concept, consciously to make
a judgement on the type of mind for which the emblem *is* adequate.
We see that as the tapestry is inadequate to represent the complexity
of a social and political structure such as " The Republic " so the
judgement of a mind which makes equivalences and simplifications
on this scale is called in question too. For people to whom " La
République " is simply a heady amalgam of glory, pride and
courage, the designs on a tapestry insignia are indeed an appropriate
way of defining them. Similarly, the eagle is the empire, the bust
of Napoleon the epitome of bravery, intelligence and leadership,
a flag can represent the history of a regiment, a bed is imbued with
the awe of its late occupant, even his poor horse and dog become
super-beasts in the iconography of idolatry.

This is not to say that the objects do not carry associations. But
what Franju is doing is making an equation between easy political
assumptions and idol-worship; and he is doing so by making an
analogy with the way easy assumptions are made by the language
of symbolism in the cinema.

Franju does something else also. He crowns his passage of
" intellectual " montage with a piece of film-making of unusual
complexity and lyrical power. The combination of slow tracking

320

shots and the song *The Dream Passes,* builds up to a moving indictment of military and patriotic sentimentality. It is not only ironical. It develops a feeling of pathos in which the soldiers are seen as the sad victims of imperial delusions. Shots *27–31* especially work on this level.

The models of the soldiers—the Hussars! The Dragoons!— whom the guide recalls so proudly—are life-like but lifeless, uncomfortable reminders of the corpses they have all become. Even the fierce horseman with his sword in *28* has become simply a toy in a museum. The eagerness of the young Hussar leaning forward so intently in the saddle in *30* is in moving contrast to his immobility. The immobility itself is given added point by the relentless and eventually *sympathetic* tracking of the camera. " They all salute," the song goes, " the Emperor whose gaze is on them." Yet this is the same Emperor—the little corporal— whose little hat, says the song, " seems to guide their shadows towards immortality." And on " immortality " we cut to a shot of Napoleon's tricorne, a pitiful relic, it seems, of his own immortality. There are many other points one could make. Note for example—by viewing it—how much use Franju makes of the idea of " shadows "—with its associations with death.

18

NOUVELLE VAGUE

Caméra-Stylo

IN a now famous critical piece[1] Alexandre Astruc, film-maker and critic, wrote:

The cinema is quite simply becoming a means of expression, something that all other arts have been before it, particularly painting and the novel. After having been successively a fairground attraction, an amusement rather like the *théâtre de boulevard*, and a way of preserving images of the times, it is becoming, little by little, a language. A language; that's to say, a form in which and through which an artist can express his thought, however abstract it may be, or translate his preoccupations in exactly the same way as he does today with the essay or the novel. That's why I call this new age of the cinema that of the *caméra-stylo* . . .

. . . The silent cinema tried to give birth to ideas and meanings by symbolic associations. We have realised that they exist in the image itself, in the natural progression of the film, in every gesture the characters make, in every one of their words and in the camera movements which bind the objects one to another, and the people to the objects . . .

. . . this implies, naturally, that the screen-writer make his own films. Better still, that there no longer be such things as screen-writers, for in this cinema the distinction between author and director no longer makes any sense. Film direction is no longer a way of illustrating or presenting a scene, but really a way of writing it . . .

Astruc's piece has not been forgotten because it did crystallise in a useful expression—*caméra-stylo*—a way in which young French intellectuals began to think of the cinema. It was an instrument of thought and feeling in which the film-writer could express himself as freely as the novelist. The camera must be used as a pen.

The film director was a writer—or to use the French word most appropriate—*auteur*. The French cinema had often been in the hands of its writers. Prévert's work for Carné, Spaak's for Duvivier spring to mind. But the writer exerted a control over the director which critics began now to feel was unproductive. Astruc and

---

[1] *Naissance d'une nouvelle avant-garde: la caméra-stylo* (L'Ecran Français, *number 144, 30 March 1948*).

his supporters drew attention to the unreal distinction between the writer and the visualiser. Excellence, as in so many other arts, should spring, they felt, from the unity of one controlling mind. The cumbersome giant of the cinema must be cut down to manageable proportions that one man, the creator, could handle.

This obviously relates to the movement we discussed in the last section. Cinéma-vérité was one response to the appeal for a more simple, life-like and personal recording apparatus, designed to interfere as little as possible with the flow of real events. To the would-be *auteurs* this was an attractive proposition. The first *nouvelle vague* films were to make extensive use of direct cinema techniques, including improvisation.

Another influence was the move towards widescreen. This was, too, in some ways a weapon in the move towards greater simplicity. The wide screen discourages, as we have seen, the temptation to over-" interpretative " editing.

So the desire to use the camera as a pen to record, with the same directness as writing, was related to this quest for simplicity. At the same time, as we shall see, this was not the only use to which the philosophy of the *caméra-stylo* was put. The same directness and simplicity (of a *process*) was to be bent to the service of expressing complexities of theme and character, common in the novel but rare, till now, in the film.

The logical development of these tendencies was soon to come to fruition in a new type of cinema. To Jean-Pierre Melville, one of its early and often neglected practitioners, we owe a useful definition of its characteristics:

A workmanlike system of production in natural locations, without stars and with less than a minimum crew, ultra-fast stock, no distribution guarantee, no authorisation and no obligations of any sort.

What he was talking about came to be known as the *nouvelle vague* or New Wave.

New Wave

We have to resist the temptation to put inverted commas around the description *New Wave*, as though we didn't believe in it. It is true, there was no such wave, in the sense that there was no clearly defined conscious movement with set aims, technical or thematic. On the other hand the term is a useful shorthand for an event beginning in France about 1958–1959 and to have international repercussions in the next few years. If the New Wave was a phrase dreamed up and sustained by journalists, it nevertheless broadly designates a sudden change in the cinema industry: a change in production methods, a change in subject matter, a change in moral attitudes perhaps; certainly a change in the style and appearance of the film. After Cannes 1959, when the first New Wave films were recognised by a larger public, the language and conventions of the cinema were perceptibly altered. The special interest to us here lies in the new methods of expression which they made current.

At the time of writing, eight years after the ballyhoo of a festival which perhaps obscured more issues than it revealed, it is interesting to remember that three films-grouped together under the heading of New Wave included *Orfeu Negro*, *Hiroshima Mon Amour* and *Les 400 Coups*. If they have anything in common it may be that their makers knew one another. It can be little else. What little there is may, however, give us our first sketchy description of the new cinema.

The New Wave directors, in so far as they had a critical voice or a discernible aesthetic aim, were grouped chiefly around the nucleus of the *Cahiers du Cinéma* critical team. Several of these critics made their first features at this time: among them, Godard, Truffaut, Rohmer, Rivette, Doniol-Valcroze, Chabrol. Some of their films were taken as typical of what the movement at its best would achieve. They sought to make cheap, saleable films, with no great box office names, but preserving the impact and freshness of a personal vision. They cut costs by cutting schedules, working fast with small, sometimes non-union crews, shooting on location, in the streets, using not only non-stars, but in some cases non-actors, friends, other directors. Above all they sought to strengthen the concept of the *cinéma d'auteur*: a cinema in which one man would be creatively responsible for conception and execution of his own idea. It was this virtue which they praised especially amongst those American directors who were most oppressed by the massive uniformity of the Hollywood system and yet managed to give a personal flavour to their work.

In a search for cheapness, and a fresh and personal treatment, some of the trends we have noted in earlier pages were obviously of importance. The spontaneous cinema with its hand-held camera and snooping microphones for one: for another, the theory of Astruc about the *caméra-stylo*, the flexible and yet complex instrument with which the new film-maker would be able to write his work on celluloid as the author did on paper. And understandably, there was a determination to break in subject and spirit with the dead hand of *qualité*, the traditional scenarist's cinema in

324

France in which the writer produced a literary script and took little further interest in the film's visualisation.

In one way, then, the three films said to have ushered in the New Wave at Cannes in 1959 did have something in common: they were all *films d'auteur*. They were films bearing the imprint primarily of one man, expressing a personal vision and doing it in a personal style. By a stroke of good fortune some of the new films caught the public imagination and were financially successful. The New Wave was splendidly launched. The result was that what might have been simply a short-lived, indiosyncratic and domestic revolution in style was given international currency overnight. By the time backers withdrew with burnt fingers from the inevitable anti-climax the new language was familiar—and was being copied —throughout the world.

It was copied most of all, of course, in France. There, about a hundred and fifty new directors made their first feature films between 1959 and 1962. Some are still unseen. Newcomers with scarcely any experience even as assistants were encouraged to get behind the camera by the revolutionary cries of the 'veterans':

> All you need to know to be a film director can be learnt in four hours
> (Claude Chabrol, *Arts* 658, 19 Feb. 1958)
> Anybody can be a director or an actor
> (François Truffaut, *Arts* 619, 15 May 1957)

In the cases of Truffaut and Chabrol the claims were justified. They, along with others of their generation, produced a crop of successful films between 1959 and 1962. Apart from those we have mentioned, such films as Chabrol's *Le Beau Serge* and *Les Cousins*, Louis Malle's *L'Ascenseur pour L'Echafaud* and *Les Amants*, Jean-Luc Godard's *A Bout de Souffle* (*Breathless*), Truffaut's *Tirez sur le Pianiste* (*Shoot the Pianist*), are typical of the early days of the movement. Many of the films were financed personally by their directors—*Le Beau Serge* and *Les 400 Coups* among them. They were often autobiographical, like these two, and their makers still very young, having had a literary or philosophical education, sometimes as critics, but having served no apprenticeship in the industry. Malle was twenty-five when he made *Les Amants*. Chabrol confessed that he made *Le Beau Serge* very slowly since he spent such a long time in the course of it learning " the technical side." *Shoot the Pianist* caused widespread dismay in the press when it appeared since it was quite unlike Truffaut's first film *Les 400 Coups*. *Breathless* astonished everybody by being like nothing in the world.

The new cinema was knowing and self-conscious. By training critics, as we have said, many of the new directors had a deep knowledge of the cinema and its history which gave them a wide area of reference. They used it liberally. Familiar with the cinema's historical development in subject-matter and technique they were able to pick from its resources, past and present, what seemed to them most useful. They were able to play on our sense of nostalgia, to use old forms in a new way, to mix moods more abruptly than ever before, to coax audiences with a mixture of lyricism and violence, reverence and iconoclasm, into an awareness of new possibilities in the medium.

The marks of this are visible, as ever, in the style, and it is that with which we are chiefly concerned. But before taking brief examples of this, there is one general point which it might help us to broach first.

Some of the surprise expressed at the new films was due not only to the novelty of their style but to what we might describe as their novelty of theme. That is to say that their makers showed less interest in the formality of plot, of the " good story."

This is especially true, for example, of *Hiroshima Mon Amour*, where the " action " in the present consists simply of a lover's meeting. In Resnais' next film, *L'Année Dernière à Marienbad* (*Last Year in Marienbad*), it is not even clear that the lovers ever met. Other films substitute for a plot a slice of life more or less screwed into focus by a personal crisis in the hero's life. Thus *Cléo de Cinq à Sept* (Agnes Varda) deals with two hours in the life of a girl waiting to know the result of a crucial X-ray. Or Jacques Demy's *Lola* uses a tradition knowingly and goes to formal extremes in a complex fugue-like love story in which the parallels between couples multiply into infinity like an image in a hall of mirrors. Others again, like *Breathless*, almost ironically take a very strong plot form—the B-feature gangster thriller—and bend it till it breaks, or force it, as in *Shoot the Pianist*, into fantasy.

These developments are not the result of youthful exhibitionism. They are intended to show that the plot is a convention, like any other, and that it is not necessary, in order that a work shall have meaning, for it to have a logically progressing story line. A great deal of modern literature shows mistrust of the processes of logic and causality. Life is not seen as a continuous and ordered progression towards the good, or towards sanity, or towards civilisation. The framework of external values—religion, morality, patriotism—has buckled and collapsed. It is up to the individual, it seems to

326

say, to work out his own values, and he can only do this by looking into himself, since *he* is what he knows best, or at least he is what he must first know. The ordered progression of events leading to a climax and a reward—a plot in fact—seems in this context to be an irrelevance. The new cinema, too, is less concerned with the outer world, a good deal more with the inner: with thought processes, with our experience of memory, of time passing, with our individual ideas of good and evil.

For the logic of geography and chronology then we must expect to see substituted the logic of the brain's thought processes: jumpy, allusive, fragmentary, discontinuous, making unusual connections we should find it hard to defend in words. Once we have grasped that, we are a good deal nearer understanding the choppy illogic which is often the first impression we get from the films of the New Wave.[1]

The subject of the modern film is, therefore, often not so much in the " story " as in the relationship between the director and his material. This means that, as we have suggested, he adopts a tough and unconventional attitude to the traditional tools. One of the first things to disappear in the new cinema has been the use of the dissolve and the fade as blanket devices to indicate passage of time and change of location. Not that the dissolve and fade have disappeared themselves. Far from it. Instead of being conventional signs they have once more become flexible

[1] *An interesting view of the assumptions of some New Wave directors is put forward by Eric Rhode and Gabriel Pearson in* Sight *and* Sound, *Autumn 1961, p. 164. The whole article, " Cinema of Appearance," is relevant to the new methods in the cinema which we are discussing. We summarise some of the assumptions they notice below:*

(a) *A world in which all appearances are equally valid is a world of discontinuity. The self is a series of events without apparent connection; its past and future are a series of actions, but its present is a void waiting to be defined by action. The self is therefore no longer seen as stable. It is without an inner core—without essence.*

(b) *Other people are likewise without essence: since they too are an infinite series of appearances, they remain unpredictable. Only objects—i.e., " things " with an essence—can be understood. People remain mysteries.*

(c) *Since there is no longer a stable reality, traditional morality proves untrustworthy. It seeks to essentialise appearances, order them so that they can be predicted, and so conceal from men their true condition in a discontinuous world—utter isolation. Each is responsible for improvising his moral imperatives; to accept any one role (i.e., to fix one's identity as " bandit," " pianist " or " intellectual ") is an evasion of responsibility and becomes " bad faith." Such " bad faith " dehumanises and turns man into an object. Existentially, he dies.*

(d) *Conversely, to avoid bad faith, morality must be an endless, anguished process of improvisation. One no longer acts to fulfil ideals like goodness and decency, but to initiate one's own self-discovery, the only " moral " goal left. Hence action is necessarily opportunistic.*

(e) *In consequence, each act is unique and without social precedence, and so to others will appear motiveless since there is no stable self on which to pin a motive. From this arises the seemingly absurd notion of a motiveless act (l'acte gratuit).*

tools. In more films than it would be worth citing the passage of time is indicated now not by a dissolve but by a straight cut. The dissolve is thereby restored to its usefulness as, for instance, a sensuous device for linking soft images, or as an intellectual device for tacitly indicating a connection. At one point in *Shoot the Pianist*, for instance, the hero is seen in bed with his wife. The smiling image of her lover lingers between them as the dissolve closes down.

Perhaps more attention has been paid to the trickery and gimmickry the New Wave has made familiar, than the more constructive of its achievements in style. But even the tricks are not without point, and if they are sometimes frivolous, they rarely lack charm. Truffaut's fondness for freezing frames has often been commented on. He did it in *Les 400 Coups*: as Antoine has his photo taken for the dentention centre; and again, at the end, on the beach as he runs into the sea and turns and faces us, the frame is frozen. In *Jules and Jim*, he frequently freezes Catherine's face. Truffaut resuscitates silent devices—the iris for example—then splits the screen, Abel Gance-like, into three irises with the talking head of the same villain in each. (Plyne in *Shoot the Pianist*.) At most, it means that Plyne is devious and two- (or three-) faced. But the gesture is an affectionate homage to the silent cinema as much as anything, though it has perhaps started a vogue.

In other places, Truffaut lifts the idea of dynamic frame, masking off parts of the screen he doesn't want to use, or wants to hide temporarily. Again, he uses 1914 War footage in the Dyaliscope *Jules and Jim*, stretching the old frames to fit the new ratio, so that the image appears flattened and widened, but perfectly acceptable.

The lesson that we may take from these sort of innovations is perhaps this: that all weapons are useful if they are used with skill and intelligence and made to work in a precise way—that is, if the impetus of the idea forces its way through the device. If a director is strongly in control of his medium, he re-defines its weapons and signs as he uses them, as a poem might change permanently the meaning of some words.[1]

One final general example must suffice before we go on to discuss particular film-makers and their work. It is a curious shot in Chabrol's *A Double Tour*. It is unlikely that it would have found its way into any film before the days of the New Wave.

---

[1] *Because Truffaut is in control, he can get away with the most outrageous jokes, which, to say the least, do not advance the story. His most celebrated joke occurs in* Shoot the Pianist. *One of the semi-comic crooks swears he is telling the truth with some such formula as "May my old mother drop dead if I'm not." In a brief iris-shot suddenly inserted at that point, his mother is seen to be doing just that.*

A Double Tour is the story of an infatuation and of jealousy leading to murder. A well-to-do bourgeois lives with his family next door to a very beautiful girl, Léda. He is obsessed by her and plagued by his own, understandably rather hysterical family, who know of this affair. The strongest possible contrast is made between his environment and Léda's: his house, to say nothing of his wife, is ugly and gloomy; Léda's house is light, airy and beautiful. She herself is exquisite. The imagery of her house with its colours and objects, and the colours and textures of her clothes make of her a sort of rare and beautiful bird: a bird because of her plumage, as it were, and equally, in a way, because of her inarticulacy. She is foreign, she smiles a great deal but rarely speaks. The crux of the film is that she is strangled by the family's eldest son, mad with jealousy of his father and with what the affair is doing to his mother. We do not see the murder, though we have a shrewd suspicion of who the murderer is. The latter part of the film is taken up with a police investigation. During the course of it the events leading up to the murder are seen more than once from the point of view of different suspects. At one point in the narrative Chabrol suddenly introduces an unexplained shot of a peacock rising up from the undergrowth in panic, presumably disturbed by someone's invisible and stealthy progress through the garden between the two houses. A little later, during someone else's version of the story, the same shot is repeated. Again no explanation is offered.

At first we are inclined to assume that it is there as a reference point to synchronise the two narratives. Much later though it becomes clear that the shot marked the actual moment of Léda's death, which we did not see. The shot then takes on an astonishing force. It gathers a kind of retrospective beauty by virtue of its obliqueness. We see that the peacock's fright, the soft flurry of its feathers, the image of beauty and grace disturbed, are an image of the girl's death. But it is all the more powerful for not being made explicit. It is a new refinement of metaphor: the second term of the comparison appears before we know what the first is. Cinema metaphor has come a long way from the days when Stroheim represented the young couple in *Greed* as lovebirds at the mercy of the prowling cat, Marcus; or when Eisenstein pictured the might of the working class as a bull. It is at moments like these that we see how much the new cinema has benefited from its knowledge of the past.

19

PERSONAL CINEMA IN THE SIXTIES

WE have been able to illustrate various editing devices until now by reference to genres of films in which they were appropriately used. So action sequences demand one type of cutting, and we have discussed thrillers; comedy another, and we have looked at comedies; dialogue sequences, documentary realism, newsreels, instructional films, similarly . . . It now becomes more difficult to follow this scheme. The reason is one we have mentioned often enough in the last section. The cinema at its most representative and advanced in the sixties is such a personal medium that the only category it makes sense to divide our discussions into is that of individual directors. The film director, as we have seen and shall see in more detail, uses the medium now less to tell stories effectively, more as an instrument of thought. As in other arts, the cinema's very devices have become increasingly part of its meaning. The pan, the track, the dissolve, the fade, the zoom, like the brush-stroke, or a form of words, can be looked at as well as through.

The four directors whose work we shall look at in this way are Truffaut, Godard, Resnais and Antonioni.

François Truffaut

Truffaut has said in an interview that what he is aiming at is " un éclatement de genres par un mélange de genres "—" an explosion of genres by a mixture of genres." He always tries, he says, to confound his audiences' expectations, to keep them constantly surprised. When the film seems to be going in one direction he likes to turn it round and send it off in another. He thinks of his films as circus shows with a dazzling variety of turns, and likes at the end to take the audience out into the country or to some idyllic scene—snow or the sea—as a reward for being cooped up in the dark for nearly two hours.

330

It should not be thought that Truffaut is being simply frivolous in saying this. In the first place his films bear out the thesis: each of them[1] does flick from moods of despair to exhilaration and does contain scenes of black comedy alternating with scenes of real tragedy or simply good-hearted unaffected joy. As for locations: the last scene of *Les 400 Coups* has the boy hero running to the sea: the last scene of *Shoot the Pianist* takes place in a snowstorm by a mountain chalet of fairy-tale improbability. *Jules and Jim* is such a lyrical medley of sea, river, alp and forest that few spectators can surely have suffered from being cooped up with it. *Fahrenheit 451* ends in a snowstorm, in a forest.

Nor are Truffaut's aims the result of simple contrariness. They are the reflection of his philosophy. It is clear from his films that he celebrates what Rhode and Pearson call " the philosophy of discontinuity."

The swift changes of mood and pace which characterise his films are an attempt to match his form more nearly to the way life usually develops. We don't live life according to " genres." Nor is life, according to the way we think today, a taut unbroken chain of significant purposeful acts, linked by logic, as it is sometimes made to appear according to the editing pattern and plot development of the traditional cinema. Indeed, plot often disappears, as it virtually does in *Les 400 Coups*. Antoine's life is described not so much by a series of dramatic events as by a string of non-events: roaming the streets, playing truant, visiting the fairground, mooning about the flat, avoiding doing his homework.

The action is handled in long unbroken medium-shots lasting as long as physically possible. The cuts come when they're unavoidable: when a character leaves the room or goes out of sight down the stairs. It is clear to see from *Les 400 Coups* that Truffaut is a pupil of André Bazin. When the shot lasts too long for comfort, but Truffaut wants to use the beginning and the end, he is not above chopping a bit out of the middle. In one scene involving Antoine's friend and the friend's father, the father goes out of sight through a doorway on his way to the kitchen. He soon reappears in the kitchen, some way away at the end of a dark passage. But between leaving this room and reappearing in the other one there has been a longer time lag than we are led to believe. A cat lazing on a shelf in the top left-hand corner of the frame makes a sudden " jump " to a slightly different position and

---

[1] Les 400 Coups, Tirez sur le Pianiste, Jules et Jim, La Peau Douce, Fahrenheit 451.

betrays that there is footage missing. Or it could be that the camera was stopped and locked off in the end position in the first half of the shot and picked up again when the father had had time to get into position for the continuation of the shot. The point is that rather than cut to a new set-up, Truffaut tries to preserve the sense of continuity. Similar examples occur elsewhere in *Shoot the Pianist*. Truffaut disguises a jump cut between two different takes by joining the shots when Fido, the kid-brother, realises he is being shadowed by the " crooks " in their big American car. Again, in Theresa's long, apparently one-shot, confession to Charlie/ Edouard in their flat just before she commits suicide, Truffaut has very skilfully disguised the fact that he has used the first half of one take and the second half of another by finding a cutting point where the images are almost identical for a moment. The question of intention arises. Truffaut confesses that " he saves all his films in the cutting room," It isn't that these things had never been done before. But the New Wave directors take more risks, do them more frequently and with more boldness, and more often than not demonstrate that only if the audience is already confused will it be further confused by unconventional technique.

But in *Les 400 Coups* the mysterious interview with the psychiatric social worker is a classic case of how not to do it, in traditional terms. During the interview the boy's answers are joined by dissolves and we never see the interviewer at all. As a " dramatic " scene, or as a treatment of social problems, the scene is a failure. But of course that isn't its purpose. The real subject is internal and that is what the method is designed to deal with. The subject is the boy's own internal world. He takes no interest in the interviewer. We don't see her because, for him, she hardly exists.

At the end of the film Antoine escapes from the detention centre where he has been sent for stealing a typewriter. He runs to the sea, which he has never seen. The action is chiefly described in a very few, very long tracking shots taken from a car while the boy runs alongside. The sequence lasts several minutes. It is not so much an event as a state of mind of which the form of the shot is an apt expression. We feel the freedom of his flight as a great release after the various sorts of imprisonment, mental and physical, which he has suffered in the course of the film. In this example, and in that of the dissolves, too, the form of the shots has been as much a part of the meaning as any content they have " described."

332

More so than *Les 400 Coups*, *Shoot the Pianist* extends the vocabulary of the new cinema in interesting ways. The story concerns a concert pianist, Edouard Saroyan, who discovers that his career really began when his wife slept with his impresario, Schmeel. She begs his forgiveness, but momentarily he turns from her in disgust. She commits suicide. He retires from society, changes his name to Charlie Koller and becomes a café-player. He has a liaison with a new girl but is once more, after a series of adventures, indirectly the cause of his girl's death.

Charlie goes to Schmeel's flat for an audition. While he is waiting outside the door, he hesitates before pressing Schmeel's bell. He puts out a finger to it, and stops. There then follow two or three bigger and bigger close-ups of his finger and the bell button getting closer. The shots provoke a whole string of reactions: (1) They are funny. (2) They are menacing, as all moments are when the action slows up, or the cutting begins to go into a great deal of detail. So they should be, in view of what we later know is happening (but we don't know it then.) (3) They are psychologically accurate since they represent his timidity. (4) They draw attention to a notorious *temps-mort*, that time which we all spend standing outside doors that won't open, or waiting for lifts that won't come. At those moments the universe shrinks to the dimensions of a doorbell which seems for a time to have more reality than oneself. And here we reach perhaps the most central consideration of all. (5) Charlie is a protagonist who embodies the philosophy of discontinuity. His life is a search for wholeness; the wholeness of success, the wholeness of an ideology, of a successful love affair, of a scale of values he can believe in. He looks for confidence and for trust. He doesn't succeed. The representation of his failure is carried in a sequence of images of increasing fragmentation. He is constantly seen reflected in a mirror which hangs over his piano in the café. We are introduced to him in the café's Gents, where he is knotting his tie and looking into the mirror. At the end of the film in the mountain chalet, sheltering from the police after he had accidentally killed a man, he stares into a little cracked shaving mirror and repeats to himself the words of his criminal brother: " Now you are one of us." His relinquishing of himself to Schmeel, the impresario, is marked by the completion of a portrait of him of which Schmeel says, " Thanks to this painting, I can look at you every day." Charlie's wife also speaks of being cut in two by the spider, Schmeel. In the context of this abounding fragmentation, it is not difficult to see the finger-on-bell shots as an indication that for Charlie the universe, the world of objects, is irretrievably breaking up beyond his power to control it.

The opposite process is implied by a similar series of shots in *Jules et Jim*, Truffaut's next film. The shots themselves are three or four simple close-ups of Jeanne Moreau (Catherine) at the driving wheel of her car, switching on, starting up, putting it in gear and driving off.

Again it is necessary to go into some detail about the story and the theme in order to explain the framework in which to read these shots.

Catherine is beloved by two friends, Jules and Jim. She is a determined experimenter with new forms, not least in love. She is anxious to create new natural forces and combinations, and, for example, to make a *ménage à trois* not only work but appear almost grudgingly ascetic. All three of them do their best to live without jealousy. Jim more actively pursues the affair on his side. Jules, a naturalist, patiently observes, determined, at whatever sacrifice to himself, to hold the circle of friendship unbroken. Catherine, in her vain attempt to create new laws, makes both them and herself unhappy. Finally, she drives her car off the middle of a broken bridge into the river, taking Jim to his death with her. Jules watches from a nearby café terrace.

The film's imagery stresses the naturalness of circular patterns of growth, and the naturalness of plant and insect life. The triangular human relationships fit awkwardly into a cyclical world. In Jules resides the lesson of natural morality: observe and adapt. He hopes, one day, if he is lucky he says, to write a love story in which the characters will be insects. Instead of observing and adapting, Catherine wishes to impose herself on the universe, to adapt it to *her* rather than the other way around. She experiments constantly with the elements. Around her fires are always starting: smoke rises from the vitriol she pours down the sink. When she jumps into the Seine in exasperation one day, little ringlets of reflected light spread out, like fire, across the water. Her attempts to fuse the elements are doomed to failure. Her power to manipulate the material world is only partial. This is where the car-driving close-ups are important. They show her easy mastery of some forms of *artificial* power. But, as if to warn us that this is not enough, the description is fragmented and dislocated out of any possible unity. Gear stick, wheel, accelerator are *tokens* of power only. They bring with them an illusion of mastery. When she drives off the bridge—a broken circle—it is the water, a natural force, which kills her and not the car.[1]

These two examples, from *Shoot the Pianist* and *Jules and Jim*, should show us that even in the, apparently, simple close-up there lies a way into the core of the film's meaning. We are a long way from the days in which the close-up was an answer to the complaint " I can't see what's going on."

Let us look at a sequence from *Shoot the Pianist* which is typical of Truffaut's work in its range of moods and technical dexterity.

SHOOT THE PIANIST[2]

			Ft. fr.
1	A newspaper front page which announces the suicide of Theresa, Charlie's wife. This is superimposed on a barely discernible view of a scrap yard across which the *camera begins to pan right* immediately. (The newspaper shot has been superimposed on the previous shot, of Theresa lying in the road, dead.) The paper fades and the pan reveals now cars in the junk yard, now a roadway, now a café exterior in a poor quarter.	Newspaper reads " Wife of noted pianist throws herself from fifth floor." *Charlie's characteristic piano music starts.* *Lena's voice* You disappeared. You began a new life. Edouard Saroyan became Charlie Koller. You visited your brothers in the snow and asked them to let Fido live with you. One day you found yourself at Plyne's. *The piano music stops.*	29
2	*M.L.S.* Interior café by day. Plyne is mending a table. Charlie is sweeping the floor. Charlie opens the keyboard. Sabine, Plyne's mistress, enters and picks up Charlie's cleaning utensils and walks towards camera. Charlie sits at piano.	You must have swept that floor a thousand times. There was a little upright battered piano in a corner. *A distant engine hoot.* You spent all your time— —looking at it, walking all round it, looking at it again. One day you asked Plyne: *Charlie:* Can I play a bit? *Plyne:* Eh? *Charlie:* I think I know how. *Plyne:* Go ahead then. But you better arrange it with Sabine.	48 6

[1] *Some of these reflections derive from a fine article about the film: " Elective Affinities " by Roger Greenspun, Sight and Sound, Spring 1963.*
[2] *Director: François Truffaut. Editor: Cécile Decugis. Films de la Pléiade. 1960. Fido, a boy of about twelve, is Charlie's youngest brother. Theresa is his former wife. Plyne is the proprietor of the café. Lena is a waitress at the café.*

3   *B.C.U.* Full face of Charlie, left profile, seated at piano. He looks down at keyboard, serious, then begins to play.
The *camera slowly swings right and pans left and tilts down* his arms and on to the keyboard. Then it *tilts up* on to the hammers, seen clearly through the open front of the piano.

MIX TO

Classical piano music begins.

Music mixes to Charlie's cafe tune.

4   *M.S.* Interior of café. Night time. In a rectangular mirror above the piano Charlie is seen playing. *Camera pans down left* on to Charlie. He is enjoying himself.

Lena's voice   16
Who is Charlie Koller? Little known. He's a pianist. He looks after his little brother. Above all, he wants no trouble.

5   *M.L.S.* Charlie and two other musicians on the stand. People are dancing.

Thanks to you, the local people 10 8 started coming every evening to dance, and it got to be quite a place. Plyne took on extra staff, and some musicians.

6   *M.C.S.* Victor the drummer.

Victor the drummer, who was 4 8 always laughing without knowing why.

7   *M.C.S.* François the bass player.

And his brother François the bass 3 4 player—

8   *C.S.* François' hands on the bass.

—with his long hairy hands.   4 2

9   *M.S.* Exterior of the café. Night. The camera begins a *long tracking shot from left to right* along the pavement outside the café, looking in. It passes over, after a while, the poster on the outside wall advertising " Charlie Koller."

And then there was me—whom 27 you looked at all the time without ever seeing.

The jaunty music of the café piano gradually mixes to a quieter, more dreamlike theme.

MIX, starting at about 24 ft. and clear in shot 10 at about 30 ft. from the beginning of shot 9.

10   *M.S.* Interior of bedroom (Lena's). 9 is still panning when 10 begins. 10 too begins with a *pan* which continues throughout the shot, *a full 360 degrees.* But this *pan* is in the opposite direction i.e., *from right to left.* The shot begins on a poster on the wall announcing a concert to be given by Edouard Saroyan. *After 5 ft. of this pan,* a *close-up* of Lena and Charlie kissing each other gently is superimposed and held throughout the shot until, at

64

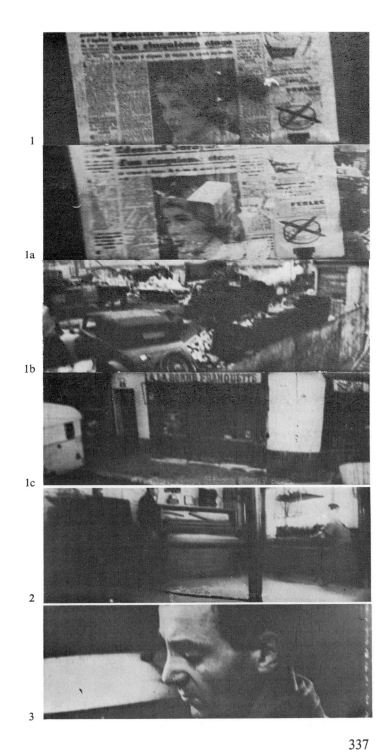

1

1a

1b

1c

2

3

$54\frac{1}{2}$ ft. in, it starts to disappear. The objects which the pan reveals on its course round the bedroom are in turn, the door, a radio, a window, a bowl of goldfish, a bust (i.e., a piece of sculpture), a bra and other clothes on a chair, and finally the bed with Charlie and Lena in it. The superimposed close-up of them fades completely just before the pan reaches the bed.

11   C.S. Charlie and Lena in bed.

Lena's voice
On my birthday, when I kissed   22
everybody, it was just so that I
could kiss you, you know. Then I
saw you looking at me, and I
looked at you, too.

MIX lasting $\frac{1}{2}$ second.

12   M.S. Charlie and Lena in bed, moving in their sleep. *The image is clear for little more than a foot.*
                                                2   4[1]

MIX lasting $\frac{1}{2}$ second.

What were you thinking about   7   8
when we were walking together
in the street last night?

13   As 11.

14   M.S. As 12, same lengths of dissolve out of 13 and into 15. *Clear image* for 2 ft. 12 frs.

MIX to

15   C.S. As 13.

Did you like me right away? Do   11
you remember the evening you
said to me—

16   As 14 exactly in lengths.

MIX to

17   As 15.

When I took your arm I was afraid   9   12
you'd be shocked.

18   As 16. *Clear for 2 ft. 8 frs.*

MIX to

19   As 17.

I wanted you so badly to take   7   8
mine.

MIX to

20   As 18.

MIX to

21   C.U. Lena in bed.
                                                10

[1] *Since the dissolves are so unusually short, and the shots too, it isn't very helpful to quote a precise length of shot.*

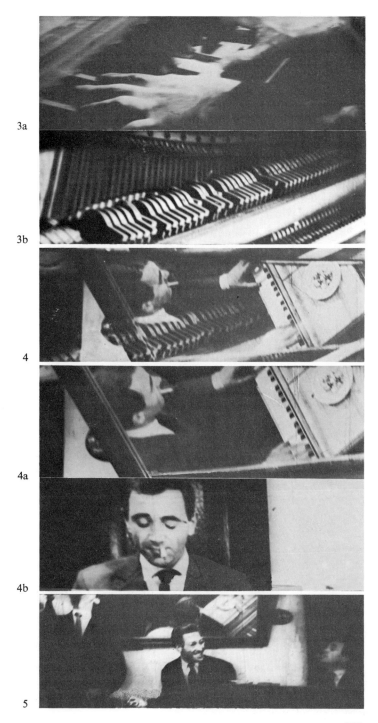

3a

3b

4

4a

4b

5

The most interesting thing about this extract is that although it employs a great diversity of styles and tones it has, on the screen, a surprising homogeneity. This is only partly because of the unity brought to it by the narrator's voice.[1]

In *1-4* we have moved from Theresa's suicide to Charlie's new life as the café pianist. In that time we have also established the locale and tone of the café and learnt a little about its people. We have learnt especially about Lena's early feeling for Charlie. All the four shots seem leisurely. *1* and *3* especially have a strong lyrical feeling in them. But they still perform a valuable function in conveying information and drawing character.

Shot *1* associates the sadness and squalor of Theresa's death (she had thrown herself from a window) with the junkyard of old cars, by having the newspaper superimposed over both shots. The junkyard suggests the spiritual depths to which Charlie has been plunged by his wife's suicide. It also tells us, of course, what sort of area he has chosen to bury himself in in order to get away from the bright lights and all his former friends. Lena's affectionate regard comes through in the commentary (especially in the description of Charlie's fascination by the piano), but the lightness of tone is not allowed to detract from the seriousness with which we are to treat Charlie. In the next shot his excellence as a pianist is brought to our attention by the intensity of the moving close-up, which seems to give him dignity. In no way does this cast any reflection on Lena's slight playfulness about him. It is this constant delicacy in balancing tones of feeling, in commentary/dialogue and image, which gives Truffaut's film the curious flavour of sadness and joy which it has.

In the next section the jokes are about, but not at the expense of, Victor and François. Charlie, in *4* and *5*, is happily jogging in time to the music. But they are not just jokes. Lena is talking about the three of them, and so we see Charlie at the piano, then the three on the stand, then Victor, then François, and François' hairy hands. But when she mentions herself it seems to be her characteristic modesty which prevents her from appearing when

---

[1] *The narrator has long been a popular figure in French cinema. He provides a useful third dimension in addition to the audience and the screen. Or he can be an objective voice when the " author " wants to comment. The literary parallel is useful since the narrator is of course a literary device, and the French cinema has always had a strong literary tradition, which New Wave directors have generally been keen to preserve. The narrator is also a popular figure in the American thriller-school, a tradition that the New Wave have equally revered. Perhaps an interim stage of adoption can be seen in such films as Melville's* Bob Le Flambeur *(1956), which is intermittently narrated. At any rate the narrator makes frequent appearances in the contemporary French cinema, notably in Truffaut's third film,* Jules et Jim.

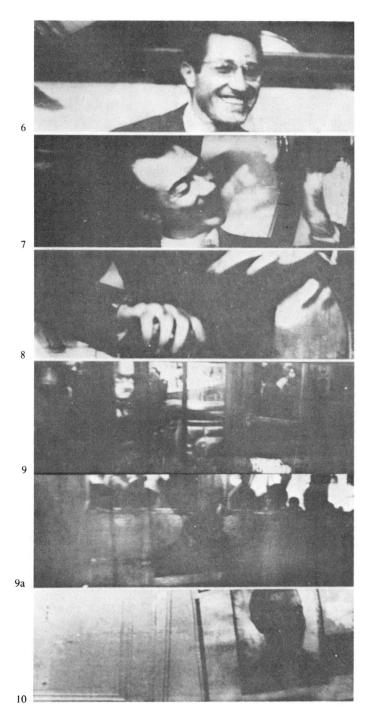

6

7

8

9

9a

10

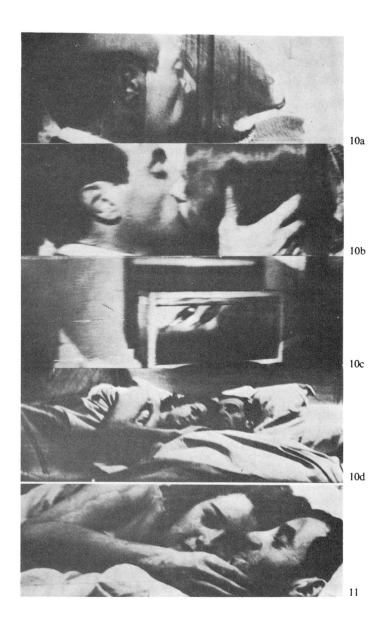

10a

10b

10c

10d

11

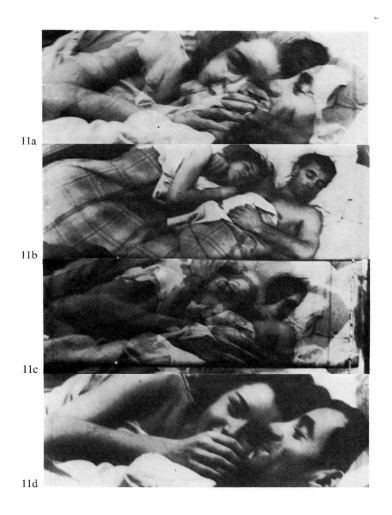

11a

11b

11c

11d

we should most expect it. Instead of her we see the exterior of the café, and in a long tracking shot past the windows, watch the happy couples inside. It is almost as though Lena is silently telling us that she feels she is shut out from this happiness. We know that that is how Charlie feels about his own life. A link between them is tacitly suggested, almost entirely by the absence of an expected shot, and the form of another.

But the exterior tracking shot is not simply a metaphorical device. The shot continues until we pan across a poster announcing the attraction of " Charlie Koller " playing at the café. With perfect logic this suggests the poster of Edouard Saroyan which we know is hanging in Lena's bedroom. In a curious dissolve the poster of Saroyan, with something of a metaphorical force, since it represents as it were the wishes of Lena, appears to displace the stand-in, Charlie Koller. So we see, too, that the movement of the camera along the pavement and away from the café was a way of expressing the movement of Lena's mind away from the café and towards her own bedroom where she lies now with Charlie.

The dissolve is curious because, breaking all the rules, it not only begins at the end of *9* on movement, not only continues in *10* on movement, but the movements are in opposite directions. The effect mixes the images in such a way as to suggest pleasant reverie, though it doesn't pretend that it is a picture of what Lena herself is seeing.

The pan from the poster of Saroyan on the bedroom wall is the longest shot in the sequence. Because of the close-up of Charlie and Lena superimposed over it, the underlying images of the bedroom are hard to discern. This is what makes the moment when the goldfish bowl swims into view particularly delicate. For a few seconds as the camera pans over them, the four goldfish are seen, in long shot, nibbling the surface of the water in exactly the same way as the lovers are nuzzling each other's faces. The superimposition disappears just before the pan completes its circle and we come back to the bed again. The next eleven shots are a most unusual device. The short alternate shots into and out of which we dissolve so quickly show the lovers stirring vaguely in the abandoned attitudes of sleep. They take liberties with our conventional idea of the time scale, and they work, literally, like a charm.

Jean-Luc Godard

I have made four films in three years, and I would like to pause for a while.

This is Jean-Luc Godard in an interview.

Since making this pronouncement, Godard has made ten more full-length features as well as sketches in portmanteau films. He has, therefore, made fourteen films, apart from the sketches, in nine years. There are two things to say about this. One, he is unpredictable. Two, few people are able to keep up with his output and it is therefore difficult to make any pronouncement about his work which he doesn't immediately call in question a few weeks later with a new film.

One further thing seems clear: he makes films with rare fluidity, and the films' surface appearance bears out this diagnosis. Even more than Truffaut, perhaps, he is an exponent of the *caméra-stylo* philosophy. He is widely read, his films are stuffed with literary and philosophical allusions, not to say poetry readings; they are made with the freedom one associates with the typewriter rather than the camera, and he has spoken of his growing disinterest in the carefully composed image:

> What worries me is that I find I am no longer thinking in terms of cinema, but I don't know whether this is a good or a bad thing. When I was making *Breathless* or my earlier shorts, a shot of Seberg would be made from a purely " cinematic " point of view, making sure that her head was just at the right cinematic angle and so on. Now I just do things without worrying how they will appear cinematically.[1]

Of all the new film-makers of the sixties, Godard provoked the most violent reaction. His unconventional style earned him infuriated criticism from those who felt that *Breathless* had been flung on the screen with total disregard for screen language or conventions, or for the audience. What do his films look like?

They are not smooth in the conventional sense. He uses frequent jump-cuts, that is to say, cutting together two discontinuous parts of a continuous action without changing the set-up. He cuts abruptly from one scene to another with little warning and no attempt at smoothness. His ruthlessness with parts of the action in which he is not interested is more thoroughgoing than ever before in the cinema. He makes no concessions to the spectator who would be glad of a dissolve to help him across the hours or the miles. He will have no truck with inherited rules about general-shots, medium-shots and close-shots. At first sight he appears

---

[1] *From the interview quoted above: Tom Milne,* Sight and Sound, *Winter 1962–1963, p. 12.*

never to have heard of the dangers of boring or offending the audience. He has the effrontery to present his audience with highly literate films built on the framework of an American B-feature thriller. (*Breathless* is dedicated to Monogram Pictures.) But he is as wayward about moods as they are predictable. He veers from tragedy to farce with indifference. He tricks us by concerning us with an absurd plot in *Breathless*. In *Pierrot le Fou* even the tenses are mixed. Its curious chronology shows us scenes from present and future in continuous shots and in a continuous geographical location; not, in other words, as the obvious projections of one character's mind. Above all, there is no comfortable morality propounded by the editing style.

The angles, the lengths of shot, the rhythm, fail to tell us who to love, who to disapprove of. Godard encouraged Coutard, his cameraman, constantly to strive for natural effects and to " keep it simple " by preserving the appearance of natural light. But sometimes this meant in practice anything but simplicity for Coutard, who had to devise ways of making the camera as sensitive and flexible as the human eye. Only two scenes in *Breathless* are lit with film lights.

In *Breathless*, as we shall see, he alternates cascades of short shots during the chase sequences with long one-shot near-improvisations between Michel (Jean-Paul Belmondo) and Patricia (Jean Seberg). The whole film was shot wild, and the dialogue post-synchronised. During long takes his camera often seems to be afflicted with a kind of nervous shuffle which appears neither functional nor lyrical. But it is deliberate and frequent, and we might attempt to put some kind of construction on it.

Rather than go on making generalisations about his methods, it may be more useful if we examine a typical sequence from his first film *Breathless*.

BREATHLESS[1]

			Ft. fr.	
1	M.S. The radiator grille of a car travelling behind the camera car crosses the white line in the road, from screen left to right.	*Musique concrète*	1	9
2	M.C.S. Taken from the backseat of the car, including the driver's head, looking through the windscreen as he overtakes a lorry.		3	3
		Michel, the driver: Oh, oh, the cops.		
3	M.S. *Pan screen right to left* of car overtaking lorry.	*Sudden roar of car engine.*	1	5

[1] *Director: Jean-Luc Godard. SNC 1959.*

346

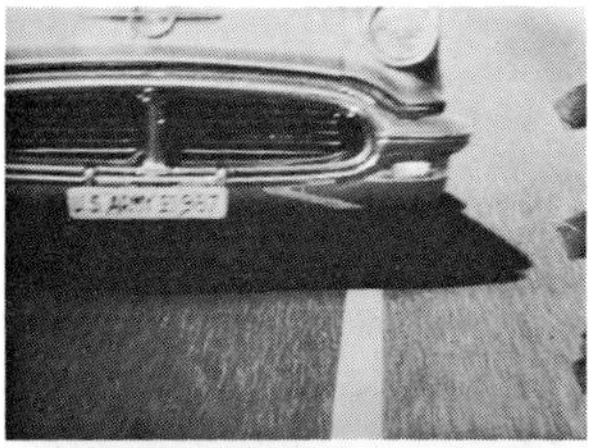

1

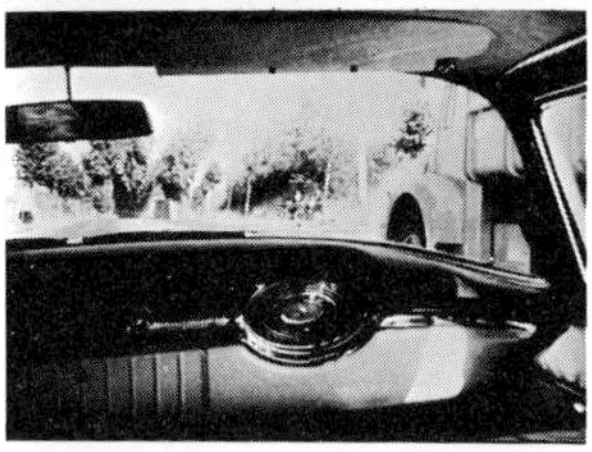

2

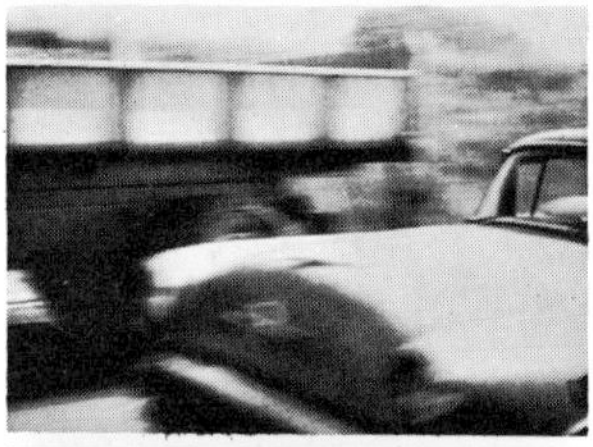

3

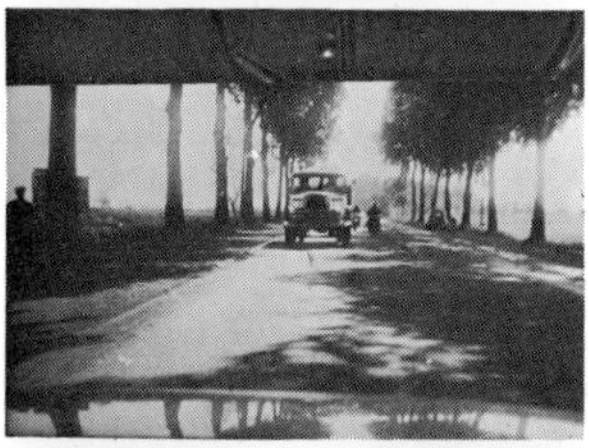

4

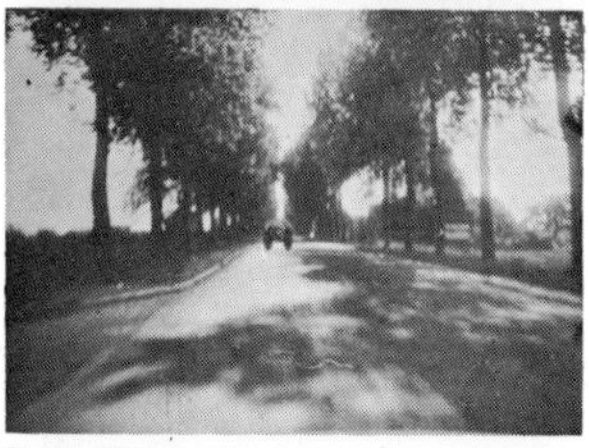

5

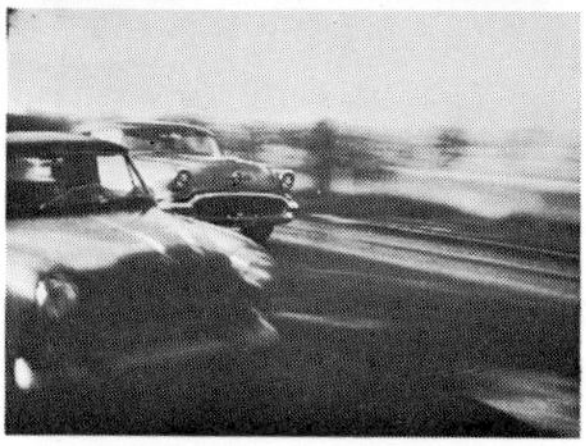

6

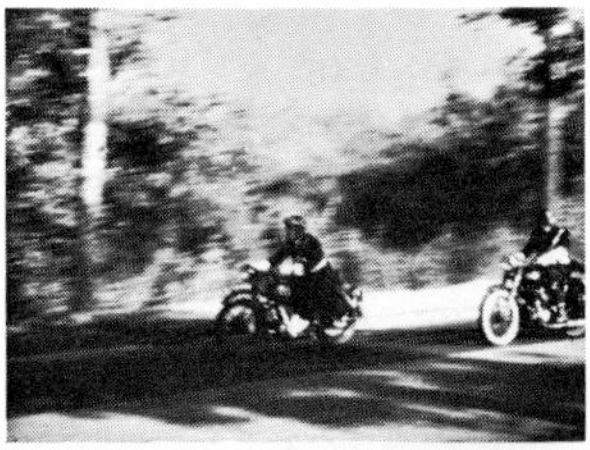

7

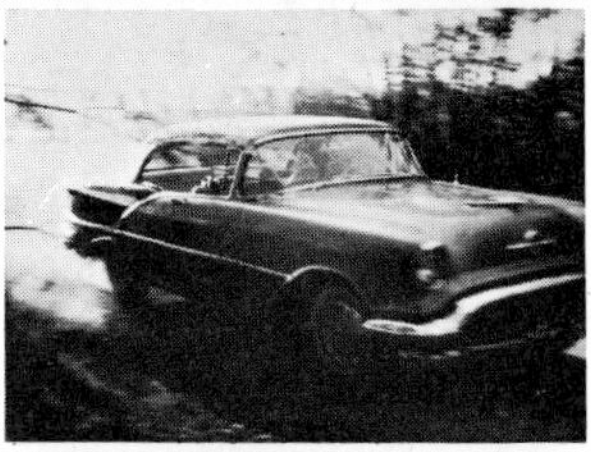

8

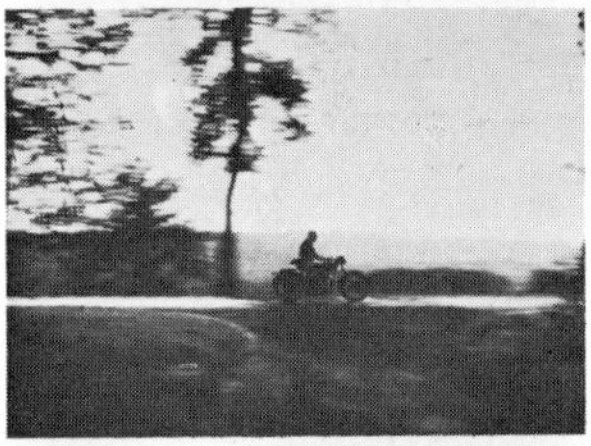

9

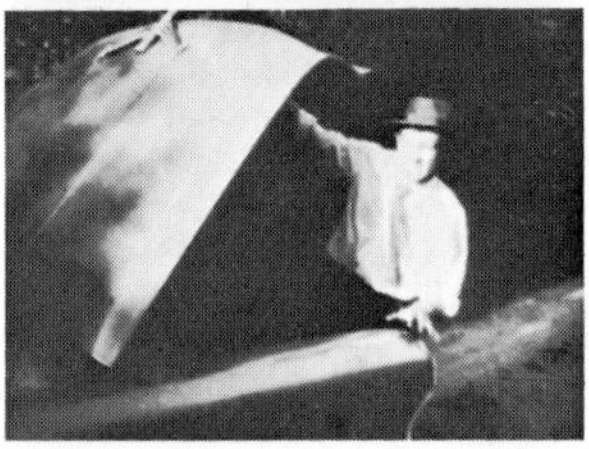

10

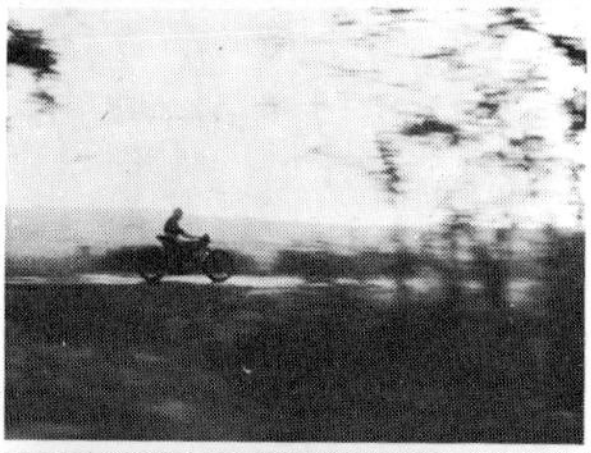

11

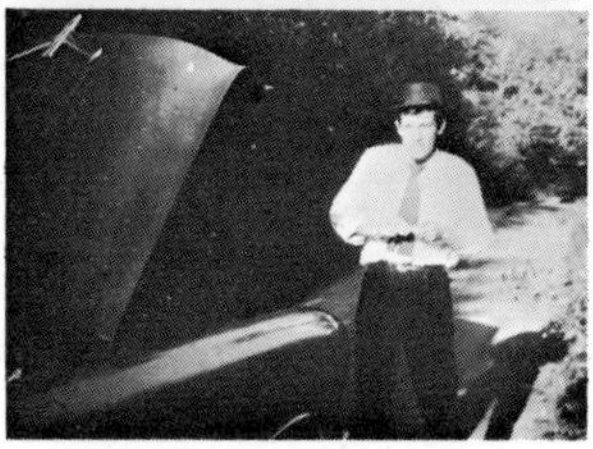

12

4	*M.C.S.* As 2, *panning* immediately off *right to left* to look out of rear window. Police motor-bikes are seen overtaking the lorry behind.	5 5
5	*L.S.* As 4. Through rear window, the police are still there, the lorry has disappeared.	5 11
6	*M.S.* Shot from kerb. Car over-takes another, screen left to right.	2 4
7	*M.S.* The two police motor-bikes roar past right to left.	2 6

8	*M.S.* The car turns off the road down a slope towards the *camera*, which *pans round* left to right with it as it draws up in MS. Michel looks behind him out of the car window.	*Screech of brakes.* Michel: Oh, my clamps have come off.	8 2
9	*M.L.S.* One motor-bike passes along the road left to right.	*Motor-bike noise.* Michel: The fools have fallen into the trap.	1 3
10	*M.S.* He goes to front of car, opens bonnet and begins to fiddle with the engine. He hears further motor-bike noise and looks up.	*Second motor-bike noise.*	7 13
11	*M.L.S.* The second motor-bike passes along road left to right.		1 13
12	As 10. He continues to fiddle with engine part. He looks up as the motor-bike noise increases.	*Motor-bike noise fades and swells again.*	7 10
13	*M.S.* The second motor-cyclist rides down the slope towards the car. *Camera* as for 8.	*Squeal of brakes.*	5 6
14	*M.S.* Michel runs back to the driver's door and leans in through the open window.		5 7
15	*C.U.* Michel's head. The *camera pans down* first over his hat and then on to his face. He is looking out screen right.	Michel: Don't move or I'll shoot.	2 12
16	*B.C.U. Pan* along his arm from *left to right.* He is holding a gun. He cocks the gun.		2 2
17	*Extreme B.C.U.* The pan con-tinues along the revolver barrel.	*Click of gun being cocked.*	2 1

348

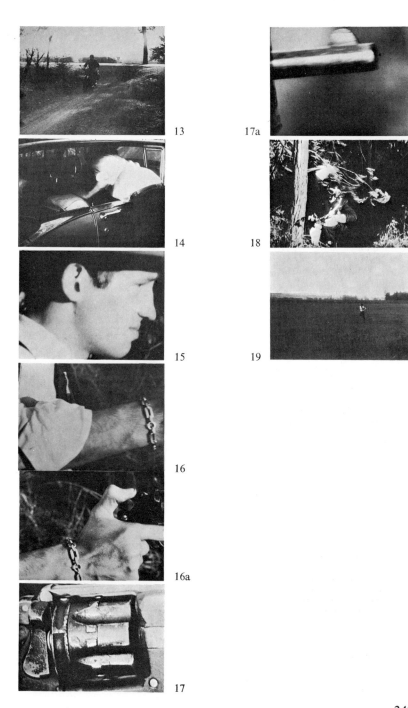

13

17a

14

18

15

19

16

16a

17

349

			Ft. fr.
18	M.S. The policeman, barely glimpsed, falls backwards clutching a branch he breaks off, into the trees.	*The gun fires.*	3 8
19	L.S. Michel running right to left across a bare field. *FADE*	*Big band " dramatic bridge " type of music begins and finishes on the fade.*	24

This extract illustrates well the nature of Godard's impact on screen language. It is not baffling; except for a couple of curious changes of direction we can follow the action perfectly clearly. And yet it is sufficiently different from a conventional treatment of this kind of sequence to make us sit up and take notice. What is the difference?

We can set aside those weapons which Godard deploys in company with the rest of the industry and which have been amply described elsewhere in this book: the use of short shots for pace and their alternation with longer shots, (notice particularly *8, 10, 12* and *then 13*, where the break in pace is, as it were, transferred to the police motor-cyclist); the use of the cocking click to cut from *16* to *17*, the release of the scene's tension in the long—four times as long as any other, almost—shot at the end of the sequence (*19*). There are other aspects of the extract which we might investigate in more detail.

In the first place, the editing apparently takes a very free hand with verisimilitude. We seem to leap unnaturally from one phase of the action to the next. There is less apparent connection between shots than we are used to. But then we must remember that our idea of screen verisimilitude is itself a convention. For example, the convention whereby a cut-away for a few seconds to the hunter allows the hunted to travel an improbably long distance in the interval. Or the convention according to which the participants in a chase must be seen to move over the same territory. These conventions are developed in the interests of economy and efficiency. They are logical and useful devices. What the extract here shows is that Godard does not flout logic but rather pushes it further towards its extreme. Thus we get a slightly less connected account of the action, but we get all that is necessary and, we might say, *only* what is necessary. Successive developments of the action are shown to us as they would strike us if we were spectators in real life. Nothing is prepared or led up to. No " clues " are laid as to imminent action. We are given no insight, we have no omniscience. We have to accept, without knowing how, that the police are on Michel's trail. We accept that he decides suddenly to turn off the road, though we have been given no indication that he needed to repair his engine; and that he finds it appropriate—let us not say necessary—to shoot the patrolman. We accept these things just as we accepted that he was a car thief without knowing why (we are offered no social or psychological explanation for his activity), or just as we had to accept that he should leave his girl behind (as he does at the beginning of the film when she has helped him to steal the car). The logic of the author who used to share his knowledge with us is replaced, for better or worse, by the logic of the passer-by who knows as little about it as we do. In a way Godard is confessing that he knows as little about this man as we do. We must all observe his behaviour in order to find out more. How can anyone know what he is going to do since the hero, according to the philosophy we discussed briefly earlier, is intent on inventing his own life from moment to moment?

These reflections are not irrelevant to a close look at the editing.

Shots 4 and 5 break a well-established convention of the simplest sort. In 5, in a virtually identical view of the police motor-cyclists to that in 4, the lorry the patrolmen were overtaking has abruptly disappeared. In 6, Michel's car is seen overtaking a car in the direction screen left to right, whereas the last time we had seen him, in shot 3, he was travelling right to left. Then in 7 the patrolmen succeed shot 6, pursuing Michel apparently in the opposite direction. In shot 8 Michel casually explains his stopping by muttering that the clamps (which he had fitted to start the ignition of the stolen car) had fallen off. There seemed on the evidence of the prevous shots to be hardly sufficient distance between himself and the patrolmen to make it likely that the first motor-bike would have ridden past without the rider noticing that Michel had turned off the road.

All these things, at first sight, as we've said, are obstacles to conventional smoothness and logic. Yet they are perfectly efficient in the sense that they create an impression of confusion, flight, fear, restrained violence, imminent danger, etc., while staying within the bounds of possibility. Their status, in other words, is this: that they *could* be scenes from an authentic chase, but they are not linked together in a deliberate attempt to contrive the *illusion* of continuity as would normally be the case. The editor is saying, in fact, " the habitual idea of screen continuity is merely an illusion which is in any case subsidiary to the communication of the scene's meaning. I am going to take advantage of your admission that it is unreal by rejecting it and substituting this cruder but more direct description of the action."

But from the point when the second patrolman turns back, the description of the action becomes even more sparse. We see Michel reaching into the car, we see a gun, we hear a shot, we catch sight of the patrolman falling (though only just; he's actually visible for only ten frames in shot *18*), and we see Michel running across a field. It is a kind of shorthand, and for that reason, perhaps, it is curtly efficient.

And yet it is not simply a shorthand. For what shorthand-writer would leave out the noun in any sentence as important as this? Or dwell at the same time so lovingly on the punctuation? For that's the effect of the final assembly of shots *12–19*. Any conventional thriller would have dealt more fully with the patrolman, who, after all, is about to die. We should at least have seen him before the gun went off. As it is, because the shot is pruned so tight we barely see the moment at which he is struck, but catch, as it were out of the corner of our eyes—as we might do had we been there—a glimpse of him falling backwards, vainly clutching at a branch, into the bushes.

Secondly, we see no evidence of premeditation in Michel. His thought processes are obscure and so his action is viewed obliquely and intermittently. In fact what we *hear* is a threat, uttered, with the crazy logic of real life, only a fraction of a second before the gun goes off. " Don't move or I'll shoot." If the patrolman did move we shall never know. He was given no chance. Nor were we. We might say that this style of editing gives *us* no chance to introduce of our own accord unnecessary, irrelevant or misleading knowledge. We cannot, therefore, add, as we so often do, to the image on the screen. All we know is what we can see.

Sometimes not even that. In the extrordinary tilt down across Michel's hat and face (*15*) we hear his voice but don't see his lips move. Instead of a menacing close-up or a two-shot showing the victim at bay, what we have is, in the circumstances, an almost lyrical treatment of Michel's profile, his arm and the gun. Lyrical, that is, in the deliberation of the camera movements and the pleasure taken in the compound effect of these three shots *15*, *16*, *17*: the studied 90-degree change of direction, the sudden jump into big close-up on the barrel, the metallic gleam, the ritual finger movements, the spinning chamber, the satisfying clicks—above all the shocking crack of the explosion. But what saves it from lyricism is not menace, as you might expect, but humour. The humour comes from those very elements we have just described: the minuteness, here, of the examination of the action, in the absence of any description at all in more obvious places. In a word, incongruity; the contrariness of a treatment which warns you not to classify an event nor its protagonist—in terms of fear, enjoyment or approval—solely according to your previous experience. It is only right to remind ourselves that it is the editing as much as anything else which persuades us to this conclusion.

There is probably no other film quite like. *Vivre Sa Vie*. It describes the life of a girl who decides to take up prostitution. Formally, it is unique. It consists of twelve " chapters " separated by fades, introduced by " chapter heading " titles on a black screen. Like *Breathless* it is " dédié aux films de série B." But where *Breathless* may have got by with an average B-feature audience on account of its thriller plot, *Vivre Sa Vie* wouldn't: no such sustaining fantasy supports the substance of this. It is a pretty plain and bold narrative. Many of the chapters are shot almost in one take. For example, one chapter consists entirely of a discussion between the heroine Nana (Anna Karina) and the philosopher Brice Parrain, who plays himself. Nana's contribution to the discussion is restrained. If you are not prepared to listen to a ten-minute lecture from a contemporary philosopher, you will find this sequence, in particular, boring. But Godard has never thought twice about taking liberties with the audience.

The opening sequence of *Vivre Sa Vie* starts with a view of Nana's back in a café. The camera makes one or two small movements during the rest of a rather long sequence in which she parts finally from her boy friend. Her face can be glimpsed dimly in the bar mirror, but not his. An echoing set-up occurs later in another café sequence when Nana meets the pimp who has interested her in the proposal for her new career. The scene is shot from behind the pimp's head, all in one take. Sometimes the camera swings from side to side to reveal Nana; sometimes it just stays behind him and she is blotted out.

Two films later Godard does it again in *Le Mépris*. In an interior discussion between Bardot and a man, who talk with a table and table-lamp between them, the camera crabs left and right as the discussion progresses, revealing now one and now the other. But it must be admitted that if the movements of the camera are intended to represent the sway of contending forces in the

353

discussion, then it is the table lamp which comes out of the argument best.

Godard has said of the opening scene in *Vivre Sa Vie*:

> I started with the idea that it was to begin where *Breathless* left off. Patricia in *Breathless* is a girl whom we see as it were from behind, and who faces us fully for one brief instant. So I knew that *Vivre Sa Vie* was to start with a girl seen from behind—I did not know why. It was the only idea I had, and I couldn't tell Anna much, so she cast about without knowing what I wanted, while I tried to work out my conception. We certainly improvised in the sense that I changed my mind all the time, deciding to do this, then that.[1]

If Godard didn't know exactly why he was doing it, one can't be categorical about the matter. One can say though that such proceedings, whether successful or not, clearly spring from an original look at the cinema's methods. The behaviour of the camera in these shots conveys a remarkable blend of inquisitiveness and coldness. It makes itself not so much the ordinary spectator at life's dramas, but, if anything, the rather badly placed spectator. Often in Godard's films we feel as one feels on those irritating occasions in restaurants when some domestic drama is unfolding just out of earshot. All one can do is to rock nonchalantly backwards and forwards in one's seat from time to time, and hope to catch a bit more of it. It may be felt that this is to carry the theme of unobtrusive detachment, which we are suggesting is one mark of the modern cinema, a little too far. But detachment, simplicity and elegance *can* be combined with strong feeling as other parts of Godard's work demonstrate more conclusively, and we shall try and see how he does it.

Take for example the remarkable end of *Vivre Sa Vie*. This is a scene in which the pimp is handing Nana over to two other men in exhange for a sum of money. Nana doesn't appear to know much about what's going on. Her pimp places her midway between his car and the others, some twenty yards away. They throw him the wallet. He picks it up and makes his way back to his car, abandoning Nana. When he reaches his car he discovers that they have given him less than agreed. He turns back, grabs Nana, and holding her in front of him as a hostage demands the rest of the money. The other two are not prepared to pay. One of them takes out his gun and prepares to shoot. Nana is in the direct line of fire. She cries out in fear, imploring them not to shoot. The first man turns to shoot, but the gun doesn't go off. " You shoot," he commands his sidekick, " I've forgotten to load mine." He

---

[1] *Interview with Tom Milne*, Sight and Sound, *Winter 1962–1963, p. 11.*

turns back to get into his car. The second man duly shoots, and Nana falls, hit. Her pimp is on the move back to his car. She gets up, and stumbling, tries to follow. But as she gets to the car the gunman fires again, and again she is hit. She falls beside the back wheel of the car. Her pimp is already at the wheel. He drives off without a backward glance. The camera tilts down abruptly till the crumpled body of Nana is in the top of frame. The screen fades and it is the end of the film.

All this action is contained in one shot. The camera is mounted on a dolly which runs up and down the road between the two cars when necessary, and occasionally pans from one group to another. We stay in long shot and on a wide-angle lens throughout. There are no zooms. When the first shot is fired, the camera is panning on to Nana so that we don't in fact see the gun fire but only hear it. The second shot is also fired out of vision. The opportunities for close-ups or at least medium-shots are legion. In the traditional thriller cinema this scene would be full of them. There would certainly be close-ups of Nana's agony and fear. There could hardly fail to be one of the first man's empty gun. As it is, the fact that the gun doesn't fire is not immediately appreciated. There is so much else to see in the wide and complex shot. It is complex in the sense that a lot happens in it, but it is utterly simple in form.

Something about the moral destitution of the episode is conveyed by the camera's wide-eyed stare. At first sight it seems to be that the coolness of the criminal ethic is matched by that of the camera. But beyond this there is surely a feeling that such horror demands the respect of being viewed whole. This time we are a well-placed spectator, but, as in real life, not a participant. The domestic drama unfolds, to our horror, within earshot, but, as in life, out of range.

Godard has admitted that *Vivre Sa Vie* owes very little to the editing and is really " a collection of shots placed side by side, each one of which should be self-sufficient." Part of the cumulative effect of *Vivre Sa Vie* stems from this very discontinuity of style. The lassitude with which Nana drifts through life is caught by the broken rhythms set up by the disjunctive editing.

Les Carabiniers deals with war in the same distant, wide-eyed way as *Vivre Sa Vie* dealt with prostitution. But what some critics call coldness and inhumanity in Godard's treatment might be equally seen as honesty. During a war, war films are usually monuments of unsullied patriotism in which your own side behaves with characteristic loyalty and courage while the enemy is seen at his typical brutal worst. As the war recedes into history, the enemy becomes more human—more like yourself in fact, until the point is reached when, in an access of masochism, the other side is seen to display more courage and loyalty than your own. It is felt that (often) the second type is more honest than the first. All war films more or less pay lip-service to the principle that war is evil, but they consciously or not canalise the powerful emotional reactions to violence that any audience has if shown it in operation. If our side is oppressed by enemy brutality, one can be sure it will take its revenge before renouncing violence at the end of the film. This is the pattern of most war films and many westerns.

There is nothing of this in *Les Carabiniers*. There are scenes of brutality and inhumanity, but no revenge for us. The two main culprits are indeed executed at the end, but there is no comfort in it. If this is more honest than the traditional type of war film, the open-handed style serves this honesty well. We are never allowed to identify. We are never drawn in. The distant and choppy style keeps us at arm's length, which is where Godard thinks we ought to be, in order to judge this madness with sanity.

The two soldiers, Ulysses and Michelangelo, have been, they say, around the world. Whatever they have seen, they have conquered; and their king, they say, has promised to them many of their prizes. They show their wives the prizes they have won. Out of their suitcase they pull a stack of picture postcards and flick them one by one down on the table: the Taj Mahal, the Eiffel Tower, St. Peter's, etc. What do their cards represent? We smile for a while at their naivety, and at the cheek of the device. But it dawns on us that Godard is accusing us of making the same mistake as Ulysses and Michelangelo. In the age of the photograph, we all live vicariously through images. Like the magic signs on the cave wall, the image is an attempt to gain control of the object. The image puts us instantly in touch with the appearance of things not only on this earth but, now, throughout space. At a flick of a switch we can make the President of the U.S.A. talk; climb Everest; land on the moon. That sort of familiarity brings with it the illusion of knowledge and power. It is this knowledge which Godard is questioning, not only in this little allegory in *Les Carabiniers*, but frequently throughout his work.[1]

[1] *So does Antonioni, of course, particularly in* Blow-Up.
(*In* Pierrot Le Fou, *Belmondo complains about a photo of a guy:* " *You seem to know him, but you've no idea what he was thinking at the time it was taken.*")

It doesn't mean that he succeeds. He is looking for a way of saying new things. In this case, the catalogue of conquests on picture postcards goes on, for most people's tastes, far too long. But other liberties he takes with the audience's patience are more successful.

In *Bande à Part* the group of friends challenge each other to keep silent for one minute. The challengers stare at one another for one minute in silence. The audience sits through the experience with them. What has happened? Is it just that Godard has won a private bet against us? Or is it that he has made us stop and feel the weight of time passing in a way rarely experienced in the cinema? Again, like Truffaut, he vindicates the theories of Bazin, who called for a cinema in which more respect would be paid to the integrity of the event. But by his arbitrary stifling of the sound track he reminds us, too, of the impermanence of the events surrounding us. Life is very fragile, as the end of all his films also reminds us. How then do we square this undertaking to integrity with the acknowledged choppiness and bittiness of many parts of his films—and of Truffaut's and Resnais' too?

Let us remind ourselves of the theories about the cinema of appearance put forward by Rhode and Pearson:

The self is without essence—merely a series of events without apparent connection; there is no stable reality against which to measure fantasy or truth; there are, equally, no absolute values. At the same time, a morality is as necessary as ever but it is a morality that must be invented from moment to moment.

Making pictures of a world which is in continuous flux, indefinable and unassessable, is a comforting way of attempting some understanding of it. But making pictures itself is a self-defeating process, for the pictures we make don't have the effect of re-integrating the world for us. On the contrary, unlike painting, they substitute a lesser reality and a very convincing one, fragmenting the world even further, till all we have left is a continuous stream of visual memories standing in for first-hand experiences, or, if you like, a suitcase full of postcards. " Franz did not know," says the narrator of *Bande à Part*, " whether the world was becoming a dream or a dream becoming the world."

As in dreams this world will be described by the " juxtaposition of things that don't necessarily go together." Its characters, who have no firm identity except the one they invent for themselves moment by moment, obey a logic we can't always understand. This accounts for the constant changes in pace and mood, and for

357

the bewildering "actes gratuits" of which the action consists. On the other hand, sometimes the best chance we have of coming to grips with this world is to let its confused medley of events unroll before us as uninterruptedly as we can. So the camera stands back in long shot, the take runs on, minute after minute, having nothing to add by cutting.

But what happens when the surface of the films *does* break up in an explosion of close-up fragments? When Catherine sits at the wheel of her car, for instance, in *Jules and Jim*, or when Godard entitles *Une Femme Mariée* " fragments of a film " and its heroine Charlotte is seen in bed not so much as a complete woman but as a compilation of parts, while the world outside the bedroom window is a bewildering hotch-potch of signs, arrows, flashing lights and broken words—the enemy that Lemmy Caution conquers by love in *Alphaville*?

Then we can see this language as an expression of anguish that the desire for integrating our vision of the world has broken down. It has broken down before that battery of fragments which life today has become. Our response to the increasing flood of information and sense impressions is panic: our minds reflect not a new synthesis but a meaningless kaleidoscope. According to which of those two extremes you think Godard himself has most nearly approached, so you will judge the success of his films, and his success in extending our screen language through them.

Alain Resnais

Resnais' editing style serves perhaps the most personal and idiosyncratic aim of all. However, his standpoint is similar in enough respects to other film-makers of the sixties to allow us to bracket him with them: he is obsessed by identity, being, knowledge of oneself and other people, and how it is acquired—and lost; with the effects of time and memory on each other and on ourselves. His films move as far away as any have from the traditional structure in which plot and character illustrate a theme. His second major feature, *L'Année Dernière à Marienbad*, is, to beg a few questions immediately, so much like a dream that speculations about its " plot " have proved a waste of time (as we had been told they would be by its makers Resnais and Robbe-Grillet). Resnais' subject is the human mind, the structure of his films is the mind's ceaseless cataract of images; the drama of the films is in the ebb and flow of emotion which lights up the images, or blacks them out: conviction—doubt; persuasion—resistance; love

—hate. The traditional distinction between present and past, fact and fantasy, is obliterated, not simply as a game, but out of a conviction that it is a more honest way of representing the flow of perception. A passage from the French avant-garde writer Alfred Jarry could pass as a gloss on Resnais' work:

As a result of these reciprocal relations with Things, which he could direct with his thought (but all of us can, and it is not at all certain that there is a difference even in time, between thought, will, and act: cf. the Holy Trinity), he did not in the least distinguish his thoughts from his acts, or his dreaming from his waking; and perfecting the Leibnitzean definition that perception is a true hallucination, he saw no reason against saying: hallucination is a false perception, or more precisely a feeble one, or better yet, an anticipated perception (remembered, sometimes, which is the same thing). And he thought above all that there were only hallucinations, or perceptions, and that there is neither day nor night (in spite of the title of this book, which is why it is chosen), and that life is continuous . . .[1]

Resnais' work is dedicated to the proposition that it is not at all certain that there is a difference, even in time, between thought, will and act. Without some such realisation, his work will seem confused and meaningless. Like Godard, he seems to be extending screen language in a way which appears strange now but will no doubt be common currency in time. The co-author of his second film, *Marienbad*, Alain Robbe-Grillet, describes the methods of the film:

What do all these images amount to? They are bits of imagination; and imagination, if it is vivid enough, is always in the present tense. The memories one " re-sees," the distant places, the future meetings, the episodes from the past which everyone carries in his head, re-arranging their development as time passes—these make up a kind of film which keeps running continually in our minds, whenever we stop paying attention to what is actually happening around us. At other times we're recording through all our senses an external world by which we're fairly and squarely surrounded. So the complete film as it runs through our minds allows simultaneously for fragments of actual experience, things seen and heard at the moment, and for fragments belonging to the past, the future, the remote distance, or entirely to fantasy.

It is not an accident that we quote the " author " rather than the " director " of *Marienbad*. They decided to sign the film together, since they were equally responsible for its conception, though Robbe-Grillet acknowledges the " major role of execution as Resnais'." In Resnais' work the writer has always played a large part. *Hiroshima* was written by Marguerite Duras, whom Resnais encouraged to " write literature—forget about it being a film." Robbe-Grillet, leading exponent of the French new novel, wrote *Marienbad* in the form of a shooting script. Jean Cayrol,

[1] *Jarry*, Les Jours et les Nuits, *1897.*

who wrote the script of *Nuit et Brouillard*, Resnais' film about German concentration camps, made a large contribution to *Muriel*, in writing the script. It is customary to regard the writer's role as a minor one, and the script as a kicking-off point. Not so with Resnais. (Resnais' methods are another sort of vindication of the *caméra-stylo*; but they stress the connection with the psychological density and complexity of the novel rather than simply the flexibility of the pen.) In a sense *Marienbad* is a *nouveau roman* in which it is more convenient to photograph the images than to describe them.

One of the tenets of the *nouveau roman* is briefly this: that traditional literary forms are bedevilled and distorted by the anthropomorphism of imagery, metaphor and figurative language of all descriptions. We find ourselves saying " the day was gloomy" without realising that we are attributing a feeling induced in us by the weather or by other considerations to the day itself, as though it had a personality. Natural objects are particularly prone to this kind of possessive intrusion on our part. Brooks sparkle, old houses huddle together, shadows loom. Some critics maintain that only by anthropomorphising inhuman objects can we begin to grasp their essence, and that it is not merely the natural, but the *only* form of human expression, and the only way to extend our understanding of the phenomenal world. But the writers of the *nouveau roman* maintain that it is a distortion. *Marienbad* can be seen as an illustration of this thesis. It is in one sense a discussion of how the material world is apprehended and transformed by the mind under the pressure of desire, regret, fear, and other strong emotions; and not only one mind but, perhaps, three.

These prefatory remarks are necessary in order to establish a reference point from which to discuss the appearance and editing style of the films. For they rely more than many others on the precision and order of shots, and the editing relies, with an exact correspondence, on the meaning: the editing *is* the meaning.

The events of *Hiroshima Mon Amour* are as follows: a French actress, in Hiroshima to make a documentary film about Peace, meets and falls in love with a Japanese. She is reminded, by the context, of her first love: a German soldier with whom she had an affair in her home town of Nevers during the war. He was killed on Liberation Day. For shame, her parents shaved her head and locked her (overcome with grief) in a cellar, where she almost lost her reason. But now, to her horror, she has almost forgotten what

360

the German looked like. She warns the Japanese that she will forget him too.

The theme of the film therefore concerns this familiar tragic irony that life survives only by way of death; that the fact that we need to make a film about a great act of hatred reminds us constantly of our hypocrisy in forgetting its horror. But worst irony of all, the love necessary to overcome this hatred is subject itself to the ravages of memory; only by forgetting the German could she begin to love the Japanese; and that she finds, even as she looks at him, the time approaches when she thinks of him not as her lover and a person, but as Hiroshima. She has succeeded in drowning him in the universal oblivion. The connections between these themes are made as much by the editing as by any explicit statements in the commentary or dialogue. The paradoxes are expressed by stressing the similarities between different time sequences. So the film begins with shots of the lovers' bodies entwined. They are in turn covered with ashes, rain, sweat or dew. The film was originally to have begun with the mushroom cloud of the atom bomb, but this was cut. The ashes and the dew were therefore to be seen as fallout, giving way to the sweat of love. Now that the cloud is no longer there, it is more difficult to make the connection, but not impossible. The woman tells the man that she saw everything at Hiroshima. He denies that she has. She gives instances of what she has seen: the hospital for example. And we cut immediately to images of present-day Hiroshima, the hospital, the museum. During the course of the sequence we cut backwards and forwards between the lovers on the bed, present-day Hiroshima, a Japanese reconstruction on film of the horror, and real documentary. The connection between the lovers and the war is hinted by a line of the woman's: " Just as this illusion exists in love, the illusion of never being able to forget, so I had the illusion, with Hiroshima, that I will never forget."

Time passes. She is on the hotel balcony outside her room. She is watching him lying asleep on the bed. She watches his hands move gently as children's do sometimes when they're asleep. While she's looking at his hands, quite suddenly, in place of the Japanese, there appears the body of a young man, in the same pose, but dying, on the banks of a river. His hands twitch in agony. The image is a very short one. Immediately we return to the woman, still watching the Japanese.

Later in his house, he says to her: " Was he a Frenchman, the man you loved during the war?" We suddenly see the figure of a

German soldier crossing a square at dusk. We suppose it is in Nevers. Then we return to her lying on the bed in Hiroshima. She says, " No, he wasn't French." Then she says, " Yes it was in Nevers." We see shots of Nevers in the wintertime, the old walls, ruins, trees. While she talks a little about Nevers he says, " It's there, I seem to have understood, that you are so young, so young that you aren't really anybody exactly yet. That pleases me." And again, " It's there, I seem to have understood, that I almost . . . lost you . . . and that I risked never knowing you." And again, " It's there, I seem to have understood, that you must have begun to be how you are still today."

In all these examples we can see how Duras and Resnais begin to wrap the past up in the present, not by referring one back to the other but by associating them simultaneously as part of the texture of the present. It is part of their thesis that the past not only conditions the present but in a sense *is* the present, too. So instead of past tenses being used in the dialogue, present tenses are used. As Robbe-Grillet says, images on the screen have only one tense: the present. The cinema is therefore uniquely endowed to deal with Resnais' habitual themes.

In a café at night on the banks of the river at Hiroshima, the woman drinks and reminisces about Nevers. Images of her here now and as a girl in the cellar, disfigured and distracted, replace one another constantly. Suddenly he says to her, " When you are in the cellar, am I dead?" We see a shot of the German lying in agony on the bank. Later, to an interior monologue by the woman, we track through the streets of Hiroshima and Nevers in successive shots. We can make no emotional or chronological distinction between them: for her they are landscapes full of misery. For us they have, present and past, the same emotional weight. The " flashback " is abolished. The shots were filmed by different crews at an interval of three months, but at exactly the same speed. When the woman sits on a bench at the station in Hiroshima, shots of Nevers are accompanied by the station loudspeaker announcing " Hiroshima, Hiroshima." (Apart from one cry, there is no natural sound from Nevers, it is all Japanese: river frogs, a barge hooter, a Japanese song.) She realises that Nevers has made her what she is, but despite it having marked her so deeply she has almost forgotten the man whom she loved. The German was Nevers. The Japanese is Hiroshima. She will forget him, too. " Hiroshima," she says, " is your name." " It's my name," he replies, " yes. And your name is Nevers. Nevers-in-France."

362

This was the most thoroughgoing assault ever on the conventional time-structure that editing supported in the cinema.

The assault is carried on in Resnais' next two films *L'Année Dernière à Marienbad* and *Muriel*. *Muriel* is the story of a widow who tries to re-investigate, perhaps re-light, a twenty-year-old love affair. The attempt is unsuccessful. The theme is the treacherous power of memory. The past is all we know, but it is very little help in guiding us through the present. Since it is all we know, it conditions our present apprehension of the world. So we are introduced to events in *Muriel* as it were through the agency of memory, even if they are happening now. When a customer arrives at Hélène Aughain's flat/antique shop we see a hand on the door, Hélène's face, the kettle being poured in the kitchen, an assortment of furniture. Views of wartime Boulogne are cut in suddenly with the present-day town. A picture of reality is built up from a number of, at first, incoherent details presented in not necessarily the right order. Who knows, it seems to say, what the right order is?

This does seem a quite different sort of process from the one we have been talking about with reference to other French film-makers of the sixties. Where is the much-vaunted disengagement? The detachment of the discreet widescreen camera, the long takes, the attempt to let reality declare itself by not interfering? Resnais of course works in a completely different way, but it would be wrong to say that he negates by his methods the assumptions we have made about the cinema of appearance. He is as concerned as anyone in building up the most honest picture of an unstable reality. His inquiries lead him not outward to the surface of observed life but to the fragmentation of it which goes on in the mind. His picture of the world is built up of these fragments, half-perceived and inconclusive.

Marienbad is above all a collection of fragments, fragments of memory, fragments of conjecture, images remembered and imagined. If projectionists have nightmares, they have them about *Marienbad*. It must have been shown more often with reels missing or in the wrong order than any other film ever. It would take a sharp audience to notice a mistake in the running order, for the film's chronology bears little resemblance to anything encountered in real life. We have already quoted Robbe-Grillet on the film's methods. The " plot " is as follows. In a baroque palace, which may be a hotel, three guests in particular develop a strange relationship. An unknown man, X, tells a woman, A, that they have met before, last year, in fact, in Marienbad. She had promised to go away with him. He had waited a year, now he will wait no longer. She must come. The woman denies ever having met him, resists his accounts of their time together. She is attended by another man, M, who may be her husband. But, eventually persuaded, she abandons M and leaves the palace with X.

The story is told in an elliptical fashion. No action is ever allowed to develop to its conclusion. In early scenes involving the rest of the guests Resnais freezes the frame frequently and we immediately think of the quarrel we have overheard a couple having. The man complains that he is tired of living like this with her, with her conspiracy of silence. They are like two frozen statues side by side, he says. There is much talk of the extraordinary summer of '28 or '29 when the fountain froze over for a week. X tells A that the pond had frozen last summer at Marienbad, too. People freeze into stillness just as the memory freezes them in recollection or as they are sometimes seen in a dream. In one shot a number of the guests are seen standing transfixed in an *allée* in the formal garden. Their shadows strike dramatically across the gravel. But there is an eerie feeling about the shot which is difficult to pin down. It is only gradually that we realise there are no other shadows in the picture: it is an overcast day. Resnais has had the shadows painted on to the ground. At other times he doesn't freeze the frame but simply asks the actors to stay absolutely immobile while the camera tracks past them.

Immobility—and movement. The camera is ceaselessly on the move. Indeed, it seems to have more life than the people. Without searching for any other meaning it is worth saying that Resnais employs the moving camera principally for the sheer sensuous pleasure it gives. He experiments a good deal with exposure by tracking the camera very quickly from one light area to another: sometimes of an extreme difference. One shot takes A from a dark corridor across two ante-rooms and out on the balcony in the bright sunlight. The next shot reverses the angle and we see A against the white outer wall, dressed in white, with white feathers, while on the right of the frame we can pick out details in the dark interior through the French window. Another tracking shot speeds along an immense corridor, turns a corner at the end and sweeps into a medium-shot of A in her bedroom. The corridor shot is highly over-exposed: the bedroom scene is very high key. From a shot of A in dazzling white, again, we cut to a faintly glimmering garden at dusk.

Not only do the exposures change abruptly: locations and clothes do too. There is no continuity, since we are being shown several mental processes involving different versions of, perhaps, the same event.

Let us look, finally, at a representative sequence from the film.

L'ANNEE DERNIERE A MARIENBAD[1]

(The dialogue is taken from the English edition of the book Last Year in Marienbad *by Alain Robbe-Grillet. Calder and Boyers 1962. Pp. 83–87 make an interesting comparison with the film.)*

			Ft. fr.
1	L.S. The ballroom, with the bar on the left. The woman, A, and the man, X, are seen standing at the bar. Couples are dancing on the floor.	*Music is playing, but it stops after 12 ft.*	19
2	A long view of the bar, at right angles to it. A and X are clearly seen. The dancers are drifting off the floor, and some moving to the bar. At 27 ft. a *slow tracking shot* begins, moving in to A and X. It finishes at 86 ft. A and X are now in a *two-shot*, favouring X.	X: I met you again. You had never seemed to be waiting for me, but we kept meeting each other at every turn in the path, behind each bush—at the foot of each statue—at the rim of every pond. It was as if only you and I had been there in that whole garden. (*Pause. Ballroom noises can still be heard, but above them there is a noise of feet crossing gravel.*) We were talking about anything that came into our heads—about the names of the statues, about the shapes of the bushes, about the water in the ponds—or else we weren't talking at all. At night, most of all, you enjoyed not talking.	100
3	A white bedroom in which A is standing.		9
4	A and X at bar as at end of 2.	X: One night I went up to your room.	3 14
5	Similar to 4 but a closer shot.		4 12
6	As 3		8
7	As 4		3
8	As 6		8

[1] *Director: Alain Resnais. Script: Alain Robbe-Grillet. Editors: Henri Colpi, Jasmine Chasney. Terra Film/Films Tamara/Films Cormoran/Précitel/Como-Films/ Argos-Films/Cinetel/Silver-Films/Cineriz (Rome). 1961.*

		Ft. fr.
9	As 7	2 14
10	As 8	8
11	As 9, but squarer.	2 15
12	As 10	1
13	As 11	1 8
14	As 12	1 8
15	As 13	1 6
16	As 14	1 10
17	As 15, but a *different angle*, favouring A	1 8
18	As 16	1 8
19	As 17	1 8
20	As 18	1 8
21	As 19	12
22	As 20	1 8
23	As 21	12
24	As 22	1 8
25	As 23, but a slightly *closer shot*, favouring A.	12
26	As 24	4 5
27	As 25	1 8
28	A in bedroom, sitting on stool, surrounded by pairs of shoes, some of which she appears to be trying on. She begins laughing quietly. *The waltz music heard earlier in the ballroom begins again.*	39 13
29	The ballroom. Another guest, a girl, moves away from the camera towards the bar, laughing. *The ballroom noises increase.*	1 5
30	C.S. X looking screen left.	8
31	C.S. A. The camera *reverse tracks* very quickly. A looks right.	14
32	C.S. X looking screen left.	8
33	C.S. The camera *reverse tracks.* A looking horrified.	12
34	C.S. X. As 32	8

366

26

27

28

29

30

31

		Ft. fr.
35	C.S. As 33	12
36	*Wider shot* of the bar. A steps back suddenly and collides with the girl who laughed in 29. A drops her glass. The camera *reverse tracks* very quickly.	1 9
	Sound of glass smashing.	
37	The bedroom. A, surprised, is falling backwards off the stool. X is standing on the left of frame.	4 10
	The sound is blocked off after 3ft. of this shot.	
38	C.S. Hand of waiter picking up smashed glass from floor in front of bar.	17 5
39	M.S. Waiter picking up glass fragments.	10 7
40	*High-angle L.S.* Waiter picking up glass.	24 7

This passage is particularly good at illustrating a point made often in this book: that the apparent duration of a shot depends not only on its length, the size or complexity of the image, etc., but also on its context. In any other context, shot *26* would seem quite short, lasting as it does just under three seconds. In fact, here it seems to last a long time. Partly to match the sudden slowing in tempo, partly to prepare us for *28*, *27* is twice as long as the last three shots of A have been.

There is very little else one can say about this sequence which isn't obvious from a consideration of the shot-lengths. The eight shots *29–36*, for example, take only about $4\frac{1}{2}$ seconds of screen time. One point which should be mentioned is that the ballroom scenes are very dark, the bedroom scenes unnaturally bright and lit in a very high key. Though it is often argued—and we have argued it here—that Resnais' methods are an attempt to mirror the movements of the mind, it can be seen here that the technique at its most extreme is not in any way naturalistic. (Neither is the dialogue, of course, which, like the images, depends on constant slightly changing repetitions. See *2*.) The cutting backwards and forwards between scenes here is a formal device meant to represent the battle of X's mind against A's, to convey his attempt at persuading her that something had happened which she is doubtful about. The indication that his version of the events is gaining the upper hand in her mind comes in the mid-point of the battle, around shots *13–19*. Here he is, as it were, transporting her by the power of his mind, from the ballroom to the bedroom, and across a year of time (and us, too, of course). Gradually, her consciousness of her presence in the ballroom fades under the power of his reminiscence. Shot *21* is as brief as the first flashes of the bedroom had been. But our minds don't of course, work in quite this way. All one can say is that Resnais' device is an effective approximation: a metaphor, if you like, instead of a literal representation.

Michelangelo Antonioni

Antonioni is, as much as Resnais, a director whose films have a personal style which owes nothing to general theories of editing. Even less than Resnais does he have anything to do with the New Wave. It is more difficult than it was with Resnais to describe an " Antonioni style " since it has changed considerably throughout his career. Yet in so far as his style is a very personal instrument, closely adapted to his aims, his work will be very useful as our last example of the " personal cinema." We shall start with an extract from *L'Avventura* since it represents a mid-point in his development, and because it is still probably the best-known of his films.

L'AVVENTURA[1]

The story:

A group of rich Romans set out on an excursion to a barren volcanic island off the coast of Sicily. Sandro, a successful but discontented architect, is having an unhappy affair with Anna. On the island Anna mysteriously disappears and Sandro and Anna's friend Claudia are left behind while the rest of the party go to get help. Before Anna's complete disappearance is confirmed, Sandro begins to be attracted to Claudia who, to her horror, finds herself drawn similarly to him at a time when their thoughts should be wholly on Anna. They set out together through Sicily on a quest for the missing girl which soon turns in fact into a record of their love affair. The film ends when Sandro is discovered by Claudia making love to a starlet at a party. Sandro and Claudia, it is hinted, will stay together though they have had it brutally demonstrated that even the strongest emotions lack permanence. Claudia can hardly rebuke Sandro, for she has forgotten Anna in the same heedless—but inevitable—way as he has temporarily forgotten Claudia.

The extract:

The island. Sandro and Claudia and a third member of the party have spent an uncomfortable night in a fisherman's hut. They have had a brief row, during which Sandro thinks Claudia has accused him of helping to cause Anna's disappearance. It is now dawn.

Ft. fr.

I	L.S. View of the rough sea and the clifftop. After 12 ft. the *camera pans slowly left and up* across the cliff. At 31 ft. it picks up Sandro who walks uphill, turns, sits on a rock, looks over his shoulder,	*Noise of wind and sea. Stormy weather. The conditions throughout this scene are grey and blustery, despite the occasional gleams of sun.*	85

[1] *Director: Michelangelo Antonioni. Editor: Eraldo da Roma. Cino del Duca/ Produzioni Cinematografiche Europée (Rome)—Société Cinématographique Lyre (Paris). 1959–60.*

369

stands up and continues to walk left and uphill. He is about 15 yards from camera. At 66 ft. Claudia enters frame from the left and they stop facing each other.

Sandro when Claudia appears:
Do you feel better?
Claudia: 83
Forgive me for last night.

2   *Full shot.* Sandro looking out screen right, the sea behind him. It is the reverse angle of 1. He is looking at Claudia. At 12 ft.:

Sandro:
You're very fond of Anna, aren't you?
Claudia (off):
Very.

Sandro starts to walk into a two-shot at *17 ft.*, finishing up at *24 ft.* on screen left, to Claudia's right and slightly below her. She is facing the camera.

Sandro:
Didn't she ever speak to you about me?
Claudia:
Only rarely. But always **very** tenderly.

At *40 ft.* he turns away and walks deep into the frame, screen left, then comes back into a *C.U.* in front of the camera at *60 ft.*

Sandro starts while walking towards us:
You see, she has acted as if all our affection—mine, yoûrs, **even** her father's in a sense, wasn't enough for her, meant nothing to her.
Claudia at 68 ft.:
I wonder what I should have done to have prevented all this?

At 80 ft. the sound of a motor-boat engine makes them both turn their heads and look out screen left.

Sound of motor-boat.

3   Extreme *L.S.* View of the surrounding islands and the strait between them. No boat is visible.

Sound continues   19

4   *As 2.* They look puzzled and look out right of screen.

      11

5   A view of sea and cliff similar to 1, but this time from the opposite angle, with the sea on the left. The *camera pans up and right* on to the cliff. At 13 ft. Claudia walks into the frame away from the camera and continues to walk until she is a small figure at 36 ft. At 37 ft. Sandro enters the frame from the left in *C.U.* He looks round at her, but her back is towards us and he turns and continues to look out screen right.

      53

The motor-boat noise stops at 40 ft.

6   *Extreme L.S.* Another view of the sea and islands, the island we are on sloping down rockily to the sea in the lower half of frame. The island's lone fisherman is visible working his way up the hill towards us. The sun is low in the sky and shining across the water at us.

7   As at the end of 5. Sandro moves out of frame, screen right, leaving Claudia still in, a remote figure in the distance.

8

8   *M.S.* The fisherman is walking left to right along the cliff. Sandro walks in from the right to meet him at 11 ft.

39

Sandro:
    Whose boat is that?
Fisherman:
    What boat?
Sandro:
    A moment ago. Didn't you hear the noise?
Fisherman:
    At this time of the year there are so many boats—

He turns to go, but stops when Sandro speaks.

Sandro:
    Do you always get up so early?
Fisherman:
    Early? Do you call four o'clock in the morning early?

They both look up and out of screen right, and exit.

9   *L.S.* The fisherman walks off behind a rock screen right. Sandro, just behind him, looks up the hill to where the camera is. In *C.U.*, the back of her head towards us, Claudia is watching this scene. When she sees there is no news of Anna she turns and leaves the frame screen left, the *camera panning a little* with her. It stops, however, to wait for Sandro who is climbing towards us. When he is nearing the camera it begins to track backwards with him. They both stop at *36 ft.* (The fisherman leaves the frame at *3 ft.*)

36

At 4 ft. a lugubrious clarinet melody begins. Claudia turns on 7 ft.

10   *C.S.* A rock pool. Claudia's hands are in it, *the camera tilts up* to reveal that she is washing her face. The *tilt* reveals that Sandro is walking down the hill towards us, but unseen by Claudia since her face is towards camera. He

60

1   5a

1a   5b

2   9

2a   9a

5   10

372

10a 14

11 15

12 15a

13 15b

    sits on a rock a little way behind
her, watching her. She stands up,
not noticing him. At 29 ft. she
blows her nose, turns screen left
and notices him over her shoulder
at 33 ft. She begins to move up
past him.

11   *M.C.S.* She trips and almost falls   3 7
but is held up by him. She is
below him in the bottom right-
hand corner of the frame.

12   *M.C.S.* Reverse angle. She stares   4 8
at him. Favouring Claudia.

13   *M.C.S.* As 11. Slowly she begins   4 12
to recover her balance and moves
from right to left across the
frame.

14   *Full shot.* She looks down and   13 3
then moves off across left, the
camera panning with her. He is
still in the foreground with his
back to us, and he follows her.

15   *Extreme L.S.* A spur of rock fills   34
the left-hand side of frame.   *At 8 ft. the clarinet music stops.*
Beyond it can be seen the sea
between the islands, and in the
strait a boat, probably a hydro-
plane, is speeding left to right
towards us.   *Boat noise.*
After 5 ft. the camera *panning
right* picks up Claudia, closely
followed by Sandro, on the cliff-
top, who overtakes her and moves
to the left of her. They are about
15 to 20 yards from the camera.

DISSOLVE at 34 ft.

The first thing to notice here is that, by ordinary standards, this
is a very long piece of film (467 feet) for a very short piece of action.
A common complaint about Antonioni's work has been that it is
slow and empty. Without entering at this stage into a full-scale
critical defence we can, nevertheless, point to the different nature
of activity at which Antonioni seems to have been aiming.

We have said often enough before that in many of the films of
the sixties conventional ideas of plotting have been ignored.
L'Avventura is a good example of this. While " events " in the
shape of dramatic developments in the action are few and far
between, the real " story " is carried on by other means. Secondly,
in this case the locations themselves play a large part in the action,
374

both as symbols and as physical presences. If one definition of tragedy is " character as destiny " then in some of Antonioni's films it is not fanciful to suggest that the definition could be extended to include " environment as destiny." In other words, Antonioni sees a direct and not purely metaphorical link between a man's environment and his behaviour.

This was true even of his early documentary films. In *Gente del Po* (shown in 1947) the character and economic prospects of the poor people who live in the region of the Po river in Northern Italy is as depressed, flat and bleak as the river and the countryside itself. It is true, though obviously in a more oblique way, of his feature films, too. In them he tries to find the actual and not simply the metaphorical correspondence between the characters and the locations in which their story is set.

How does this relate to *L'Avventura*? It is noticeable that the most impressive " character " in this extract, if we judge by the weight given it, is the landscape. By conventional standards indeed the sequence is " badly cut." The shots go on absurdly too long—long after the apparent action is over. But we have said that the action is elsewhere. Where then?

The island is a major participant in the action but its contribution is complex and difficult to define. It is partly to be associated, in its barrenness, coldness and hostility, with the group of bored empty and non-productive people who have come to visit it. In this light it can be seen as a symbol of their society. It seems appropriate that they can think of nowhere more interesting to visit than this most inhuman and inhospitable of landscapes.

At the same time the island and the sea surrounding it have a curious quality which is not always the property of this sort of landscape. The island is volcanic: parts of it are constantly crumbling away and crashing into the sea which eats incessantly away at its outline. If the island is a symbol of their society it suggests, therefore, that the society is both petrified and in process of dissolution. If we think of the island as a kind of world, we see Claudia and Sandro's movements about it in a different light. The long, slow-moving shots become edgy, tense and uneasy.

It would be foolish to pretend that the landscape has only this symbolic meaning. The action also lies in the way the disposition of people and landscape charts the give-and-take of their growing relationship, while their mute struggle for authority is given a voice by the elements. The sequence doesn't seem over-attenuated now, because when the human characters brood and lower, the landscape too seems to glare back, but with a more ambivalent scrutiny. There is an air of menace about it, in the incessant, unlocatable, dislocated noises it makes, in the presence or threat of storm, in its wildness, in its opposition to human life. This could be at the same time a description of what Claudia, a working-class girl, feels about Sandro's fashionable society. When we can see all this we can see that the picture of Claudia and Sandro wandering impotently and at cross-purposes about its surface, staring into its frightening crevices, uncertain any longer of what they are looking for, even more uncertain of what they will find, is a complex and disturbing one.

With these general thoughts in mind, let us turn to a few more particular notes about the extract.

1. The camera is static on an empty landscape for 12 feet. There is a further 19 feet before Sandro comes into picture. 35 feet later Claudia appears. The landscape and the weather positively oppress them. In this light their drawing together in circumstances where they might be felt to be antagonistic is more understandable. In other words the landscape here takes, as we suspect it has earlier in the case of Anna, a positive hand in the action.

Throughout this shot Sandro is at least 10 yards from the camera. Even during the first exchange of dialogue between them Antonioni resists the temptation of cutting into a closer shot. The effect is to link them in their smallness and pit them against the vast power of the surrounding elements. It also suggests an equal poise of potential authority, which is in question throughout the sequence. Eventually it becomes apparent that he is the supplicant and she the stronger of the two; no small part of the film's meaning. But at first the current seems to be running his way, for the close shot, when it does come, is given to him. But she is lent a certain dignity by her off-screen reply which by its restraint makes his question seem slightly importunate. Her position is strengthened when the camera starts to pan up screen right to take him up to her in a two-shot in which she is easily dominant. His question is even more indelicate than before and her reply consistently graceful. He then moves off restlessly, and coming back towards the camera forces himself into a crudely forward position with his back to her. There is no need for a close shot on her to establish her unsought superiority, won for her by her polite immobility. Their dialogue makes explicit the meaning implicit in the *mise-en-scène*. The pretence of conversation is dropped. His complaint is selfish and peevish. Her response is to blame herself, rather than Anna, for

376

what has happened. They are no longer communicating, though it is no fault of hers. She can expect little from him in the way of suggestion or solace. She moves away.

But characteristically she does it in a politely negative way. That's to say she's not seen to turn on her heel, but walks into a panning shot (5) from behind the camera, and then away from us into the far distance. The beginning of this shot is interesting. In 4 we see a view, accompanied by the motor-boat noise, which suggests that it is their eyeline we are looking at.[1] But the manner in which she walks into the shot reveals that it cannot be hers. Antonioni has demonstrated that a distance must be kept at this stage between us and Claudia since it is a part of her delicacy to preserve it. We must not identify with her. No such inhibition attends Sandro. At the end of 5, when Claudia is a small remote figure taking her grief and perplexity privately off, deep into the frame, he bursts into it once more, in right profile, very close to the camera. Disgruntled, he looks towards her, but she is not looking at him. In shot 6 we see the tiny figure of the fisherman and in 7 Sandro moves out of the repeated shot 5 to leave Claudia still there like a small black question mark. The inference is that he goes to question the fisherman as much out of a desire to please Claudia as to find Anna. From this point on we suspect rightly that the re-appearance of Anna would be more of an embarrassment to him than a relief. One of the film's major themes is that it soon—too soon—becomes a necessity to them both that Anna shall have disappeared once and for all.

For the moment, however, Claudia is immune. She is allowed to appear in close-up from the back in shot 9 to observe Sandro's encounter with the old man. When it proves fruitless she again turns away out of shot. This leaves Sandro once more climbing earnestly up towards her, a small but gradually intrusive figure. A melancholy clarinet which seems to grow out of the natural sounds is heard now and hints that they may both be conscious of a mutual attraction. The music is repeated throughout the film and comes indeed to be associated with their love, no more tellingly than in the final scene where its plaintive note is expressive of " the sort of shared pity," in Antonioni's phrase, which is all their relationship has come to. We may suspect also that for the first time Claudia quits the shot not so much out of delicacy as of retreat.

But the most explicit encounter has still to come. In shot 10

[1] *Its function in the story, of course, is to suggest that Anna may have thrown herself, or fallen, from the cliff, into the sea.*

377

Sandro again pursues her, even, metaphorically, into the bathroom. It is one of Sandro's lesser irritations throughout this sequence that although he and Claudia are thrown together by the situation and by the elements, he could wish for a more constraining togetherness than in the bleak wastes across which he has tirelessly to pursue her. In shot *11* she stumbles when passing close to him, he steadies her and in a flurry of short two-shots—especially short in this context—their mutual attraction is established beyond question. For a moment the habitual dominance of Claudia in the frame is upset here. She has been put off balance in more ways than one.

No. *12* clinches Sandro's insidious ascendancy. We have gone close enough to them to see what we had to see. Shot *12* links all the elements of the sequence again in a complex long-shot. We see first the view of the sea and neighbouring islands, then the approaching boat bearing police and civil authorities. Claudia is the first to enter the picture as the camera pans right with the boat, but Sandro is just behind her. The music, which comes to be associated more with her than with him, since his love is faithless, now stops. He walks up to, and past her. He has overtaken her at last. He has achieved the transference of her thoughts from Anna to himself. He has, in a sense, "taken her over."

The long take has been suggested as the most characteristic mark of Antonioni's style, especially (by harsher critics) the long take in which nothing much happens and in which nobody looks at anyone else. One response to that would be to say that most films give a very polite account of how often we look at each other normally; and that it is in the moments when we are not looking at each other that we reveal most, in the dead time—the *temps mort* we talked about earlier—between deliberate gestures, action or speech that the most significant emotional decisions are taken. It is in these moments that Antonioni is particularly interested.

A great deal, for example, can be learnt about the character of Sandro from the way in which he puts his hands in his pockets, walks up and down, watches people unobserved. Or the way in which Claudia's youthfulness and good nature are suggested by her manner, when unobserved, of putting her head on one side, humming and pulling faces. There are a great many of those sort of moments on the island. The long night scene near the end when she waits in her bedroom while Sandro puts in a " courtesy " appearance at the party downstairs is, in a strict sense, a scene like this, a scene without " action." It is written in the script simply

" Claudia's room. Interior. Evening. Claudia waits for Sandro all night."

A second reply would be to say that to describe *L'Avventura* is not to describe Antonioni's films. His scenes have been longer, more " action-packed." They can also be a great deal shorter, and devoid of action whatsoever in any formal sense.

One of Antonioni's better-known early films, *Le Amiche* (1955), is an intricate study of a group of fashionable women in Turin. Some of the scenes, notably a beach-excursion, are shot in long takes involving the complex criss-crossing and interweaving of a large group of people. Continuity is strictly maintained. Their disposition and the direction of their glances indicates the relationships they are forming, or more often, would like to form. Changes of angle are designed to throw into relief the struggle and clash of personalities. " I always try to manage," said Antonioni in an interview, " so that each element of the image serves to specify a particular psychological moment. An image is only essential if each square centimetre of that image is essential." This is particularly true of this film and for that reason it is a film which could have benefited from the use of widescreen, with its tendency to let the dynamic of the sequence be dictated by the action of the characters and not by a cutting rhythm.

An earlier film than *Le Amiche*, *La Signora Senza Camelie* (1952–3) has an even smaller average number of set-ups per scene. Many of the scenes are shot in one set-up, or in the useful French phrase, in *plan-séquences*. On the normal ratio screen this meant that in the long series of two-shot, three-shot and group-shots which such a technique demands, the faces, on which Antonioni relies so heavily, were often irritatingly small. Where the background is important, too, as it is in *L'Avventura*, a widescreen ratio is essential to preserve intimacy as well as the sense of geography.

The landscape, the background, the environment in the widest sense, have always been important elements in Antonioni's work. In *La Signora Senza Camelie* the drama takes place on a film set, glamorous, unreal and impermanent like the emotions involved. In *Il Grido* (1957) the emotional journey of the hero finds a correlative in a real physical journey which is the course of the film. As we have mentioned, the same is true of *L'Avventura*. So we see that to make way for the long slow-moving *plan-séquences*, the editing has, as it were, slid lengthways to become a juxtaposition of sequences and locations. This is a particularly forceful element in

L'Avventura.[1] From the barren island the couple move to an abandoned village, to a small town in which the square is alive with a sort of sullen, prowling lust, to a frenzied Messina set on fire by the arrival of a split-skirt starlet on a publicity stunt. By contrast there are scenes in a beautiful palace-turned-police-headquarters; in another villa near Messina where the couple rejoin the group; and in a luxury hotel at Taormina, where, final irony, Sandro makes love to the starlet encountered earlier.

The form of the film as a journey makes a clear impact and its centre is an actual train journey during which the attraction between Sandro and Claudia is finally accepted by them both. At the end of the film—at the end of her journey—Claudia says to a friend, when Sandro has disappeared during the night, that she is afraid that Anna has come back. She has talked herself into a position of virtually wishing Anna dead. Each of the stages of the journey, each of the locations, sensuously, figuratively, thematically, has had its distinct contribution to make in this emotional development.[2] The art of editing is as much a matter of structure as an arrangement of set-ups.

Curiously enough the subsequent development shown in Antonioni's work points to a return to a more fragmented style which depends intimately on an arrangement of set-ups. Even at the end of *L'Avventura* the wary reconciliation of Sandro and Claudia is handled in a quite unusual flow of short, broken close-ups of heads, faces, hands. It is an interesting thought that we have touched on several times in the course of the latter section of this book, that although the technical movement in the cinema has lately been, *on the whole*, towards the longer take, the flexible camera, the inclusive image, the broad, deep, complex widescreen picture—at the same time the philosophical movement has been towards dislocation, fragmentation, dissociation; a viewpoint which would naturally find a stylistic counterpart in a sequence of short disconnected shots. We have seen this most clearly in Godard and Resnais. And, in fact, Antonioni himself has stated his allegiance to this view and his later if not his earlier films bear it out. " Cinema today should be tied to truth rather than to logic."[3]

This somewhat question-begging statement can be taken to

[1] " *In this film the landscape is not only an essential component, it is in a way the pre-eminent one.*" (*Antonioni.*)

[2] *We are not suggesting that this is a device unique to Antonioni. It has been used often in the American cinema for example, notably in the Western. A particularly fine example is Cukor's* Heller in Pink Tights, *a film which repays close study.*

[3] *Quoted in* Michelangelo Antonioni, *by Ian Cameron. Movie Magazine Ltd. 1963.*

represent his support for the disappearance of unnecessary narrative links, a practice we've already noted and which it would be hard to disapprove of. On a more thoroughgoing level it supports the oblique way in which information is delivered to us in his films—as it is in real life—and ultimately it supports his willingness to do away altogether with what we should broadly regard as " plot," which we've also seen to be a mark of the modern cinema.

Before *L'Avventura* we can detect an urge in Antonioni to find an explanation at least, if not a solution, to problems, to round out an untidy situation in real life—like *Le Amiche*—in the fuller and more satisfying shape of a connected narrative with a beginning, a middle and an end—the classic process of art in fact. But with *L'Avventura* a new movement begins in his work. An interviewer asked him what became of Anna whose disappearance and fate is never explained. "I don't know," he is said to have replied. " Someone told me that she committed suicide. But I don't believe it." It is the customary flattening rejoinder of the artist who is demonstrating, without boring himself, that if we have to ask these questions we've got hold of the wrong end of the stick. Plot, in this sense, then, doesn't count. The narrative line has begun to break up and the style, too, as at the end of *L'Avventura*, bears the unmistakeable signs of it.

It does to a greater extent in his next film *La Notte* (1961). This concerns the realisation by a slightly older couple that their marriage is dead. He is a writer, commercially successful, but like the architect in *L'Avventura*, unhappy. The tendency, which Antonioni himself pointed to in the previous film, for the landscape to become dominant is here more marked. It is linked with the breaking up of the sequences into shorter and more disconnected sections and shots. The wife, Lidia, leaving a reception for her husband's new novel, is bored and restless. She goes for a stroll through the streets of Milan. It seems clear that she is used to travelling everywhere by car. She tests her legs as though it were a unique experience long forgotten. In contrast to the soulless and uniform modernity of the area in which she and her husband live, the district she passes into is old, decrepit and interesting. Several themes have already been touched upon in the film, notably isolation and impermanence: the isolation of the individual in a world of objects which have lost human scale; the impermanence of emotions which one would hope were something to cling to in a constantly changing world. Here the themes become more explicit. Lidia sees a crying child whom she attempts unsuccessfully to

381

comfort. She investigates, behind a hoarding, an old derelict building awaiting the developers' bulldozer. She picks at a piece of flaking rust. At her feet lies a battered clock. She passes along a row of phallic-looking concrete pavement pillars. An old woman is matter-of-factly sitting on one munching her lunch . . . It could be felt that here the objects isolated by the director seem too nakedly symbolic—of youth, of the passage of time, of old age, of fertility and so on. As we have often said, themes like this are difficult to generalise about on film in the way they can be dealt with in poetry. They are certainly *objects* here rather than events, and they are isolated despite the tenuous connection given them by her walk. The passage is moving in fact towards a sort of stylisation which possibly hasn't found its proper pitch yet. But the interesting thing from our point of view is that it marks the beginning of a really disconnected and almost surreal chain of images presented as part of 'a continuing narrative.

This movement is continued and extended in each of his next three films. Here is the first hint of the theme whereby the isolation and sense of impermanence is reflected in gross contrasts of scale and perspective, echoing Antonioni's original Marxist impetus to point the contrasts between wealth and poverty. So a rich indus-trialist, Gherardino, thinks he can buy beauty by planting three hundred rose bushes, or brains by buying himself a tame intellec-tual, the writer Giovanni. So a man is seen at the honeycomb window of his tiny flat in a huge block, less as a man than as a tiny caged creature. Tommaso, the sick friend of Lidia and Giovanni, dies in a hospital reflecting ironically that it is more like a night-club, with its champagne and pretty nurses. So the society which is sending sophisticated rocketry to the moon is still fascinated by the primitive thrust of toy rockets on a piece of waste land (another scene Lidia sees on her walk), and for Lidia the rocket represents an even more primitive thrust which she and her husband, for all their intelligence, are incapable of dealing with happily.

This rather abstract speculation is closely connected with the way the film is edited. The picture Antonioni builds up—out of a hundred fragmentary details, since that is the character of the society he is portraying—is of a world upside down, wallowing in a valueless chaos with no conception of scale or perspective. (Signora Gherardino, the hostess at the party the couple attend later in the evening, greets them with: " Ah, you catch us at an informal moment: a little celebration for my horse.")

In this world of technology run riot, where capitalism and

philistinism go hand in hand, where emotions seem by contrast lamentably primitive and human values are at a discount, objects, with their apparent solidity and reliability seemed to have gained the upper hand. Antonioni has said in an interview (pp. 148–9, *L'Avventura*, Cappelli) that he cut into several sequences in *L'Avventura* shots of a documentary nature which people might have thought inessential—mostly of objects unconnected directly with the action. But for him they were indispensable because they served the idea of the film, which was the observation of given facts, or matters of fact (*l'osservazione di un dato di fatto*). He wanted to contrast this with the impermanence of the world human beings inhabit, political, moral, social and physical. The world we lived in was unstable both inside and out. Reference to known objects, therefore, he regarded as a way of combating this instability.

" There are times when a tree, a house, etc., are as important to me as a man," says Vittoria in *L'Eclisse* (1962). This film carries the idea further. Again the theme is the transcience of emotion, the permanence—even the tyranny—of objects. The first scene shows the final break-up of an affair between Vittoria and Riccardo. It is handled in a multitude of short shots and a great many close-ups. But it is the end of the film which is most extraordinary. In the last fifty-eight shots, lasing about seven minutes, neither of the two leading characters is seen.[1] Instead, there is an array of objects, occasional buses, passers-by, bus passengers, a water butt, objects mostly which have been associated with the lovers' meeting, the gutter and pavement on the corner, the side of a house under construction. The effect of the ending is as if to say: " Up to now in the ' story ' of this film you have seen a part of a pattern, a part of the complexity which is the real texture of life. But instead of being an investigation this has been in fact only an abstraction. It appeared meaningful to a certain extent only because we removed certain essential contingencies which otherwise would have obscured it. They are there in life. Our vision is only a limited and finite one, conditioned by our inadequate sense of scale in matters of time and dimension. Here, at the end of the film, we return you to the world as it is really experienced. These people look like the couple you are expecting to see." (They have a date on that street corner, but they don't turn up.) " They could be them but they're not. This water-butt, seen in close-up, isolated from human contact, could be a lake. The trickle of water a gushing torrent, the street-lamp an H-bomb, or the sun." Antonioni

[1] *For the exactitude of these figures I am indebted to Ian Cameron, op. cit.*

is fascinated by the findings of modern physics and biochemistry which show that at its extremes—that's to say the extremes as we apprehend them—the *scale* of objects becomes meaningless, merely different ways of expressing matter and energy: a metaphor in other words. And at the end of *L'Eclisse*, in isolation from human connections, it is in fact difficult to place the objects in space or in time. Antonioni seems to be suggesting that in order to be happy, man must engineer some radical alteration in the scale of his emotional life, an alteration which will make us more settled inhabitants of a complex, diverse and infinitely multiple universe of objects. Until then the world will be experienced only as a formless stream of disconnected images. A far cry from the days of the *plan-séquence*!

The hero in *Blow-Up* (1966) is a photographer dedicated to obtaining some kind of control in however brutal a way, at whatever cost to the emotions, over the world of objects. He does it by reverting to primitive magic: he makes images of the objects he covets or fears in order to conquer them, and occasionally to worship them. Objects in this context are people, too, for his constant preoccupation is to objectify all reality so that he empties it of all threat to himself.[1] When the proprietor of a junk shop he wants to buy won't sell, he takes revenge by photographing it. He tries to share in poverty by photographing a down-and-out's hostel, in love by snapping two lovers in a park. Only when this activity gives him by coincidence some real rather than imaginary power—he appears to have photographed a murder[2]—is he put in touch with the world of real events and tries for a while, but unsuccessfully, to bring his society to its senses. Eventually he joins in an imaginary game, swept up, despite himself, in the collective hysteria. He steps wholeheartedly, or perhaps mindlessly, into the imaginary world he has done so much to create.

Blow-Up is far and away Antonioni's most stylised film despite its apparent naturalistic trappings. One sequence at a discothèque operates on a purely symbolic level. The transported leader of the pop group on stage batters his guitar to pieces in a destructive frenzy and throws the pieces to the rapt congregation. The photographer wins the fight for the main piece and runs outside into the street with it. There he throws it away, where it lies disregarded. In context once more it is seen not as a piece of the true cross but

---

[1] *Proust said that photography was " the product of complete alienation."*

[2] *In the original story by Julio Cortazar the girl interestingly enough is procuring a man for her partner: an apter image of the vicarious fantasy world in which the film alleges we live.*

as a piece of worthless junk. In other words, value is a matter of scale and context.

The environment of *Blow-Up* is not a geographical one. If, as we said before, environment is destiny, the " environment " most characteristic of this film is the still photograph. The style has become heavily fractured. The long *plan-séquences* of the days of *Le Amiche* and even of *L'Avventura* are a thing of the past. Many of the shots are very short. Many of them have no people in them. The camera rarely moves.

Blow-up is clearly concerned with illusion, and with our attempts to trap or mirror reality by making representations of it. The central problem of an image-making society is that it is in constant danger of mistaking the image for the reality, the shadow for the substance. Easy familiarity with objects, people and events through images of them gives us also a flattering illusion of power over them. Antonioni is anxious to question this illusion. In company with other film makers of the sixties, notably Resnais and Godard, he no longer shows confidence in the evidence of our senses, the accuracy of our judgment, the infallibility of our reason or the resources of our memory. He reflects the fractured world in fractured images. If, by some irony, the contemporary film begins to resemble the densely worked films of Eisenstein once more in the self-consciousness of its editing it will not be for the same reason. Though they both have made of the editing process a weapon in a philosophical investigation, where Eisenstein used it to try and construct a synthesis of a whole and stable reality, contemporary film makers are, on the contrary, recording impressions of disintegration.

CONCLUSION

Two of the themes with which this book has been chiefly concerned have been the pleasure we derive from moving images, and the conscious control which we can exercise over their type, length and sequence. It will seem perhaps something of an irony that the later section of this book has largely devoted itself to describing the circumstances in which, on the one hand, this control has been gradually relinquished, while, on the other, the images themselves have frozen into immobility.

Since we have all along argued that idiosyncratic unconventionality has been the most striking mark of the cinema's style in the sixties, it may be unwise to make further generalisations. However . . .

Cinéma-vérité perhaps has shown us as much as it is capable of with the machinery available. It won't cease to be a useful device, but it may be that the cinema's next metamorphosis will be the Cinema of Immobility, a contradiction if ever there was one. Despite its greater age the still photograph exercises an increasing hold over our imaginations. We don't seem yet to have shaken ourselves free of the spell cast by its curious mute eloquence. In an age preoccupied by problems of time/space, memory and identity, ambivalence of all kinds, and in a medium passing through a period of intense self-consciousness perhaps the still image offers a new angle of approach, or at least a temporary escape from the cataract of unclassifiable information released by the moving image.

Once more it is hard to resist citing Marker as an example. His film *La Jetée* (1963) tells a space-age story of time-sequences upset, memory and imagination mixed, a future foreseen, fought off but inescapable. It is a story in which the philosophical themes of free-will and predestination are treated not as matters of specula-

386

tion, but as observable scientific facts. The whole film is composed of stills.

The Lumière brothers were rightly fascinated to see factory workers walking, and trees waving in the wind. If the cinema does move in this new direction the wheel will have come more than a full circle. Whatever happens the editing process will continue to be not only the key to the work's meaning, as it is intimately in *La Jetée*, but also, in the best films, a reflection of the major artistic and philosophical currents of the times.

APPENDIX

SELECT BIBLIOGRAPHY

ONLY books and articles having a direct bearing on editing and sound editing are mentioned.

ARNHEIM, Rudolf. *Film*, Faber, 1933.

BADDELEY, W. Hugh. *The Technique of Documentary Film Production*, Focal Press, 1963.

BALÁZS, Béla. *Theory of the Film*, Dennis Dobson, 1952.

BAZIN, André. *Qu'est-ce que le Cinéma?* I. *Ontologie et Langage*, Paris, Editions du Cerf, 1958.

BOUNOURE, Gaston. *Regards Neufs sur le Cinéma*, ed. Jacques Chevalier, Bourges, Editions du Seuil, 1953.

CAMERON, Ken. *Sound and Documentary Film*, Pitman, 1947.

CONGRES INTERNATIONAL DES ECOLES DE CINEMA ET DE TELEVISION. *Reports presented to the Congress, Vienna, May 1963*, Centre International de Liaison des Ecoles de Cinéma et de Télévision, 1965.

EISENSTEIN, S. M. *The Film Sense*, Faber, 1943.

EISENSTEIN, S. M. *Film Form*, Denis Dobson, 1951.

EISENSTEIN, S. M. *Notes of a Film Director*, Lawrence & Wishart, 1959.

FELDMAN, J. and H. *Dynamics of the Film*, New York, Hermitage House, 1952.

FULTON, A. R. *Motion Pictures: the Development of an Art*, Norman, University of Oklahoma Press, 1960.

GASKILL, A. L., and ENGLANDER, D. A. *Pictorial Continuity*, Duell, Sloan & Pearce, New York, 1947.

JACOBS, Lewis. *The Rise of the American Film*, Harcourt, Brace & Co., New York, 1947.

LINDGREN, Ernest. *The Art of the Film*, Allen & Unwin, 1948.

MONIER, P. *The Complete Technique of Making Films*, Focal Press, 1958.

NILSEN, Vladimir. *The Cinema as a Graphic Art*, Newnes, 1936.

PUDOVKIN, V. I. *Film Technique*, Newnes, 1933.

RHODE, Eric. *Tower of Babel*, Weidenfeld & Nicolson, 1966.

ROTHA, Paul. *Documentary Film*, Faber, 1936.

ROTHA, Paul (with Richard Griffith). *The Film Till Now*, Vision Press, 1949.

SPOTTISWOODE, Raymond. *A Grammar of the Film*, Faber, 1935.

VAN DONGEN, Helen. *The Cinema, 1951*, ed. Roger Manvell and R. K. Neilson Baxter, Penguin, 1951).

391

Pamphlets and Articles

ASQUITH, Anthony. *The Tenth Muse Climbs Parnassus*; in *Penguin Film Review*, No. 1.

ASQUITH, Anthony. *The Tenth Muse Takes Stock*; in *Cinema* 1950, Pelican Books.

BAUCHENS, Anne. *Cutting the Film*; in *We Make the Movies*, edited by Nancy Naumberg, Faber, 1938.

BOOTH, Margaret. *The Cutter*; in *Behind the Screen*, edited by Stephen Watts, Barker, 1938.

CLARK, James, and HARVEY, Anthony. *Putting the Magic in it*; *Sight and Sound*, Vol. 35, No. 2, Spring 1966, discussion with Roger Hudson.

COLE, Sidney. *Film Editor*; in *Working for the Films*, edited by Oswell Blakeston, Focal Press, 1947.

COLE, Sidney. *Film Editing*; British Film Institute pamphlet, 1944.

COLPI, Henri. *Debasement of the Art of Montage*; *Cahiers du Cinéma*, No. 65, December, 1956.

EISENSTEIN, S. M. *Potemkin*; *Cahiers du Cinéma*, No. 82, April 1958.

FREND, Charles. *Cutting Room Practice*; *British Kinematography*, Vol. 8, No. 3, 1945.

GODARD, Jean-Luc. *Montage, mon beau souci*; *Cahiers du Cinéma*, No. 65, December 1956.

HITCHCOCK, Alfred. *Direction*; in *Footnotes to the Film*, edited by Charles Davy, Lovat Dickson, 1938.

HITCHCOCK, Alfred. *Film Production Technique*; *British Kinematography*, Vol. 14, No. 1, 1949.

JAFFE, Patricia. *Editing Cinéma-Vérité*; *Film Comment*, Vol. 3, No. 3, Summer 1965.

KNIGHT, Arthur. *Editing: the Lost Art*; *Films and Filming*, Vol. 5, No. 9, June 1959.

LEAN, David. *Film Director*; in *Working for the Films*, edited by Oswell Blakeston, Focal Press, 1947.

RENOIR, Jean, and ROSSELLINI, Roberto. *Cinema and Television*; *Sight and Sound*, Vol. 28, No. 1, Winter 1958/59, interviewed by André Bazin.

VAS, Robert. *Meditation at 24 Frames per Second*; *Sight and Sound*, Vol. 35, No. 3, Summer 1966.

CUTTING ROOM PROCEDURE

THE mechanical operations performed in the cutting room are relatively simple. Unlike the cameraman or sound recordist, the editor does not require a great deal of specialised technical knowledge in order to be able to use his instruments. All his tools are simple to operate and perform purely mechanical functions. This short account of cutting room routine work is given here in order to acquaint the non-technical reader with the order and manner in which the editor does his practical work. It is not intended as a comprehensive guide to cutting, but merely as a simple exposition of some of the more important processes.

Synchronisation of rushes

When the first positive prints of a previous day's shooting (generally called the " rushes ") arrive in the cutting room from the laboratory, the first job is to synchronise the sound-track and picture. This is a routine job which is either done by the editor's assistant, or, in some big studios, by a special staff responsible for such work. The rushes reach the cutting room in reel lengths, each reel containing several takes of a number of different scenes. The first task is to cut these reels into shorter lengths, each containing the sound or visuals of one complete take.

During shooting a special routine is adopted to facilitate synchronisation in the cutting room. At the beginning of each take a board bearing the number of the scene is held in front of the camera ; a wooden clapper is brought down sharply on to the top of the board and the sound of this is recorded. As a result, a sharp modulation appears on the sound track which corresponds in the picture with the moment of contact between the clapper and the board. These two points are now marked on the celluloid and the

393

two tracks are placed in parallel in a synchroniser. A similar procedure is adopted for each take and the whole series of synchronised sound and picture takes are joined together by means of paper clips. The two reels, one of sound track, one of picture, both provisionally held together by paper clips, are joined on a splicer.

The assembled reel is now projected and checked for correct synchronisation. If this is in order, the two reels are passed separately through a numbering machine which prints numbers at foot intervals along the edge of the film. The same numbers are printed on the sound and picture tracks so as to mark corresponding frames with a single identification number.

The director and editor view the whole reel in a theatre and decide which of the takes will be used in the cutting.

Before the editor begins to work with the material the reel is now again cut up into lengths of one take each, and the takes which have been rejected are filed for possible future use.

Editing the film

The instrument on which the editor views the film is the editing machine, usually known by its appropriate trade name, *Moviola*, *Acmiola* or *Editola*. This is a personal viewing apparatus which has a separate sound and picture head and enables the editor to change the strips of film to be viewed quickly and conveniently. The editor merely has to slip the length of film on to the sprocket holes and bring the lens unit down over it. He can control the passage of the film through the gate by means of a foot pedal. By adjusting a switch, he can cause the film to go forward or back through the gate. Most editing machines are equipped with an additional variable speed motor : by switching over to this, the editor can vary the speed of the film with a foot pedal. The speed can be reduced well below normal to facilitate a more leisurely examination of the material. Alternatively, to save time in getting to a particular spot in the film, the speed can be increased up to three times projection rate. Most editing machines also incorporate a flywheel which is attached to the rotating axle : by applying his hand to this, the editor can slow down the movement of the film and stop it at an exact frame. When the film is stationary, the flywheel can be turned manually to take the film a few frames forward or back.

When the editor has decided where he wants a cut, he marks

the appropriate frame with a wax pencil and cuts the film with the scissors. After he has edited a substantial footage, the assistant will join the separate strips of film on a splicer and the sequence is ready for the first viewing.

The precise time during the production when the editor does his work depends on the amount of material he has available. Normally, as soon as all the material for one sequence has been shot, he proceeds to prepare the first rough assembly. At this stage he tends to leave most of the shots rather longer than will be finally necessary, and concentrates on planning the order of shots and working out the effects which he will later elaborate in detail. At this stage it is not possible to make any final decisions as the length of the film may have to be adjusted or certain effects altered in view of what happens in other parts of the film. The final editing decisions are generally arrived at in consultation with the producer and director. After repeated screening and re-screening, often going on long after the picture has come off the floor, the final continuity is evolved. On some rare occasions the sound editor or the composer may ask the editor to lengthen or shorten a particular shot for a specific reason of their own, but normally it is the editor who has the final say and the sound technicians have to accommodate their effects to the editor's requirements.

Opticals

Dissolves, fades, wipes and any other optical effects are made according to the editor's requirements. The editor decides where and at what length the opticals will be wanted and sends a form with precise instructions to the laboratory.

Sound editing

The sound editor gets to work on a picture when it has been completed in the cutting room. He runs the dialogue and picture together and checks whether all the lines are audible and well enough recorded. Any piece of dialogue which is not satisfactory is recorded again. This process involves getting the actors to speak the lines in synchronisation with the picture and is known as post-synchronising.

Post-synchronisation is not used only to cover up faulty recording. Many location sequences, for instance, are entirely post-synchronised because of the difficulty of recording sound in the open air and in some Hollywood studios it has become common to post-synchronise most of the spoken lines. The purpose of this is to let the actor concentrate on his facial expressions and " acting " while he is on the floor and let him worry about speaking his lines later.

When all the dialogue has been satisfactorily post-synchronised, the sound editor consults the editor, director and composer : together, they work out in principle all the effects which the sound editor will put into practice and the composer gets to work on the score.

Meanwhile, the sound editor's next task is to record any additional sound effects which he may need and then to lay the tracks. Laying a track involves assembling reels of sound track with the appropriate effects, interspersed with blank film in such a way that the effects synchronise with the picture. Anything up to a dozen separate tracks may have to be laid to accommodate all the different effects. There will be at least one dialogue track, at least one music track and a number of effects tracks depending on the complexity of the sound required.

With the tracks laid and the music recorded, there remains only the last stage of re-recording the sound (" dubbing "). The picture is projected on to a screen and at the same time all the tracks are played in synchronisation with it. Special equipment is used for dubbing on which the volume of each track can be varied by a separate control. Thus while the picture is being projected, the various changes in volume can be controlled and correlated with the visuals. The picture is run through several times and the technicians in charge of the controls (the mixers) rehearse the timing of the precise volume changes of each track while viewing the picture. Special dubbing charts are prepared to indicate to the mixer the point at which he is to make a particular up or down adjustment. When the rehearsal is found satisfactory, the film is run through again and the total sound resulting from the mixing of the various tracks is recorded on to a single track. This is used in the final version of the film.

It now only remains for the laboratory staff to cut the picture negative in exactly the same way as the editor has cut the positive. From this cut negative and the negative of the re-recorded composite sound-track, a married print is prepared which is ready for projection to cinema audiences.

GLOSSARY OF TERMS

A ACCELERATED MOTION. Means whereby movement in a shot is represented as taking place at greater speed than it did in reality; opposite of SLOW MOTION.

ACTUAL SOUND. Sound whose source is visible on the screen or whose source is implied to be present by the action of the film: e.g., words spoken by a character on screen; words spoken by a character whose presence has been previously visually established; the ringing of a bell which is either visible on screen or accepted to be present in the room. *The term is used throughout the text of this book in this specially defined sense.* See also opposite: COMMENTATIVE SOUND.

ANGLE. See CAMERA ANGLE.

ASSEMBLE. To carry out the first process in film editing, namely, to collect together the required shots and join them in provisional order, thus producing a ROUGH CUT.

B BACK-LIGHTING. Where the main source of light is directed towards the camera thus tending to throw the subject into silhouette.

BACK PROJECTION. Projection of a film on to a translucent screen from a projector (placed behind the screen) in order to provide a moving background for actors working in a studio.

BIG CLOSE-UP. *Abbr.* B.C.U. Shot taken with the camera nearer to the subject than would be necessary for a close-up; in relation to a human subject, a shot of part of the face only. See also CLOSE-UP

BLOOP. Small opaque patch over a splice in a positive sound-track designed to smother any intrusive noise which the splice might otherwise produce.

BRIDGING SHOT. Shot used to cover a jump in time or other break in continuity.

C CAMERA ANGLE. Angle of view subtended at the lens by the portion of the subject included within the picture area.

CAMERA-STYLO. The camera-pen, a word coined in 1948 to suggest the delicacy and flexibility of the instrument with which the new young French writer/directors would make their films.

CEMENT. Cellulose solvent used for joining cinematograph film.

CHANGE-OVER. Transition made from one reel on one projector to the next reel on a second projector during the continuous projection of a multi-reel film programme.

CHANGE-OVER CUE. Small spot or other mark made in the top right-hand corner of certain frames near the end of a reel to give the projectionist a signal for the change-over.

CHEAT SHOT. Shot in which part of the subject or action is excluded

397

from view in order to make the part which is recorded appear different from what it actually is (e.g., a shot of a man falling from the top of a building into a net spread six feet below, but with the net out of view in order to suggest that he has fallen a great distance).

CINEMASCOPE. 20th-Century Fox's trade name for their widescreen process, employing a ratio of $1 : 2.5$.

CiNEMA-VERITE. A way of filming real-life scenes without elaborate equipment. A *cinéma-vérité* crew would consist perhaps of only two men, using a hand-held 16 mm. camera (with fast film-stock and no lights), linked to a portable tape-recorder and microphone. Such a unit is more mobile than the traditional one, as well as being quicker and more unobtrusive, though occasionally at the expense of technical quality.

CLAPPER. Pair of boards hinged together at one end which are banged together in view of the camera at the beginning of a take to enable the sound cutting print and the picture cutting print to be synchronised in the cutting room. (The bang appears as a pronounced fluctuation on the sound track, and this is related to the first frame in the picture print showing the boards in contact. The clapper is usually attached to the number board.)

CLAPPER-BOY. Junior technician who works the clapper.

CLOSE MEDIUM SHOT. *Abbr.* C.M.S. Shot between a close-up and medium shot; of a human subject roughly from knees to head. See also CLOSE-UP.

CLOSE-UP. *Abbr.* C.U. Shot taken with the camera very close to the subject, revealing a detail only; in relation to the human subject, a shot of the face only, the hands only, etc.

(The terms BIG CLOSE-UP, CLOSE-UP, CLOSE MEDIUM SHOT, MEDIUM SHOT, LONG SHOT have precise meanings relating to shots of the human subject; in relation to other subjects, only the terms CLOSE-UP, MEDIUM SHOT and LONG SHOT are commonly applied.)

COMMENTARY. Descriptive talk accompanying film.

COMMENTATIVE SOUND. Sound whose source is neither visible on the screen nor has been implied to be present in the action. Sound which is artificially added for dramatic effect, e.g., music, commentary, subjective sounds heard as if through the mind of a character. *This term is used throughout the text of this book in this specially defined sense.* See also opposite: ACTUAL SOUND.

CONTINUITY GIRL. Technician responsible for recording the details of each take during shooting in order to ensure that no discrepancies occur between shots when the material is edited.

CONTINUITY TITLE. Title designed to bridge a break in the pictorial continuity.

CRAB. To move the camera sideways on a dolly.

CRANE SHOT. Moving shot taken by the camera on a specially constructed crane.

CROSS-CUT. To intermingle the shots of two or more scenes in the course of editing so that fragments of each scene will be presented to the spectator's attention alternately. See PARALLEL ACTION.

CUTTER. Technician who carries out the more mechanical operations of editing. In practice, the terms *cutter* and *editor* are frequently used interchangeably.

CUTTING-PRINT. The particular positive print which the editor assembles and on which he works.

D   DAILIES. See RUSHES.

DEPTH OF FIELD. Distance between the nearest and furthest points from the camera at which the subject is acceptably sharp.

DIRECT CINEMA. See *CINEMA-VERITE.*

DISSOLVE. Gradual merging of the end of one shot into the beginning of the next, produced by the superimposition of a fade-out on to a fade-in of equal length.

DOLLY. Vehicle on which the camera and cameraman can be wheeled about during a take.

DOLLY SHOT. Shot taken while the camera is in motion on a dolly.

DUB. 1. To re-record the sound-track of a film, substituting for the speech of the language originally used, a spoken translation in some other language. 2. To re-record (q.v.).

DUPE. To print a duplicate negative from a positive.

DUPE NEGATIVE. Negative made from a positive print; negative which is not the original negative.

DUPING PRINT. Special soft print (lavender or fine grain) made from an original negative so that a dupe negative can subsequently be made from it.

E   EDITOLA. Trade name of one model of editing machine.

EFFECTS TRACK. Sound-track of sound effects other than speech and music.

ESTABLISHING SHOT. Shot (usually long shot) used near the beginning of a scene to establish the inter-relationship of details to be shown subsequently in nearer shots.

F   FADE-IN. 1. (*n.*) Beginning of a shot which starts in darkness and gradually lightens to full brightness.
2. (*v.*) To bring up sound volume from inaudability to required volume.

FADE-OUT. Opposite of FADE-IN.

FLASHBACK. Sequence in a film which takes the action of the story into the past; used either as a reminder to the audience of an earlier event or to indicate the recollections of one of the characters.

FOCUS PULL. To re-focus the lens during shot so that a part of the image further from or nearer to the camera is brought into sharp focus, so allowing the first subject to go " soft."

FOOTAGE. Length of a film measured in feet.

FRAME. One single transparent photograph of the series printed on a length of cinematograph film.

FREEZE-FRAME. At a chosen point in a scene a particular frame is printed repeatedly, so giving the effect of arresting, " freezing " the action.

FULL SHOT. *Abbr.* F.S. Shot in which an object or figure is just visible whole within the frame. See also CLOSE-UP.

I   INTERCUT. See CROSS-CUT.

IRIS. Circle-shaped mask (q.v.) and diminishing circle.

IRIS–IN and OUT. A decorative fade-in or -out in which the image appears or disappears as a growing or diminishing oval. Much used in the silent cinema.

J   JOIN. See SPLICE.

JUMP CUT. Cut which breaks continuity of time by jumping forward from one part of an action to another obviously separated from the first by an interval of time.

K   KEY-LIGHTING, HIGH or LOW. A high-key image is one with a characteristic all-over lightness achieved by soft, full illumination on a light toned subject with light shadows and background. Low-key is the reverse of this.

L   LAP-DISSOLVE. See DISSOLVE.

LEAD, LEADER, LEADER STRIP. Length of film joined to the beginning of a reel for threading through the camera, projector, etc.

LIBRARY SHOT. Shot used in a film but not recorded specially for it; shot taken from a library or store of shots kept for future use.

LONG SHOT. *Abbr.* L.S. Shot taken at a considerable distance from the object. A L.S. of a human figure is one in which the whole figure appears less tall than the height of the screen. See also CLOSE-UP.

LOOP. Short length of film joined together at its ends to form an endless band which can be passed through the projector to give a continuous repetition of its subject. (Used by actors when rehearsing the timing for post-synchronising dialogue; or in re-recording, when a particular sound—e.g., of machine-gun fire—is needed intermittently.)

M   MARRIED PRINT. Positive print of a film carrying both sound and picture.

MASK. Shield placed before the camera to cut off some portion of the camera's field of view.

MASTER SHOT. Single shot of an entire piece of dramatic action taken in order to facilitate the assembly of the component closer shots of details from which the sequence will finally be covered.

MEDIUM CLOSE SHOT. *Abbr.* M.C.S. See CLOSE MEDIUM SHOT.

MEDIUM SHOT. *Abbr.* M.S. Shot taken with the camera nearer to the object than for a long shot but not so near as for a close-up; in relation to the human subject, a shot of the human figure approximately from the waist upwards. See also CLOSE-UP.

MID-SHOT. See MEDIUM SHOT.

MIX. 1 (*Optical*). See DISSOLVE. 2 (*Sound*). To combine the sound of several sound tracks for the purpose of re-recording them on to a single track.

MIXER. 1. Technician in control of mixing sound-tracks for the purposes of re-recording. 2. Apparatus on which sound-tracks are mixed.

MONTAGE. See the detailed descriptive definition given in the first paragraph of Chapter 6, p. 112.

MOVIOLA. Trade name of an American model of editing machine. The term is commonly used instead of EDITING MACHINE.

MULTIPLE EXPOSURE. Two or more exposures made on a single series of film frames.

MUTE NEGATIVE. Picture negative of a sound film, without the sound-track.

MUTE PRINT. Positive print of the picture part of a sound film without the sound-track.

N   NARRATAGE. Method whereby one of the characters in a story film is depicted as telling the story of the film.

NOUVELLE VAGUE. New Wave. Description applied, chiefly by journalists, to an assortment of young writers, critics and technicians whose first feature films began to appear at the Cannes Film Festival in 1959. The term was also used to identify the originality, youthfulness, freshness of vision and technique, low budgets, unknown actors, " frank " dialogue and other attractions of their films. Since confusingly applied in other countries to other people and to so many different kinds of film that its usefulness as a description of anything, except novelty and vagueness, is limited.

NUMBER BOARD. Board momentarily held before the camera and photographed at the beginning of a take, recording the title of the film, number of the take and scene, in order to facilitate identification for the editor. (Number board and clapper are usually combined in one unit.)

O OPERATOR. Usually the lighting cameraman's first assistant, he actually operates the camera during shooting. On a small unit, e.g., a *cinéma-vérité* unit, the operator may be the cameraman and perhaps even the director as well.

OPTICAL. Any device carried out by the optical department of a laboratory requiring the use of the optical pirnter, e.g., dissolve, fade, wipe.

OPTICAL PRINTER. Apparatus for enabling images from one film to be photographed on to another film by means of a lens, used in making reduction prints and for special effects and trick work.

P PAN. To rotate the camera about its vertical axis during a shot.

PANNING SHOT. Shot taken with a panning camera.

PARALLEL ACTION. Device of narrative construction in which the development of two pieces of action is represented simultaneously by showing first a fragment of one, then a fragment of the other, and so on alternately. See CROSS-CUTTING.

PLAN-SEQUENCE. A long and usually complex shot involving much camera movement during which a whole scene is shot in one take without cuts.

PLAY-BACK. Reproduction of a sound-track in a studio during shooting to enable action or additional sound or both to be synchronised with it.

POST-SYNCHRONISATION. Recording and adding sound to a picture after the picture itself has been shot.

PRINT. Positive copy of a film.

R RELATIONAL EDITING. Editing of shots to suggest association of ideas between them.

RE-RECORD. To make a sound record from one or more other sound records; especially to make a single sound-track from the several component tracks of a film.

RE-TAKE. Repetition of a take.

RE-WIND, RE-WINDER. Apparatus for re-winding film.

ROUGH CUT. First assembly of a film which the editor prepares from the selected takes, joining them in the order planned in the script but leaving finer points of timing and editing to a later stage.

RUSHES. Prints of takes which are made immediately after a day's shooting so that they can be viewed on the following day.

S SET-UP. Camera position.

SLOW CUTTING. Cutting and joining of shots so lengthy that they follow each other in slow succession on the screen.

SLOW MOTION. Means by which movement in a shot is represented as taking place more slowly than it did in reality. Opposite of ACCELERATED MOTION.

SOUND-TRACK. Narrow path normally running along one side of the frames of cinematograph sound film, in which the sound is recorded in the form of a light trace varying in its light transmission.

SPECIAL EFFECT. Any effect which is introduced into a film after shooting by the special effects department, e.g., matte shots, " ghost " images, special montages.

SPLICE. 1. (*n.*) A film join. 2. (*v.*) To join film.

STOCK-SHOT. See LIBRARY SHOT.

SUPER-IMPOSE. To print two shots, one on top of the other, on the same length of film, so that when projected on the screen each can be seen through the other.

SYNC. See SYNCHRONISE.

SYNCHRONISE. To place, during editing, the sound-track in such a position relative to the picture track that on projection a particular selected sound will be heard at the same instant as a particular selected image is seen. In most cases, this is done in order to make the reproduced soind coincide with the appearance on the screen of the sound's natural source.

SYNCHRONISER. Apparatus which facilitates the mechanical operation of synchronising two tracks.

SYNCHRONOUS SOUND. Sound which has been synchronised with the picture.

T   TAKE. Single recording of a shot.

TILT. To turn the film camera up or down in shooting so that the axis of the lens rotates through a vertical plane.

TRACK. 1. (*n.*) Abbreviation of SOUND-TRACK. 2. (*v.*) To move the camera bodily forward or backward.

TRACKING SHOT. Shot taken with a tracking camera.

TROLLEY. Wheeled vehicle on which the camera can be moved while taking a shot.

TRUCKING SHOT. Shot taken when the camera is in movement on a truck or trolley.

TWO-SHOT. Shot framing two people, usually from the waist up.

W   WIDE-ANGLE LENS. Lens of short focal length with a wide angle of view and great depth of field.

WIDESCREEN. Screen ratios wider than the 1 : 1·33 of the traditional sound cinema. Inaugurated in the form of Cinemascope (q.v.). Later adopted throughout the industry in a variety of forms with ratios of 1 : 1·65 and wider.

WILD SHOOTING. Shooting the picture of a sound film without at the same time recording the sound of the action.

WILD TRACK. Sound-track recorded independently of any picture with which it may subsequently be combined.

WIPE. Form of transition from one shot to another in which a line appears to travel across the screen removing, as it travels, one shot and revealing another.

Z   ZOOM. To magnify a chosen area of the image by means of a zoom lens (variable focal length), so appearing to move the camera closer to the subject.

INDEX

403

405

ACKNOWLEDGEMENTS

THE knowledge and views which have gone into the following pages are those of the *British Film Academy* committee which was formed to write this book. Individual members made specific contributions as follows : Reginald Beck on the early stages of planning ; Roy Boulting on Chapter 2, and the passage from *Brighton Rock* ; Sidney Cole on the historical and theoretical chapters and the section on comedy ; Jack Harris on action sequences and the excerpts from *Great Expectations* and *Once a Jolly Swagman* ; Robert Hamer on the historical material ; David Lean on dialogue sequences and the excerpts from *Great Expectations* and *The Passionate Friends* ; Ernest Lindgren on the historical and theoretical sections (he also gave permission to base much of the theoretical discussion on arguments put forward in his book *The Art of the Film* and to use many of his definitions in the Glossary) ; Harry Miller on sound editing and the passage from *Odd Man Out* ; Basil Wright on all the documentary chapters and the excerpts from *Night Mail, Diary for Timothy* and *Song of Ceylon* ; Thorold Dickinson, as chairman, on every phase of the writing.

Others who helped the committee were : Geoffrey Foot who contributed the analysis of the passage from *The Passionate Friends* and gave much patient advice on the complexities of cutting room procedure ; R. K. Neilson Baxter who supervised the chapter on instructional films ; G. T. Cummins and N. Roper who supplied the information on newsreels ; Jack Howells and Peter Baylis who spent much time with me on the excerpts from *The Peaceful Years* and made written contributions ; Paul Rotha who advised on *The World is Rich* ; Wolfgang Wilhelm who advised on dialogue scripting ; J. B. Holmes who gave an account of his work on *Merchant Seamen* ; and R. Q. McNaughton who provided the analysis and break-down of the passages from *Merchant Seamen* and *Night Mail*.

From U.S.A. we received the advice of Viola Lawrence on *Lady from Shanghai* and James Newcom on *Topper Returns*. Helen van Dongen's long contributions about the editing of *Louisiana Story* are printed in full : to her we owe perhaps the greatest individual debt.

Dr. Rachael Low gave freely of her time and knowledge of film history in discussion and Julia Coppard gave invaluable help in the preparation of the manuscript. Dr. Roger Manvell of the British Film Academy and A. Kraszna-Krausz provided sympathetic help—and patience.

I also wish to thank the following :—

Miss Norah Traylen and Mr. Harold Brown of the British Film Institute for a great deal of help in the preparation of the stills ;

The cataloguing staff of the National Film Library for permitting me to use their editola ;

The film companies which have enabled me to use stills and reproduce excerpts of dialogue as follows : Associated British Picture Corporation (*Brighton Rock, The Queen of Spades*), Associated British-Pathé (*The Peaceful Years*), Central Office of Information (*Diary for Timothy, Merchant Seamen, Night Mail, The World is Rich*), Columbia Pictures Corporation Ltd. (*Lady from Shanghai*), General Film Distributors (*Great Expectations, Naked City, Odd Man Out, Once a Jolly Swagman, The Passionate Friends*), London Films Ltd. (*Louisiana Story*), Ministry of Education (*Casting in Steel at Wilson's Forge*), R.K.O. Radio Pictures, Inc. (*Citizen Kane*), Hal Roach Studios Inc. (*Topper Returns*), Shell Film Unit (*Hydraulics*), Warner Bros. Pictures Ltd. (*Rope*) ;

The authors and publishers who have allowed me to quote from their publications as follows (full particulars of quotations are given in the text) :— Allen & Unwin Ltd. (*The Art of the Film*, by Ernest Lindgren, 1948) ; Faber & Faber Ltd. (*Documentary Film*, by Paul Rotha, 1936 ; *The Film Sense*, by Sergei M. Eisenstein, 1943) ; Dennis Dobson Ltd. (*Film Form*, by Sergei M. Eisenstein, 1951) ; George Newnes Ltd. (*Film Technique*, by V. I. Pudovkin, 1933) ; Harcourt Brace & Co. (*The Rise of the American Film*, by Lewis Jacobs, 1939) ; The British Film Institute (*Film Editing*, by Sidney Cole, 1944) ; Sir Isaac Pitman & Sons Ltd. (*Sound and the Documentary Film*, by Ken Cameron, 1947).

K.R.

Acknowledgments to Part II

I am grateful to the British Film Institute and especially to Mr Colin Ford, for their co-operation and help in obtaining films, and to Messrs. Frank Holland and Harold Brown of the National Film Archive at Aston Clinton for the preparation of the frame enlargements.

I should like to thank *Sight and Sound* for permission to reproduce several passages, notably from the essay "Cinema of Appearance" by Eric Rhode and Gabriel Pearson; and Calder and Boyars Ltd. for permission to reproduce a section of dialogue from the English edition of *Last Year in Marienbad*.

I wish to thank the following companies for their invaluable co-operation in supplying prints of the films and in permitting us to reproduce selected frames:

The Rank Organisation for *El Cid*;
Contemporary Films Ltd. for *Le Joli Mai*;
Sebricon Films for *L'Année Dernière à Marienbad*;
British Lion Films Ltd. for *Shadows*;
United Artists Corporation Ltd. and Compton-Cameo Films Ltd. for general willingness;
and the staff of the Institut Français for *Hôtel des Invalides* and *Toute la Mémoire du Monde*

Most of all my thanks are due to Karel Reisz and Professor Thorold Dickinson for their careful reading, necessary corrections and sound advice. To Thorold Dickinson particularly I owe a year as a Slade Film Student during which time Part II of this book was obliquely brewing.

410

A Note on the Illustrations

It will be noticed that there are no production stills in Part II. All the illustrations are frame enlargements from the celluloid. In a work of this kind this is clearly a necessity but in the case of widescreen films it presented great problems. The photographic unit at the National Film Archive has pioneered the reproduction and enlargement of anamorphic frames in this country. The difficulties are considerable and in some cases the photographic loss of quality on the page is considerable too. Any imperfections in the illustrations are therefore to be attributed to the intractability of the material rather than to carelessness.

G. O. M.